THE POLITICS OF EDUCATION

THE POLITICS OF EDUCATION

*The Seventy-sixth Yearbook of the
National Society for the Study of Education*

PART II

By
THE YEARBOOK COMMITTEE
and
ASSOCIATED CONTRIBUTORS

Edited by

JAY D. SCRIBNER

Editor for the Society

KENNETH J. REHAGE

Distributed by THE UNIVERSITY OF CHICAGO PRESS • CHICAGO, ILLINOIS

The National Society for the Study of Education

The purposes of the Society are to carry on investigations of educational problems and to publish the results of these investigations as a means of promoting informed discussion of important educational issues.

The two volumes of the seventy-sixth yearbook (Part I: *The Teaching of English* and Part II: *The Politics of Education*) continue the well-established tradition, now in its seventy-seventh year, of serious effort to provide scholarly and readable materials for those interested in the thoughtful study of educational matters. The yearbook series is planned to include at least one volume each year of general interest to all educators, while the second volume tends to be somewhat more specialized.

A complete list of the Society's past publications, including the yearbooks and the recently inaugurated series of paperbacks on Contemporary Educational Issues, will be found in the back pages of this volume.

It is the responsibility of the Board of Directors of the Society to select the subjects to be treated in the yearbooks, to appoint committees whose personnel are expected to insure consideration of all significant points of view, to provide for necessary expenses in connection with the preparation of the yearbooks, to publish and distribute the committees' reports, and to arrange for their discussion at the annual meeting. The editor for the Society is responsible for preparing the submitted manuscripts for publication in accordance with the principles and regulations approved by the Board of Directors.

Neither the Board of Directors, nor the Society's editor, nor the Society is responsible for the conclusions reached or the opinions expressed by the Society's yearbook committees.

All persons sharing an interest in the Society's purposes are invited to join. Regular members receive both volumes of the current yearbook. Those taking out the "comprehensive" membership receive the yearbook volumes and the volumes in the current series of paperbacks. Inquiries regarding membership may be addressed to the Secretary, NSSE, 5835 Kimbark Avenue, Chicago, Illinois 60637.

Library of Congress Catalog Number: 76-44919

Published 1977 by
THE NATIONAL SOCIETY FOR THE STUDY OF EDUCATION
5835 Kimbark Avenue, Chicago, Illinois 60637

Copyright, 1977, by KENNETH J. REHAGE, Secretary

No part of this Yearbook may be reproduced in any form without written permission from the Secretary of the Society

First Printing, 9,000 Copies

Printed in the United States of America

Officers of the Society
1976-77

(Term of office expires March 1 of the year indicated.)

JEANNE CHALL
(1977)
Harvard University, Cambridge, Massachusetts

N. A. GAGE
(1979)
Stanford University
Stanford, California

JACOB W. GETZELS
(1978)
University of Chicago, Chicago, Illinois

A. HARRY PASSOW
(1978)
Teachers College, Columbia University, New York, New York

KENNETH J. REHAGE
(Ex-officio)
University of Chicago, Chicago, Illinois

HAROLD G. SHANE
(1979)
Indiana University
Bloomington, Indiana

RALPH W. TYLER
(1977)
Director Emeritus, Center for Advanced Study in the Behavioral Sciences
Stanford, California

Secretary-Treasurer

KENNETH J. REHAGE
5835 Kimbark Avenue, Chicago, Illinois 60637

The Society's Committee on The Politics of Education

JAY D. SCRIBNER

(Chairman)
Dean, College of Education
Temple University
Philadelphia, Pennsylvania

ALONZO A. CRIM

Superintendent, Atlanta Public Schools
Atlanta, Georgia

LUVERN L. CUNNINGHAM

Novice G. Fawcett Professor of Educational Administration
Ohio State University
Columbus, Ohio

BARBARA HATTON

Assistant Professor of Education
Stanford University
Stanford, California

WILLIS D. HAWLEY

Associate Professor of Policy Sciences and of Political Science
Associate Director, Institute of Policy Sciences and Public Affairs
Duke University
Durham, North Carolina

RICHARD C. SNYDER

Director, Mershon Center for Education in National Security
Ohio State University
Columbus, Ohio

ARTHUR E. WISE

Visiting Scholar, Education Policy Research Institute
Washington, D.C.

Associated Contributors

NORMAN DRACHLER

Visiting Professor of Education
Stanford University
Stanford, California

ASSOCIATED CONTRIBUTORS

RICHARD M. ENGLERT

Assistant to the Dean, College of Education
Visiting Assistant Professor of Urban Education
Temple University
Philadelphia, Pennsylvania

LAURENCE IANNACCONE

Professor of Education
University of California
Santa Barbara, California

FRANK W. LUTZ

Professor of Education
Pennsylvania State University
University Park, Pennsylvania

DALE MANN

Chairperson, Department of Educational Administration
Associate Professor of Educational Administration
Teachers College, Columbia University
New York, New York

EDITH K. MOSHER

Associate Professor of Education
University of Virginia
Charlottesville, Virginia

GERALD E. SROUFE

Director of Instruction, National Ed.D. Program for Educational Leaders
Nova University
Fort Lauderdale, Florida

HARVEY J. TUCKER

Research Associate, Center for Educational Policy and Management
Visiting Assistant Professor of Political Science
University of Oregon
Eugene, Oregon

TYLL VAN GEEL

Assistant Professor of Education
University of Rochester
Rochester, New York

L. A. WILSON, II

Assistant Professor of Political Science
University of Nevada
Las Vegas, Nevada

ASSOCIATED CONTRIBUTORS

FREDERICK M. WIRT
Professor of Political Science
University of Illinois
Urbana, Illinois

HARMON ZEIGLER
Professor of Political Science
Program Director, Center for Educational Policy and Management
University of Oregon
Eugene, Oregon

Editor's Preface

The study of the politics of education has never been of greater importance than it is today. The magnitude and rapidity of change in today's world is without precedent in human history. A multitude of societal demands impinge upon the process of policy making in education. New discoveries, new knowledge, and technological inventions shape educational policy in particular ways. Conflict erupts and power balances change as numerous lay and professional interest groups attempt to influence policy makers, as minorities press for equal rights and justice, and as court mandates call for equalizing opportunities for children born into different circumstances. Changes in state and federal policies and prevailing economic conditions add further pressure on local decision makers. How such forces are channeled, how they are processed, the nature of the policies they effect, and the impact of new or changing policies are matters of concern both to those whose needs have not been met and to those who must comply with policy changes. Clearly, the predominant process for educational change is political.

The purpose of this volume is to suggest the kinds of concerns of the politics of education as a relatively new field of disciplined inquiry and to present some of the current research efforts. The contributors to the volume include both practitioners and scholars, educators and political scientists. This balance is largely the result of the process by which the yearbook came into existence. In 1974, I sent a letter to 136 persons involved either in the theoretical or in the practical aspects of the politics of education, inviting them to critique a preliminary outline of the proposed yearbook and to nominate potential contributors. The sixty-five persons who responded nominated 300 potential authors, submitted in-depth comments on the tentative outline, and expressed overwhelming support for a yearbook dealing with the politics of education. Those nominated were invited to submit proposals to the yearbook committee. The response was impressive. Ninety proposals were sent to the committee for consideration. Many respondents declared their enthusiastic support for the manner in which contributions were being solicited.

The yearbook committee selected the proposals it considered to fit best with other proposals selected. With some exceptions, the volume is the result of that process. Plans were made originally to include chapters dealing with the contributions of political science to education, the politics of community-school interaction, and the politics of the local school site (that is, the school building). For a variety of reasons, these chapters could not be included, although the areas with which they were to deal are clearly significant for practice in the politics of education.

The yearbook may be viewed as having five sections. The first chapter provides a brief overview of the field. The two following chapters deal with concepts and methodologies, addressing four concepts that have had an enduring quality over the years. In chapters 4 through 7 attention is turned to major influence systems at national, state, and local levels of government, including the interrelations of those systems as they influence educational policy. In a fourth section (chapters 8 through 10) consideration is given to selected aspects of the policy-making process: decision making, communication, change, and evaluation. A final section (chapter 11) raises the question of directions the study of the politics of education might take in the future.

In our opening chapter, Richard M. Englert and I describe the circumstances that led to the emergence of the field of educational politics, noting how developments in political science, especially since World War II, led to a broadening of the scope of that discipline and how educators increasingly came to the realization that the making of educational policy at all government levels involves actions that are essentially political. The chapter concludes with a description of the field of educational politics in terms of its central concern with interactions surrounding the authoritative allocations of values in education.

In chapter 2, Frank W. Lutz draws upon several models related to the central concept of "power" and shows how these models can be applied to educational politics. His work is an outgrowth of the studies of community power structure and decision making that go back to the 1930s, but he is not limited to those works. Rather, he demonstrates how the earlier studies are related to new models in educational politics. He systematizes the entire set of models into a comprehensive framework, thus providing a dimension often missing from earlier studies in the field.

In chapter 3, Dale Mann addresses three other concepts that have emerged again and again in recent educational practice and research: participation, representation, and control. Participation is presented in the context of a range of options for involvement. He examines representation in the context of some prominent studies and indicates that this concept is intertwined with both legislation and administration. Control is viewed in its essential relationships with the other two concepts.

In chapter 4, Edith K. Mosher discusses the patterns of American federalism, considering especially how intergovernmental relationships influence education. She describes the historical development of these relationships, stressing particularly the growth in centralization that has produced strong national influences upon education. Her analysis of the relationship between federalism and the responsiveness to citizens in educational governance deals with a persistent theme in political theory: how responsiveness varies with changing structures of governance.

The involvement of federal courts in education provided a great impetus to the emergence of the politics of education by revealing many instances of school conflict. In chapter 5, Tyll van Geel analyzes an important dimension of that involvement: the perception of the Supreme Court of its own proper role in addressing societal conflict. When the justices practiced great restraint, school systems were allowed great leeway in handling real or potential conflict. But when justices became more active in entering certain kinds of controversy, school systems necessarily became more open, and certain kinds of conflict emerged more readily. Van Geel's chapter also provides sets of criteria for the two models of court involvement—criteria that might have predictive value for determining what kinds of areas could be subject to judicial scrutiny.

Frederick M. Wirt examines state and regional cultures that account for variations in school politics. His basic concept is that of "centralization," a concept that has concerned educators over the past century. Wirt attacks the problem of centralization in a unique fashion, using a procedure he devised for comparing state centralization patterns with each other. Not only is his discovery of regional cultures of educational policy significant, but his research paradigm, built upon the work of David Easton, also offers the promise of shedding some much needed light on questions of spending-outcomes and even perhaps of pupil gains in relation to kinds of structural and environmental inputs.

Norman Drachler, formerly a superintendent of a large-city school district, examines influences upon education at the local level. He points out political and educational implications of demographic transformations occurring in large cities since 1950. The issues he raises have been prominent in the literature of the politics of education: collective bargaining, desegregation, decentralization, tax referendums, and citizen participation. Drachler's chapter reinforces the findings of many earlier studies that have shown the enormous political effect of forces in the wider society upon education and its operations.

In chapter 8, Harmon Zeigler, Harvey J. Tucker, and L. A. Wilson report upon one phase of their longitudinal study of structures of school governance. In the past, many studies of school decision making have been quite limited in scope. These authors, however, have collected a broad range of data in representative school districts over a long period of time. Moreover, they focus upon the flow and content of communication and upon the relationship of this communication to school decision making. As in the case of the Wirt study, the work of Zeigler and his associates has value not only for its content but also for its systematic and comprehensive approach. Their study will likely provide a wealth of data for analysis of local educational systems.

In chapter 9, Laurence Iannaccone describes and explains political change in education. He proposes three ways of looking at change, each of which revolves around a different facet of educational systems. Whereas the separation of education and politics historically focused attention on incremental policy changes, more recent events have forced education to deal directly with changes in its system for managing political conflict. Iannaccone suggests

that both of these kinds of change are preludes to a real revolution in the politics of education.

Gerald E. Sroufe's chapter illustrates the widening horizons of research in educational politics. In the past some educators might have considered evaluation to be entirely apolitical, but Sroufe shows how politics and evaluation are intimately related. He traces the development of paradigms of both political science and evaluation, and then demonstrates the political nature of evaluation. His description of political elements in specific evaluation studies is a positive contribution not only to the politics of education but also to the development of educational evaluation.

In the final chapter, Willis D. Hawley raises the question, "So what?" He suggests that while studies of the politics of education have explored policy processes and even policy outputs, the actual outcomes of policy (that is, how the policies affect the clients of education) are largely unknown. He challenges researchers in the politics of education to examine several very specific issues in future studies in order to determine the effects of governmental actions. Thus, while the beginning of this volume looked to the past, its last chapter looks forward. Hopefully, the yearbook will assist further development in the politics of education.

I wish to express deep gratitude to all who have made this volume possible. Special thanks are due to each member of the yearbook committee for the ideas and energies they have lent to the entire project; to each of the persons who responded to the several mass mailings for their constructive criticism, incisive comments, and interest; to the authors of the chapters for their cooperation and suggestions; to Herman G. Richey for preparing the index; and to the Board of Directors of the National Society for the Study of Education for their willingness to authorize the preparation of this volume and for their great patience throughout the process of its preparation.

JAY D. SCRIBNER
Philadelphia, January 1977

Table of Contents

	PAGE
THE NATIONAL SOCIETY FOR THE STUDY OF EDUCATION	iv
OFFICERS OF THE SOCIETY	v
THE SOCIETY'S COMMITTEE ON THE POLITICS OF EDUCATION	vii
ASSOCIATED CONTRIBUTORS	vii
EDITOR'S PREFACE, *Jay D. Scribner*	xi

CHAPTER · PAGE

I. THE POLITICS OF EDUCATION: AN INTRODUCTION, *Jay D. Scribner and Richard M. Englert* 1

    Emergence of the Field. Describing the Field.

II. METHODS AND CONCEPTUALIZATIONS OF POLITICAL POWER IN EDUCATION, *Frank W. Lutz* 30

    Introduction. Methods for Studying Power and Politics in Education. Models and Concepts Applied to Educational Politics. Summary. Conclusions.

III. PARTICIPATION, REPRESENTATION, AND CONTROL, *Dale Mann* . 67

    Introduction. Participation. Representation. The Future of Control.

IV. EDUCATION AND AMERICAN FEDERALISM: INTERGOVERNMENTAL AND NATIONAL POLICY INFLUENCES, *Edith K. Mosher* . . 94

    Education in the Context of General Government: Bridging Islands of Inquiry. The Architecture of the Federal System of Educational Government. The Federal System of Educational Government in Historical Perspective. Responsiveness to Citizen-Consumers in the Federal System of Educational Governance.

V. TWO MODELS OF THE SUPREME COURT IN SCHOOL POLITICS, *Tyll Van Geel* 124

    Introduction. The Model of Restraint. The Model of Activism. Restraint and the Minimization of Costs. Activism and the Maximization of Benefits. The Model of Activism and the Warren Court. The Model of Restraint and the Burger Court. The Models and Local School Politics. Conclusions.

CHAPTER	PAGE
VI. SCHOOL POLICY CULTURE AND STATE DECENTRALIZATION, *Frederick M. Wirt*	164

The Setting of the State's Role. A Paradigm for Comparative Research. Research Design. The Data for Analysis. Distribution of Centralization among the States. The School Policy Cultures of American Regions. Local Consequences of State Centralization.

VII. EDUCATION AND POLITICS IN LARGE CITIES, 1950-1970, *Norman Drachler* 188

Introduction. Demographic Transformations in Large Cities. Educational Implications in an Age of Anxiety. Political Implications. Some Reflections about Education and Politics.

VIII. COMMUNICATION AND DECISION MAKING IN AMERICAN PUBLIC EDUCATION: A LONGITUDINAL AND COMPARATIVE STUDY, *Harmon Zeigler, Harvey J. Tucker, and L. A. Wilson, II* . . 218

Who Governs Public Schools? A New Approach. What Is the Agenda of School Board Meetings? The Nature of Communication. Who Sets the Agenda? Who Proposes Policy Decisions? Decisions. Conclusions.

IX. THREE VIEWS OF CHANGE IN EDUCATIONAL POLITICS, *Laurence Iannaccone* 255

Introduction. Administrative Politics: The Politics of Educational Change. Political Adjustment: Political Change in Education. Political Ideology: The Key. A Change in the Politics of Education. Conclusion.

X. EVALUATION AND POLITICS, *Gerald E. Sroufe* 287

Toward an Understanding of Politics and Evaluation. An Expanded Definition of the Politics of Education. Evaluation and Politics. Politics of Evaluators and Evaluation Agencies. Prognosis for the Politics of Evaluation.

XI. IF SCHOOLS ARE FOR LEARNING, THE STUDY OF THE POLITICS OF EDUCATION IS JUST BEGINNING, *Willis D. Hawley* 319

Policy Studies and the Field of American Political Inquiry. Research on the Politics of Education. Final Comment.

INDEX 335

CHAPTER I

The Politics of Education: An Introduction

JAY D. SCRIBNER AND RICHARD M. ENGLERT

Man is by nature a political animal.
                                   Aristotle, *Politics*

> *Get thee glass eyes;*
> *And, like a scurvy politician, seem*
> *To see the things thou dost not.*
>   Shakespeare, *King Lear*

Politics are now nothing more than a
means of rising in the world.
                                   Samuel Johnson,
                            Boswell's *Life of Johnson*

Emergence of the Field

This volume is the first in the yearbook series of the National Society for the Study of Education, now in its seventy-sixth year, to address explicitly the topic of the politics of education. Some previous yearbooks have touched indirectly upon this domain, but those volumes typically portrayed either a stronger sociological orientation[1] or a more general emphasis on social and behavioral science approaches to basic inquiry and problem solving in educational practice.[2] It is significant that the interrelationships of education and politics—two pillars of American society—have so long evaded comprehensive examination by the Society. The reason lies

---

1. See, for example, C. Wayne Gordon, ed., *Uses of the Sociology of Education*, Seventy-third Yearbook of the National Society for the Study of Education, Part II (Chicago: University of Chicago Press, 1974).

2. See Ralph W. Tyler, ed., *Social Forces Influencing American Education*, Sixtieth Yearbook of the National Society for the Study of Education, Part II (Chicago: University of Chicago Press, 1961) and Daniel E. Griffiths, ed., *Behavioral Science and Educational Administration*, Sixty-third Yearbook of the National Society for the Study of Education, Part II (Chicago: University of Chicago Press, 1964).

not in any oversight by the Society, but rather in a peculiar set of historical developments in both education and political science. A brief overview of these developments sheds light on the field of the politics of education and its relatively late emergence in the pages of educational journals.

THE SPECTER OF EDUCATIONAL POLITICS

At the beginning of the twentieth century a reform movement blossomed that staked out the dimensions of educational politics for the next sixty years. At that time many school systems exhibited overtly political structures and activities. Decentralized systems flourished on the bases of ward politics and large governing boards. In the opinion of some observers, such political machines were the source of much that was wrong about education during those years.[3]

Perhaps some of the criticism was misplaced. Certainly, dramatic growth in industrialization and immigration presented monumental problems for schools.[4] At the same time, increasing emphasis on secondary education,[5] growing school enrollments,[6] and a lack of qualified teachers[7] did little to alleviate these stresses. The sum total

---

3. Frederick M. Wirt and Michael W. Kirst, *The Political Web of American Schools* (Boston: Little, Brown and Co., 1972), pp. 5-9; David B. Tyack, "Needed: The Reform of a Reform," in *New Dimensions in School Board Leadership*, ed. William E. Dickinson (Evanston, Ill.: National School Boards Association, 1969), pp. 29-51.

4. Henry Bamford Parkes, *The United States of America: A History*, 3d ed. (New York: Alfred A. Knopf, 1969), pp. 395-414. A total of 26,277,000 persons immigrated from 1870 to 1920, with a peak decade total of 8,795,000 from 1901 to 1910. Ibid., pp. 468-72.

5. Martin Trow, "Two Problems in American Public Education," in *The Sociology of Education: A Sourcebook*, ed. Robert R. Bell and Holger R. Stub, rev. ed., (Homewood, Ill.: Dorsey Press, 1968), p. 26.

6. Martin Burlingame, "American Politics and Education: A Prospective" (Unpublished manuscript, June, 1974), p. 5; Abbott L. Ferriss, *Indicators of Trends in American Education* (New York: Russell Sage Foundation, 1969), pp. 376-417.

7. "The education of teachers, general and professional, was in fact limited; few teachers even in the cities had more than twelve years of formal education. . . . The tasks of the teacher did not require the making of decisions and his limited knowledge did not enable him to make sound ones." Raymond E. Callahan and H. Warren Button, "Historical Change of the Role of the Man in the Organization: 1865-1950," in *Behavioral Science and Educational Administration*, p. 76.

of all social and economic forces at the end of the nineteenth century produced challenges that educators seemed most incapable of assuming.

What particularly irked several observers were some of the more blatant failings of educational systems at the time. Corruption was evident. Spoils system privileges, including the awarding of jobs and contracts by ward bosses, were widely exercised. The decentralized, ward-based, overtly political school systems became symbols of the general inability of education to cope with demands made upon it. Reform was logically constructed in terms of changing such systems and removing these abuses.[8]

Reformers borrowed from theories of efficiency in industry[9] and a perennial distrust of politics (see the epigraphs at the beginning of this chapter) to propose a platform based on nonpartisanship, at-large elections, smaller governing boards, and professionalization of education.[10] Nonpartisanship was aimed at decreasing dependence on political parties. The ward system with large school boards representing parochial interests was to be replaced by smaller boards, elected at large and thus presumably more responsive to the interests of the community as a whole. Emphasis on professionalization paralleled the emergence of educational administration as an area of inquiry. This emphasis culminated in the centralization of school administration, the rise of stronger, more independent

---

8. Wirt and Kirst, *The Political Web of American Schools*; Tyack, "Needed: The Reform of a Reform"; Michael B. Katz, *Class, Bureaucracy, and Schools: The Illusion of Educational Change in America* (New York: Praeger Publishers, 1971), pp. 113-25.

9. "[The muckrakers] *solution of many of the problems was through the application of modern business methods.* . . . It was, therefore, quite natural for Americans, when they came to reforming the schools, to apply business methods to achieve their ends." (Italics in original) Callahan and Button, "Historical Change of the Role of the Man in the Organization," p. 78. See also Frederick Taylor, *Scientific Management* (New York: Harper & Bros., 1947) and Franklin Bobbitt, J. W. Hall, and J. D. Wolcott, *The Supervision of City Schools*, Twelfth Yearbook of the National Society for the Study of Education, Part I (Bloomington, Ill.: Public School Publishing Co., 1913).

10. L. Harmon Zeigler and M. Kent Jennings, with G. Wayne Peak, *Governing American Schools: Political Interaction in Local School Districts* (North Scituate, Mass.: Duxbury Press, 1974), chap. 4; Joseph M. Cronin, *The Control of Urban Schools: Perspectives on the Power of Educational Reformers* (New York: Free Press, 1973), pp. 9-12; Wirt and Kirst, *The Political Web of American Schools*.

superintendents, and the separation of administration (and the superintendent) from overt politics.[11]

The reformers were successful—so successful that "city school governmental arrangements remained stable for the thirty-year period following 1925."[12] Yet, stability was not the reformers' only legacy. Some later researchers claimed that the new reforms removed from power the lower-class workers, mostly immigrants, and placed in their stead middle- and upper-class professionals.[13] Others stated more pointedly that the reform merely placed a professional elite in power, thus only exchanging one brand of politics for another.[14] In other words, politics was still present, only in a different guise. No matter what the reality, though, the rhetoric of the reformers prevailed: politics and education were to be kept separate. Education was said to be in the hands of professionals, not politicians.

This "apolitical myth"[15] of education, however, could never have endured so long without the aid of the professional educator. Several very relevant reasons existed for educators to preach, and even believe, the myth.[16] First, the spoils system abuses and cor-

11. The development of the administrative function in schools is described in Callahan and Button, "Historical Change of the Role of the Man in the Organization." The efforts of superintendents to free themselves of lay (and therefore political) control were paramount at the turn of the century and are described in Burlingame, "American Politics and Education," pp. 7-8. See also Raymond E. Callahan, *Education and the Cult of Efficiency: A Study of the Social Forces That Have Shaped the Administration for Public Schools* (Chicago: University of Chicago Press, 1962), pp. 179-221; idem, "The History of the Fight to Control Policy in Public Education," in *Struggle for Power in Education*, ed. Frank W. Lutz and Joseph J. Azzarelli (New York: Center for Applied Research in Education, 1966), pp. 16-34. The theory behind the separation of administration and politics is enunciated in Frank J. Goodnow, *Politics and Administration: A Study in Government* (New York: Macmillan Co., 1900), p. 15.

12. Cronin, *The Control of Urban Schools*, p. 12.

13. Tyack, "Needed: The Reform of a Reform," p. 35; Zeigler and Jennings, *Governing American Schools*, p. 55; Samuel P. Hays, "The Politics of Reform in Municipal Government in the Progressive Era," *Pacific Northwest Quarterly* 55 (October 1964): 163.

14. See the chapter by Laurence Iannaccone in this volume.

15. Wirt and Kirst, *The Political Web of American Schools*, p. 5.

16. Stephen K. Bailey et al., *Schoolmen and Politics: A Study of State Aid to Education in the Northeast* (Syracuse, N.Y.: Syracuse University Press, 1962), pp. viii-x.

ruption of the early 1900s were genuinely feared, and many associated them with "politics." Second, the world of the intellect was somehow considered superior to that of politics:

> Our culture is steeped in the notion that in matters spiritual and intellectual neither the crassness of the market place nor the power-seeking of the hustings should have any substantial influence.[17]

A third reason for educators' separation of education and politics involved extreme hesitancy to align with one political party or another. Politics was defined as partisanship, and many educators believed that bipartisan support of education insured financial (and other) backing no matter which political party was in power. This was particularly evident in eastern school districts whose budgets were dependent upon approval of town and city councils. Finally, educators, in seeking to gain public support for education, attempted to stress "high principle" and "social responsibility" and thus zealously avoided identification with anything hinting at "self-seeking" or partisanship—that is, politics.

In such a historical and ideological context it is easy to see how the area of the politics of education could be overlooked by educators. Past practices and present realities argued in favor of keeping the two concepts quite separate. But educators were not alone in shunning this area.

DEVELOPMENTS IN POLITICAL SCIENCE

While the historical and ideological reasons for educators' avoidance of the politics of education are reasonably clear, the reasons for avoidance by political scientists are somewhat more difficult to identify. One might think that educational systems would contain a wealth of data for study by political scientists: enormous public expenditures, a large number of local school districts as legal subdivisions of the state, numerous elections of board members, and countless tax overrides and bond elections. Surprisingly, though, only rarely did studies of education by political scientists appear before the early 1960s. One group of political scientists surveyed the scene in 1962 and lamented the neglect of education by political scientists. But they admitted that they could not assign a cause for

---

17. Ibid., p. viii.

such a state of affairs.[18] While there are no clear solutions to this puzzle, a brief review of the development of political science offers some possible solutions and at the same time helps explain some of the early beginnings of the politics of education.

The historical evolution of the field of political science can be conceptualized as having occurred in four major stages.[19] In the initial period, the study of politics, like the social sciences, was considered a part of moral philosophy. Beginning with the ancient Greeks (Plato and Aristotle) and continuing until the nineteenth century, the study of politics was intertwined with knowledge of the moral world, that is, an understanding of the "good life." Practical problems of the day provided the specific content of study, and the approach used was usually a decidedly normative one.

During the nineteenth century, a second stage took shape, one that could be described by the term "legalism." Traditional philosophic inquiry into the ends of the state and government formed the basis. But the emphasis shifted away from the general "good life" to a legal study of the state. Initially the state was narrowly defined as a collection of legal norms, so description focused on formal legal structure. This focus gradually broadened into investigations of the nature and origin of the legally defined state, including its sovereign properties and the growth of the law. Throughout this stage the seeds were sown for breaking with the tradition of moral philosophy and for the adoption of greater empiricism in method.

The third stage, "realism," was identifiable at the end of the nineteenth century and continued into the 1930s. This stage began with a de-emphasis of legalism and the addition of nonlegal and informal processes as concerns for investigation. This approach

---

18. Ibid.

19. This historical description is based on the writings of three political scientists: David B. Truman, "Disillusion and Regeneration: The Quest for a Discipline," *American Political Science Review* 59 (December 1965): 865-73; Gabriel A. Almond, "Political Theory and Political Science," in *Contemporary Political Science: Toward Empirical Theory*, ed. Ithiel de Sola Pool (New York: McGraw-Hill Book Co., 1967), pp. 1-21; David Easton, *A Framework for Political Analysis* (Englewood Cliffs, N.J.: Prentice-Hall, 1965), pp. 11-13; idem, "Political Science," in *International Encyclopedia of the Social Sciences*, vol. 12, ed. David L. Sills (New York: Macmillan Co., 1968), pp. 282-98.

grew into a focus on group activities and eventually evolved into a study of struggles for power, a development that paved the way for the next stage. At its best, the stage of realism constituted a much needed break with a normative and legalistic past by emphasizing empirical facts and concrete description. But at its worst, it was overly optimistic about political change, degenerated into empiricism for its own sake, and neglected the development of theory. Eventually, dissent against realism became more pronounced, and a new system emerged.

The fourth stage, "behavioralism," is essentially a post-World War II approach, even though many of its bases can be found much earlier. It overcame the crude empiricism of realism by adding a theoretical dimension concerned with the development of general theory. Methods of investigation were now considered to be problematic, especially in the sense that they needed to be rigorously constructed, examined, and never taken for granted. Content became more diversified to include emphases on "policy" and different kinds of political systems. Overall, the approach of behavioralism can be described in eight statements:

1. In the political realm regularities exist that can be expressed in explanatory and even predictive generalizations.

2. Such generalizations must be testable.

3. Means for gathering and analyzing data must be examined, refined, and validated.

4. Precision requires measurement and quantification.

5. Ethical values are different from empirical explanations.

6. Theory and research should be parts of a coherent, orderly body of knowledge.

7. Practical application is based on theoretical understanding.

8. Political science should be integrated with other social sciences.[20]

Thus, behavioralism represents the completion of the break of political science with its philosophical, normative past and the application of the methods of modern science to the sphere of politics.

20. See Easton, *A Framework for Political Analysis*, p. 7

This historical development of political science has ramifications for an understanding of the politics of education. For example, the past of political science offers a possible explanation of its neglect of education. As long as political scientists viewed politics in terms of "state" or "formal government," and as long as educators perpetuated a myth of separateness from other governmental structures, the likelihood of interaction was greatly reduced. Moreover, even in the years of "realism," when political scientists placed more emphasis on pressure group activities and conflict, much of education still might not have seemed to qualify for consideration. The apolitical myth stressed nonpartisanship, unity of community interest, and professionalism. Much conflict was stifled since legal channels did not exist for its articulation and open resolution. The educational profession was considered "united" with little conflict between teacher and administrator. The entire educational enterprise seemed most bent on maximum consensus and agreement and minimum overt conflict. Such actions might have seemed to many to be largely apolitical, and hardly the environment for endeavors of political scientists.

It was no coincidence, then, that the politics of education arose at a time when behavioralism began to be in vogue. Emphasis on policy and on comparative political systems seemed more likely to include education. The concern for building a general theory of politics similarly demanded a comparative approach that included more than state, government, and partisanship. The attempt to integrate political science with other social sciences likewise brought it more closely to education. As political science began to be examined, redefined, and restructured as a field of inquiry, it was necessarily broadened to include investigations of new horizons. In this context, education certainly came under scrutiny.

The historical development of political science has one further implication that should be mentioned here. As the field of the politics of education emerged and as educators consequently began to study their own political activities, the theory and methods they most naturally used were those developed by political science. Since every present research theory is largely affected by its own peculiar evolution, it is incumbent upon educators to understand the history of political science when studying educational politics. Since research is a cumulative process, the study of past concepts, generalizations, and methods is an essential prerequisite to present conceptualizing and theorizing in the politics of education.

ADVENT OF THE POLITICS OF EDUCATION

Precipitating forces. Given a history in which educators claimed education to be apolitical and political scientists inexplicably avoided education, the question arises, "What provided the impetus for the emergence of the politics of education?" There is no clearcut answer. But several precipitating forces seem likely, insofar as they chronologically accompanied the early evolution of the field and can be logically related to that beginning.

In the 1950s and 1960s the federal government enlarged its role in education and consequently helped highlight political aspects of schools. Federal court decisions signaled a willingness to encroach upon educational territory whenever basic constitutional rights were involved and to take a more aggressive posture in defining those rights.[21] Judgments involving religion in schools, racial segregation, rights of students, teachers, and others under the First, Fifth, and Fourteenth Amendments to the Constitution opened to adjudication matters that were previously determined mainly by educational professionals.[22] Perhaps the key focal point (as far as schools were concerned) for this entire judicial posture was the celebrated *Brown* decision in 1954.[23] This decision surely opened the schoolhouse door to judicial scrutiny and at the same time provoked a seemingly endless stream of controversies that could leave no doubt that conflict (and therefore politics) was an essential part of the educational scene.

The federal government also increased its involvement in schools

21. See Tyll van Geel's discussion of the model of judicial activism in chapter 5 in this volume.

22. Some key cases in the 1950s and early 1960s included *Sweatt v. Painter*, 339 U.S. 629 (1950); *McLaurin v. Oklahoma State Regents*, 339 U.S. 637 (1950); *Adler v. Board of Education*, 342 U.S. 485 (1952); *Zorach v. Clauson*, 343 U.S. 306 (1952); *Wierman v. Updegraph*, 344 U.S. 183 (1952); *Brown v. Board of Education of Topeka* 347 U.S. 483 (1954); *Brown v. Board of Education of Topeka*, 349 U.S. 294 (1955); *Sweezy v. New Hampshire*, 354 U.S. 234 (1957); *Shelton v. Tucker*, 364 U.S. 479 (1960); *Engle v. Vitale*, 370 U.S. 421 (1962); *Sch. Dist. of Abington Twnshp., Penna. v. Schempp*, 374 U.S. 207 (1963). For later cases, see John C. Hogan, "Law, Society, and the Schools," in *Uses of the Sociology of Education*, pp. 411-47. Also see Tyll van Geel's chapter in this volume.

23. *Brown v. Board of Education of Topeka*, 347 U.S. 483 (1954).

through legislation in the 1950s and 1960s. Of course, national legislation affecting education had been much more prominent before 1950 than many people commonly thought.[24] But after 1950 that commitment was considerably strengthened, in terms of both amount of funds and degree of control. A flow of legislation with its apex in 1965, when the Elementary and Secondary Education Act was enacted,[25] deepened the relationship of the federal government to the schools. Such an interrelationship increased the likelihood that education would be viewed as being engaged in political activities. Moreover, governmental support for educational research was unprecedented during the 1960s. The perceived need for better intellectual approaches to research in education led to legislation that provided for funding of research and development, which in turn encouraged private initiative in this area.[26]

Accompanying this federal aid, and at times causally related to it, was a growing criticism of the effectiveness of education. In the decade following 1950 a succession of attacks upon schools occurred. In the era of McCarthyism, charges of "communism" were leveled at schools and educators alike.[27] With the decline of Progressivism, its effects were criticized by defenders of "basic" educa-

---

24. The following testify to the great extent of that involvement: land grant college acts (for example, the Morrill Act of 1862), vocational education acts (for example, the Smith-Hughes Act of 1917 and extending legislation), depression legislation (with educational aspects of the Civil Works Administration, the Public Works Administration, the Civilian Conservation Corps, and the National Youth Administration), the Servicemens' Readjustment Act of 1944 (G.I. Bill), and funds for federally impacted areas (1941 and 1950).

25. Other legislation of the period included: establishment of the National Science Foundation (1950), the Cooperative Educational Research Act (1954), the National Defense Education Act (1958), the Manpower Development and Training Act (1962), the Vocational Education Act (1963), the Higher Education Act (1965), and the Education Professions Development Act (1967). For a review and discussion of federal aid programs, see Roald F. Campbell et al., *The Organization and Control of American Schools*, 2d ed. (Columbus, Ohio: Charles E. Merrill Publishing Co., 1970), pp. 21-38.

26. See *Research for Tomorrow's Schools: Disciplined Inquiry for Education*, ed. Lee J. Cronbach and Patrick Suppes (New York: Macmillan Co., 1969), especially chap. 6, "Improving the Research Effort."

27. Robert M. McClure, "The Reforms of the Fifties and Sixties: A Historical Look at the Near Past," in *The Curriculum: Retrospect and Prospect*, Seventieth Yearbook of the National Society for the Study of Education, Part I, ed. Robert M. McClure (Chicago: University of Chicago Press, 1971), p. 47.

tion.[28] The launching of Sputnik in 1957 encouraged further debate about the effectiveness of education.[29] Concern for the disadvantaged in the 1960s provoked spirited discussion of the ability of education to meet the needs of large segments of the population.[30] These criticisms exuded strong currents of conflict over the basic aim of schooling and led to attempts to influence the formulation of educational policy. On both counts, the political dimensions of education were revealed.

In addition, the aura of professionalization was also challenged during this period. Growing teacher militancy, especially the New York teachers' strike of 1960, shattered the image of a unified profession of educators.[31] Demands for decentralization of school districts and community control of education raised new questions about the desirability of "apolitical" institutions run by professionals seemingly unresponsive to community demands.[32] Furthermore, the need for education to compete for finances with other public services in the face of taxpayer resistance induced further doubt about the effectiveness of a bipartisan approach in procuring

28. Lawrence A. Cremin, *Progressivism in American Education: 1867-1957* (New York: Alfred A. Knopf, 1961), pp. 338-53.

29. McClure, "The Reforms of the Fifties and Sixties," p. 48.

30. See Mario D. Fantini, "Community Control and Quality Education in Urban School Systems," in *Community Control of Schools*, ed. Henry M. Levin (Washington, D.C.: Brookings Institution, 1970), pp. 40-75; Kenneth B. Clark, "Alternative Public School Systems," in *School Policy and Issues in a Changing Society*, ed. Patricia Sexton (Boston: Allyn & Bacon, 1971), pp. 411-26.

31. See Michael Moskow, "Teacher Organizations," in *Collective Negotiation for Public and Professional Employees*, ed. Robert J. Woodworth and Richard B. Peterson (Glenview, Ill.: Scott, Foresman & Co., 1969), pp. 315-29. For a history of the development and decline of the "united profession" model as embodied in California public policy, see Richard M. Englert, "California Policies for Teacher Employment Relations, 1930 to 1975" (Ed.D. diss., University of California, Los Angeles, 1976).

32. Robert F. Lyke, "Political Issues in School Desegregation," in *The Politics of Education at the Local, State, and Federal Levels*, ed. Michael W. Kirst (Berkeley, Calif.: McCutchan Publishing Corp., 1970), pp. 111-32; George R. LaNoue and Bruce L. R. Smith, *The Politics of Decentralization* (Lexington, Mass.: Lexington Books, 1973); Jay D. Scribner and David O'Shea, "Political Developments in Urban School Districts," in *Uses of the Sociology of Education*, pp. 380-408.

needed funding.³³ Failures of local tax election referendums meant greater dependence on state and federal sources.³⁴ All of this necessarily implied more stress on overt political action.

One final set of forces leading to the emergence of the politics of education as a relatively discrete area of inquiry came from academia. From the 1930s through the 1950s a number of social science studies on community power structures were published.³⁵ These studies influenced many educators and sparked the realization that political concepts and structures were integrally related to educational systems.³⁶ At the same time, widespread concern for improving the training of educational administrators and for developing theory and research in educational administration provoked changes within this field. The establishment of the National Conference of Professors of Educational Administration (NCPEA) in 1947, the support of the Kellogg Foundation for the Cooperative Program in Educational Administration (CPEA) in 1950, and the establishment of the University Council for Educational Administration (UCEA) in 1956 were all influences that led to development of the field of educational administration.³⁷ Much of this development involved wider use of concepts and methods from the behavioral sciences.³⁸ Ultimately, the politics of education became a natural complement of other social science disciplines (especially sociology) already used in this field.

Research on community power structure and the developments in educational administration inspired related investigations of

33. Wirt and Kirst, *The Political Web of American Schools*, p. 10.

34. "For those who believe that state governments must share an even larger burden of the cost of public education in the years ahead, the lesson is clear. The road to increased state aid is political." Bailey et al., *Schoolmen and Politics*, p. 108.

35. For an overview of the works of Robert S. and Helen M. Lynd, W. Lloyd Warner, Floyd Hunter, Robert A. Dahl, and others, see Campbell et al., *The Organization and Control of American Schools*, pp. 407-24.

36. Cronin, *The Control of Urban Schools*, p. 18.

37. Andrew W. Halpin, "The Development of Theory in Educational Administration," in *Administrative Theory in Education*, ed. Andrew W. Halpin (Chicago: Midwest Administration Center, University of Chicago, 1958), pp. 1-19.

38. For example, see *Behavioral Science and Educational Administration*.

school board-community relationships in education. Goldhammer focused upon the relations between school board members and community power structures and concluded that the political affairs of schools (especially the succession of school board members) are closely tied to the affairs of the wider community.[39] Gross interviewed 105 Massachusetts superintendents to get their perceptions of relationships among superintendents, board members, and the community (particularly interest groups).[40] McCarty investigated the perceptions of fifty-two school board members and their motives in relation to a series of variables, including the extent of community orientation.[41] In the context of the numerous manifestations of political activity mentioned above, works such as these provided a logical stepping-stone to further study of politics in education.

Early studies in the politics of education. Political scientists took the lead in deliberately attending to many political aspects of education and in defining the boundaries of this area of study. An essay by Eliot, written in 1959, is often regarded as the initial attempt to conceptualize the politics of education during this period.[42] While sympathetic with some of the reasons for the historical separation of education and politics (for example, the prevention of patronage and the abuses of ward politics), Eliot nevertheless emphasized that educators were engaged in political activities "whether they like it or not." [43] He called for an exorcism of what he termed the educators' taboo of politics and proposed that "if all the significant political factors are revealed, the people can more rationally and effectively control the governmental process." [44] He

39. Keith Goldhammer, "Community Power Structure and School Board Membership," *American School Board Journal* 130 (March 1955): 23-25.

40. Neal Gross, *Who Runs Our Schools?* (New York: John Wiley & Sons, 1958).

41. Donald J. McCarty, "Motives for Seeking School Board Membership" (Ph.D. diss., University of Chicago, 1959). See also idem, "School Board Membership: Why Do Citizens Serve?" *Administrator's Notebook* 8 (September 1959): entire issue.

42. Thomas H. Eliot, "Toward an Understanding of Public School Politics," *American Political Science Review* 53 (December 1959): 1032-51.

43. Ibid., p. 1035.

44. Ibid., p. 1036.

also put forward a working hypothesis (based on the concept of "professionalization of education") to focus later research and suggested a number of areas for further study:

> In all such studies, the realization that public policy in education is the product of discernible professional-lay interaction (sometimes conflict) at different governmental levels may serve as a unifying conception.[45]

This series of challenges provided a spur to activities by political scientists and educators alike.

Eliot's essay was quickly followed by the Syracuse studies, conducted by a number of social scientists and published in the form of twelve monographs on the economics and politics of education.[46] In the first of these, Bailey et al. focused upon political processes surrounding state aid to education in eight northeastern states. The authors specifically challenged the apolitical myth and noted that:

> Education is one of the most thoroughly political enterprises in American life—or for that matter in the life of any society. The fact that this monograph is one of the first serious attempts to illuminate the politics of education is in itself worthy of comment.[47]

The authors examined the political processes of the states in great detail and concluded that the efforts to get more funding for education from the state would be seriously hampered to the extent that educators avoided political activities, since state aid was observed to be specifically the result of political struggles at the state level. The political scientists emphasized:

> The future of public education will not be determined by public need alone. It will be determined by those who can translate public need into public policy—by schoolmen *in* politics.[48] (Italics in original)

Martin similarly stressed the end of the isolation of education from politics in his study of suburban school districts.[49] He depicted

---

45. Ibid., p. 1051.

46. For a list of the monographs and a discussion of their import, see Wallace S. Sayre, "The Politics of Education," *Teachers College Record* 65 (November 1963): 178-83.

47. Bailey et al., *Schoolmen and Politics*, p. viii.

48. Ibid., p. 108.

49. Roscoe C. Martin, *Government and the Suburban School* (Syracuse, N.Y.: Syracuse University Press, 1962).

the educational system as a closed one in which the professional bureaucracy optimizes its power and consequently minimizes citizen action. Martin's conclusions were based on a nation-wide sample of more than 200 representative school systems and an in-depth analysis of twelve systems. Sayre commented on the Martin study as follows:

The shape, focus, and methodology of his study are thus impressively pioneering and persuasive in a field where systematic data and analysis are exceedingly sparse and usually tangential.[50]

Munger and Fenno explored the same apolitical theme on the national level and blamed the peculiar isolation of education from politics for the failure of any general aid packages to be enacted into federal law.[51] The other Syracuse studies likewise questioned the separation of education from politics and examined local, state, and national activities in the context of concepts and methods of political science, economics, and sociology.

From these seminal works, the politics of education grew into diverse investigations of political phenomena at all levels of educational government. In the following pages we have attempted to describe briefly some of the earlier studies, grouped according to certain themes.[52]

One group of early studies extended the inquiries regarding community power structures in school systems, and power structures were often related to the central concept "decision making." Kimbrough studied decision-making processes at the local level and concluded that top policy decisions are greatly influenced by in-

50. Sayre, "The Politics of Education," pp. 181-82.

51. Frank J. Munger and Richard F. Fenno, *National Politics and Federal Aid to Education* (Syracuse, N.Y.: Syracuse University Press, 1962). See also Sayre, "The Politics of Education," pp. 179-80.

52. Two cautions are needed, however. First, no matter how many works are listed, it is inevitable that some significant works will be left out. Hopefully, those who are offended by such omissions will realize that the purpose of the authors of this chapter is to "introduce" the politics of education as a field, not to exhaust its content. Moreover, many important works are mentioned elsewhere in this and succeeding chapters of this volume. Second, for the sake of brevity and coherence the earlier studies are grouped in a partly chronological, partly thematic manner. At times, this approach does injustice to true links among different individual works.

formal elites, informal interest groups, and informal interactions.[53] Minar investigated voting data for board elections and tax referendums and discovered a close relationship among community characteristics, community political behavior, and decision-making styles in school districts.[54] In a follow-up study comparing four suburban school districts Minar concluded that the decision-making system in a school district was strongly conditioned by the social context.[55] McCarty ascertained that a superintendent's tenure was dependent upon how well that administrator fit into the power structure of the district,[56] while Cunningham reviewed studies of community power and explained their implications for educators.[57] In an undertaking involving 122 school districts in four states, Johns and Kimbrough related power structures to a number of significant variables. For example, they discovered that community influentials in "low financial effort" districts had developed much more closed social systems than had those in "high financial effort" districts.[58] Thus, this study reinforced the earlier studies of power structure and decision making and underscored the close relationship between educational decisions and political structures and activities in the community at large. Empirical data were found to contradict the apolitical stance of education.

Concurrently, several studies at Stanford University were devoted to economic and political determinants of educational decision

---

53. Ralph B. Kimbrough, *Political Power and Educational Decision-Making* (Chicago: Rand McNally & Co., 1964).

54. David W. Minar, "Community Characteristics, Conflict, and Power Structures," in *The Politics of Education*, ed. Robert S. Cahill and Stephen P. Hencley (Danville, Ill.: Interstate Printers & Publishers, 1964), pp. 125-43.

55. David W. Minar, *Educational Decision-Making in Suburban Communities*, Cooperative Research Project no. 2440 (Washington, D.C.: U.S. Office of Education, 1966).

56. Donald J. McCarty, "How Community Power Structures Influence Administrative Tenure," *American School Board Journal* 139 (May 1964): 11-13.

57. Luvern L. Cunningham, "Community Power: Implications for Education," in *The Politics of Education*, ed. Cahill and Hencley, chap. 2.

58. Roe L. Johns and Ralph B. Kimbrough, *The Relationship of Socioeconomic Factors, Educational Leadership Patterns, and Elements of Community Power Structures to Local School Fiscal Policy*, OE 5-10-146 (Washington, D.C.: U.S. Office of Education, May, 1968).

making. James, Thomas, and Dyck found no difference between fiscally independent and fiscally dependent school districts, as far as patterns of expenditure were concerned.[59] This effectively undercut one rationale for fiscal independence (and thus separation from other political structures). James, Kelly, and Garms concentrated upon the governmental arrangements under which wealth was allocated and demands were satisfied. They identified a number of determinants of educational expenditures in urban areas, including involvement of mayors in resolving certain kinds of conflict and informal relations between school administrators and community leaders. Significantly, the role of the board of education in the budget process was found to be mostly one of balancing conflicting pressures that arose.[60] James also stimulated a series of dissertations investigating political components of school systems. For example, Cronin used historical means to analyze school boards in large cities[61] and Scribner examined selected school board meetings by application of a "functional-systems analysis" approach.[62] All in all, the Stanford studies, under the leadership of James, provided an impetus to the study of the politics of education, especially in relationship to basic concepts of the economics of education.

In addition to the Syracuse studies, the investigations of community power and decision making, and the work at Stanford, a number of other research efforts in the politics of education were undertaken in the 1960s. Many of these focused upon the local school districts, especially the political interactions involving boards, superintendents, and the larger community. The Claremont studies in the mid-sixties found that school systems were somewhat responsive to the pressures of communities, to the extent that superintendents were often replaced when even a single board member had

59. H. Thomas James, J. Alan Thomas, and Harold J. Dyck, *Wealth, Expenditure, and Decision Making for Education* (Stanford, Calif.: School of Education, Stanford University, 1963).

60. H. Thomas James, James A. Kelly, and Walter I. Garms, *Determinants of Educational Expenditures in Large Cities of the United States* (Stanford, Calif.: School of Education, Stanford University, 1966).

61. Joseph M. Cronin, "The Board of Education in the 'Great Cities,' 1890-1964" (Doct. diss., Stanford University, 1965).

62. Jay D. Scribner, "A Functional-Systems Analysis of School Board Performance" (Doct. diss., Stanford University, 1966).

been defeated for reelection.[63] Salisbury argued convincingly for "a greater measure of local political leadership in education and coordination of the schools with other portions of the community." [64] Masotti described a decision-making fiasco that resulted when a superintendent, quite naive politically, lost contact with his constituents.[65] Lipham, Gregg, and Rossmiller undertook a comprehensive study of the school board engaged in an essentially political set of activities: conflict resolution.[66] These and other studies of local school systems made the same point again and again: political expertise within school districts was an important variable in responding to demands of the community and of the school system.

While not as numerous as the local studies, several investigations of the politics of education followed the lead of Bailey and his associates in analyzing state-level phenomena. For example, Masters, Salisbury, and Eliot compiled case histories in Missouri, Illinois, and Michigan to determine how and by whom power is exercised when state policy decisions are made on school matters. They found that emphasis on avoidance of conflict and consensus (two traditional strategies of educators) was entirely disadvantageous whenever divisions and strains occurred in the political system.[67] Campbell, Sroufe, and Layton examined the different organizational plans for administering education at the state level. They concluded that state departments of education needed to be stronger, especially as agencies of political leadership that help link educational professionals, the public, and political leaders.[68]

63. See Laurence Iannaccone, *Politics in Education* (New York: Center for Applied Research in Education, 1967), pp. 89-98.
64. Robert H. Salisbury, "Schools and Politics in the Big City," *Harvard Educational Review* 37 (Summer 1967): pp. 408-24.
65. Louis Masotti, *Education and Politics in Suburbia: The New Trier Experience* (Cleveland, Ohio: Press of Western Reserve University, 1967).
66. James M. Lipham, Russell T. Gregg, and Richard A. Rossmiller, *The School Board as an Agency for Resolving Conflict* (Madison, Wis.: University of Wisconsin, 1967).
67. Nicholas A. Masters, Robert H. Salisbury, and Thomas H. Eliot, *State Politics and the Public Schools: An Exploratory Analysis* (New York: Alfred A. Knopf, 1964). See also Iannaccone, *Politics in Education*, p. 28.
68. Roald F. Campbell, Gerald E. Sroufe, and Donald H. Layton, eds., *Strengthening State Departments of Education* (Danville, Ill.: Interstate Printers & Publishers, 1967).

Such state studies agree in recommending more attention to political structures and activities lest leaders in education be impotent at the state level.

Research emerged also at the federal level, although it certainly lagged behind local and state studies. Meranto reviewed the political factors surrounding the question of federal aid to education. Whereas several roadblocks had historically obstructed the passage of general aid to education bills, he found that changes in the political environment and structures led to the enactment of the Elementary and Secondary Education Act of 1965.[69] Yet a law only sets general policy. Bailey and Mosher demonstrated how this same act was put into effect through the rules and regulations developed by administrators of the law in the U.S. Office of Education. The system for administration of laws was observed to have significant political antecedents, concomitants, and consequences to such an extent that the Office of Education had become a major shaper of educational policy.[70] These works were convincing proof that politics in educational policy making are evident at every governmental level and in every phase of operation.

The proliferation of studies on educational politics in the 1960s was dramatic witness to the new concern for the politics of education. The field, however, had a significant drawback—there were many different research efforts, but few attempts to integrate all into a cohesive whole. Two mid-1960 works are exceptions to this statement. In 1965, Campbell, Cunningham, and McPhee produced a comprehensive work in educational administration.[71] Using "control" as their unifying concept, they drew heavily upon concepts and findings from research in the behavioral sciences, including political science. Their statement that "educational policy

---

69. Philip Meranto, *The Politics of Federal Aid to Education in 1965: A Study in Political Innovation* (Syracuse, N.Y.: Syracuse University Press, 1967).

70. Stephen K. Bailey and Edith K. Mosher, *E.S.E.A.: The Office of Education Administers a Law* (Syracuse, N.Y.: Syracuse University Press, 1968).

71. Roald F. Campbell, Luvern L. Cunningham, and Roderick F. McPhee, *The Organization and Control of American Schools* (Columbus, Ohio: Charles E. Merrill Books, 1965).

making at all governmental levels is immersed in politics and by definition educational policy making is political action"[72] was a significant departure from a tradition in educational administration that often concentrated on legal governance, administrative professionalization, and separation (especially in fiscal matters) from other governmental bodies. This work represented a high level of integration of past practices with an emerging new emphasis. While not devoted exclusively to the politics of education, the work of Campbell and his associates showed how the study of educational politics could be interrelated with other fields. Two years later, Iannaccone brought together most of the significant research on the politics of education to that date. His work, structured principally along the lines of the three levels of government and emphasizing the central concept of "change," contributed a much needed unified view of the entire field of the politics of education.[73]

In the late 1960s and early 1970s, researchers in the politics of education came to the realization that comprehensive frameworks for looking at this field as an entirety were seriously lacking. Following the lead of Iannaccone, other researchers produced either comprehensive reviews of research or frameworks for conceptualizing the diverse elements that make up educational politics. Kirst and Mosher reviewed what they termed a "policy-science orientation" in educational research and concluded that the emergence of the politics of education as a field was more associated with developments in educational policy and less with any distinctive kinds of theory or methodology.[74] In addition, Kirst combined essays of prominent researchers in educational politics with a conceptual framework based on intergovernmental relations, systems analysis, and five general conceptual questions.[75] Wirt categorized research literature in a system-analytic framework and raised basic conceptual and methodological questions about research in the politics

---

72. Ibid., p. 404.

73. Iannaccone, *Politics in Education*.

74. Michael W. Kirst and Edith K. Mosher, "Politics of Education," *Review of Educational Research* 39 (December 1969): 623-40.

75. Kirst, ed., *The Politics of Education at the Local, State, and Federal Levels*.

of education.[76] In a later work, Wirt and Kirst centered on the "political system" as their unit for analyzing local and state educational systems and policy-making areas in public education.[77] Iannaccone and Cistone examined "the state of the knowledge" of the politics of education in 1974.[78] These works represent comprehensive attempts to organize and unify the diverse research endeavors in the politics of education. To the extent that the field has gained coherence, these studies have provided frameworks for understanding; but to the extent that many aspects of the politics of education yet remain unconnected, these works provide models for further research.

Describing the Field

A main reason for lack of synthesis in the area of the politics of education has been confusion, or disagreement, over the kinds of phenomena that might be considered "political." As was pointed out earlier, in the past politics was essentially associated with formal government. While this kind of conceptualization was relatively clear, it was by no means broad enough. As this early definition changed and more concepts came to be included under the umbrella of "politics," the precise meaning of the term became blurred. By the 1960s any number of concepts were associated with the political realm: conflict and its resolution; struggle to gain and maintain power; pressure group activities; government institutions, structures, and actions; policy and policy making; attempts to influence others; decision making; activities of political parties; voting behavior; civic training for citizens; and any number of related ideas, including the age-old "dirty politics." The trouble was that as the concepts proliferated, the politics of education became more and more inclusive. When politics is found under every bed and in

---

76. Frederick M. Wirt, "Theory and Research Needs in the Study of American Educational Politics," *Journal of Educational Administration* 7 (May 1970): 53-86; idem, "American Schools as a Political System: A Bibliographic Essay," in *State, School, and Politics*, ed. Michael W. Kirst (Lexington, Mass.: D. C. Heath & Co., 1972), pp. 247-68.

77. Wirt and Kirst, *The Political Web of American Schools*.

78. Laurence Iannaccone and Peter J. Cistone, *The Politics of Education* (Eugene, Oreg.: ERIC Clearinghouse on Educational Management, University of Oregon, 1974).

every closet, the distinction between the politics of education and other areas of study becomes quite blurred.

A BASIC NOTION OF POLITICS

In the late 1960s one solution to the problem of conceptualizing began to gain wide acceptance as a unifying definition. The notion of politics as *the set of interactions that influence and shape the authoritative allocation of values* provided a frame of reference that was simultaneously broad enough to include most significant concepts of the past and sufficiently discriminating in comparison with nonpolitical viewpoints. This notion is based on the basic principle of scarcity. Every society has a number of valued things that are scarce enough to be the source of potential conflict among its members. To avert chaos, society sets up mechanisms to make decisions (that is, allocations) that members of society will find acceptable (that is, authoritative). Thus, as individuals and groups attempt to influence these authoritative allocations, they are exhibiting what we would call "political" behavior.[79]

This notion is directly applicable to the realm of education on two levels. First, educational systems, such as the local school system, are legal subunits of state government. As such, they have the authority to allocate values (for example, education, public funds, jobs) for large segments of the population. Insofar as individuals, groups, and agencies attempt to influence either the allocation process or its outcomes, those individuals are engaged in political activities within the school system. But on a different level, educators and even the educational system itself can be viewed as engaged in trying to influence the authoritative allocation processes or products of the wider society (for example, the state or national governments). Thus, insofar as individuals in education, groups interested in education, or educational systems exhibit behavior aimed at affecting the authoritative allocation of values by state or federal governmental bodies, politics is occurring. In this context, therefore, much behavior in the educational realm is clearly political.

---

79. See Easton, "Political Science," pp. 285-88.

CENTRAL CONCEPTUAL CATEGORIES

From this basic notion, a number of operational concepts can be defined. Such concepts can be logically organized under four categories: government, power, conflict, and policy. Ultimately, each of these categories is included under the basic notion, "the set of interactions that influence and shape the authoritative allocation of values." A review of these four categories indicates the kinds of operational concepts that have been used to study politics in education.

Perhaps one of the oldest notions associated with politics is that of "government" or "state." As was pointed out above, this concept was emphasized in the stage of realism in political science. In the politics of education, this notion has four aspects. First, insofar as an educational system is a legal subdivision of the state, its legal aspects can be studied. Thus, traditional theory of educational administration usually included a legal analysis of the connection of the school system with state government. In spite of the apolitical myth, this kind of study was touching upon political concerns, whether or not anyone admitted it. Second, insofar as an educational system interacts with other governmental units, it can be analyzed for the kinds and degrees of these interactions. In the politics of education this involves study of American federalism,[80] as well as traditional studies of fiscal dependence and independence. A third aspect is derived from a Weberian notion of a state monopoly of power within a given territory.[81] A school system has the authority to govern its own territory. Traditionally in education the school system was considered a separate governmental entity, and school governance was studied from that perspective.[82] But

---

80. See Daniel J. Elazar, *American Federalism: A View from the States* (New York: Thomas Y. Crowell Co., 1966). See also chapter 4 by Mosher in this volume.

81. H. H. Gerth and C. Wright Mills, trans. and eds., *From Max Weber: Essays in Sociology* (New York: Oxford University Press, 1946), pp. 77-78.

82. Phillip Monypenny, "A Political Analysis of Structures for Educational Policy Making," in *Government of Education for Adequate Policy Making*, William P. McLure and Van Miller, eds., (Urbana, Ill.: Bureau of Educational Research, College of Education, University of Illinois, 1960). See also chapter 4 by Mosher in this volume.

governance in the politics of education is now conceptualized in much wider terms. For example, Zeigler and Jennings concentrated on the measurement of traditional educational approaches to governance in relation to the criterion of traditional democratic theory, which involves more open competition in elections and political structures.[83] A fourth aspect of the notion of government involves the long-standing question of whether education shapes the directions of the state, or the state shapes the purposes of education.[84] In the politics of education this aspect is studied through investigations of civics learning and political socialization.[85]

A second general concept associated with the term politics is "power." Lasswell and Kaplan proposed power as a central element in their framework for inquiry into political phenomena,[86] but March emphasized that the concept of power was not all-inclusive, for it must be used in conjunction with other central terms in order to understand certain kinds of decision making that are unexplained by power.[87] Also associated with power are terms like "control," "authority," and "influence." The latter has been particularly prevalent in research in political science. For example, Banfield developed several conceptual questions based on the concept of influence.[88] In the politics of education, these concepts have wide appeal. As was pointed out earlier, the concept of power was crucial to the studies of community power structure of the 1950s and 1960s. Cronin emphasized control in his examination of his-

83. Zeigler and Jennings, *Governing American Schools.*

84. See Wirt and Kirst, *The Political Web of American Schools*, pp. 21-27.

85. For example, see Willis D. Hawley and William G. Cunningham, "The Implicit Civics Curriculum: Teacher Behavior and Political Learning" (Working paper, Institute of Policy Sciences and Public Affairs, Duke University, March, 1975).

86. Harold D. Lasswell and Abraham Kaplan, *Power and Society: A Framework for Political Inquiry* (New Haven, Conn.: Yale University Press, 1950).

87. James G. March, "The Power of Power," in *Varieties of Political Theory*, ed. David Easton (Englewood Cliffs, N.J.: Prentice-Hall, 1966), pp. 39-70.

88. Edward C. Banfield, *Political Influence* (New York: Free Press, 1961). See also Kirst, ed., *The Politics of Education at the Local, State, and Federal Levels*, pp. viii-ix.

torical and contemporary proposals for reform of urban schools.[89] A central theme in many investigations of educational politics has to do with who has how much power over whom and how that power (or influence, authority, or control) is exercised. This theme is especially apparent in the days of demands for community control and decentralization. Also logically included under studies of power might be works dealing with attempts of political parties to gain and maintain power and similar studies of patterns of partisanship.

A third prevalent concept is that of conflict. Schattschneider considered this term so crucial to political study that he called conflict the root of all politics and the contagiousness of conflict the central political fact.[90] Included under this concept might be the activities of interest or pressure groups, which Truman placed at the center of the governmental process,[91] and all kinds of bargaining activities, including formal collective bargaining structures. In the politics of education a host of works have documented conflict situations in education. An example would be the volume edited by Lutz and Azzarelli, in which the conflict attending the growth of teacher power in the early 1960s was investigated.[92] Another example is found in the work of McCarty and Ramsey, who developed an approach to educational administration through a model built on a combination of power and conflict that was based on earlier studies of community power structure.[93]

Finally, a fourth notion of politics that has developed is the concept of policy. Easton emphasized the making of policy, both the process and the policy that results, as a central theme of politics.[94] Some of this concern with policy and policy making

89. Cronin, *The Control of Urban Schools.*

90. Elmer E. Schattschneider, *The Semisovereign People: A Realist's View of Democracy in America* (New York: Holt, Rinehart & Winston, 1960), p. 2.

91. David B. Truman, *The Governmental Process: Political Interests and Public Opinion* (New York: Alfred A. Knopf, 1965).

92. Lutz and Azzarelli, eds., *Struggle for Power in Education.*

93. Donald J. McCarty and Charles E. Ramsey, *The School Managers: Power and Conflict in American Public Education* (Westport, Conn.: Greenwood Publishing Corp., 1971).

94. David Easton, *The Political System* (New York: Alfred A. Knopf, 1953).

has evolved from the work of social psychologists and management theorists concerned with decision-making processes. Thus, Simon understood the decision-making process to be at the core of administrative behavior.[95] In the area of the politics of education, Crain compared case studies of school desegregation in a framework of decision making, community structure, and policy making.[96] Mann disagreed with the traditional distinction between policy and adminstration (as contained in the apolitical myth) and identified five characteristics of policy problems, which he described as public in nature, very consequential, complex, dominated by uncertainty, and involving competing interests.[97] Thompson provided a comprehensive analysis of educational policy making through a systems approach.[98] "Policy" and "policy making" have emerged as major concerns of the politics of education.

Thus, one basic definition—interactions influencing the authoritative allocation of values—and four conceptual categories (government, power, conflict, and policy) can be said to describe what constitutes the field of politics of education. One obvious value of the description is that it subsumes past traditional studies of educational governance while still leaving room for newer approaches deriving from emphases on behavioral sciences. But a drawback of this description also exists. Many of the past studies that have touched upon political matters were developed from perspectives other than political. For example, the earlier studies of community power structure could more properly be said to have used sociological or anthropological approaches, not political ones. To say that something involving "power" always involves a political approach is not accurate. Therefore, while the above description is helpful in describing the historical emergence of the politics of

---

95. Herbert A. Simon, *Administrative Behavior* (New York: Macmillan Co., 1947).

96. Robert L. Crain, *The Politics of School Desegregation: Comparative Case Studies of Community Structure and Policy-Making* (Chicago: Aldine Publishing Co., 1968).

97. Dale Mann, *Policy Decision-Making in Education: An Introduction to Calculation and Control* (New York: Teachers College Press, Columbia University, 1975), pp. 10-17.

98. John Thomas Thompson, *Policymaking in American Public Education: A Framework for Analysis* (Englewood Cliffs, N.J.: Prentice-Hall, 1976).

education and some of the continuing concerns of that field, the description is not the same as a theory of the politics of education and hardly explains relationships among the above concepts or methods for studying them.

THEORETICAL APPROACHES

Principally because of the writings of political scientists like Almond and Easton, the politics of education has of late become more and more concerned with questions of theory.[99] The abundance of unconnected explorations of almost any kind of "politics" has been a sign that the field needs more attention to theory.[100] So it is particularly encouraging that the politics of education has adapted some theoretical approaches from other disciplines, notably from political science.[101] For the sake of brevity only two of these will be mentioned.

Mazzoni and Campbell used two conceptual frameworks (or theoretical approaches) in their study of influentials in educational policy making: political systems theory and allocative theory.[102] Political systems theory views policy making as a process through which inputs (in the form of demands and supports) are converted (through a political system) into outputs (one kind of which is the authoritative decision), which result in certain kinds of outcomes (for example, consequences of the decisions) that in

99. For a more comprehensive discussion of the importance of theory, see David Easton, *A Framework for Political Analysis*, chap. 1, and idem, *A Systems Analysis of Political Life* (New York: John Wiley & Sons), chap. 1.

100. Iannaccone provides this critique of the eclecticism of the politics of education: "Bits and pieces of political science jargon are ripped from context, consumed by use in a single journal article, and discarded." Laurence Iannaccone, *Education Policy Systems: A Study Guide for Education Administrators* (Fort Lauderdale, Fla.: Nova University, 1975), p. 26.

101. The term "theoretical approach" is deliberately used to contrast with "theory" in the sense of the physical sciences. The theoretical approaches used by the politics of education are hardly theory in the purest sense of the term. See Easton, *A Systems Analysis of Political Life*.

102. Tim L. Mazzoni, Jr., and Roald F. Campbell, "Influentials in State Policymaking for the Public Schools," *Educational Administration Quarterly* 12 (Winter 1976): 1-26. Mazzoni and Campbell trace their use of systems theory to Easton, *A Framework for Political Analysis*, and allocative theory to Harold D. Lasswell, *Politics: Who Gets What, When, How* (New York: McGraw-Hill Book Co., 1936).

turn can feed back into the political system as new demands or supports. Minar used a political systems framework when he focused upon context, political process, and policy in his study of four suburban school districts.[103] Scribner found that the operations of a school board could be adequately described by systems analysis.[104] Dye studied the effects of political and economic inputs upon policy outputs and discovered a strong relationship between policy and economic antecedents.[105] Wirt and Kirst applied this approach to an entire range of educational activities.[106] According to allocation theory, on the other hand, the relationships of actors are dominated by conflict and attempts to influence the decisions made by the authoritative policy-making body (for example, the school board). Thus concern is directed toward the kinds and amount of influence that can be aggregated (often dependent on resources, willingness to use them, and application of them) and formal and informal structures through which that influence operates. Using allocation theory, Campbell and Mazzoni also studied state policy making, especially the influences of key institutions, actors, and groups.[107] The existence of both political systems and allocative frameworks emphasizes the directions that the politics of education is now taking in terms of the development of theory.

In summary, then, the politics of education can be described in the following manner. It is centrally concerned with interactions surrounding the authoritative allocation of values in education, especially insofar as the concepts of government, power, conflict, and policy are concerned. Moreover, while this field of inquiry is currently engaged in theory development that has resulted in conceptual frameworks such as political systems and allocative

---

103. Minar, *Educational Decision-Making in Suburban Communities*.

104. Scribner, "A Functional-Systems Analysis of School Board Performance."

105. Thomas R. Dye, *Politics, Economics, and Public Policy: Outcomes in the American States* (Chicago: Rand McNally & Co., 1966).

106. Wirt and Kirst, *The Political Web of American Schools*.

107. Roald F. Campbell and Tim L. Mazzoni, Jr., *State Policy Making for the Public Schools: A Comparative Analysis of Policy Making for the Public Schools in Twelve States and a Treatment of State Governance Models* (Berkeley, Calif.: McCutchan Publishing Corp. 1976).

theories, no true theory has yet emerged. Considering the reign of many years of the apolitical myth in education, it is no mean accomplishment that the politics of education has developed even this far since the early 1960s.

CHAPTER II

Methods and Conceptualizations of Political Power in Education

FRANK W. LUTZ

Introduction

Everyone involved in politics, from ward heelers to statesmen, from the naive beginner in the study of politics to the most eminent political theoretician, needs some kind of conceptual framework in order to understand or to affect political power. That conceptualization may be a "seat of the pants" guide, a "feel" for politics learned in the school of "hard knocks," or it may be a sophisticated combination of methods and theories of politics. In any case some conceptual map is required if a person is to find a way through the maze of power, authority, and influence that constitutes politics.

Although some still insist that educational policy making and politics *should* be separate, few, if any, still contend that they *are* separate. Walsh emphasizes the necessity for the superintendent to comprehend and understand the power structure of the community and school board and the operation of politics in education.[1] Substantiating that position, Zeigler and Jennings state:

> We can infer that when educational government is *not* depoliticized, the arena will be structured to devalue the resources of the superintendent and inflate the resources of the board and the community-interest groups. It is frequently argued that educational decision making is becoming more involved with the political process.[2]

If superintendents are to survive in this political process they must understand the politics of education.

---

1. John E. Walsh, *Educational and Political Power* (New York: Center for Applied Research in Education, 1964), p. 40.

2. L. Harmon Zeigler and M. Kent Jennings, *Governing American Schools* (North Scituate, Mass.: Duxbury Press, 1974), p. 158.

No less a practically oriented organization than the American Association of School Administrators has admonished school administrators to become more involved in politics.

> If America's superintendents want more federal [and state] school dollars, . . . then they will have to become much more involved in the blood and sweat of practical politics.[3]

If superintendents are to survive in that ominous sea, they need some navigation aids to guide their voyage.

At the other end of the practitioner-researcher continuum, Dahl specifies the very practical kinds of appraisals that influence decisions in politics:

> 1. . . . one's decisions depend on what one considers to be the alternative courses of action, if any, that are "open" or "available."
> 2. . . . one's decision depends on what one believes are the *likely consequences of pursuing each of these alternative courses of action.*
> 3. . . . one's decisions depend on the *value* one assigns to the consequences of each alternative.
> 4. . . . then, in situations of uncertainty, one's decision depends on one's guesses, hunches, or estimates, concerning the *probability that the various consequences will actually occur.*
> 5. . . . in situations of uncertainty, your decision will depend on your *orientations toward risk, uncertainty, and gambling.*[4]

But recognizing alternatives, consequences, values, probabilities, and orientations depends on conceptualizations available to the political participant. As Dahl points out:

> If politics is inescapable, so are the consequences of politics. . . . The best reason for improving one's skill in political analysis, is this: political analysis helps one to understand the world he lives in, to make more intelligent choices among the alternatives he faces, and to influence the changes, great and small, that are an inherent aspect of all political systems. . . . Whenever students of politics scrupulously test their generalizations and theories against the data of experience by means of meticulous observation, classification, and measurement, then political analysis is scientific.[5]

3. "Congressmen Prescribe More Political Activity for School Administrators," *School Administrator* 31 (June 1974): 117.

4. Robert A. Dahl, *Modern Political Analysis*, 2d ed. (Englewood Cliffs, N.J.: Prentice-Hall, 1970), pp. 101-2.

5. Ibid., p. 1.

THE EXERCISE OF POWER IN EDUCATION

One of the important questions in the study of politics is always, "Who makes the decisions and who benefits from them?" Whether the system is machine or reform, monopolistic or pluralistic, the decisions of a governance system in the end serve the interests and values of the power holder. Those decisions may incidentally benefit others as well. In general, however, because interests and values differ in a society, because resources are always limited, and because political decisions benefit one group's values and interests, those decisions must also disadvantage others. Lord Acton is reported to have said, "Power corrupts and absolute power corrupts absolutely." The critical question then may not be, "Who governs?" but "Who has access to modify the governance, under what conditions, and how?" If there is a tendency toward the "Iron Law of Oligarchy,"[6] if "power corrupts and absolute power corrupts absolutely," and if those who exercise power sooner or later do so in their own best interest, then the only political difference in governance systems is whether the power is absolute or whether, when other interests are sufficiently unattended, those others can alter the governance system and by what means.

Forty years of research has demonstrated that power and politics are important elements of the governance of education and that generally such power has been exercised by the upper and middle classes and their decisions have benefited those classes.

It should be made clear that the above statements rest upon none of the works of Karl Marx. Rather they are based upon the findings of Lynd and Lynd, Warner, Hollingshead, and Vidich and Bensman.[7] All found that the public schools of the United States were governed by school boards recruited largely from the upper and middle classes and their decisions tended to benefit those classes. While Dahl found dispersed inequalities with no single elite power structure making all decisions, his data tended to support the

---

6. Robert Michels, *Political Parties* (New York: Free Press, 1966).

7. Robert S. Lynd and Helen Merrell Lynd, *Middletown* (New York: Harcourt, Brace & World, 1929); W. Lloyd Warner, *Democracy in Jonesville* (New York: Harper & Brothers, 1949); August B. Hollingshead, *Elmtown's Youth* (New York: Doubleday & Co., 1949); Arthur J. Vidich and Joseph Bensman, *Small Town in Mass Society* (Garden City, N.Y.: Doubleday & Co., 1960).

notion that educational decisions were made by a coalition of upper- and middle-class individuals and served their interests and values.[8] Iannaccone and Lutz found that while a middle-class school board could be politically overturned, the conflict was between rural middle-class and suburban middle-class values.[9]

The consistency of these data over such an extended period of time indicate that (a) politics and power are components of decision making in education; (b) those in power tend to govern in ways that enhance their own values and interests; and (c) upper- and middle-class values and interests have dominated educational decisions to the detriment of the interests and values of the lower economic class and minority groups. Some may think this reflects the leadership responsibilities of the elite; others may decry it as unjust, even immoral. Some may contend this situation exists because power and its resources are concentrated within the wealthy upper classes; others may contend that power is based on a system of dispersed inequalities that permits lower-class influence through coalitions. While explanations of the empirical reality may differ, they do not change it. If we are either to maintain it, or to change it, it will be necessary to understand the politics of the exercise of power in educational decision making. One needs a model of politics to guide data collection, analysis, interpretation, and application.

Methods for Studying Power and Politics in Education

Five methods used to gather data in order to answer questions about power in politics will be reviewed briefly in this section: (a) survey analysis; (b) reputational analysis; (c) issue analysis; (d) socio-anthropological field analysis, and (e) comparative analysis.

SURVEY ANALYSIS

Perhaps the first analytic political use of demographic data was in 1662 in John Graunt's *Natural and Political Observations Made*

---

8. Robert A. Dahl, *Who Governs?* (New Haven, Conn.: Yale University Press, 1961).

9. Laurence Iannaccone and Frank W. Lutz, *Politics, Power and Policy: The Governing of Local School Districts* (Columbus, Ohio: Charles E. Merrill Publishing Co., 1970).

upon Bills of Mortality.[10] Modern demographic methods are heuristic if only because of the abundance of demographic data. United States census data by tract and enumeration district are available on computer tape. Standard demographic data are thus available to describe the entire United States and many of the areas of interest to research in the politics of education. These include such data as family income categories, level of education, home ownership, age categories, certain racial designations, and other information often important in assessing possible educational constituencies. Lutz and Iannaccone provide a list of such variables.[11]

Given the total demographic description of the geographic area of concern to the researcher, a stratified random sample may be selected to approximate the total population and to answer very complicated political questions about, for example, political values and voter predisposition and opinion. Nunnery and Kimbrough as well as Conway, Jennings, and Milstein provide comprehensive reviews of polling techniques related specifically to education.[12] Given such information the computer can simulate a particular condition and predict voter response. These methods have been successfully used in party politics for two decades.[13] Their use in education has been much less extensive and considerably less sophisticated; such methods may also be used, however, to predict the likelihood of public acceptance or rejection of educational innovations, new building programs, curricular changes, and the like.

REPUTATIONAL ANALYSIS

There are perhaps as many variations of the reputational analysis in determining the power structure as there have been studies using

10. John Graunt, *Natural and Political Observations Made upon Bills of Mortality*, ed. Walter F. Willcox (Baltimore, Md.: Johns Hopkins Press, 1939).

11. Frank W. Lutz and Laurence Iannaccone, *Understanding Educational Organizations: A Field Study Approach* (Columbus, Ohio: Charles E. Merrill Publishing Co., 1969), p. 42.

12. Michael Y. Nunnery and Ralph B. Kimbrough, *Politics, Power, Polls and School Elections* (Berkeley, Calif.: McCutchan Publishing Corp., 1971); James A. Conway, Robert E. Jennings, and Mike M. Milstein, *Understanding Communities* (Englewood Cliffs, N.J.: Prentice-Hall, 1974).

13. Paul Lazarsfeld et al., *The People's Choice* (New York: Columbia University Press, 1948); Ithiel de Sola Pool et al., *Candidates, Issues and Strategies* (Cambridge, Mass.: M. I. T. Press, 1965).

the approach. The original method was developed by Hunter, who field tested this method in Popular Village in the late 1940s.[14] He used a refined version in Regional City. There he identified 175 reputed "influentials" in areas of social, civic, governmental, and business concerns. A panel of six judges reduced the original pool to ten influential individuals in each of the four categories, resulting in a reputed "power elite" of forty persons. These persons selected by reputation (thus reputational approach) were thought by Hunter to be the decision makers in all important areas using either overt or covert power.

Hunter's study of Regional City in the late 1940s found that no one nominated black people except other black people. From that he concluded that there was a power structure, composed only of blacks, that was subservient to the top power structure in all issues. That situation probably is no longer accurate for Regional City; still it is well to recall that such "mini" power structures may exist in any community. Leaders cannot act autonomously, but must frequently obtain the cooperation of these other groups. Thus the power elite of the reputational approach simulates to some extent, under certain conditions, the coalition of the pluralists.

As with any research method the reputational approach has both strengths and weaknesses. Perhaps its major strength is the fact that it is far less expensive in time, energy, and money than other methods. Its major weakness is that it assumes covert power. Whether or not one chooses to influence a decision, his reputation covertly influences that decision. Additionally, the very use of this method not only assumes a single top power elite but guarantees the discovery of such an elite as an artifact of the method. It should be noted, however, that prominent political scientists have found similar power systems when using both reputational and issue analysis methods in the same community.[15]

ISSUE ANALYSIS

Unlike the reputational approach, issue analysis neither assumes covert power nor does it necessarily conclude with the discovery

---

14. Floyd Hunter, *Community Power Structure* (Chapel Hill, N.C.: University of North Carolina Press, 1953).

15. Robert E. Agger and Daniel Goldrich, "Community Power Structures and Partisanship," *American Sociological Review* 23 (August 1958): 383-92.

of a power elite. Issue analysis does not rely on a single method of data collection. It utilizes historical methods as well as observation of present issues. It may include interview and questionnaire methods. Its fundamental technique is, however, the selection of and the direct study of particular issues presently being decided and the process of deciding about those issues. In his classic study of New Haven, Dahl selected three issue areas: (a) political nomination, (b) public education, and (c) urban renewal.[16] From his study of these three areas and his historical analysis of past political power in New Haven, Dahl concluded that power had shifted from one oligarchy to another. This fact tends to deny the rule of a single power elite, for if such an oligarchy rules in its own best interest and holds all power, why would it be unable to perpetuate itself? More importantly, Dahl found different power groups operating in different issue areas, thus providing evidence of a shift from oligarchy to polyarchy in New Haven. Perhaps polyarchy (rule by a coalition of power groups) is but oligarchy in transition. But even this pessimistic view is a modification of Michels's "Iron Law of Oligarchy."[17] Perhaps there is a tendency toward this "Iron Law" but that tendency moves in another direction when the people choose to exercise their dispersed, albeit unequal, power. This important fact has often escaped schoolmen. Perhaps the power of a citizen or parent is but a pebble compared to the power of the educational elite. But an avalanche of pebbles has covered many a boulder.

Perhaps if the persons using the reputational approach would follow the lead of their sociometric predecessors by selecting specific issues and then asking who influences each issue, they would discover separate but overlapping power structures.[18] Miller used a technique with the results hypothesized above.[19] In spite of the

16. Dahl, *Who Governs?*

17. Michels, *Political Parties.*

18. Gardner Lindzey and Edgar F. Borgatta, "Sociometric Measurement," in *Handbook of Social Psychology*, ed. Gardner Lindzey (Reading, Mass.: Addison-Wesley Publishing Co., 1954), vol. 1, pp. 405-18.

19. Delbert C. Miller, "Decision-making Cliques in Community Power Structures: A Comparative Study of an American and an English City," *American Journal of Sociology* 64 (November 1958): 299-310.

fact that certain researchers find issue analysis to be consistently superior to the reputational approach,[20] other equally eminent researchers have found the use of both methods to produce substantially the same results.[21]

Of considerable importance in using the issue analysis method is the careful selection of the issues to be studied. Assuming that the pluralists are correct, it is possible that the most powerful organizations and persons do not choose to exercise that power except on rare occasions and in a very narrow range of issues. For instance, when studying the national power structure, Hunter found the American Medical Association ranked second among top influencers.[22] Noting that the AMA had not influenced national issues between his data collection and the publication of the study, Hunter questions this ranking: "I have heard little of the American Medical Association since, and in general the doctors are individually and collectively not considered a power-laden group—nor do they want to be."[23] What is more likely is that on certain issues the AMA is and wants to be the *most* influential of all organizations but on other less relevant issues cannot and certainly will not *use* its power. That is the problem with reputational approach. Thus, issues are important when one is studying power.

The selection of the issues to be studied is critical to the issue analysis method. Bachrach and Baratz have pointed out that power and influence are sometimes exercised to prevent issues from being joined by political bodies, policy formulators, and decision makers.[24] Thus, the observer looking for petitions, notions, and debates will fail to notice the issue at all for it never is introduced. Bachrach and Baratz refer to this as the nondecision. Such a nondecision usually operates like a covert veto. It effectively says "no" to some

20. Nelson W. Polsby, *Community Power and Political Theory* (New Haven, Conn.: Yale University Press, 1963).

21. Robert Presthus, *Men at the Top* (New York: Oxford University Press, 1964).

22. Floyd Hunter, *Top Leadership, U.S.A.* (Chapel Hill, N.C.: University of North Carolina Press, 1959).

23. Ibid., p. 15.

24. Peter Bachrach and Morton S. Baratz, *Power and Poverty: Theory and Practice* (New York: Oxford University Press, 1970).

interest and value without overtly saying it. Thus overt controversy is avoided. Similarily, Schattschneider has noted that the ability to control the agenda, thus preventing issues from becoming issues, is an important element in the study of power and influence.[25] These types of power may escape the issue analysis proponent unless the student of politics is aware of these problems and defines "issues" so as to allow a topic of concern to be defined as an issue even if it never appears on the agenda. Kelly provides a rather extensive analysis of the influence of the American Medical Association that can be interpreted as supporting this position.[26]

SOCIO-ANTHROPOLOGICAL FIELD ANALYSIS

The field method as defined here is based primarily on the use of participant observation. In addition, historical examination of records, minutes, policy and regulations, newspaper accounts, and written materials about the culture, society, or organization, its important issues, decisions, and individuals are used. Buttressing participant observation, the researcher examines all formal or informal accounts of the activities observed and makes use of informant descriptions, informal interviews, and, depending on the role of the observer and the nature of the problem, certain questionnaire surveys and polls.

The field study approach does not assume the power elite of the "reputationalists." Nor does it assume the existence of important issues as does issue analysis. It only assumes that there are decisions to be made and asks, "Does anyone govern?" Only after that question is answered does it ask, "Who governs, who influences, under what conditions, how are conflicts resolved and decisions made, and whose interest and values do they serve?" Lutz and Iannaccone have described the use of this method, including data collection, analysis, and report writing, in the study of educational organizations.[27]

Two aspects will be briefly treated here—the role of the ob-

25. Elmer E. Schattschneider, *The Semisovereign People: A Realist's View of Democracy in America* (New York: Holt, Rinehart & Winston, 1960).

26. Stanley Kelly, Jr., *Professional Public Relations and Political Power* (Baltimore, Md.: Johns Hopkins Press, 1956).

27. Lutz and Iannaccone, *Understanding Educational Organizations*.

server and the sample of data to be collected. For more extensive treatments of participant observation and field work the reader is referred to Junker, to McCall and Simmons, and to Wax.[28]

Briefly, the role of the participant may vary from (a) the active participant who maximizes participation with the observed in order to gather more accurate or meaningful data to (b) the inactive participant who attempts to minimize interaction with the observed in the notion that interaction contaminates the data and therefore the conclusions. The observer's research role and objectives may be known or hidden from the observed. Of paramount importance, regardless of the observer's role, is the necessity for the researcher to do all possible to guard against observer bias. On the one hand, bias stems from preconceived values, assumptions, and models about the phenomena being observed. As the observer stands aloof and uninvolved with the society being observed, observer bias tends to be reduced. On the other hand, the more active the participation of the observer the greater the possibility of "going native," that is, losing objectivity by integrating or empathizing completely with the observed society and accepting its "unscientific" explanations as the truth.

Of major importance are the time span during which data will be collected and the breadth of observation. In general, there should be observation through one cycle of the environment with which the system must interact. Because field work was introduced in largely agrarian, nontechnical societies, a minimum of one year has become the standard. In education the same period of time seems reasonable due to the nature of school (that is, school opening, budget, board elections, examinations, graduation, school closing, summer session). The time period, however, is best defined by the sequence of important environmental impingements on the decision-making body that might affect the political process being studied. Most field investigators are prone to want to gather more data and should be cautioned to specify the time when data collection will be terminated and then abide by that decision, with only minor variations.

28. Buford Junker, *Field Work* (Chicago: University of Chicago Press, 1960); George J. McCall and J. L. Simmons, *Issues in Participant Observation* (Reading, Mass.: Addison-Wesley Publishing Co., 1969); Rosalie H. Wax, *Doing Field Work* (Chicago: University of Chicago Press, 1971).

The question of how far to broaden the data collection base must also receive an ambiguous answer: "As narrow as possible but as broad as necessary to understand the process." The researcher does not purposely push data collection out of the school board meeting to the local cocktail lounge where important decision makers meet after the regular meeting. But based on empirical evidence, the researcher must move to the lounge at certain times and for certain data. Another researcher however may be in the same lounge, a focal data point, collecting data on an entirely different research problem. Only as these separate issues converge will their observations center on the same behavior. These and other issues concerning participant observation have been summarized by Lutz and Ramsey.[29]

While the socio-anthropological method avoids many of the weaknesses of methods previously discussed, its major weakness is the expense incurred in avoiding those weaknesses. Where "grounded" empirical field work has laid the foundation for testing theoretically based and compelling hypotheses, field methods are to be avoided because of the expense.

COMPARATIVE ANALYSIS

The term comparative applies to any of the above methods if the research involves the study and comparison of two or more political systems. These may be two systems from the same culture (for example, two American school boards) or systems from different cultures (for example, the study of urban education in London and New York). It may also include the comparison of two methods of studying the same system (for example, comparing the power structure discovered through reputational approach with the power system described by issue analysis in the same city).

Comparisons of political systems of the same kind (for example, school boards), either in the same culture or cross-culturally, or comparisons of different kinds of government (for example, a school board with a local city government), are all too few and are to be encouraged both for their practical and theoretical value.

---

29. Frank W. Lutz and Margaret A. Ramsey, "The Use of Anthropological Field Methods in Educational Research," *Educational Researcher* 3 (November 1974): 5-8.

This, of course, assumes that any type of comparative analysis attempts to draw generalizations concerning similarities and differences about the systems compared and not merely to report a description of the separate systems. Even this latter accomplishment is worthwhile when another researcher can use these descriptions as data (assuming both method and data are well described) in order to build generalizations and models.[30]

Models and Concepts Applied to the Politics of Education

In this section various models useful in the study of the politics of education are described under the following six classifications: general systems models, class structure models, ideal typical models, participation models, comparative-descriptive models, and political-psychological models.

GENERAL SYSTEMS MODELS

All of the models explained under this classification can be said to involve some application of general systems principles as set forth by von Bertalanffy.[31] As such, they involve variables of: (a) inputs, (b) outputs, and (c) a processing system through which inputs are converted to outputs, and, in the case of a cybernetic or open system, with a feedback-feedforward mechanism. McClelland has correctly defined general systems as standing "for an approach; it is a certain point of view. It might be characterized also as a conceptual framework within which observations are held."[32] The following are general systems models.

Almond-Coleman model. This system classifies major components of a political system as (a) inputs, (b) conversion functions, and (c) outputs in the political process.[33] Developed orig-

---

30. Examples of comparative political power studies include Robert Agger, Daniel Goldrich, and Bert E. Swanson, *The Rulers and the Ruled* (New York: John Wiley & Sons, 1964) and Arthur J. Vidich, Joseph Bensman, and Maurice R. Stein, *Reflections on Community Studies* (New York: John Wiley & Sons, 1964).

31. Ludwig von Bertalanffy, *General Systems Theory: Foundations, Development Applications* (New York: George Braziller, 1968).

32. Charles A. McClelland, "General Systems and the Social Sciences," *ETC.* 18 (February 1962): 449-50.

33. Gabriel Almond and James E. Coleman, eds., *The Politics of Developing Areas* (Princeton, N.J.: Princeton University Press, 1960).

inally as a model of developing nations, Scribner tested the model for its utility in the analysis of school board behavior.[34] Scribner classified the official minutes of six meetings of a school board. Several functional subcategories of school board behavior were developed. He concluded that a school board is a political system and that the adopted Almond model is useful in classifying school board political behavior by using the readily available data of public board minutes. While there is serious doubt as to the completeness of most public minutes of school boards, they do constitute the official record of governmental function.

Easton model. Easton has developed a rather sophisticated macro-model he calls "a dynamic response model." [35] This model includes: (a) inputs (demands and supports), (b) a conversion political system (where demands are converted) and (c) outputs (including a feedback loop to the demand-support element). Wirt and Kirst utilize and adopt this model to examine local, state, and national politics in education.[36] In particular, the application of Easton's model as suggested by Wirt and Kirst is useful and explanatory. It is capable of explanation and hypothesis development at both macro and micro levels depending on the operational categories selected.

Tri-systems model. Combining the systems variables from Homans,[37] which explain the behavior of individuals in groups, Loomis's "processually articulated model" explaining the behavior of groups with other groups,[38] and the general systems concepts of von Bertalanffy [39] and of McClelland [40] describing the macro move-

34. Jay D. Scribner, "A Functional-systems Framework for Analyzing School Board Action," *Educational Administration Quarterly* 2 (Autumn 1966): 204-15.

35. David Easton, *A Systems Analysis of Political Life* (New York: John Wiley & Sons, 1965).

36. Frederick M. Wirt and Michael W. Kirst, *The Political Web of American Schools* (Boston: Little, Brown & Co., 1972).

37. George C. Homans, *Social Behavior: Its Elementary Forms* (New York: Harcourt, Brace & World, 1961).

38. Charles C. Loomis, *Social Systems: Essays on Their Persistence and Change* (New York: Van Nostrand Co., 1960).

39. von Bertalanffy, *General Systems Theory.*

40. McClelland, "General Systems and Social Sciences."

ment of elements with the environment, Lutz and Iannaccone suggest a model that moves from the micro to the macro in political behavior.[41] At one level their model deals with power of individuals within groups. At another it explores important elements as groups form coalitions against other groups. At the most general level it suggests that all human systems are open systems and governed by the principles of general systems theory. Like many systems models it has the advantage of "explaining" all systems and the disadvantage of often failing to explain the differences among various systems without the assistance of additional models. A possible application of the tri-systems model that has not been tried is in the development of political simulation games. Rigorous measurement of the variables in the model, carefully operationalized and manipulated within the parameters of a computer program, could result in interesting hypothesis testing and prediction.

CLASS POWER MODELS

All social class models are predicated on the assumption of oligarchical elites. Power in these models is assumed to be a result of membership in a particular class (for example, military, business, social-economic) rather than any particular power assets. The fact is, however, while actual power assets may be correlated with class membership (for example, wealth with upper class) class membership does not guarantee nor is it perfectly correlated with power. This is perhaps the major weakness of social class models.

The power elite. One of the better known models attributing power to an elite class or group of classes is that described by Mills in *The Power Elite*.[42] Mills postulates a configuration of military, industrial, and religious leaders that dominates all national decisions. Given the diminution of the clergy in American society, the model attributes power to the military-industrial complex and indicates the undemocratic aspect of such a power elite. Any class power model is undemocratic if it attributes almost total power to an elite. It is not only that the power elite described by Mills is

41. Lutz and Iannaccone, *Understanding Educational Organizations*.

42. C. Wright Mills, *The Power Elite* (New York: Oxford University Press, 1959).

undemocratic but many feel it dangerous to mankind. In a society that permits an expenditure of more than $110 billion a year for "defense," and given the disclosures about the Central Intelligence Agency and other military intelligence groups both at home and abroad, it is difficult to dispute Mills's notion entirely. But as pointed out by Etzioni, "*The Power Elite* provides a perspective on American society, but scarcely considers other categories of sociological knowledge." [43]

The application of notions like Mills's power elite leaves certain kinds of political decisions unexplained, but it may provide interesting insights and hypotheses regarding congressional behavior related to education bills. For instance, why was the term "defense" used in designating the first omnibus education bill to pass the national Congress—the National Defense Education Act? Why did the Land Grant Act include the establishment of ROTC units in land grant colleges? Why was there an aspect of military, business, or agriculture in every education bill passed by the Congress prior to the first NDEA Act?

Social class model. The most noted researcher in social class is Warner, and the best single example of his works in this arena is perhaps his *Social Class in America*.[44] The most comprehensive volume covering his work and that of other researchers in this area is Kahl.[45] Kahl not only provides a number of methods for determining the class structure of a community and the theory providing the prodigious leaps from social class to political power. He also cautions: "There is a tendency for judges of high status to degrade persons of low status and for persons of low status to raise their colleagues a bit," and "We must remain suspicious concerning claims that the informants will agree about decisions into clear-cut strata." [46] These cautions should be remembered by those using a social class conceptual model and the reputational method as well.

---

43. Amitai Etzioni, "Nonconventional Uses of Sociology as Illustrated by Peace Research," in *The Uses of Sociology*, ed. Paul F. Lazarsfeld et al. (New York: Basic Books, 1967), p. 830.

44. W. Lloyd Warner, Marcia Meeker, and Kenneth Eells, *Social Class in America* (New York: Harper & Bros., 1960).

45. Joseph A. Kahl, *The American Class Structure* (New York: Holt, Rinehart & Winston, 1957).

46. Ibid., p. 41.

The social class model categorizes individuals into one of six classes. These classes each have prescribed a rather distinct lifestyle, ideologies, values, and patterns of interaction that, along with their power assets, produce a configuration of political power. As noted earlier, most studies of education and power have found public education to be governed by the upper and middle classes; the interests of these classes have been served by that governance to the detriment of the lower classes. While Warner's class model is not as narrow or centralized as Mill's power elite, it too fails to recognize the power potential, if not the actual power, of lower-middle and lower classes. Recent national legislation on education benefiting poor and minority groups would be difficult to explain within purely social class models of power except by recognizing the power of the lower classes. This is not to say that social class models explain nothing. Their application is derived from the empirical reality of the past and this reality lingers into the present. Class models become useful as one recognizes that power is dispersed among classes, that power and its resources rest not only in the upper classes, and that the exercise of class power (status politics) is often an ugly affair whether the oligarchy is an upper- or lower-class oligarchy.

Class polyarchy model. Class models generally are in some manner, to a greater or lesser extent, wed to oligarchical rather than pluralistic notions of the exercise of power. Class models, however, need not be so narrow in their assumptions. Almost twenty years ago, Miller questioned the validity of certain assumptions about the top power elite found by most reputationalists, particularly the sweeping generalizations about the influence of business leaders and inherited wealth in that power structure.[47] He found somewhat varying patterns in three cities he studied in three geographically different locations.

In what may be described as a classic work on social class and power, Bendix and Lipset have compiled an anthology of class theories and related variables permitting the application of class theory to notions of political pluralism and issue analysis methods.[48]

47. Miller, "Decision-making Cliques in Community Power."

48. Reinhard Bendix and Seymour Martin Lipset, *Class, Status and Power: A Reader in Social Stratification* (Glencoe, Ill.: Free Press, 1953).

Given the assumption of social class structure and the attending clusters of interests, norms, and cultural values, then assigning potential power assets within each of the given classes, it might be possible to analyze the potential power of various class coalitions and predict their likely attempts to exercise that power given specific educational issues.

Allowing the belief in class power, but combining with it the pluralistic notions that power is a system of dispersed inequalities resting not solely within a single social class but dispersed within all classes and that the exercise of this power depends on the perceived saliency of the issue as related to particular class values, then one can ask questions about who is likely to attempt to influence a particular educational decision, how, and with what effect. Given the demographic description of a community one can distribute the population within various social classes. Based on carefully selected class studies one can describe value structures and interaction patterns within and among social classes. Reasonable guesses can then be made about likely power configurations. By matching issues with the values of particular classes, a prediction can be made about the likely use of that power to influence educational decisions. For instance, one might have been able to speculate about the exercise of power and the manifestation of that power as it is related to busing decisions in Boston in the mid-1970s.

IDEAL TYPICAL MODELS

"Ideal typical" models as defined here follow the lead of Weber in developing a set of criteria for organizational or system prototypes that epitomize a pure type at the end of a continuum.[49] It is assumed that while real systems will only approximate the "ideal" prototype, they can be classified along the continuum, at least in rank order, based upon the degree to which they achieve the "ideal" state. There is no valuing of "ideal" in this ranking; that is, "ideal" simply defines the approachable but unattainable state.

Oligarchy-polyarchy (elite-pluralistic). This conceptual continuum follows the traditions, methodologies, and assumptions of

---

49. Max Weber, *Wirtschaft und Gesellschaft* (Tübingen, Germany: J. C. B. Mohr, 1922).

Hunter and his notions of power elite at one end of the continuum[50] and of Dahl and his notions of pluralism at the other.[51] Thus political systems can be classified as tending toward oligarchy if they are constituted of a single and rather static power structure that makes all decisions either through overt or covert intervention and rules in its own best interest. At the other end of the continuum, political systems may be classified as a configuration of competing individuals and subsystems each holding some power (unequal but dispersed). As no single subsystem has sufficient power to rule, coalitions are formed. These coalitions change depending on the issue. When one coalition becomes powerful enough, a decision is made in a particular area. Thus the power to decide is not vested in a single elite but in a shifting, ever changing, pluralistic coalition of subsystems—rule by polyarchy.

While the work of no researcher in educational politics rests totally at either end of this continuum, Kimbrough is more of the Hunter tradition and toward the oligarchy end.[52] Zeigler and Jennings are more of the Dahl theoretical tradition, toward polyarchy.[53] In addition, it is possible, using either reputational or issue analysis methods, to place school governance systems on the continuum based on the answer to the question, "Who governs and whose interests are served?" Such data reveal answers to questions about public education and its role in the American society. One should note the kinds of methodological biases that lead one researcher to a particular theoretical position while a different bias leads another researcher to a different one.

Sacred-secular. Moving from the work of Becker and his classification of communities along a sacred to secular continuum,[54] Iannaccone and Lutz applied Becker's ideal typical definition to school board behavior.[55] They indicate that the local school

50. Hunter, *Community Power Structure*.

51. Dahl, *Modern Political Analysis*.

52. Ralph B. Kimbrough, *Political Power and Educational Decision Making*, (Chicago: Rand McNally & Co., 1964).

53. Zeigler and Jennings, *Governing American Schools*.

54. Howard P. Becker, *Through Values to Social Interpretation* (Durham, N.C.: Duke University Press, 1950).

55. Iannaccone and Lutz, *Politics, Power and Policy*.

governance systems, whether oligarchically or polyarchically constituted, may govern in a sacred or secular tradition. Sacred governance systems tend to operate out of the public view. They value the traditional ways and abhor change. Decisions are made in private sessions and consensus usually reached. Decisions are ritualistically enacted in the legal public arena, usually by unanimous vote. The rules of influence are the folkways of informal politics and known only, or at least best, by the "priesthood" of the ruling educational experts, particularly the school board and the superintendent. Secular governance systems, however, desire change and value it nearly as an end in itself. The rules of political participation are public and the decisions are made in public where influence and political response can be seen by all participants. While it may be more likely that a sacred school board will operate as a ruling oligarchy and a secular board will govern by a coalition formed from the polyarchy, the models are not coincident and should not be used interchangeably. It is possible for an elite board to operate in a secular fashion or for a pluralistic board to operate nearer the sacred end of the continuum. This model best describes not who governs, but *how* the system governs, responding to questions and hypotheses within the process category.

Machine-reform (private- or public-regarding). In their book *City Politics*, Banfield and Wilson describe a model of city politics that capitalizes on the pluralist model.[56] Their model follows and is interwoven with their notion of "public- vs. private-regarding." As will be noted later, the failure to separate the two is perhaps one reason this model has not been applied to the politics of education very often.

A machine system is based on specific and material inducements while a reform system (although not made explicit by Banfield and Wilson) is based on generalized and nonmaterial inducements. Interwoven with this reward-inducement dichotomy is the psychological value of individuals and the cultural ethics of systems, either private- or public-regarding. Private-regarding seeks those specific and material rewards that benefit one's self or group while public-regarding seeks the generalized and nonmaterial rewards that benefit the greater

---

56. Edward C. Banfield and James Q. Wilson, *City Politics* (New York: Vintage Books, 1966).

good, the public at large, and presumably do not directly benefit self. Apparently Banfield and Wilson believe that the exercise of power in itself, the acquiring of rank or authority, the ability to allocate values and resources authoritatively, and the right to "serve" through public office are not rewarding or self-serving. Such an argument flies in the face of other social science research.[57] Banfield and Wilson indicate that material rewards sought by the poor and emergent masses through the machine constitute private-regarding while the "service" motive of the middle and upper class is public-regarding. Such a view seems to provide a philosophical foundation for the rule of the elite upper class. Another view would suggest that both groups seek what they have least and need most.[58] The poor seek material rewards and the wealthy, already possessing material rewards, seek prestige. Is one more moral than the other? Probably when one achieves office in either machine or reform system one is more likely to benefit from both kinds of rewards. Banfield and Wilson admit that one of the most important rewards the machine can offer is friendship, hardly a material inducement.

The above argument is presented to posit the possibility that either machine or reform systems of governance can be operated by either public- or private-regarding persons and with some combination of self-interest and public interest. Should anyone doubt this possibility he may recall the "reform" New York City school board that was removed by the state legislature in 1960 for various private-regarding activities including charges of irregularities in school construction contracts and personal gain from their office.

On the other hand, can machine governance, operating in the public interest (at least as far as education is concerned), produce good public education? The record indicates that it was in the early 1900s during the height of machine government in many American cities that urban education was strongest and, according to some, best. It was after reform took hold of practically every

57. See Wallace S. Sayre and Herbert Kaufman, *Governing New York City: Politics in the Metropolis* (New York: Russell Sage Foundation, 1960), pp. 736-38, in political science; Homans, *Social Behavior*, p. 79, in social psychology; and Marvin Harris, *Cows, Pigs, Wars and Witches* (New York: Random House, 1974), p. 111, in anthropology.

58. Abraham H. Maslow, *Motivation and Personality*, 2d ed. (New York: Harper & Row, 1970), pp. 53-66.

American city's public school board that urban education declined. This is not to demonstrate that the decline was because of reform (although that argument could be made) but that reform politics and public-regarding did not stay that decline.

It is important to note that Banfield and Wilson state that it is the poor, minority group, slum dwellers who find support from machine government. Is it possible that whoever governs does so in their best interest and that the public interest of reformers is congruent with middle- and upper-class values and interests and rewards those classes, while the private interest of machine government rewards the *specific but not immoral* interests of the poor? The careful application of the machine-reform (private- or public-regarding) model might provide answers to some very interesting questions about urban education and its ability to handle inputs and respond with meaningful outputs to a clientele of poor, minority, slum dwelling people who prefer machine governance and find no support in reform governance systems.

Elite-arena. Bailey has posited two ideal typical council types.[59] Others working in political anthropology have used these concepts to study various noneducation councils.[60] Lutz has attempted to apply this model to local school boards.[61]

According to Bailey, elite councils (a) think of themselves as guardians of and separate from the people, (b) strive for consensus and decide in private meetings, and (c) legislatively enact those decisions in public by unanimous vote. They tend to rule in a narrow area and include executive-administrative as well as legal-judicial functions as council concerns. Arena councils (a) are "community in council" and their members think of themselves as representatives of specific factions and interests, (b) decide issues in public by debate and counter-debate, and (c) make decisions in public session by majority vote. They tend to rule in broad areas

---

59. F. G. Bailey, "Decisions by Consensus in Councils and Committees," in *Political Systems and the Distribution of Power*, ed. Michael Banton (London: Tavistock Publications, 1965).

60. Audrey Richards and Adam Kuper, eds., *Councils in Action* (Cambridge, England: Cambridge University Press, 1971).

61. Frank W. Lutz, "The School Board as Meta-Mediators," (Paper presented at the annual meeting of the American Educational Research Association, Washington, D.C., 1975), ERIC 105 563, 1975.

of governance and the executive function is independent from but responsible to the council for carrying out its decisions.

It might be hypothesized that elite council behavior is more akin (more desired or acceptable) to *Gemeinschaft*, sacred, homogeneous communities. Also, arena council behavior is more akin (more desired or acceptable) to *Gesellschaft*, secular, heterogeneous, and fractionated communities. Bailey has suggested that individuals or groups who perceive that they are consistently ignored and disadvantaged ("worsted," he says), often by "crooked means," have no confidence in elite councils. He continues: "In such circumstances the underprivileged are not likely to feel that they are governing themselves and not likely to become enthusiastic about working . . . when all the benefits go to the wealthy." [62]

It should be possible to classify school boards along an elite-arena council continuum. The elite-arena conceptualization might provide the basis for interesting hypotheses about urban education and an insightful reexamination of the very foundations upon which the governance of public education is based.

Iannaccone state model. Most of the conceptualizations presented have been applied to local school politics (although there is no reason they might not be applied at the state or perhaps federal level). The Iannaccone state model proposes a continuum of state politics of education consisting of four types of legislative process through which states enact state educational policy and law.[63] The continuum includes four types: (a) disparate, where local issues and self-interest prevail, (b) monolithic, where education interests (professional and lay) speak with a rather unified voice, (c) fragmented, where interest groups compete and (d) syndicated, where there exists a legal and publicly known mechanism where competing factions have representation and conflict can be resolved before legislative action. The application of this model could examine questions pertaining to state legislative process types and (a) total state allocations for education, (b) public employee legislation and teacher benefits and influence, (c) urban vs. rural educational legis-

62. Bailey, "Decisions by Consensus in Councils and Committees," p. 19.
63. Laurence Iannaccone, *Politics in Education* (New York: Center for Applied Research in Education, 1967).

lation, and (d) legislative-executive relationships in educational policy.

PUBLIC PARTICIPATION MODELS

Included in this category of conceptual political models are selected models that account for, describe, explain, or predict public participation in educational politics.

Voter turnout model. The voter turnout model is based on work by Carter and Sutthoff.[64] Data gathered in 1,954 school districts showed that the greater the voter turnout in school tax and bond referendums the more likely those issues were to be defeated. While numerous other variables, including psychological predisposition of the voter, personal influence, and community size, were considered in the study, percent of voter turnout was the most significant and memorable finding. Most school politicians (school administrators) operate on this model. Operationally the model holds that such elections should be kept "low key" in order to keep the turnout light, resulting hopefully in the approval of the tax or bond issue.

Such behavior, however, ignores Carter's own caution:

> Administrators viewing these results might well be dismayed. . . . That is, the issues which failed were those which drew larger voter turnout. . . . The inference to be drawn is that increased turnout is potentially dangerous if no selectivity is to be found among the new increments of votes. . . . A campaign can be waged [however] among voters known to be favorably disposed toward the issue.[65]

An excellent, accessible, and more complete description of the turnout model is provided by Wirt and Kirst,[66] whose work builds on the work of Carter and others. Basically, however, the turnout model suggests the seemingly "undemocratic" behavior of the sacred politics of education. Piele and Hall have provided the most recent

---

64. Richard F. Carter and John Sutthoff, *Communities and Their Schools*, (Stanford, Calif.: Institute for Communication Research, 1960), chaps. 4 and 5.

65. Richard F. Carter and William G. Savard, *Influence of Voter Turnout on School Board and Tax Elections*, Cooperative Research Monograph no. 5 (Washington, D.C.: U. S. Office of Education, 1961), pp. 21-22.

66. Wirt and Kirst, *The Political Web of American Schools*, pp. 98-109.

research updating the Carter turnout model in education and providing some links into the crosspressure model briefly described below.[67]

Crosspressure model. Actually explicit in the research upon which the turnout model is based but submerged in its single overriding postulate is the nature of the electorate: who they are and how they are influenced and why they turn out or stay home. A model concerned less with the size of the turnout and more with the latter variables is the crosspressure model. Lazarsfeld has described this model as related to partisan national elections.[68] Agger has described the nature of crosspressure theory in local school politics[69] and Nunnery and Kimbrough have related crosspressure theory to the broad spectrum of the politics of education.[70]

Basically crosspressure theory indicated that persons who find themselves in some sort of value conflict about a specific election will either change their habitual voting behavior or simply not vote at all. Changing a habitual voting pattern (for example, from a Republican to a Democratic ticket, or from opposition to tax increases to support for a bond referendum to build a new high school) is in itself a value conflict. The more likely result of crosspressure is that the voter will "stay at home"—not vote.

Operating on this model, the school politician assumes that the individuals and groups or factions are predisposed one way or the other in their voting behavior. That is, they are either habitual "yes" or "no" voters in tax elections. There are considerable data to support the notion that individuals are, through generations of family values and voting behavior, either Republicans or Democrats. There are data to support the notion that habitual voting behavior carries over into nonpartisan school tax and bond elections.

67. Philip K. Piele and John Stuart Hall, *Budgets, Bonds, and Ballots: Voting Behavior in School Financial Elections* (Lexington, Mass.: Lexington Books, 1973).

68. Lazarsfeld et al., *The People's Choice.*

69. Robert Agger, "The Politics of Local Education," in *Governing Education: A Reader on Politics, Power, and Public School Policy,* ed. Alan Rosenthal (Garden City, N.Y.: Doubleday & Co., 1969), pp. 44-85.

70. Nunnery and Kimbrough, *Politics, Power, Polls and School Elections,* pp. 40-57.

Based on these assumptions, the school politician does not attempt to change people's minds or get them to vote in opposition to their predisposition. Rather he attempts to relieve any possible crosspressure operating on those who are predisposed to vote for the referendum and places as much crosspressure as possible on those predisposed to vote "no." Thus all possible "yes" voters vote—and they vote as they are predisposed to vote, while large numbers of "no" voters stay at home. The bond issue passes because those who opposed it stayed home. This is a much different operational model from the voter turnout model. Its use may prove very effective in analyzing school tax and bond referendums and in guiding school boards and administrators in their preparation for such referendums.

The political science literature, obviously, is rich in research relating to voter behavior and electoral politics. In *The Responsible Electorate* Key argues that "voters are not fools," since rational choices govern how a person casts a ballot.[71] The theory and practice of party politics and presidential strategy is carefully analyzed by Polsby and Wildavsky in *Presidential Elections*.[72] An exhaustive treatment of this literature is precluded here; however, voter behavior in local school district elections deserves further amplification.

Factional politics. A model of factional politics is somewhat like or at least parallel to the "class polyarchy model," for that model attributes to identifiable social classes certain values and norms that predispose them to action or apathy depending on the issue. It is a more flexible model, however, in that the factional model is not determined only by social class variables and the factions may cross class boundaries. For instance, a taxpayer's group may be comprised of upper-, middle-, or lower-class individuals. It may include the interests of laborers, business owners, and professionals, all of whom are concerned about raising taxes and potentially opposed to increases in school operating budgets and bond issues for new buildings.

71. V. O. Key, Jr., *The Responsible Electorate: Rationality in Presidential Voting 1936-60* (New York: Vintage Books, 1968).

72. Nelson W. Polsby and Aaron B. Wildavsky, *Presidential Elections: Strategies of American Electoral Politics* (New York: Charles Scribner's Sons, 1964).

Factional models depict the politics of education without the coalescing structure of political parties as dependent upon participation within interest groups. Such a conglomerate of public power is described by Lutz and Iannaccone.[73] Wirth described the partyless politics of factions in the following manner:

> Being reduced to a stage of virtual impotence as an individual, the urbanite [or resident of a school district] is bound to exert himself by joining with others of similar interests into organized groups to obtain his ends.[74]

Wirth was describing urbanism exclusively but his description, with the bracketed addition, describes the plight of the citizen attempting to influence public school policy removed from the normal party politics of the rest of American government.

Zeigler and Jennings present a model of factional politics.[75] Briefly, two variables are of important consideration: (a) "mass support," the active or apathetic community support of the school governance; and (b) organizational intensity, the active attempts to influence, criticize or make demands upon the board. They state that, "As the population [the notion of a single public] becomes more supportive of the politics of the board, organized group activity diminishes [the notion of many publics]." They continue, ". . . as public confidence in board policy declines, the decline in confidence is articulated and given explicit focus by interest groups." [76]

It is important to note that factioned groups do not merely describe formally organized interest groups but include *also* the temporal group, organized for the specific purpose of influencing a single issue and uniting individuals from a varying range of other classifications because they share common and strong interest in that single issue.

Factional models are also interwoven in machine models as it is those "specific interests" that are of concern to the machine. Banfield and Wilson describe four types of factions: (a) machine (less

---

73. Lutz and Iannaccone, *Understanding Educational Organizations*.

74. Louis Wirth, "Urbanism as a Way of Life," *American Journal of Sociology* 44 (July 1938): 20.

75. Zeigler and Jennings, *Governing American Schools*, pp. 97-117.

76. Ibid., p. 101.

than city-wide), (b) personal following, (c) the interest group, and (d) the political club.[77] While types (b) and (c) seem self-explanatory, types (a) and (d) require some explanation as related to educational politics. "Machine" describes the interest group (less than district-wide) that relies upon specific and material inducements to hold it together. The particular educational issue is of consequence only as it affects the broader interest of the machine as it functions to reward specifically with material benefits. (In general, a taxpayers' association is not so well organized and more generally would be classified as an interest group rather than as a machine.) The "political club" not infrequently enters educational politics covertly, almost never overtly. Through overlapping memberships, where prestigious club members are also elected school board members, various interests of the club become important in educational decision making (for example, purchase of insurance, food, materials, building contracts, and jobs). In some ways both machine and club factions may overlap. Personal following and interest group factions are likely to be more temporal in nature. Some factions will be classified as mixed among pure factional types. For instance, if the PTA can be considered a club with a particular interest, it becomes a mixed group interest club.

Due to the fact that even in states where school board members are elected on partisan tickets (e.g. Pennsylvania), there appears to be little partisanship in the politics of education, and the party structure provides no mechanism for resolving interest group conflict. Factional models are useful for describing and understanding participation in the politics of education.

Political styles. Based on a comprehensive study of the politics of education in New York City during the late 1960s and early 1970s, Lutz, Lonsdale, and Bloland place participatory behavior in local school decisions into three styles of politics: (a) expertise, (b) pluralistic, or (c) status politics.[78] The first two are related respectively to two models already described—sacred-secular and oligarchy-polyarchy. The notion of status political style is based

77. Banfield and Wilson, *City Politics*, p. 128.

78. Frank W. Lutz, Richard Lonsdale, and Harley Bloland, "Educational Politics in New York City," unpublished research report for the Danforth Foundation, 1973.

on the work of Gusfield[79] and relates in part to the notion of the specific and material rewards of the machine model.

Status politics, while always just below the surface of any political process, emerges full-blown when one category of the governed perceives itself to be greatly disadvantaged by the governance system in power and finds no way or hope of altering that relative position within the established structure or by other political styles. Status politics states demands in moralistic, nonnegotiable terms and uses "face smashing" tactics and disruption of the present power structure as its major weapons. It tends to see situations as zero sum games (what you win, we lose). Its leadership is informal, often shifting, and very close to the grassroots politics of "people."

Expertise politics is the politics of the reform movement operating in a sacred norm. It holds that there are those individuals (usually board members and top level administrators) who because of certain expertness know better than the "people" what is good for and should be done for the "people." Certain selected outsiders and prestige groups are often counseled with regarding decisions, but these groups only influence, they do not decide. Usually these groups are support groups for the top power elite and are not expected to make public demands on that power structure that have not been agreed to in advance.

Pluralistic politics in education seems to be of two types. One allows another group of experts into the arena, usually through collective bargaining procedures. As a form of pluralistic politics, it often is but a broader form of expertise politics, for the most likely group in this type of pluralism is the teacher group. A broader form of pluralistic politics recognizes the pluralistic power of the competing interest groups within the diverse school district community. Community control, if it exists in its secular form (as opposed to operating within a type of status politics), is the extreme participatory example of pluralistic politics in education.

This model not only allows one to analyze the type of politics being exercised in attempts to influence educational decisions, but it permits speculation and hypothesis building about types of politics

---

79. Joseph Gusfield, *Symbolic Crusade* (Urbana, Ill.: University of Illinois Press, 1963).

that may be exercised by which groups, under what conditions, and with what results.

COMPARATIVE-DESCRIPTIVE MODELS

It is difficult to describe comparative models because these models borrow their conceptual notions from other theories in the social sciences and either compare two or more systems based on that model, or test the notion that a model generated in one political system can account for behavior in another type of political system, or are simply descriptive of a single system providing the opportunity for others to explore its utility in other systems. Some research in the politics of education that can be classified within this type should be mentioned as possible models for additional research or as guides to practicing educational politicians.

A model of political culture. Using the private- or public-regarding model, Cistone tested the notion that that concept, as part of a local political culture, would pervade the political arena from city government to educational government.[80] Specifically, he predicted that areas that choose city manager government would also elect school boards that would give their school superintendents greater professional latitude than did areas choosing a strong mayor form of government. He found that the public-regarding reform values did carry over to educational government.

Urban-state model. Utilizing the New York community control legislation struggle in the state legislature, Iannaccone has developed a model of the state politics of education as it differs from the usual politics of education and as it responds or fails to respond to specific educational demands in the great cities.[81] Central to this model is the notion of the "local unity norm" calling for "legislators to support local [urban] representatives when they are united in requesting legislation affecting only their locality." [82] Although not

---

80. Peter J. Cistone, "Formal Government Structures and the School Board-Superintendent Relationship" (doctoral diss., Pennsylvania State University, 1970).

81. Laurence Iannaccone, "Norms Governing Urban-State Politics of Education," *Toward Improved Urban Education*, ed. Frank W. Lutz (Worthington, Ohio: Charles E. Jones Publishing Co., 1970), pp. 233-53.

82. Ibid., p. 243.

tested in other states, this descriptive hypothesis could prove fruitful in investigating particularistic legislation affecting major cities. For instance, in 1975 Mayor Daley, who seldom lost a political fight, lost in his effort to restore educational funds for Chicago that had been cut by the state legislature. Was the local unity norm violated in some fashion?

Comparative-descriptive model. The work of both Bailey et al. and Masters et al. is noteworthy in this regard.[83] Although each uses different methods of data collection, each provides a comparative description of the state politics of education in several different states, the former in New York, New Jersey, and New England states and the latter in Missouri, Illinois, and Michigan. Models from comparative-descriptive research in the politics of education are noteworthy and capable of providing interesting hypotheses for research in the politics of education.

Power-process model. At the federal level Summerfield[84] has provided a model of the policy process for education in the administration, the Congress, the lobbies, and their interrelationships. His model is intended to explain the dynamics of the structure of federal politics and illustrates that not only does power make the system work, but also the effect of power shapes the subtle, and often vital, elements of the system itself. Summerfield demonstrates that although the federal policy process, like any policy process, can be described and characterized, it cannot thereby be stabilized and predictable in terms either of its process or its policy outcomes. From the notion that power shapes the process, he does demonstrate, however, that building a federal system will have powerful impact on dependent systems, both state and local.[85] Thus, in exercising power we must not only be aware of the immediate power outcomes but also of the effects that the patterning of power has on the future structure of the political system itself.

Urban-rural biases model. This model depicts a special applica-

---

83. Stephen Bailey et al., *Schoolmen in Politics* (Syracuse, N.Y.: Syracuse University Press, 1962); Nicholas A. Masters et al., *State Politics and the Public Schools: An Exploratory Analysis* (New York: Alfred A. Knopf, 1964).

84. Harry Summerfield, *Power and Process* (Berkeley, Calif.: McCutchan Publishing Corp., 1974), chap. 5.

85. Ibid., chap. 6.

tion of the power-process model and the operation of the federal Congress as it produces legislation with particular relevance to education. Guthrie suggests an urban-rural bias (favoring rural values) that operates in the process from the House (most rurally biased) to the Senate (less rurally biased) to the President (most likely to support urban requests and needs).[86] He suggests the bias favoring rural interests and values is produced by (a) the process of recruitment, election, and reelection to federal political office and (b) the operation and committee structure of the Congress (modified at least legally since Guthrie's positing of the model). Guthrie cites data supporting the claim that this bias is an extreme disadvantage to urban education. He describes the process and role of rural ideologies and values likely to be held by the majority of federal officeholders. In this fashion this model is linked to the power-process model that describes the process through which one individual and then one group is influenced to accept some version of another's ideology in the process of forming coalitions in order to pass legislation. Both are in this sense linked to some notion of political-psychological models referred to below.

POLITICAL-PSYCHOLOGICAL MODELS

Some of the models presented above may well have been classified, at least in part, within the rubric of political psychology. Particularly those elements of models involving political attitudes, beliefs, and values fall within the domain of political psychology. How does one become a Democrat or Republican, or pro or anti public education? Why does it seem impossible for a politician to act in ways "dissonant" to his previous investments, actions, and values? What are the elements of crosspressure that keep voters at home? Why do certain groups prefer reform government and others prefer machine government? These and other questions can be addressed by using concepts from political psychology.

Political research dealing with concepts mentioned earlier, such as public- or private-regarding, machine-reform, urban-rural bias, all have their roots in concepts of political psychology (for example, political socialization).

86. James E. Guthrie, "City Schools in a Federal Vise," in *Toward Improved Urban Education*, ed. Frank W. Lutz, pp. 273-305.

For two reasons no major effort will be made here to outline or describe the models available in political psychology. First, the personal bias of this author leads him to models that explain group political activity rather than individual political behavior. Without debating the independencies and differences between these two points of view, it is clear that there exist interdependencies between individual behavior and group activity but that the group is clearly different from the individual. The choice of this author is toward explanations due to group behavior. This bias has led to a greater familiarity and use of group models rather than the psychological models in explaining political action.

Second, the space limitations of this chapter prohibit the possibility of covering this area as completely as it should be covered given the emphasis in chapter 1. A recent comprehensive and excellent publication edited by Knutson covers the field of political psychology including the following areas of interest to students and practitioners of the politics of education: political attitudes; patterns of political belief; political socialization; anomie, alienation, and political behavior; and patterns of leadership.[87] As with most of the work in political science, the area of education and the application of the political models to education are not dealt with in this work. The relationship between the topics mentioned and the models previously presented in this chapter should be evident to political practitioners and researchers alike.

Summary

Theoreticians create models of politics, but politicians create power systems. When the two are empirically incongruent, resulting in the model's failure to predict or explain reality, theoreticians should check their observations and then reformulate our model and theory. The following figure is an attempt to show how the various conceptual models are theoretically related (for example, sacred-secular grows out of Gemeinschaft-Gesellschaft). Empirically, political systems have not always operated as they are theoretically designed. The dotted lines in figure 1 indicate empirical shifts under certain conditions.

87. Jeanne N. Knutson, ed., *Handbook of Political Psychology* (San Francisco, Calif.: Jossey-Bass Publishers, 1973).

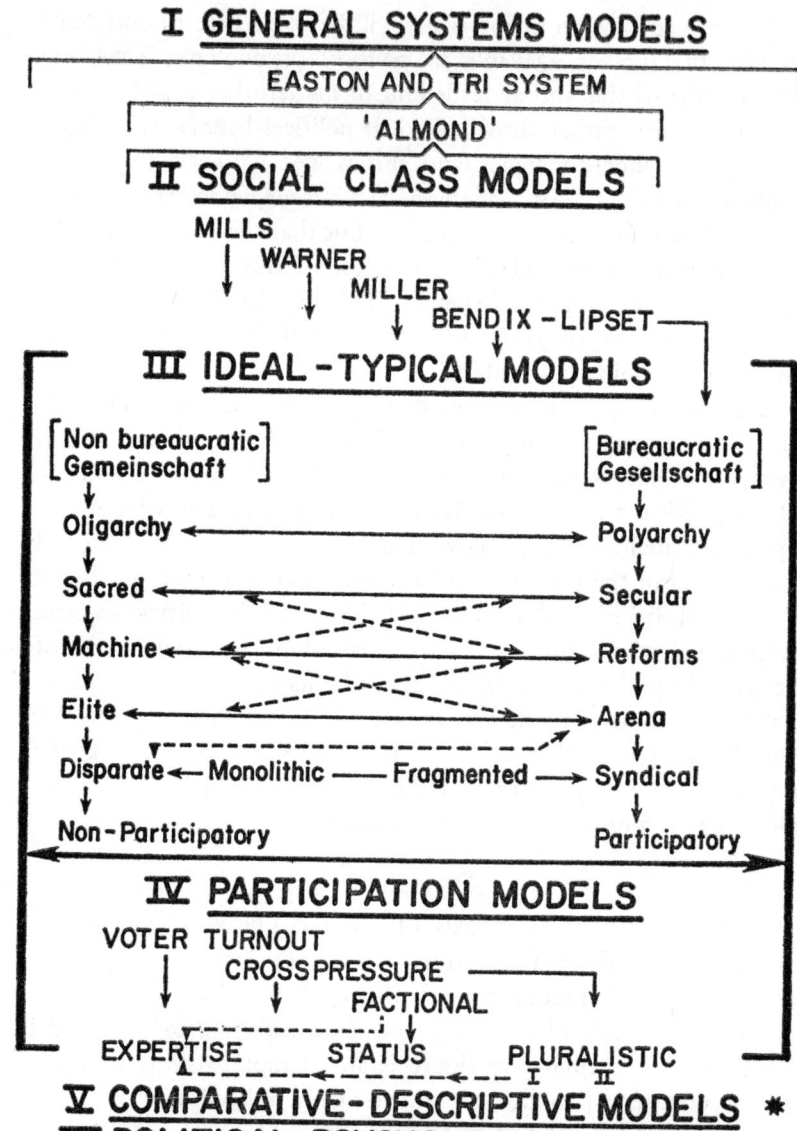

Fig. 1. Political models along participation-nonparticipation continuum

Of particular concern in figure 1 is the relationship between the ideal typical models of governance form and participation models of political style within the structure of educational politics. Both of these model types are portrayed (as are the other model types) along a participation continuum. That continuum is indicated between the ideal typical and participation model types. The brackets uniting those model types signify the important relationship between them, for the former describes the governance form of the structure and the latter describes the process of participation within the structure. Unfortunately space does not permit an extensive elaboration of those interesting and interdependent relationships.

Figure 1 attempts to relate the various models presented in this chapter to one another according to conceptual linkages and along a participatory continuum. As such, the general systems model as articulated by von Bertalanffy is a macromodel providing a conceptualization within which all other models can be subsumed and evaluated. The Easton and tri-systems models have a narrower application but still are macro in explanatory power. The Almond model as operationalized by Scribner has even a narrower application. All could, however, explain or predict behavior regardless of the degree of participation and indicate the if-then condition.

Social class models all fall toward the nonparticipatory end of the continuum. Progressively, the models of Mills, Warner, Miller, and finally the class polyarchy model based on the Bendix and Lipset volume depict and derive from increasingly broader versions of the dispersion of power, influence, and political participation.

The ideal typical models outlined in this chapter are all seen as related to, if not actually derived from, the Weberian model of bureaucratic behavior and linked to the concepts of Gemeinschaft-Gesellschaft social organization. In this regard, oligarchy not only prohibits the participation of pluralistic community groups but operationally denies the legitimacy of such demands upon the authoritative allocation of resources in order to serve those pluralistic interests. At the other end of that continuum, the concept of polyarchy not only attributes power to a system of dispersed inequalities and recognizes the diverse nature of interests in the broad "public," but specifically values such participation. The sacred-secular continuum derives directly from the Gemeinschaft-Gesellschaft community and describes the political process satisfying such communities. Additionally, traditional secular politics is specifically bureaucratic in values and organization.

While the reformists seek the secularism of the political structure as their goal, formalizing that structure according to bureaucratic principals in order to move politics into the open and away from the sacred politics of the machine serving the particularistic requirements of a Gemeinschaft community, the reverse process may be viewed in education, at least under certain conditions. Having removed education from "politics" of the people, supposedly opening the structure in a secular fashion, an elite oligarchy emerges. An oligarchy of experts rules, protected by the bureaucratic nature of the civil service structure, generated by secular intent, and protected by the "moral" ideology of reform politics. This trend can be best viewed as within the *tendency* toward Michels's "Iron Law of Oligarchy." The dotted lines between the sacred-secular and the machine-reform continuums depict this operational tendency.

In such a manner a reform government becomes an elite council. Also, a machine government may be viewed as an arena council, depending on the range of interests served in a particular fashion and represented by the machine, although the debate over an issue is likely to be more private and *within* the machine. While reform government is intended to be secular in nature, the reform board tends to view itself as an elite council ruling in the best interests of a monolithic public and fails to represent, in any reasonable fashion, the particularistic interest groups of the pluralistic secular society. This again is indicated by dotted lines, here between the machine-reform and elite-arena continuums.

Although not so clearly demonstrable, the disparate classification in the Iannaccone state education governance model is composed of so many factions that no coalition strong enough to rule is possible. Therefore, governance is likely to be by the strongest single oligarchy or by the unlikely coincidence of complete consensus. While the disparate classification is a multiplicity of factions (in arena fashion), those factions end up with no representation except through possible veto power. More obviously monolithic, fragmented, and syndical classifications move progressively from elite toward the structured representation of arena councils, representing pluralistic interest groups in state educational policy making. As the three classifications to the right side of the continuum are progressively more arena, secular, and participatory, only one dotted line is required indicating the operational fact that the many groups of the disparate classification produce only a weak factional representation and are thus likely to result in a powerless "rabble" permitting the rule of an elite or a machine governance, but in either case a sacred oligarchy.

Regarding participation models, the voter turnout notion of school politics is clearly based on elite nonrepresentative politics. The very aim of such politics is to keep public participation low. The crosspressure notion, depending on the number of interest groups perceived, appeared to consider and interact with at least two groups and may result in factional or rather pluralistic politics. This model does not view the governing body or the political issue as simply a reactive element of the political process, but views it as a proactive one as well. This fact alone can account for the small attention crosspressure theory has received in the politics of education. Although they seldom behave in such a fashion, educational politicians have always contended that politics and education are separate and that they are merely the pitiful recipients of political pressure. As is the case in most primitive forms of politics, the actors in the politics of education are "true believers."[88] That is, they actually believe their ideology and find ways of rationalizing behavioral discrepancies without damaging their cherished myths.

Factional models, while having many interest groups, often operate with a "divide and conquer" behavior. This model views the factions attempting to influence educational decisions as selfish and narrow interest groups unrepresentative of the will of the monolithic "people." This view of the politics of education has resulted in monolithic, elite political behavior and expertise styles of politics. When the interests of a particular faction are sufficiently neglected in the authoritative allocations of values and resources by the monolithic elite, and when the faction is sufficiently frustrated in its attempts to influence and change the elite governance structure,

88. Eric Hoffer, *The True Believer* (New York: New American Library, Mentor Books, 1951).

it tends to turn to status political styles in their more overt and unpleasant forms.

Thus one comes to political styles, the last model in the ideal typical group. Here expertise politics depicts participation within the rule of the elite group of educational experts, and status politics as the attempt of factions to use "face smashing" methods to influence and modify that expertise style. Pluralistic politics may be divided into two forms. Pluralism I permits an adjustment in the circle of experts who make the decisions through negotiation with powerful teacher associations and unions (thus the dotted line). Pluralism II opens the politics of education to the pluralistic concepts of Dahl and the participation in decision making and the governance of the polyarchy.

As indicated in figure 1, no attempt is made here to classify either comparative-descriptive nor political-psychological models along the participatory-nonparticipatory continuum.

Conclusions

This chapter provides the researcher and practitioner with some data collection methods and some conceptual models for studying and participating in the politics of education. For the researcher an attempt was made to provide theory for hypothesis generation and methods for investigation. The practitioner in the politics of education is provided with models for evaluating, understanding, and making predictions that could guide such a "politician" through the web of politics in which education is meshed.

The chapter was not designed, however, to provide examples of how to apply either the data collection methods or the political models described. Even with the limited tasks, sufficient space was not available to describe completely all methods or models. It is again suggested that practitioners and researchers read the original works cited. In *The Last Hurrah* by Edwin O' Conner, the old time politician Frank Skeffington tells his young nephew that politics is the nation's greatest and largest "spectator sport." Given the methods and models suggested above, some of those spectators may become participants.

CHAPTER III

Participation, Representation, and Control

DALE MANN

Introduction

In democratic societies people have a general expectation about self-government. They expect to be able to take part in decisions about public matters that affect them. Most of the time, it is enough that they are consulted or that decisions reflect some part of what they would like to see happen. They consent to the result. But occasionally decisions are of such consequence that they will want to try to guarantee a result that conforms exactly to their wishes. Sometimes they seek to control.

Political science studies the distribution of benefits or public goods and the process through which that distribution takes place. The higher the stakes, the more likely it is that more people will seek control. The ways through which people seek control over significant issues can be important to the outcome. We can approach the analysis of participation, representation, and control by asking which is more important to the individual. Would one rather be able to participate in a decision, to be represented in a decision, or to control a decision? Control is clearly preferable, and some individuals may not care much about how it is achieved. Participation rests on personal involvement. In representation someone else is doing the work. As long as both yield the same amount of control, representation is the better and less costly choice. Are there qualitative differences in the nature or in the amount of control delivered to an individual by others' representation as opposed to one's own participation? Are there systematic gains and losses in terms of one's ability to control as one moves from one form to the other? Are there limits on participation? What are the shortcomings in representation?

A common language definition of *control* will suffice here. Control is a determinate, or at the very least a dominant influence. There is an idea of sufficient command in controlling.[1]

Verba and Nie define *political participation* as "those activities by private citizens that are more or less directly aimed at influencing the selection of governmental personnel and/or the actions they take."[2] The definition reflects a consensus among political scientists that the participation of ordinary citizens in national politics is confined to trying to do something to or about the "real participants"—government officials and interest groups. But the politics of education happens at every level, and at the level of the local school, citizens are often in direct and unmediated contact with the school. Thus, in addition to wanting to influence which sets of people will make decisions and the substance of those decisions, citizens sometimes intend that their involvement or participation should itself directly control the outcomes. We may define participation as direct or unmediated involvement by citizens with the intent of affecting what happens in schools.

Representation involves "re-presenting," or making present again something that is not in fact present. Someone acting as our political representative acts for us, sometimes instead of us, sometimes on our behalf. In the outstanding theoretical work on representation, Pitkin presents a root definition of substantive representation as "acting in the interest of the represented, in a manner responsive to them."[3]

In this chapter the limits of participation and representation as control devices are stressed, especially from the point of view of the individual citizen. The barriers that keep an individual from realizing effective control are emphasized in part because so much of the drive for citizen involvement in educational matters springs from intensely personal (parental) interests and in part because

---

1. An excellent treatment of the more formal definitions of control is available in Dorwin Cartwright, "Influence, Leadership, Control," in *Handbook of Organizations*, ed. James G. March (Chicago: Rand McNally & Co., 1965), pp. 1-47.

2. Sidney Verba and Norman H. Nie, *Participation in America: Political Democracy and Social Equality* (New York: Harper and Row, 1972), p. 2.

3. Hannah F. Pitkin, *The Concept of Representation* (Berkeley, Calif.: University of California Press, 1967), p. 209.

recent expectations for more responsive schools have been premised on a model of policy outputs matched to individual demands. Participation, representation, and control recur throughout the politics of education. In this chapter we look briefly at the traditional question of who controls the schools, then at some of the forms of participation, and then at representation. A concluding section returns to the overall concern with school control.

Like most questions, "Who controls the schools?" has some complex answers. Schooling and education are different things. Schooling is the official and institutional provision of teaching and learning. Schooling is one part of education, but education also includes the teaching and learning that goes on through the family, the peer groups, the media, and the surrounding culture. The frustrating hunt for effects of schooling (What features of the institutional portion of education can be manipulated to provide desired outcomes?) combined with the extreme potency of, for example, the family-as-educator or the media-as-educator suggests that if we intend to maximize learning, we should look beyond the school. Yet very little is known about control of those powerful nonschool educational forces.

But if by schooling we mean what takes place in the neighborhood school building, the level at which the service of the system is delivered, then there is a more substantial body of knowledge. The microlevel of schooling is affected by several different forces. National actors (the Congress, the executive agencies, the interest groups, the courts) legislate, regulate, and encourage some parts of what is done in schools. The publishing industry provides a quasi-national curriculum. State level forces (legislatures, state departments of education) provide the local schools with signals that sometimes conflict with and sometimes reinforce those from the other levels. Academics and researchers affect the practices of the local school by developing new knowledge and through the socialization of professionals in training. Traces of these influences from the suprasystem can be found in every school building, but they are only traces. The determinate impact of any of these groups is surprisingly small. The Supreme Court may declare a national ban on segregation or forbid prayer in the schools, but the local microlevel compliance is only hesitant, partial, temporary. The

Congress and the executive branch may declare war on certain social ills and make assistance available to thousands of individual schools, but those schools will bend such assistance to their own purposes. The research and development community is notorious for its lack of effect. Thus, while there are traces of influence, there is no determinate control of the schools from these forces. Superordinate actors are not powerless but neither do they have the most control over what goes on in the local school. That role is reserved for more proximate local actors.

Participation

Participation has been one of the most widely praised, hotly debated, and poorly understood techniques for affecting what schools do, especially in the cities. Part of the impetus for increasing citizen participation beyond the low levels that had until recently characterized school governance was the political climate of the 1960s in which "maximum feasible (client) participation" was a popular slogan. But in the arena of schooling much of the advocacy about participation was based on confusion between involvement as a parent and involvement as a citizen. The demonstrated association between intensive parental involvement and high levels of student achievement was often used to justify increased civic involvement by parents and others in school decision making. But the two situations are not comparable—parents are not the whole of the community, the school is not the home, policy decisions are not personal decisions only, and participation in decision making is not equivalent to parental participation. This chapter concentrates on political not parental involvement.

What forms has participation taken? One way to classify types of participation is by the amount of input required and the amount of control yielded. Some participation makes only minimal demands on the citizen in terms of time, preparation, personal commitment, and risk. Other forms are far more expensive. In general, the control that follows from any individual's participation is directly related to the investment represented by that form. For example, exposing one's self to political stimuli or being compliant toward the government are types of participation that are almost passive and yield little if any control in terms of the individual's agenda.

Voting requires slightly more investment and yields some more control. Joining a group, becoming active in a group, and leading a group all increase both the investment and the potential for control. Finally, election to public office makes intense personal demands but also has the highest probability of maximizing that person's influence on public events.[4] What is known about the major forms of participation in the governance of schooling?

In theory, a vote expresses a policy preference; one candidate is selected over another because the voter favors something about the preferred candidate.[5] A series of dissertations supervised by Iannaccone indicated that in politically unstable southern California school districts, the defeat of even a single member of a five-member school board tended to be followed by the involuntary departure of the superintendent.[6] Since, as Iannaccone points out, superintendents are the de facto leaders of their boards, there may be some aggregate policy consequences of personnel voting. Selecting school board members who share the voter's preferences gives the individual voter an opportunity for influence. In this chapter, we are examining two of the ways in which control happens—through participation and through representation. The citizen's attempt to control is expressed through the vote, but for personnel elections the amount of control associated with the voting act is indicated by the subsequent behavior of the representative. Thus,

---

4. For a discussion of the hierarchy of political involvement, see Lester W. Milbrath, *Political Participation* (Chicago: Rand McNally & Co., 1967), p. 18.

5. The ability of the masses to pursue their own self-interest is called issue voting. See the arguments and extensive citations in *American Political Science Review* 66 (June 1972) in the following articles: Gerald M. Pomper, "From Confusion to Clarity: Issues and American Voters, 1956-1968," 415-28; Richard W. Boyd, "Popular Control of Public Policy: A Normal Vote Analysis of the 1968 Election," 429-49; Richard A. Brody and Benjamin I. Page, "Comment: The Assessment of Policy Voting," 450-58; John H. Kessel, "Comment: The Issues in Issue Voting," 459-65; Gerald M. Pomper, "Rejoinder to 'Comments' by Richard A. Brody and Benjamin I. Page and John H. Kessel," 466-67; Richard W. Boyd, "Rejoinder to 'Comments' by Richard A. Brody and Benjamin I. Page and John H. Kessel," 468-70. Robert E. Agger and Marshall N. Goldstein touch provocatively on this issue in *Who Will Rule the Schools: A Cultural Class Crisis* (Belmont, Calif.: Wadsworth Publishing Co., 1971).

6. Laurence Iannaccone, *Politics in Education* (New York: Center for Applied Research in Education, 1967), p. 91.

in personnel elections, voting already verges toward representation.

In finance elections, the choice offered the voter is to approve the budget or not, to approve the bonds for the new buildings or not, to approve the new tax rates or not. Our major interest is in the control that comes from the act of voting. But the voter enters the booth with a host of predetermining factors that shape the vote at least as much as the fact of the immediate choice presented by the ballot. Piele and Hall found that "studies of voting behavior agree . . . in assuming that an array of forces predetermine or shape the choice of most voters."[7] What are these factors? In their extensive review of the literature Piele and Hall include a useful inventory of propositions for which there is some empirical evidence. In general, the outcome of school finance elections may be attributed to combinations of the following factors:

1. Economic self-interest. Both the size of a tax increase and the amount of benefit accruing to the voter shape voters' opinions.

2. Socioeconomic status. Income and educational status are both positively related to support for finance issues.

3. Community responsibility and social distance. Those with strong ties in a community, those who believe themselves to be important participants in community affairs, and those who participate in several information networks are more likely to support finance issues.[8]

Thus, the more a combination of such factors as parents with school-age children, high incomes, high education, and a trusting attitude toward government is present (at the individual or the aggregate level), the more likely it is that there will be a supportive vote on finance issues. In addition, black voters are more likely than white voters to support finance issues.[9]

But what about the link between a voter's ballot and the voter's personal priorities? For discretionary, new, or additional activities (sometimes called "frills"), the voter's participation may be determinate. But where the voter is being asked to approve state-

---

7. Philip K. Piele and John Stuart Hall, *Budgets, Bonds, and Ballots* (Lexington, Mass.: D. C. Heath & Co., 1973), p. 140.

8. Ibid., pp. 142 et seq.

9. Ibid., pp. 151 et seq.

mandated functions, then a rejected proposition usually results in a new election with a slightly different option until a level is reached that is acceptable to the voters and the state. In some states, continued rejection of bond issues results in the state superseding the local education authority until such time as the voters will assent to a budget. Even in finance elections, the amount of control from voting participation is far from determinate. Of course, some inescapable properties of votes also diminish the amount of control that can be realized through them. In general, any single vote is: (a) an intermittent act that occurs only at widely spaced intervals that seldom coincide with critical decisions about schooling; (b) a binary expression of approval or disapproval for an issue or of one candidate over others; (c) a tiny fraction of the total vote; (d) unlikely to be the critical determiner of the outcome; (e) an imperfect summarization of many attitudes and opinions on a variety of inconsistently structured issues; (f) no reflection of the intensity of the voter's attitudes; and (g) no indicator of the degree of the voter's information, experience, wisdom, or "correctness" with regard either to personal or public interests in the issue. From the individual citizen's point of view these characteristics of a vote reduce the incentive to vote, especially in the absence of political parties or groups.[10] From the point of view of the official whose behavior is supposed to be controlled by such votes, their characteristics make them ambiguous, diffuse, and thus subject to interpretation, manipulation, or indifference. We shall return to these problems in the discussion of representation.

The amount of control from voting is limited by these characteristics. But other forms of participation may be more important for the operation of the local school. Voting is a somewhat remote and diluted form of participation, especially from the perspective of the local school. Where parents and other community members take a more direct part in decisions about schooling, there is evidence that the institution becomes more responsive to them. According to Yin et al., who studied several types of citizen participation, moving from participation that is advisory to participation that has governing authority results in a substantial increase in the

10. Anthony Downs, *An Economic Theory of Democracy* (New York: Harper & Row, 1957).

responsiveness of social welfare institutions to community members.[11] Rosenthal and Jacobson, in discussing the Pygmalion effect of teacher attitudes toward students' achievement, reported that children who profited from positive changes in teachers' expectations of the children's ability *all* had parents who had evinced interest in their child's development and who were distinctly visible to the teachers.[12] Bridge demonstrated that involvement of parents is most likely to be effective where their acceptance of a decision is critical and where the decision itself rests on information that only parents have.[13] Participation in groups also yields responsiveness on the part of institutions. Mann found that in communities lacking education-related interest groups, 87 percent of the school administrators were quite willing to substitute their own preferences for those of the community. Where PTAs existed, 69 percent of the administrators rejected being responsive, and where in addition to the PTA there were independent interest groups working on educational problems, only 55 percent of the administrators were willing to try to override community preferences.[14]

The cumulative effect of voting, plus expressing interest and being visible at school, plus being involved in one or more education-related interest groups may increase the influence for an individual or for a group. Yet very few people are so concerned about schools that they exercise all of those options, and thus the vast majority of people fail to have the impact that they might otherwise have. Moreover, general political participation is strongly related to social class. The upper classes participate far more than do the lower classes.[15] Although poor people have the most to gain from the school, they are the least likely to participate.

11. Robert K. Yin, William A. Lucas, Peter I. Szanton, and James A. Spindler, *Citizens Organizations: Increasing Client Control over Service* (Washington, D.C.: Rand Corporation, 1973), p. vii.

12. Robert Rosenthal and Lenore Jacobson, *Pygmalion in the Classroom* (New York: Holt, Rinehart & Winston, 1968), p. 94.

13. R. Gary Bridge, "Parent Participation in School Innovations," *Teachers College Record* 77 (February 1976): 367-86.

14. Dale Mann, *The Politics of Administrative Representation: School Administration and Local Democracy* (Lexington, Mass.: D. C. Heath & Co., 1976), p. 59.

15. Milbrath, *Political Participation*, chap. 5.

Grievances account for many of the nonelectoral inputs that citizens make to schools. A national survey by Jennings of the school-related grievances held by parents disclosed that white parents were more likely to express grievances than were black parents. Higher income people had more grievances than poor people. The associations between socioeconomic status and grievances, however, were very slight. Those who were only marginally involved with the school and those who could be described as alienated from it did not account for a disproportionate number of grievances. Instead, those who were high on their own sense of personal efficacy, on social trust, and on group involvement also tended to have the most grievances. Teacher actions prompted the most parental grievances.[16]

Jennings also demonstrated that, despite the elaborate public relations programs of many schools, parents were almost entirely dependent on their children for their knowledge of the school. The reliance of parents on children for information about the school points up one of the impediments to more effective individual participation. Knowledge is an obvious precondition for successful participation, but it is very difficult for most people to obtain in a quasi-technical area such as schooling. Moreover, the enormous disparity in information possessed by most lay people and most professionals puts the citizen at a disadvantage.[17] Verba has outlined the other conditions for participation: material resources (especially leisure time and money); social resources (contacts, organizational allies); a willingness to exploit those personal and social resources because of a recognition of the stakes and of a belief that one's participation will make a difference; structural conduciveness (legal channels, regular access); and cultural conduciveness (especially the belief that schooling is a proper arena for personal influence by lay people).[18] These conditions are a

16. M. Kent Jennings, "Parental Grievances and School Politics," *Public Opinion Quarterly* 32 (Fall 1969): 363-78.

17. Dale Mann, "Democratic Theory and Public Participation," in *The Polity and the School*, ed. Frederick M. Wirt (Lexington, Mass.: D. C. Heath & Co., 1975), pp. 5-21.

18. Sidney Verba, "Democratic Participation," *Annals of the American Academy of Political and Social Science* 373 (September 1967): 53-78.

considerable barrier to much widespread participation in an area that is of only marginal interest to many people anyway. Although the reservoir of public good will toward the schools has declined, 67 percent of the public still give a positive confidence rating to schools. Similar ratings are given to the Congress by 40 percent of the public, to organized labor by 38 percent, and to big business by 34 percent.[19]

The characteristics of votes dissuade many people from that form of participation. More intensive forms yield some more control; but only a very few people have the predisposing conditions —including the interest or the incentive—to invest themselves in personal, face-to-face encounters with the school. Moreover, the school itself poses formidable barriers to such participation. The traditions of academic freedom and professional self-determination make most classrooms inviolate. Teacher unions protect their members from the teachers' adult clientele. Tenure for the teaching and administrative staffs produces insulation from public control (just as it was designed to do). The multiple levels of bureaucracy, especially in big cities, provide even more insulation. In the absence of definitive knowledge about the causes of effective teaching and learning, the large numbers of decentralized units like school buildings and especially classrooms are left to their own autonomous devices. And finally, the self-justification of administrators has persuaded much of the public that schools are best left to school administrators.

Historically, schools had been one of the proud examples of direct democracy. Lay school boards, chosen from very small jurisdictions, hired teachers and actually determined what they did. Especially in rural nineteenth-century America, the visibility of the one-room schoolhouse in tiny communities made direct and detailed participation in a wide range of school affairs quite feasible and effective. Then participation declined; "those activities by private citizens that are more or less directly aimed at influencing the selection of governmental personnel and/or the actions they take"[20] waned in school affairs. Callahan argues that a good deal

---

19. George H. Gallup, "Seventh Annual Gallup Poll of Public Attitudes toward Education," *Phi Delta Kappan* 57 (December 1975): 228.
20. Verba and Nie, *Participation in America*, p. 2.

of the explanation for that trend lies in the persuasiveness with which administrators got school board members to relinquish control over school matters.[21] But even had that not been the case, other forces would have precluded direct democracy. It is simply logistically impossible for everyone affected by a government action to participate in its determination. There are too many people, too many decisions that affect them, and the decisions are often too technical for them. Besides, they have other things to do. Direct democracy rests on widespread individual participation, which turns out to be impossible.

Direct democracy has been replaced with "polyarchal" democracy. The basic tenets of polyarchy are that (a) elites decide issues on behalf of masses (or leaders on behalf of followers, or representatives on behalf of constituencies), and (b) the masses, followers, or constituencies have periodic opportunities through elections to replace one set of elites with another. In direct democracy, the people could be assured that the government, in our case the schools, acted in their interests because popular participation was intended to guarantee that. In polyarchy, government is controlled in the people's interests not by their own actions but by competition among the alternative sets of elites. Those in office would rather not be replaced so they attend to the preferences of the followers.[22] As a control system, polyarchy solves several of the problems of direct democracy. First, it harnesses the leader's self-interest (retaining office) to the satisfaction of public wants. Second, it reduces the information, interest, and personal investment demands on the individual participant by confining that participation to intermittent choices between one set of elites or another. Of course such solutions are not without their price. It has been argued convincingly that elites benefit far more than do masses, that the de-emphasis of citizen participation atrophies those civic muscles needed to guard public interests, and that access to

---

21. Raymond E. Callahan, "The American Board of Education, 1789-1960," in *Understanding School Boards*, ed. Peter J. Cistone (Lexington, Mass.: D. C. Heath & Co., 1975), pp. 19-46

22. Robert A. Dahl and Charles E. Lindblom, *Politics, Economics, and Welfare: Planning and Politico-economic Systems Resolved into Basic Social Processes* (New York: Harper & Row, 1953), chaps. 10 and 11.

the ranks of the elite is unfairly restricted.[23]

There are arguments that lend credence to such criticisms in the governance of schooling. Some maintain that the professionally run school is an agency of social stratification, serving to keep the poor in their place by failing to boost them up the ladder of social mobility (although dramatic improvements cannot be expected from tactics such as community involvement).[24] The halting start-up process of decentralization in most cities demonstrates how few civic skills were available in the governance of schooling. Discriminatory qualifying exams or certifications are evidence of unfair restrictions on access to elite ranks. Still, despite reservations about its normative desirability, most observers agree that polyarchal democracy is an accurate description of government. And within polyarchy, representation is a central component.

Representation

Redford has stated the case bluntly but well: "The first characteristic of the great body of men subject to the administrative state is that they are dormant regarding most of the decisions made about them."[25] The number of people in a constituency, the number of different decision-making bodies that affect them, the complexity of the decisions, and the lack of interest of most people in civic affairs combine to make representation the standard vehicle of what we loosely call self-government. The business of representation is carried on by two groups of people in education. First, representation occurs through elected or appointed officials who

---

23. Two leading critics are Peter Bachrach, *The Theory of Democratic Elitism: A Critique* (Boston, Mass.: Little, Brown & Co., 1967) and Jack L. Walker, "A Critique of the Elitist Theory of Democracy," *American Political Science Review* 60 (June 1966): 285-95. Also useful is Robert J. Pranger, *The Eclipse of Citizenship: Power and Participation in Contemporary Politics* (New York: Holt, Rinehart & Winston, 1968). A temporary summation of a continuing argument may be found in the *American Political Science Review* 65 (December 1971) in articles by Raymond E. Wolfinger, "Nondecisions and the Study of Local Politics," 1063-80; Frederick W. Frey, "Comment," 1081-1101; and Raymond E. Wolfinger, "Rejoinder," 1102-1104.

24. See Dale Mann, "Ten Years of Decentralization: A Review of the Involvement of Urban Communities in School Decision Making," *IRCD Bulletin* 10 (Summer 1975): 1-18.

25. Emmette S. Redford, *Democracy in the Administrative State* (New York: Oxford University Press, 1969), p. 66.

serve on formal legislative bodies like school boards. But professional educators are also involved in the business of representation, since many decisions are not made by the public but by the professionals on behalf of the public. In addition to legislative representation, we will also examine administrative representation.

Regardless of whether the representation is done by legislators or by administrators, there are some general expectations that apply. In her analysis of representational theory, Pitkin identifies four ways through which representation occurs.[26] "Formalistic representation" happens in the act of authorizing someone to be a representative. Administrators who stress their certification by a state agency as a warrant to act for their communities are stressing formalistic representation. "Descriptive representation" stresses the similarity between the representative and the represented on allegedly salient features (race and social class, to use topical examples), not the congruence between what the constituency wants and/or needs and what the representative does. "Symbolic representation" is even less concerned with the substantive identity between actions and desires. Symbolic representation stresses how people feel about their representatives. Those people who support a representative because "he's one of us" (not because of his actions) are satisfied with symbolic representation. Those who object to the tokenism that often characterizes minority employment practices are not satisfied with symbolic representation. The fourth category, "substantive representation," is the heart of the matter since it deals with relations between the desires and interests of the representative and of the represented. Pitkin's root definition of substantive representation is, "acting in the interest of the represented, in a manner responsive to them."[27] The central idea is that there should be a correspondence between what the representatives do and what the represented would have them do.

Two other ideas enter this equation. The first has to do with the interest of the community. The representative's actions should forward the community's welfare. Second, the representative should be responsive to the constituency. Responsiveness is not replication;

26. The following discussion draws on Pitkin, *The Concept of Representation*.

27. Ibid., p. 59.

here it means acting with reference to the community. Thus, where a community wants one thing and where the representative recognizes that desire but does something else on the ground that the community's interests are thus better served, there is still responsiveness within this meaning of the term.

That of course brings up the problem of conflict. When both parties agree, then the process of representation moves smoothly. But instances of disagreement are so critical for our expectations of democratic government that they can serve as a major classifying principle for the analysis of representation. Any person who undertakes to represent another is faced with a number of practical and ethical dilemmas. Essentially, he must choose a style of representation. The major choices and their normative rationalizations have been nicely expressed by Pitkin:

> The majority of theorists argue that the representative must do what is best for those in his charge, but that he must do what he thinks best, using his own judgment and wisdom, since he is chosen to make decisions for (that is, instead of) his constituents. But a vocal minority maintain that the representative's duty is to reflect accurately the wishes and opinions of those he represents. Anything else they consider a mockery of true representation.[28]

These two choices for a representational style are distinguished by whether the representative acts as a "trustee" or as a "delegate." Briefly, a trustee is someone whose decisions are based on his own values, even though the represented may disagree. A delegate reverses the priority and is guided by expressed citizen preferences even at the expense of his own best judgment. A third position, somewhat between the trustee and delegate decision-making styles, is usually called a "politico." A representative acting in the style of a politico borrows from either the trustee or delegate styles as dictated by situations but has some internally consistent rationale for doing so. The politico does not merely waffle but rather enacts a trustee or a delegate orientation according to the dictates of circumstance.

This trustee/delegate/politico orientation captures the essence of people's expectations about government action. If it is not

28. Ibid., p. 4.

possible to guard one's interest by direct participation, then at least the representative should act to maximize that interest. Still, there are no clear guidelines in this area. The representative should act in the interests of the constituency, but what if the two disagree? People sometimes misidentify their interests; representatives can make the same mistake on the people's behalf. Constituencies are seldom monolithic; their interests change across issues and over time. These are all difficulties that confound representation.

What sort of representation do citizens get from their school boards? Zeigler and Jennings report the most comprehensive survey investigation of the subject ever undertaken.[29] Their analysis of the question of shared preferences between the leaders and the led was done first in terms of expectations for leader behavior. Did the two agree that a school board member should act as an instructed delegate or as an independent trustee? While the public had expectations of a rather weak form of trustee independence, the school board members themselves were far more adamant in endorsing the trustee style. Zeigler and Jennings note:

> There is virtually no relationship between how the constituents and their (usually) elected leaders interpret the classic representational roles. Typically, the understanding of the basic contract between the two is not at all well understood or agreed upon. . . . Little wonder that violent clashes sometimes emerge between the public and the board not only over substantive issues, but also over the decisional rules to be used.[30]

Zeigler and Jennings inquired into substantive representation by looking at the congruence of attitudes toward a number of issues between the "attentive public" and the sampled board members. Only 60 percent of their national sample had sufficient knowledge of schooling issues to discuss them. Boards and the attentive part of the public agreed that finance was the premier problem for schools and there was also agreement about teacher staffing as an area of concern. Even in the matter of race, boards and the public tended to agree about its importance on the district agenda. How-

---

29. L. Harmon Zeigler and M. Kent Jennings with G. Wayne Peak, *Governing American Schools: Political Interaction in Local School Districts* (North Scituate, Mass.: Duxbury Press, 1974).

30. Ibid., 124.

ever, agreeing that a problem exists and agreeing on its solution are two different things. They found that "the majority of the mass public has only the slimmest grasp of cause-effect relationships with respect to school district problems and their solutions."[31] In fact, there were so few people (even in the attentive public) who could propose *any* solutions to the problems they identified, that Zeigler and Jennings were unable to test the congruence between constituent wishes and board member actions. The problem thus posed for the representative is substantial. Where the constituency clearly wants actions on a given problem, they are often silent or at best inchoate about what they want done, and that puts a real premium on the representative's judgment. If there is to be correspondence between constituency desires and official actions, then "the attitudes and opinions of representative decision makers have a direct bearing on the translation of constituency preferences into policy."[32] The authors point out that the central role of the representative's attitudinal structure is best demonstrated in studies of the Congress.[33] Thus they conclude that the chances of representation are greatest where public and official attitudes are already the most congruent, a finding that emphasizes the stress in polyarchy not on direct access or widespread participation but on periodic determination of the leadership cadres.

What then are the factors that affect that determination? One of the central features has to do with the complex patterning of the constituency to be represented. The more diverse the constituency, the more difficult is the representative's task of determining how to act in its interests. From the point of view of individual citizens, the welter of diverse interests may diminish the likelihood of having their own interests enacted. The evidence from studies of this phenomenon indicates that as complexity increases, especially as metropolitanism increases, school board representatives shift their attention from cues coming from individuals to those coming from groups. "Regardless of the measure used, the more complex the school district is, the more responsive the board is to group demands.

31. Ibid., p. 131.
32. Ibid., p. 142.
33. Ibid., p. 143.

Pluralism and complexity enhance rather than impede responsiveness [to groups]."[34] Part of the explanation lies in the fact that organization becomes a necessity as the size of the constituency increases. Thus Zeigler and Jennings found that "organizational intensity," the extent to which organizations come to the board's attention, increased as social complexity increased.[35]

Zeigler and Jennings also looked at the effect of appointment versus election to the board. They concluded that elections were not delivering the much vaunted responsiveness, at least in part because school board elections are unlike other elections. In the first place, relatively few board members (one in five) aspired to higher positions,[36] so that the responsiveness to constituencies generally associated with ambition was not a factor in school board politics. Second, relatively few board seats (53 percent) were contested,[37] and in the absence of competition among alternate sets of elites, there was little incentive to pay much attention to the masses whose intermittent votes do not determine one's fate. Still, where electoral factors such as competition, forced turnovers, office sponsorship, and coterminous referenda are present, they do have an impact on the responsiveness of school boards. "It seems probable, therefore, that tinkering with the legal framework and fostering more competition for office would sooner or later affect the response linkage between constituents and school boards."[38]

At the end of their important study, Zeigler and Jennings conclude:

Measured against the yardstick of a classic democratic theory of leadership selection, school district governance hardly comes through with flying colors. There are, indeed, certain broad prerequisites which might well be considered discriminatory. Competition is limited, sponsorship and pre-emptive appointments common. Challenges to the status quo are infrequent; incumbents are but rarely challenged and more rarely still defeated. There are often no issue differences at all in an

---

34. Ibid., p. 80.
35. Ibid., p. 100.
36. Ibid., p. 41.
37. Ibid., p. 90, table 5-5.
38. Ibid., p. 92.

election, and when there are they seldom deal with the educational program, per se.[39]

In a careful look at a single metropolitan school board, Lyke found that representation in the sense of responding to constituencies was simply not something board members did. In general, these board members felt that citizen demands were (a) irrelevant (the board members preferred to listen to expert advice); (b) beyond their charge or powers as board members (they wanted someone else, primarily educators, to be responsive); (c) irresponsible (by which they meant antagonistic or unfair); and (d) illegitimate (not authorized by a public selection process).[40] Thus, Lyke's board despaired of performing its representational function, and in so doing diminished its prospects for control. Zeigler and Jennings end their book on a similar note: "School boards should govern or be abolished."[41] Wirt has summarized several pressures that have moved boards away from their ability to be responsive governors of schools. Among these factors are the growth of state and federal regulation, the increased intensity of competing interest groups, and the more acute differentiation of political cultures (rural, suburban, inner-city, money-providing/service-demanding, and so forth) within which boards must operate. A fourth factor cited by Wirt, "an intensification of professionalism in the delivery of school services," is particularly important.[42]

Representation is a function that we ordinarily associate with legislators. But the demands of representation recur throughout school administration as well. Should a superintendent resist majority opinion about school integration? Which clientele should get a new principal's first attention—those served by a reform in grouping practices? by ethnic studies? by a new reading curriculum? How do administrators determine how much or how little

39. Ibid., p. 244-45.

40. Robert F. Lyke, "Representation and Urban School Boards," in *Community Control of Schools*, ed. Henry M. Levin (Washington, D.C.: Brookings Institution, 1970), pp. 142-49.

41. Zeigler and Jennings, *Governing American Schools*, p. 254.

42. Frederick M. Wirt, "Social Diversity and School Board Responsiveness in Urban Schools," in *Understanding School Boards*, ed. Peter J. Cistone (Lexington, Mass.: D. C. Heath & Co., 1975), p. 190.

of what that phantasm, the community, says it wants will indeed be reflected in the policies and services of the school? How do they choose among competing claims or conflicting criteria? How, as professionals in the public service, do they weigh multiple criteria?

There is no doubt that administrators are having to pay increased attention to their representational roles. New York City's first guidelines to decentralization stated:

> A major goal is to reduce the gap between the source of important decisions and the place of impact. Decentralization should result in making all administrative and supervisory services more readily responsive to the needs of the children and to the ability of the schools to cope with these needs. It is to be hoped therefore that as much authority as possible will be delegated by local school boards to the schools, so as to make it possible for them to operate more independently and thus more efficiently and more responsively to local needs.[43]

The dominant (though not sufficient) position of school administrators in the control of school affairs is well documented. Koerner, for example, observes: "The school administration, not the local board and not the teachers, remains the primary focus of control over educational policy and over its implementation."[44] As compared with school boards, the power of the administrator is well summarized by the title of Kerr's article, "The School Board as an Agency of Legitimation."[45]

Still, school administrators and other educational professionals resist acquiring a political interpretation of their role. Easton's frequently cited definition of politics is "the authoritative allocation of values for society."[46] Since schools never have enough

---

43. Board of Education of the City of New York, *Guidelines to Decentralization for the Period Ending June 30, 1969: Prepared for the Use of Local School Boards and Local (District) Superintendents* (Brooklyn, N.Y.: Board of Education, 1968), p. 5.

44. J. D. Koerner, *Who Contols American Education? A Guide for Laymen*, Boston, Mass.: Beacon Press, 1968. See also Morris Janowitz, *Institution Building in Urban Education* (New York: Russell Sage Foundation, 1969), pp. 2-9.

45. Norman D. Kerr (pseudonym), "The School Board as an Agency of Legitimation," *Sociology of Education* 38 (Fall 1964): 34-59.

46. David Easton, *A Framework for Political Analysis* (Englewood Cliffs, N.J.: Prentice-Hall, 1965).

money, good teachers, or relevant curricula to satisfy all the demands on them, it is inevitable that there must be decisions about how to distribute the scarce resources among those competing demands. The first value distributed by schools, despite valid criticisms of their performance in doing so, is social mobility. Of course, schooling credentials are no proof against racial discrimination. Course work is less useful than connections. Schooling is less potent than other educating institutions. But exactly because of the power of these other nonschool factors, the school's role is enhanced for people who have access to none of the other forces for upward mobility. The school remains society's foremost consciously designed, systematically supported institution through which poor people *may* bootstrap themselves into different circumstances.

The second of the values allocated by schools is that of norms: competition over cooperation, science over art, individual effort over collective work, cognitive over affective responses, plus, of course, ideas about good citizenship, racism, sexism, "agism," and deference to authority. Third, schools are big business—$68 billion in 1974 for public elementary and secondary education. Access to teaching jobs, textbook adoptions, construction and insurance contracts add up to the distribution of substantial material values. There is little doubt that the administrators' role in all of this is an authoritative one. The state delivers a captive audience by compelling attendance, it provides tax money, and it provides formal state sanction to administrative decisions through its credentialing, licensing, and certifying of administrators. Politics is the process of the authoritative allocation of values, and school administration has important and unavoidable components of that process.

But schooling is also at least a quasi-scientific field of decision making. To the extent that it is scientific, it can be argued that schooling decisions should be arrived at by reason not influence, by merit not pressure. Unfortunately, there is no technology of teaching and learning that is even vaguely adequate to the demands of schooling decisions. After an exhaustive search of the empirical literatures, Averch et al. concluded that:

"Research has not identified a variant of the existent system that is consistently related to students' educational outcomes. . . . *Research has found nothing that consistently and unambiguously makes a difference in student outcomes.*"[47] (Italics in original)

Thus school administrators, along with all the other things they do, must also be political representatives.

Mann has researched the ways in which school administrators go about their representational tasks. It will be recalled that there are three choices for the style of representation. Those who follow the style of the "trustee" base their decisions on their own values, even when there is disagreement with the community. The "delegate" reverses that priority and is guided by expressed citizen preferences, sometimes even at the expense of the delegate's own judgment. The third position, the "politico," will borrow from either the trustee or the delegate style as dictated by particular circumstances and by an internally consistent rationale (that is, the politico does not simply vacillate through events). Of 161 administrators studied, 61 percent were trustees, 30 percent were delegates, and only 9 percent were politicos.[48] The predominance of trustee representation can be a source of difficulty since trustees will by definition choose to override the expressed needs and interests of their communities when they do not agree with that expression. When people lose confidence in the conduct of the schools or when they seek to expand their own participation and hence control over school affairs, then the trustee stance of administrators can be a source of real contention. Moreover, because administrators determine so much about schooling, their attitudes toward the incorporation of community wishes in their decisions as administrators are an important indicator of school responsiveness.

The trustee position is the least responsive to community preferences. A belief in personal expertise is a powerful rationale for excluding other people in decision making. Of those who described their own job performance as being in some fashion expert, 72 percent were trustees.[49] Similarly, those who conceived themselves

47. Harvey A. Averch et al., *How Effective is Schooling? A Critical Review and Synthesis of Research Findings* (Santa Monica, Calif.: Rand Corporation, 1972), p. x.

48. Mann, *The Politics of Administrative Representation*, p. 38.

49. Ibid., chap. 3.

as being responsible only to other bureaucrats within the organizational hierarchy, those who were organizationally furthest removed from the board of education, and those who defined their jobs as working with other professionals, tended also to take trustee orientations toward the community. With respect to the structure of authority, school administrators were most constrained (that is, least likely to take trustee orientations) by boards with direct electoral legitimation and direct oversight of their work. The more sources from which an administrator received representational cues —community associations, taxpayers' groups, parents' associations —the less likely it was that those sources would be overridden.

However, neither the size of the school being administered nor the complexity of its program organization was related to the trustee orientation. The only exception was for very small schools (which are also more likely to be homogeneous in their clientele) where noticeably more administrators were trustees. If administrative decentralization is a tactic designed in part to increase school responsiveness, then this finding suggests a lower limit on the size of such units (that is, about 500 enrollment). Elementary, junior high/intermediate, and high school principals were about equally likely to be trustees.

Suburban communities were found to have a higher proportion of trustees than either urban or rural communities.[50] Among large urban districts, New York City did not have more trustees than did other cities. The variations within urban districts seemed to be related to the social class composition of the district. In a finding that is consistent with those of Zeigler and Jennings, the complexity of the constituency was associated with responsiveness. Schools dominated by single groups from either end of the social class scale were likely to be administered by trustees. Trustee administrators were found in 80 percent of the predominantly welfare-class schools and in 75 percent of the schools at or above the upper middle-class level, although for very different reasons. The addition of significant numbers of working-class parents was associated with a decline in the administrator's tendency to be a trustee. It seems likely that the working-class parents, feeling threatened by their

50. Ibid., chap. 4.

welfare-class neighbors and unable to escape to either private schools or the suburbs, become actively involved in their own schools and that involvement presents clear representational signals, increasing the likelihood of delegate behavior by the administrator.

A related phenomenon has to do with the degree of organization about schooling matters in the community. As previously reported, the more organized the community, the more responsive its school administrators were likely to be. Similar gains in responsiveness came as the visibility of the administrator's decisions was increased. Thus, both the presence of outside watchdog groups and the visibility of administrative decisions (required budget hearings, mandatory appearances before review boards, and so forth) pressed administrators away from the trustee style.

Community participation in the career-determining decisions of its administrators also yielded a bonus in responsiveness. If the fate of one's predecessor in a position had been an unhappy or involuntary one, 20 percent fewer of the new administrative incumbents were trustees. Where the community played a strong role in hiring, retaining, and promoting there was a similar effect. The relationship between the administrator's ambition and responsiveness to the public was similar to that found in other areas of public life. As ambition decreased, the tendency to take a trustee orientation increased. Thus ambition appears to be making school administrators along with school board members more responsive to their constituencies.

The personal characteristics of the administrator have been the focus of much agitation by groups who want their schools run by administrators who share the community's racial or ethnic characteristics. But that "virtual representation" did not reduce the tendency of administrators to take trustee orientations, perhaps because of the powerful effect of professional (homogeneous) socialization or because of the belief by administrators that exactly because they so much resembled their communities they could therefore make decisions instead of them or on their behalf. Those few administrators from minority groups who appeared in the sample incorporated community needs and interests into their decisions in a fashion distinctly different from that of their colleagues from majority groups. Fewer than half as many were trustees; more were delegates; and many more were politicos. The politico role accounted for the smallest part of the sample (9 percent) and was associated with great conflict where the situational demands precluded adoption of a stable or consistent representational role orientation. The overrepresentation of politico roles among administrators from minority groups probably reflects the practice of appointing a minority group person to calm a conflict-ridden school.

The Future of Control

The politics of education is concerned with the question of who benefits and how those benefits are determined. Polsby's trilogy "who participates, who gains, who loses"[51] is an accepted formulation of the question about who controls. In democratic theory the individual has to be able to protect his own interests. Thus the theoretical importance of participation. In behavioral analysis, the axiom of self-interest means that those who participate gain the most. Thus the practical importance of participation. But those forms of participation that are least expensive to employ—expressing an opinion, voting—also yield the least direct control in terms of an individual's agenda. Dahl's classic study of New Haven demonstrated that in each of a number of key sectors of public policy, a few persons have great *direct* influence on the choices that are made; most citizens, by contrast, seem to have rather little direct influence.[52] Yet it would be unwise to underestimate the extent to which voters may exert *indirect* influence on the decisions of leaders by means of elections. The point for the educational sector is that the influence carried by electoral participation may be extremely indirect and in the case of the local school it may never arrive at all. In a moment we shall consider some recent evidence on the remarkable obdurateness of the school building as an institution. Before that, we should briefly recapitulate some of the evidence about nonelectoral citizen participation. Teachers recognize parents who are vigorous in pressing for the school to

51. Nelson W. Polsby, *Community Power and Political Theory* (New Haven, Conn.: Yale University Press, 1963), p. 4.

52. Robert Dahl, *Who Governs?* (New Haven, Conn.: Yale University Press, 1961).

serve their interests and teachers act accordingly. Organizing to pursue those interests pays some dividends in the responsiveness of the school. But participation is a class-linked phenomenon. Those who have most to gain from it are least likely to possess the resources of time, energy, knowledge, self-confidence, and allies that are necessary precursors to its exercise.

For these and logistic reasons, representation, not participation is the principal vehicle for attempts at the control of schools. Representation is one giant step removed from participation as a way to guarantee the satisfaction of one's interests; in representation individual interests must somehow be aggregated and someone else must act on that aggregation. Studies of school boards indicate that boards are in fact rather insulated from the communication of interests from much of their diverse constituuency, and boards themselves are not much inclined to translate the representational responsibilities into attempts to control schools. Large parts of the task of representing the wishes and welfare of the public thus fall to professional educators, especially school administrators. This group, standing at the key intersection between the community and the delivery of schooling services, views its representational functions in ways that stress personal and professional autonomy, often at the expense of the community's expressed preferences.

Political scientists have been rediscovering the importance of the level of government at which service is delivered as the final arbiter of what is—and what is not—done through public policy. Some recent evidence in the area of school-based innovation points up the potency of the local school as the nearly sufficient determiner of policy. The Rand Corporation undertook an analysis of several federally-supported programs that had been designed to bring about innovation in schools. These change-agent projects were undertaken with a number of favorable circumstances—a thrust toward improvement; extra money; a concentrated and specialized project focus; the availability of what was generally the state-of-the-art in educational technology; and endorsement by the federal government, state agencies, and the local board.[53]

53. Dale Mann, "Making Change Happen?" *Teachers College Record* 77 (February 1976): 313-415. The interested reader is referred to the complete

What happened? In time virtually every project simplified its treatments; slowed the pace of its activities; became less ambitious about the range of its intended effects; decreased its expectations about how many people would be affected; and decreased its expectations about the amount of changed behavior to be elicited from any given individual. In general these efforts emerged after the change-agent projects had moved their efforts to the local schools. School sites and the projects were locked in a kind of arm wrestle (or "partisan mutual adaptation") to change the other. The schools have won with stunning regularity. In all of this, the building principal was the key actor for desirable teaching assignments, free time, scheduling cooperation, and exemption from scores of harassing, petty regulations. The change-agent project was temporary; the principal was permanent. Thus every project identified the principal as a critical force. Where the principal supported the project, there was substantial change. More often the principal opposed the project, and the direction of the ensuing change ran from the school to the project, which then was co-opted, eviscerated, and dismantled.

It is important to note that the process through which this is done is nothing so blunt as overt opposition. The ways in which administrators work their will are far more subtle but also more effective. Bachrach and Baratz have employed a concept called "nondecision making" to study processes that appear similar to those at work here.[54] Nondecisions come in at least four guises: (a) default nondecisions (denial of authority to decide, buck-passing); (b) abstention (selective failure to intervene, benign neglect); (c) covert decision making (hidden choice); and (d) false consensus (the manipulation of symbolic values). All nondecisions

---

reports from the first year of the Rand project on change. See especially Peter W. Greenwood, Dale Mann, and Milbrey Wallin McLaughlin, *Federal Programs Supporting Educational Change*, vol. 3, *The Process of Change* (Santa Monica, Calif.: Rand Corporation, 1974). Other volumes relevant to the first year of the project are vol. 1, *A Model of Educational Change*; vol. 2, *Factors Affecting Change Agent Projects*; vol. 4, *The Findings in Review*; and vol. 5, *Executive Summary*.

54. Peter Bachrach and Morton S. Baratz, "Decisions and Nondecision: An Analytic Framework," *American Political Science Review* 57 (September 1963): 632-42; idem, "Two Faces of Power," *American Political Science Review* 56 (December 1962): 947-52.

share some characteristics. They stop challenges to existing values and/or they attempt to prevent something from reaching the stage of a decision. Additionally, the normative implications of nondecisions is that they are profoundly conservative. Nondecisions achieve their aims by suppressing participation and conflict.

John Kenneth Galbraith has called conflict the engine of change. Schattschneider's arena theory of political process explains how that happens.[55] Ordinarily issues are decided by the interaction of protagonists in the arena of public affairs. But occasionally the loser of a contest will protest the outcome and attempt to attract new allies from the spectator groups into the arena. Those new resources, attached as they are to the previously losing side, will provide the impetus for change in public policy. But note how that came about—through the agency of conflict. Thus, preempting conflict, through nondecision making for example, also stops change and consolidates control in the hands of existing decision elites.

Participation and representation even in their most concentrated forms seldom yield much control to individuals. Schooling governance has too many participants, too many facets for that participation, and is too subtle a process for it to be otherwise. A more adequate understanding of that process and hence better informed actions may rest on advances in areas that are as difficult to research as nondecision making.

55. Elmer E. Schattschneider, *The Semisovereign People: A Realist's View of Democracy in America* (New York, N.Y.: Holt, Rinehart & Winston, 1960), chap. 1.

CHAPTER IV

Education and American Federalism: Intergovernmental and National Policy Influences

EDITH K. MOSHER

Education in the Context of General Government: Bridging Islands of Inquiry

A student of American government and its subsystems for the government of public education cannot escape a nagging question: Why are these domains of political analysis so isolated from each other? No matter what sources of information and opinion one consults—researchers, theoreticians, practitioners, journalists, elected policy makers—the duality is apparent, and it resembles a divorce more than an amicable separation. Specialists in many fields—policy studies, governmental planning, budget and personnel administration, urban and metropolitan studies, comparative state and local politics, intergovernmental relations, voting behavior—describe and analyze the minute workings of "general government"[1] and typically omit any reference to educational governance. Recent writings about educational administration depict interdisciplinary kinships with law, history, philosophy, psychology, sociology, and business administration, but, by comparison, pass lightly over the literature of political science and public administration. These lacunae might not be such an anomaly were education not the most pervasive and costly of domestic governmental services. They cannot be dismissed as scholarly oversights that would be readily corrected by expending a little more time and effort.

---

1. "General government" is the generic term for those units not restricted to one or a few functions. It refers to towns, cities, counties, states, and national government, in contrast to "special units," such as school districts and others limited to specific functions described in their titles: sanitary districts, highway authorities, flood control or irrigation districts, etc. See Herbert Kaufman, *Politics and Policies in State and Local Governments*, 3d ed. (Englewood Cliffs, N.J.: Prentice-Hall, 1965), p. 55.

In fact, the isolation of the institutions of educational governance as objects of inquiry has deep roots that have been nourished by intensely partisan research preoccupations. For several decades educational professionals have highlighted the distinctive aspects of the services they provide and the autonomous aspects of the school systems they administer, delegating the attributes shared with other governmental entities to a dimly lit background. Political scientists tend to treat educational functions and structures at the national and state governmental levels as parallel with those of the other specialized public programs, subject to common legal and political constraints. Until recently, the local educational agencies were largely beyond their purview.[2] These number in the thousands and vary widely on every dimension, including degree of independence, and present formidable tasks of investigation and generalization. Only recently have a few political scientists given priority to empirical study of the domain that is best known and defended by the educationists.[3] Across a scholarly chasm wing critical pronouncements by political scientists and policy makers committed to rationalizing governmental organization and strengthening the authority of elected officials accountable to a broader constituency. Some have contended that the narrow representational and professional base for educational policy making violates the principles of democracy in which the schools purport to instruct their clientele.[4] Others simply have shrugged off educational governance as the

---

2. Phillip Monypenny, "A Political Analysis of Structures for Educational Policy Making," in *Government of Education for Adequate Policy Making*, ed. William P. McLure and Van Miller (Urbana, Ill.: Bureau of Educational Research, College of Education, University of Illinois, 1960), p. 8.

3. Dating from the late 1950s, this development is documented in several recent "state of the art" summaries and bibliographies. See Laurence Iannaccone and Peter J. Cistone, *The Politics of Education* (Eugene, Oreg.: ERIC Clearinghouse on Educational Management, University of Oregon, 1974); Michael W. Kirst and Edith K. Mosher, "Politics of Education," *Review of Educational Research* 39 (December 1969): 623-40; Paul E. Peterson, "The Politics of American Education," in *Review of Research in Education*, vol. 2, ed. Fred N. Kerlinger (Itasca, Ill.: F. E. Peacock Publishers, 1974), pp. 348-89. For a review of research activity focused on intergovernmental relations in American education, see Edith K. Mosher, "The School Board in the Family of Governments," in *Understanding School Boards*, ed. Peter J. Cistone (Lexington, Mass.: D. C. Heath & Co., 1976), pp. 79-102.

4. Jesse Burkhead, *Public School Finance: Economics and Politics* (Syracuse, N.Y.: Syracuse University Press, 1964), p. 152.

"fourth branch of government." Educational professionals, wary of attacks on their integrity and independence, tend neither to deny nor affirm this disdainful epithet. As a result, the study of the educational component of the American federal system has suffered neglect.

Disciplinary hostilities die hard and the scholarly search for alternative frames of reference to map so vast an area proceeds slowly. Still, some demythologizing about educational governance has already occurred. It is now widely recognized that the American educational enterprise, like other governmental activities, is infused with competing public values, responds to common social and environmental influences, and must be powered by public money. In other words, it is inescapably political and somehow locked into, or linked to, other governmental structures, processes, and purposes. When its isolation and autonomy are viewed as relative rather than absolute attributes, the inquiry problem is perceived as that of exploring the linkages that exist or should exist, how they came about, and whether they may be expected to change in the future. This change of perspective does not, however, obviate the difficulties posed by the size and intricacy of the federal structure of American government and its educational sector. The admonition to researchers given by Zeigler and Jennings recognizes the problem and also comports with the common focus and purpose of chapters in this yearbook:

An account of various relationships among the myriad actors at local, state, and federal levels and an account of the variations in the structural relationships among the formal institutions of government and the informal centers of power are needed to provide such a descriptive framework. Such an undertaking would be not only herculean, but also would result in a decidedly unparsimonious theory of educational control. Understandably, therefore, those who have attacked questions pertaining to educational government have confined the breadth of their discourse to one or another segment of that whole.

Although this division of labor is a legitimate and probably a necessary way of approaching a more complete understanding of the subject, it does raise an additional, unresolved problem—how do all of the discrete pieces of information and the various subareas of investigation fit together? Unless it is theoretically possible to link the findings of the highest quality of research concerning the political control of education to the product of that control, the classroom student, then the major benefits of the research are lost. And from the standpoint of *educational* scholarship, the research represents little more than an academic exercise.[5]

This chapter will address the question: How do the sectors and processes of general governmental and educational policy making, largely writ, fit together? To this end we shall describe and analyze educational governance as a subarea of the overarching system of American federalism, and introduce, but intrude as little as possible upon, the analysis of the constituent influence systems of educational governance in the chapters that follow. We shall give more detailed attention to the most unitary of the major influence systems, namely, legislative and executive policy making at the national level of government.

The Architecture of the Federal System of Educational Government

About the only consensus to be found in contemporary political science writings about the term "federalism" is that it refers, in its "purest" meaning, to relationships between a national government and its constituent state governments. As government became a more prominent factor in the lives of Americans, and the state and local governments developed "from sleeping pygmies (or at least dwarfs) into active giants," [6] the term has acquired almost as many meanings and modifiers as users, who have attempted, without notable clarity, to distinguish between such varieties of federalism as "national," "creative," "collective," "cooperative," and "new." Leach recently identified twelve stereotypes of perspectives that are involved in analyzing the phenomenon of federalism.[7]

Wright advocates the use of the term "intergovernmental relations" (IGR) to apply to all the permutations and combinations of relations among the units of American government. He states that the system of American federalism provides the context within

---

5. L. Harmon Zeigler, M. Kent Jennings, with the assistance of G. Wayne Peak, *Governing American Schools* (North Scituate, Mass.: Duxbury Press, 1974), pp. 9-10.

6. Richard H. Leach, "Federalism: A Battery of Questions," *Publius* 3 (Fall 1973): 13.

7. Ibid., 15-21.

which intergovernmental relations occur but does not comprise the totality of those relations.[8] Even greater analytical complexity is suggested by Kaufman, who characterizes the contemporary scene in metaphorical terms:

> Relations among the levels of government thus fall into no simple, symmetrical pattern. They are more like a tangled web of rubber bands —intricate, elastic, capable of accommodating all sorts of pressures yet retaining their shape, under the tension of many forces and counterforces, and very taut much of the time.[9]

In his recent book on policy making in American education, Thompson draws upon the literature of political science and sociology to distill three uniquely American conditions that gave the educational enterprise its most distinctive features: federalism, localism, and sectionalism or multistate regionalism.[10] His comprehensive model of the "federal" system for educational policy making combines Kaufman's concept of "tautness," attributable to its structural underpinnings in socioeconomic, demographic, and political conditions and in the legal structure and powers of government, with the "pressure-accommodating" linkages among the national, state, interstate/regional, and local communities and governmental units (fig. 1). Congruent with the unique degree of decentralization that characterizes American education is the placement of the local school system at the vortex of interacting influence systems, a conceptualization that accords with that of Zeigler and Jennings but departs from the more usual modeling of intergovernmental systems in hierarchical form, by levels.[11]

Thompson relies on analysts of urban politics for his broad view of the dynamics of educational policy making, including the processes by which schools adapt to environmental challenges and problems. This treatment enlarges and complements the segmented

8. Deil S. Wright, "Intergovernmental Relations and Policy Choice," *Publius* 5 (Fall 1975): 4.

9. Herbert Kaufman, *Politics and Policies in State and Local Governments* (Englewood Cliffs, N.J.: Prentice-Hall, 1963), p. 32.

10. John Thomas Thompson, *Policy Making in American Public Education* (Englewood Cliffs, N.J.: Prentice-Hall, 1976), pp. 17-35.

11. Zeigler and Jennings, *Governing American Schools*, p. 10; Frederick M. Wirt and Michael W. Kirst, *Political and Social Foundations of Education*, rev. ed. (Berkeley, Calif.: McCutchan Publishing Corp., 1975), pp. 147-52.

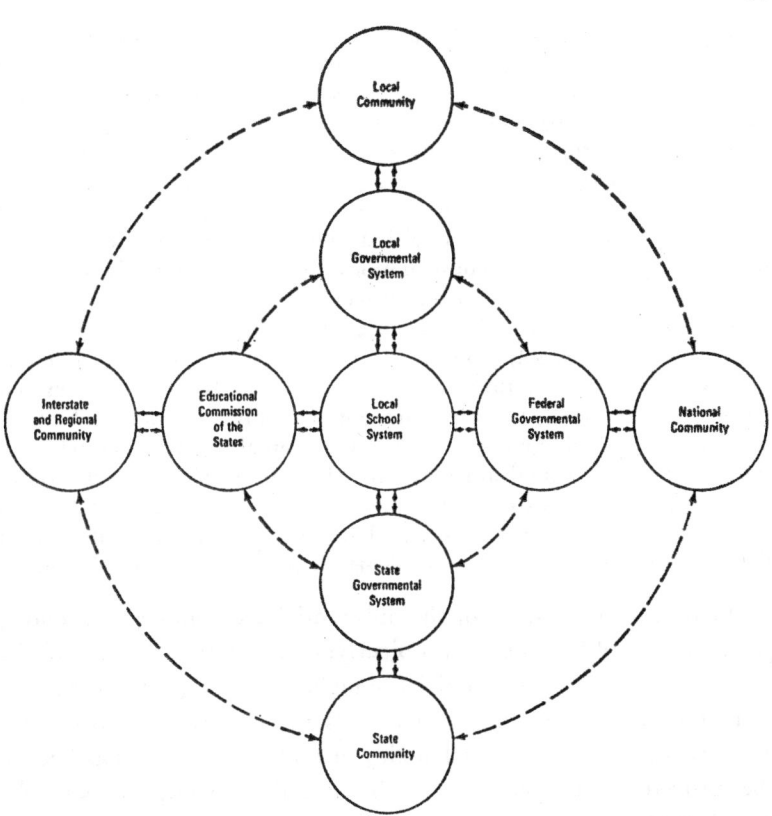

FIG. 1. Model of the policy-making system of American education
SOURCE: John Thomas Thompson, *Policymaking in American Public Education* (Englewood Cliffs, N.J.: Prentice-Hall, 1976), p. 30.

model of the stages of public policy formation set forth by Campbell et al.[12]

Herbert Kaufman has provided a unifying theoretical framework for viewing the growth and elaboration of American governmental institutions. He states:

Men build their governments as they build their houses—in many ways, to serve many purposes. . . . The design of houses and governments represents, among other things, compromises among all the competing purposes which those structures might possibly fulfill. . . . In the evolution of the structure of state and local governments in the United States

12. Roald F. Campbell et al., *The Organization and Control of American Schools* (Columbus, Ohio: Charles E. Merrill Publishing Co., 1965), pp. 37-39.

there is discernible a search especially for an accommodation among three values or objectives: representativeness; technical, nonpartisan competence; and leadership. The first refers to the demand for election of public officials by some (at first) or many (later) or virtually all (a twentieth-century innovation) adult citizens over which the officials exercise jurisdiction. The second refers to the demand for officials having training and experience qualifying them for the jobs they do, and to the insistence that their official decisions and actions be based on technical and professional considerations rather than on partisan political premises. The third refers to the demand that the actions and decisions of officials be coordinated at some central point so that government programs are reasonably consistent and efficient. . . . At any point in history, elements reflecting all three values can be discerned in our governmental system; the three are not mutually exclusive. Indeed, all have left their distinctive marks on governmental organization, with the result that governmental organization today represents a combination of devices introduced earlier and innovations constituting responses to more recent needs and desires. . . . Excessive emphasis on only one of the values tends to set in motion demands for redressing the balance.[13]

In Kaufman's analysis of the differential accommodations among these three public values or objectives in the functioning of the executive, legislative, and judicial branches of American government and of its constituent levels, one finds the congruent substructure and processes of educational policy making. At the national level, the procedures established for the President, Congress, and the courts apply to education as they do to the other areas of concern. At the state level, educational governance is subject to a mixture of general and special governmental procedures, statutes, and fiscal provisions. The latter, like those regulating other specific state functions and services, supplement and do not supersede across-the-board controls of general state governance.

At the local level one finds that education falls into Kaufman's category of "special" government, since the preponderant number of school districts have significant revenue-raising and expenditure powers and independence from the cities and counties within whose territorial limits they may be contained in whole or in part. He states that in these and in the other types of special government, which have proliferated in recent decades, accommodation of only

---

[13]. Kaufman, *Politics and Policies in State and Local Governments*, pp. 33-35.

two of the core values of the polity is discernible: representativeness, through the provision of elected school boards; and technical, nonpartisan competence by delegation of policy making to professionals.[14] The origins and operations of the special governments provide little evidence of concern for enhancing centralized authority of general governmental officials or for coordinating specific functions and services. Instead, leadership, program coordination, and a consistency of policy otherwise incompatible with localism can be traced to another cross-cutting channel of communication and influence that students of intergovernmental relations term "vertical functional specialization." This refers to the formal and informal linkages among educational professionals performing official and unofficial roles at all levels of government.

Political scientists have tended to emphasize the unitary adherence of the educational professionals to isolationist politics, which is marked by hostility to general governmental controls and competition for resources with other public services.[15] However, the professionals are by no means agreed about the goals and priorities of public education or about their own expertise. As is the case among other functional specializations, their internal conflicts add to the fragmentation and centrifugal tendencies inherent in the American system of federalism.

An adequate study and comparison of instances of intergovernmental policy making would require identification of all the relevant participants from a lengthy roster of both general and educational agencies and of extralegal groups, lay and professional. Within each cell of the model in figure 1 is a multiplicity of agencies and actors whose interactions are to some degree comparable across all regions, states, and localities, but may also be different in significant aspects. The combined impact of the subnational units on the highly variable local school systems produces further idiosyncratic consequences.

The methodological and data collection problems in conducting

---

14. Ibid., p. 55. See also Mosher, "The School Board in the Family of Governments," pp. 84-85 and William M. Boyd, "School Board—Administrative Staff Relationships," in *Understanding School Boards*, ed. Peter J. Cistone (Lexington, Mass.: D. C. Heath & Co., 1976), pp. 105-109.

15. Kirst and Mosher, "Politics of Education," 625.

such research are so demanding that it is not surprising to find it a virtually untouched field of inquiry.[16] Table 1 provides a simple typology that illustrates the range of participants whose potential influence on educational governance, no matter how tangential, must be considered in the study of particular situations or issues.

The Federal System of Educational Government in Historical Perspective

Given the range of participants and complexity of their present intergovernmental relationships it is unlikely that local school governments are actually as isolated or autonomous as is popularly believed. Yet the past intrudes on the present in two interconnected ways.[17] Attempts to meet contemporary educational needs are carried on in a context suffused with emotional support for localism, which is basic to the grass roots theory of democratic government. Further, the formal federal structure of governmental responsibility for education has remained essentially unchanged since the nineteenth century. The United States Constitution gave to the separate states all functions not specifically reserved to the federal government; and the states have delegated much formal authority to local government. The system that emerged was defined by scholars as "dual federalism," meaning that, until comparatively recent decades, the functions and administrative activities of the three levels were well delineated and separable. Advocates of decentralized control of education tend to espouse this historic view of federalism as protective of grass roots ideology and authority.

A competing interpretation has recently emerged, associated with the "marble-cake" metaphor in describing integovernmental relations, which holds that "dual federalism" never characterized the American political system. Instead, from the beginning there was a high degree of shared activity and responsibilities among

---

16. For a discussion of methodological problems, see chapter 2 of a pioneering study of federal-state-local relations: Joel S. Berke and Michael W. Kirst, *Federal Aid to Education: Who Benefits? Who Governs?* (Lexington, Mass.: D. C. Heath & Co., 1972).

17. See Geraldine Joncich Clifford, *The Shape of American Education* (Englewood Cliffs, N.J.: Prentice-Hall, 1975), chap. 1.

the levels of government, indeed as much sharing in the period 1790–1860 as there is today.[18] This view lends the weight of historical precedent to any contemporary centralization of power that is accompanied by arrangements for the sharing of administrative functions. Scheiber has recently criticized the "marble-cake" construct because its proponents did not examine the full spectrum of state policy concerns and administrative activities, did not establish plausible criteria as to what were trivial or important instances of intergovernment cooperation, and did not consider the basic issues of relative power distribution among levels of government.[19] He counters the claim of system continuity with evidence that American federalism has gone through major transformations from 1790 to the present. To put the history of educational governance into parallel perspective, it is instructive to examine these stages of development.

EARLY LOCAL, SECTIONAL, AND STATE INFLUENCES, 1790–1860

During the pre-Civil War period strict adherence to the wording of the Constitution characterized the division of responsibilities between the government and the states. In domestic affairs, the latter exercised a wide range of powers with minimal interference, especially in the areas of policy crucially important to the economy of the expanding nation: money and banking, land, taxation, transportation, conditions of labor, and civil rights. Intense sectional, interstate, and intrastate rivalries led to a balkanization of the American market, despite the Constitution's obvious intent otherwise.[20] The states also began to assert jurisdiction, through constitutional and statutory controls, in many other fields in which even today they play a dominant role: property rights, business organization, family life, social relations, criminal and civil law, local government, elections, education, and conservation. How-

18. Morton Grodzins, "Centralization and Decentralization," in *A Nation of States*, ed. Robert A. Goldwin (Chicago: Rand McNally & Co., 1963), pp. 3-4, 7.

19. Harry N. Scheiber, "The Condition of American Federalism: A Historian's View," in *Controversies of State and Local Political Systems*, ed. Mavis Mann Reeves and Parris N. Glendening (Boston, Mass.: Allyn & Bacon, 1972), pp. 64-92.

20. Ibid., p. 70.

TABLE 1
AGENCIES PARTICIPATING IN THE GOVERNMENT OF EDUCATION

Unit of Government	Structure	
	Legal	Extralegal
Local Community Units 1. Educational agents	1. Public school systems (districts) 2. Township school trustees (custodians of school funds, property)	1. Professional groups, e.g., teachers' associations 2. Parent-teacher associations 3. Citizens' education advisory committees
2. General governmental agents	1. Municipalities 2. Township officials 3. Local courts 4. Law enforcement agents	1. Community planning groups 2. Civic clubs 3. Religious groups 4. Labor unions 5. Philanthropic organizations 6. Political groups 7. Business groups
Regional Units (Intrastate) 1. Educational agents	1. County superintendent of schools 2. District school superintendents 3. Boards of cooperative educational services 4. Junior college districts 5. Institutes and technical colleges	1. Professional and lay advisory groups
2. General governmental agents	1. County board of supervisors 2. Boards for library services 3. Agricultural extension service	1. Associations of governmental officials 2. Political groups 3. Civic groups 4. Farm organizations
Regional Units (Interstate) 1. Educational agents	1. Southern Regional Education Board 2. Midwest Interlibrary Center 3. Laboratories for educational research and development	1. Educational Commission of the States 2. Associations of public school systems and institutions of higher education for accreditation and other purposes 3. Athletic associations
2. General governmental agents	1. Public health programs of the federal government 2. Social security programs of the federal government	

State Central Units		
1. Educational agents	1. State department of education (administrative agents)	1. Associations of teachers and other professional groups
	2. State boards of education for vocational education, elementary and secondary education, all public education, all higher education, groups of higher educational institutions, single institutions of higher education, teacher certification, teachers' retirement systems, museums, libraries	2. Parent-teacher associations
	3. Educational commissions for general school problems, scholarships, higher education, educational surveys	3. Association of school boards
	4. School building authorities	4. Citizens' education advisory committees
	5. Special institutions for schools for handicapped persons, corrective institutions, vocational and technical schools	
	6. Colleges and universities	
2. General governmental agents	1. Legislatures	1. Taxpayers' associations
	2. Executive departments for revenue, health, and highways	2. Labor unions
	3. Courts	3. Chambers of Commerce
	4. Commissions for children and youth, athletics, handicapped children	4. Agricultural associations
		5. Manufacturers' associations
Federal Unit		
1. Educational agents	1. Department of Health, Education, and Welfare, U.S. Office of Education, National Institute of Education	1. "Big Six" interest groups: National Education Association and affiliates; Council of Chief State School Officers; National School Boards Association; National Congress of Parent-Teacher Associations; American Federation of Teachers; American Association of School Administrators
	2. National Science Foundation	2. American Council on Education and affiliates
		3. Foundations
2. General governmental agents	1. U. S. Congress	1. President's Commission on School Finance
	2. President and White House staff agencies	2. Citizens' advisory groups for federal educational programs
	3. Courts	
	4. Eight departments of cabinet rank	
	5. Other commissions, bureaus, boards, agencies	

SOURCE: Adapted from William P. McClure and Van Miller, eds., *Government of Education for Adequate Policy Making* (Urbana, Ill.: Bureau of Educational Research, College of Education, University of Illinois, 1960), pp. 24-26.

ever, the financial support actually provided for public services was very modest, and it came predominantly from local resources.

The governmental structure of education reflected these early characteristics of the American federal system. Before 1790, educational services were limited, private, and local. When a movement for providing elementary education at public expense developed in the early 1800s, the responsibility remained with local citizens. The westward movement of population disseminated geographical patterns of school governance that are identifiable at present in sectional diversities with regard to local school district organizations and state funding provisions.[21] Jefferson and Washington, as well as other early friends of education, proposed that national and state institutions be created to promote public acceptance of the idea of public instruction and to encourage uniformity of programs and goals among existing schools, but their ideas did not bear fruit for several decades. The reformist impulse found expression in the work of Horace Mann and other leaders who were distressed by laissez-faire localism and spearheaded the move for establishment of state superintendencies and state boards of education.[22] These legislative actions are cited as the genesis of a special governmental status for education.[23] The program of federal land grants to the states for educational purposes, initiated by the Land Ordinances of 1785 and 1787, and the other subventions made during this period were important as symbolic expressions and concrete precedents for a national concern in fostering education rather than as evidence of invasion or sharing of the power of the states.[24]

CENTRALIZING FEDERALISM, 1860-1933

Partly as a result of the Civil War and partly in response to

21. Robert H. Salisbury, "State Politics and Education," in *Politics in the American States*, ed. Herbert Jacob and Kenneth N. Vines (Boston, Mass.: Little, Brown & Co., 1971), p. 410.

22. Donald R. Warren, *To Enforce Education: A History of the Founding Years of the United States Office of Education* (Detroit, Mich.: Wayne State University Press, 1974), pp. 25-47.

23. Campbell et al., *The Organization and Control of American Schools*, pp. 50-51.

24. Rufus E. Miles, Jr., *The Department of Health, Education, and Welfare* (New York: Praeger Publishers, 1974), pp. 139-40.

the new national dimension of business and labor organizations and the consumer problems of an increasingly urbanized society, the national government preempted functions and policy making powers formerly lodged in the lower levels of government.[25] Programs of cash grants to the states became more important, especially for highways, accompanied by matching requirements and constraints of planning, reporting, and quality standards. Such shared activity was very limited; for example, in 1927 federal grants provided only 1.7 percent of state and local revenues. A second development integral to the operative federal system occurred during this period: the emergence of the functional bureaucracies. Government officials in the various specialized programs began to develop a sense of professional community that cut across intergovernmental levels and even bridged the public and private sectors. As suggested by Kaufman, the "core value" of neutral competence took precedence over representativeness in policy making and was reinforced by the criteria of rationality associated with the scientific management movement. The third event that profoundly affected the future of intergovernmental relations was the enactment in 1913 of the constitutional amendment that gave the national government power to collect income taxes, the most productive, flexible, and efficient of revenue sources.

By 1933, the educational enterprise had been vastly expanded by population growth and the addition of secondary schools, and it had become bureaucratized at the state and local levels. The trend to consolidate small school districts into larger units was well underway. Education was immune from the centralizing effects of national actions such as those for interstate commerce, monetary and banking policy, and labor organizations; however, a precedent for federal categorical cash grants to the states for vocational education was set by the Smith-Hughes Act of 1917. This legislation required matching funds, development of a state plan, appointment of a state administering agency, and periodic reports. The U.S. Office of Education was established in 1867, primarily as an agency for gathering statistics and disseminating information. It had few powers and remained largely a token of federal concern for education.

25. Scheiber, *"The Condition of American Federalism,"* pp. 71-72.

The centralizing movement in which education fully shared was the growth of professionalism at all levels of government. As educators increasingly dominated the policy-making processes of larger-scale enterprises, the delivery system for educational services changed from "consumer-oriented" to "producer-oriented." The reforms of the late 1800s and early 1900s that favored nonpartisan expertise also accelerated the separation of local educational agencies from those of general government. The latter development was an American phenomenon, since central authorities in other countries were more likely to reorganize the local governments to increase their viability for delivery of welfare or educational services.[26]

THE NEW DEAL AND COOPERATIVE FEDERALISM, 1933–1958

The New Deal and World War II were crucial in shaping modern federalism. A twenty-five year period brought dramatic centralization as the national government assumed leadership in combating first the depression and then external challenges to national survival. Intergovernmental programs proliferated, with a commitment of federal funds that dwarfed previous levels. The shift to support of welfare programs during the 1930s represented a major break with a narrow programmatic scope, which had been principally on highways and vocational education. The war years were significant for involving state and local officials in the administration of federal programs, notably for draft conscription and rationing. Cooperative government became a reality, creating new forms of intergovernmental linkage and relying heavily on the financial resources of the national government. During the postwar period, the number of categorical grants-in-aid continued to increase, but became more concentrated and selectively chan-

26. "U.S. and Britain, both of which had strong nineteenth-century local self-government traditions, shifted their institutional structures at the turn of the century in dramatically opposed directions. The British abolished . . . an assortment of autonomous school boards at one stroke through the Balfour Act of 1902 and transferred their powers to the general local authorities. . . . One equivalent attempt, a 1917 New York State Act which sought to require rural school boards to hand their powers over to local governments had to be repealed because the school boards simply refused to abide by it." Arnold J. Heidenheimer, "The Politics of Public Education, Health, and Welfare in the U.S.A. and Europe: How Growth and Reform Potentials Have Differed," *British Journal of Politics* 3 (July 1973): 327.

neled into capital outlays to meet deferred wartime needs and respond to the suburbanization movement.

President Roosevelt's innovative leadership was crucial in promoting acceptance of expanded governmental action, but the prime mechanism and the enduring legacy of the new intergovernmental partnerships were fiscal in character. For example, Congress began to mandate new detailed formulas for determination of state eligibility and to follow equalization principles designed to adjust payments to state needs and resources. The legislative reorganization in 1946 created standing committees and subcommittees with explicit program and fiscal responsibilities that paralleled the increasingly specific grant-in-aid structure. The legislative focus was on devising fiscal provisions and controls rather than promoting the implementation of broad social programs.[27]

Some other distinctive features of cooperative federalism have had persistent impact, as follows:[28]

1. *A bypassing tendency.* The national government made grants-in-aid for many new purposes to local agencies of government, bypassing the states. Special-purpose and regional units were funded which cut across traditional political jurisdictions.

2. *A skewing effect.* Local and state administrations tended to allocate their revenues to programs that commanded federal matching funds rather than those requiring full funding from their own resources.

3. *Fractional responsibility.* In the grant-supported programs crosscutting the levels and agencies of government the growing community of specialist civil servants took charge in their respective areas, and it became increasingly difficult to fix clearcut responsibility for program impact on the officials of general government or on those at any one level of government.

4. *Demonstration and activist programs.* The New Deal period witnessed the initiation by the national government of several demonstration and activist programs that were organized outside

---

27. Deil S. Wright, "Intergovernmental Relations: An Analytical Overview," *Annals of the American Academy of Political and Social Science* 416 (November 1974): 7-9.

28. Scheiber, "The Condition of American Federalism," pp. 75-77.

the existing functional networks, such as agriculture, and competed with them for grass roots citizen support.

5. *Planning and administrative support.* The national government encouraged the planning efforts of state and local officials, both on a broad scale and, in a more limited way, on organizational and procedural improvements in the grant-supported programs. Growing professional influence brought pressures on the subnational governments to elevate levels of service to nationally recognized standards.

During this ferment of intergovernmental change, education at first remained remarkably unaffected. The national government bypassed the existing school establishment in implementing such emergency New Deal programs as the National Youth Administration and the Civilian Conservation Corps. However, the sudden buildup of industrial and military installations during World War II and the Korean War became a justification for temporary and later continuing direct aid to school districts in areas that were overburdened by nontaxable federal installations.[29] Subsequent Congresses supported these unrestricted formula grants as a peacetime substitute for payment in lieu of taxes. Determined efforts by a succession of presidents have been unsuccessful in eliminating or even reducing them. The Servicemen's Readjustment Act of 1944, commonly called the GI Bill of Rights, extended the scope of federal benefits to include education, but it was administered by the national government and had little impact on the elementary and secondary educational structure.

In the postwar "baby-boom" period, proponents of federal aid to education lobbied vigorously and gained supporters in the executive branch and Congress, notably the fiscally conservative Republican Senator Robert Taft. But for more than a decade they were unable to win their fight against the combined opposition of those wedded to localism, to racial segregation in the schools, and to inclusion of church-related schools as beneficiaries.[30] These fruitless efforts were directed to obtaining grants that were unrestricted

---

29. Miles, *The Department of Health, Education, and Welfare*, p. 143. The legislation authorizing such "impact aid" was the Lanham Act of 1941 and PL 81-815 and PL 81-874, first passed in 1950.

30. Burkhead, *Public School Finance*, chap. 10.

or limited to construction of buildings and supplements to teachers' salaries—grants that would fully preserve the autonomy of state and local school administration. When success finally came in 1958, with the passage of the National Defense Education Act, it was attributable in large part to the expression of a national purpose —to build up scientific and technical capacity—and to specification in the Act of grant-in-aid categories. Thus education became subject to the influences of cooperative federalism that had suffused other public welfare services for more than two decades.

CREATIVE FEDERALISM (1958-1968) AND NEW FEDERALISM (1969-1976)

The most recent expressions of American federalism have occurred under the leadership of two Democratic presidents, Kennedy and Johnson, and two Republicans, Nixon and Ford, whose administrations juxtapose highly contrasting political philosophies and strategies related to a common problem, that of managing increasingly pervasive and intricate relationships with the subnational governments.

"Creative Federalism" applies to a decade of decisiveness rather than drift in American politics. Until the Vietnam War strained the nation's resources, a rapidly growing economy provided a surplus for funding public services. Federal grants jumped from $4.9 billion in 1958 to $23.9 billion in 1970, while state aid to the localities rose from $8 billion to $28.9 billion in the same period. According to the Advisory Commission on Intergovernmental Relations, forty major federal grant programs were enacted before 1958; and ten years later, 160 major programs, 500 specific legislative authorizations, and 1,315 different assistance activities could be identified.

Wright singled out two major national policy themes of the 1960s: an urban-metropolitan emphasis and attention to disadvantaged persons in American society. He stated that the political milieu of intergovernmental relations was distinctive in its stress on unity of purpose and strategies for building consensus.[31] The design of the Model Cities program well exemplifies this creative

---

31. Wright, "Intergovernmental Relations," 10-11.

aspect of the Johnson years and its use of three novel and widely-adopted grant mechanisms: program planning, project grants, and popular participation. Ironically, these mechanisms intensified rather than reduced the centrifugal trends of earlier decades because they fragmented the grant structures, made their administration more technical, and increased the autonomy and discretion of the professional specialists. While three-quarters of all aid funds were channeled to and through state governments during the Johnson years, a number of new intergovernmental programs were created that competed with existing policy-making structures. Categorical grants proliferated, professionals and participation-minded clients clashed, and the problems to which federal assistance was targeted proved unsolvable within politically imposed deadlines and funding constraints.[32]

President Nixon countered the objectives of his predecessor with a concept of intergovernmental relations that was called the "New Federalism" but was, in fact, a nostalgic rendering of earlier views of the American governmental system. Graves defines the concept as follows:

The New Federalism is a deep-seated commitment to bringing government closer to its citizens, to restoring faith and credibility to government at all levels, and to strengthening state and local governments in ways that will foster the wise and responsible local level leadership which gave this nation so much strength and vitality in the earlier days of the republic. This concept guided many of the policies of the Nixon administration and was reflected in the budget, legislative proposals, rules, and regulations, and other executive branch actions.[33]

President Ford continued to follow these Nixon precedents, as well as Mr. Nixon's efforts to curtail federal spending on social welfare programs. Predictably, the Democratic Congress, the functional bureaucracies, and their interest group supporters resisted moves to decentralize power, funds, and authority to the subnational governments. In a climate of deep suspicion and exchanges of bitter rhetoric the conflict between the executive branch and the Congress has escalated in many forms: vetoes and veto overrides; impound-

32. Ibid., p. 12.

33. Thomas J. Graves, "IGR and the Executive Branch: The New Federalism," *Annals of the American Academy of Political and Social Science* 416 (November 1974): 41-42.

ment of appropriated grant funds; and efforts to consolidate or eliminate grant categories or entire programs identified with Great Society objectives. Yet the implementing strategies of the protagonists of Creative Federalism and New Federalism have not been at odds in all instances, since both camps stress partnership, the sharing of revenues and responsibilities, and activism at all levels of government.

From 1966 to 1974, federal grant expenditures to subnational governments increased to $43.6 billion, a rise from 2 percent to 3.1 percent of the gross national product. During the same period total state and local expenditures increased from $81.8 billion to $203.3 billion, with the amount derived from federal grants rising from 18.1 percent to 21.2 percent of the total. The total state and local expenditures rose from 11 percent of the gross national product to 14.7 percent.[34] Clearly the arena of intergovernmental action is still expanding, but, according to David Walker of the Advisory Commission on Intergovernmental Relations, an appreciation of the accompanying jurisdictional and administrative conditions is yet to be attained. He described the situation as follows:

As the nation approaches the Bicentennial, the condition of American federalism and of the countless intergovernmental relations sustaining it, roughly resembles that of the British Constitution and of the mother country/colonial relationships of two hundred years ago. Conceptually, the so-called system is in ferment. Fiscally, it is in a state of flux and of some fear. Managerially, it is in considerable confusion. In terms of the public, its major institutional components enjoy remarkably low esteem in the electorate's eyes. In short, the nonsystematic system is in a time of major transition.[35]

Walker's analysis of the present condition of American federalism probably understates the situation of the educational sector in which the launching of new forms of intergovernmental collaboration was comparatively sudden and traumatic. The pressures to obtain federal aid for schools, which had backed-up for two decades, finally prevailed in the enactment in 1965 of the Elementary and Secondary Education Act (ESEA). Several analyses of this complex

34. *National Journal Reports*, 22 February 1975, p. 282.
35. David B. Walker, "How Fares Federalism in the Mid-Seventies?" *Annals of the American Academy of Political and Social Science* 416 (November 1974): 18.

legislation and its early implementation indicate the fragile compromises that it embodied and the nervous uncertainty with which the U.S. Office of Education approached the task of inducing the state and local agencies to achieve broadly defined and novel national goals, particularly with regard to compensatory education for disadvantaged children.[36] Unquestionably, the priority set by President Johnson for education, the massive amounts of funding that did not require matching state and local funds, expanding resources of both professional specialists and administrative generalists, and the challenge to break new educational ground were yeasty ingredients for the new partnership. Still, barriers to creativity and healthy growth were severe. The federal policy makers were insensitive to the diverse capabilities of the recipient agencies, their need for preliminary planning time, and the difficulties of articulating the interlevel fiscal and personnel practices and timetables. The state and local school administrators were disappointed that the long-awaited funds were not free of constraining requirements and that amounts actually appropriated fell short of the visionary levels of authorized support. Particularly galling were the invasions of local turf epitomized by the designation of types of student beneficiaries and the mandated collaboration with church-related schools, with parent advisory groups, and other public agencies. Racial tensions in many areas escalated when the availability of federal funding brought educational agencies within the purview of the Civil Rights Act of 1964.

36. Important scholarly works include Stephen K. Bailey and Edith K. Mosher, *ESEA: The Office of Education Administers a Law* (Syracuse, N.Y.: Syracuse University Press, 1968); Berke and Kirst, *Federal Aid to Education;* Ronald G. Corwin, *Reform and Organizational Survival: The Teacher Corps as an Instrument of Educational Change* (New York: John Wiley & Sons, 1973); Eugene Eidenberg and Roy D. Morey, *An Act of Congress: The Legislative Process in the Making of Educational Policy* (New York: W. W. Norton & Co., 1969); John F. Hughes and Anne O. Hughes, *Equal Education* (Bloomington, Ind.: Indiana University Press, 1972); Milbrey Wallin McLaughlin, *Evaluation and Reform* (Cambridge, Mass.: Ballinger Publishing Co., 1975); Philip Meranto, *The Politics of Federal Aid to Education in 1965* (Syracuse, N.Y.: Syracuse University Press, 1967); Miles, *The Department of Health, Education, and Welfare;* Jerome T. Murphy, "Title I of ESEA: The Politics of Implementing Federal Education Reform," *Harvard Educational Review* 41 (February 1971): 35-63; Jerome T. Murphy, *State Education Agencies and Disretionary Funds* (Lexington, Mass.: Lexington Books, 1974); James L. Sundquist, *Politics and Policy* (Washington, D.C.: Brookings Institution, 1968), chap. 10; Norman C. Thomas, *Education in National Politics* (New York: David McKay Co., 1975).

Many of the leading architects of the federal aid policies in Congress, the executive branch, and the scholarly community did not really trust the educational establishment, including the U.S. Office of Education, to carry out broadly defined innovative programs, but it was not feasible to create an additional network of subnational units for educational services as was done with the poverty program and many other developmental programs. The alternative taken was to enact a succession of narrow, special purpose grants rather than broadly discretionary ones, and the outcome was similar to what had occurred earlier in other functional program categories. Numerous vested interests developed at local and state levels around these earmarked funds, all with a new realization that to keep the money flowing they had to develop effective lines of communication with Washington.[37]

The results of rapidly heightened politicization were mixed. The thrust of federal leadership efforts was blunted by some shifts of fiscal power, such as the transfer to state administration of the innovative and supplemental programs authorized by Title III of ESEA. To ease the fiscal planning headaches reported by the state and local agencies, Congress expedited the passage of separate appropriations bills for education and provided for advance funding authorizations. However, the compliance shortfalls of the state and local agencies began to be publicized, especially by civil rights groups, and the federal policy makers countered with requirements for accountability and additive uses (termed "comparability" measures) of federal funds, requirements that at least in theory went to the heart of local school site prerogatives and performance. In short, Congress began to take its policy making and oversight responsibilities seriously. Concurrently, many state and local school administrators had become adept at federal grantsmanship and in employing strategies that used federal funding resources to meet their own perceived needs and strategies.[38]

Federal subventions to education are more controllable by the President and the Congress in the annual budgetary and appropriations process than are the social welfare programs whose continuing

37. Miles, *The Department of Health, Education, and Welfare*, p. 164.

38. David O. Porter with David C. Warner and Teddie W. Porter, *The Politics of Budgeting Federal Aid: Resource Mobilization by Local School Districts* (Beverly Hills, Calif.: Sage Publications, 1973).

costs are mandated by authorizing legislation. Presidents Nixon and Ford took advantage of this vulnerability to propose a succession of retrenchment measures that Congress, with unprecedented support from interest groups that coalesced around the issue of "full funding" of all authorized programs, was largely able to thwart. The state and local educational officials continued to deplore the confusion and workload associated with federal funding, but they were so wary of greater exposure to funding cutbacks that they remained aloof from supporting the Nixon proposal for "special revenue sharing" for education, which would have consolidated numerous grant programs and increased subnational discretionary authority to manage them.[39] Table 2, which indicates the contributions to total

TABLE 2

ELEMENTARY AND SECONDARY SCHOOL REVENUES, BY SOURCE, FOR SELECTED FISCAL YEARS, 1942-1973

Source of Funds	1973	1971	1966	1957	1942
	Total (in millions)				
Federal	$ 4,129	$ 3,129	$ 2,003	$ 366	$ 132
State	21,319	17,371	9,915	4,400	753
Local	26,949	22,938	13,439	7,228	1,405
Total	$52,397	$43,438	$25,357	$11,994	$2,290
	Per Capita				
Federal	$ 19.68	$ 15.17	$ 10.24	$ 2.14	$ 0.98
State	101.59	84.24	50.70	25.70	5.59
Local	128.42	111.24	68.71	42.22	10.44
Total	$249.69	$210.65	$129.65	$70.05	$17.01
	As a Percent of the GNP				
Federal	0.3	0.3	0.3	0.1	0.1
State	1.7	1.7	1.4	1.0	0.5
Local	2.2	2.3	1.9	1.7	1.0
Total	4.3	4.3	3.5	2.8	1.6
	Percentage Distribution among Levels of Government				
Federal	7.9	7.2	7.9	3.1	5.8
State	40.7	40.0	39.1	36.7	32.9
Local	51.4	52.8	53.0	60.3	61.4

Source: National Education Association estimates, based on U.S. Bureau of the Census data, compiled by the Advisory Commission on Intergovernmental Relations, as reported in *National Journal Reports* 22 February 1975, p. 284.

39. Miles, *The Department of Health, Education, and Welfare*, p. 166.

educational revenues provided by each level of government between 1943 and 1973, suggests the basis for this concern. The dramatic increase in federal funds after 1966 was paralleled by a comparable decrease in the percentage contribution from local sources.

What has been the effect of ten years of national initiative in policy and programming on the federal system of educational governance? Iannaccone states that political analysts should be less concerned with the control functions of the national government, real or imagined, than with two other aspects of change. The first is the importance of the national government as an increasing revenue source. Table 2 shows that this contribution is not large compared to that of state and local units; however, the capacity of the national government to raise tax monies and redistribute funds is highly significant. Federal programs have begun to adjust the balance between poorer and richer school districts, and urban and nonurban districts, as funds have been targeted toward areas of poverty.[40] The National Education Association, as well as other professional and official study groups, advocates that the national government should assume a far larger share of educational costs in the future.[41]

Iannaccone's second alternative has to do with the symbols of national purpose offered by governmental leaders, especially presidents. Iannaccone states:

The federal political symbols of policy direction have an indirect but in long run potent effect upon the political beliefs of Americans, in particular in the areas of race, economic inequalities, and in a growing awareness of the need to accept pluralism in the delivery of educational services for different people. It is here, in the long-run impact upon the

40. Laurence Iannaccone, *Education Policy Systems* (Fort Lauderdale, Florida: Nova University, 1975), p. 139.

41. If and when significant expansion occurs, new modes of interlevel relationships and diversification of the grant structure, to include block grants and some form of revenue sharing as well as categorical forms of aid, can be expected. For an analysis of this trend see David B. Walker, "The New System of Intergovernmental Assistance: Some Initial Notes," *Publius* 5 (Summer 1975): 131-45 and Richard P. Nathan, "The New Federalism versus the Emerging New Structuralism," *Publius* 5 (Summer 1975): 111-20. Congress made a timid start in the 1974 extension of ESEA. See Stafford Smiley, "The Elementary and Secondary Amendments of 1974: The Effect of the Consolidation and Review Provisions on the Distribution of Decision-making Authority," *Harvard Journal of Legislation* 12 (April 1975): 447-94.

political ideology of Americans about education for all America that the political conflicts and events during the last twenty years are likely to have their greatest impact. . . . Federal intervention in the hearts and minds of Americans has frequently enlarged the scope of education and lifted the sights of educators, in spite of their initial opposition, to articulation of new values.[42]

THE SHAPE OF THE FUTURE

From the foregoing effort to put educational governance into perspective what further conclusions may be portents of the future? First, it is clear that localism continues to hold significant symbolic value in American federalism, but has more persistent operational consequences in education than in any other sector of governmental activity. Education followed the trend in all levels and sectors of government to rely on professional expertise and to reduce representation of lay groups in policy making. Subsequently, however, it was not drawn into the early shared partnerships between officials of general government and of other functional areas that developed when the federal government began to promote and support social welfare programs. Educators had no part in the controversies that this centralization generated: What level of government should perform which functions? How should conflicts between participants be resolved? How can programs of appropriate scale be organized and their coordination improved? And how should citizens be involved in establishing needs and priorities?

When federal funding at long last became available, education was catapulted into intergovernmental administrative arrangements that were already familiar in other sectors, improvisational and unwelcome as they may have seemed to educators. Now that the initial shocks have subsided, the latter have begun to develop political skills and wrestle with concerns comparable to those of other participating sectors, trying to sort out the dilemmas of centralized policy making and decentralized delivery of services, modes of accountability, and meaningful citizen participation. In Kaufman's conceptualization, localism and professional autonomy may be deemphasized if the values of coordination and representativeness find new and adequate expression. To predict the course of future

42. Iannaccone, *Education Policy Systems*, pp. 139-40.

intergovernmental relations in education, one should follow closely the trends in other sectors of American federalism. The record indicates that education will, in due course, adopt rather than resist the values and administrative strategies that eventually emerge from present experimentation and ferment in the broader arena.

Responsiveness to Citizen-Consumers in the Federal System of Educational Governance

The unprecedented sharing of functions among the levels of government that has occurred in recent decades should not be equated with a concomitant sharing of authority. In assessing the current state of American federalism the question of the locus of effective power—who dominates in the partnerships or cooperative arrangements—is a matter of considerable dispute. Supporting evidence for an upward thrust of power is to be found in the policies of Creative Federalism whereby the national government identified problems that transcend state and local boundaries, provided funds for the states and localities to solve them, and imposed directives and constraints on the use made of the funds. Evidence of decentralization of power is offered by the policies of New Federalism that increased the discretionary powers of states and localities in identifying problems and utilizing federal grant funds. Evidence that points to a mixed and indeterminate situation derives from experience with the two interrelated strategies that both brands of federalism had in common: program evaluation and citizen participation.

The "evaluation mandate" of Title I of ESEA was one of the most novel features of the Act and its origin is attributed in large part to Senator Robert Kennedy, who saw the requirement as a way to provide information about school effectiveness to those who had previously been uninvolved and uninformed—the parents.[43]

The evaluators of Title I, as well as those of the other federally aided programs have found, almost without exception, that the influence of the federal mandates and guidelines for programs was much diluted in passage to the point of delivering educational services. McLaughlin's statement is typical:

43. McLaughlin, *Evaluation and Reform*, p. 3.

The Title I experience shows how resistant the educational policy system is to assessment of achievements and accomplishments. . . . The structure and control of the nation's education system hampers all reporting and it may preclude the accountability and impact reports reformers wanted. . . . In a federal system of government, especially in education, the balance of power resides at the bottom, with special interest groups. Accordingly, the implementation of federal initiatives relies in large measure on the incentives and preferences of local authorities; there is little effective muscle at the top.[44]

Wayson depicts the local power system as extending to the school site and the individual classroom:

The ESEA approached the American school system as though it were made up of local districts (which it is), each operating a monolithic, hierarchically arranged decision system controlled and directed by administrators who wield power through rational means (which it is not). The ESEA failed to achieve its purposes in many instances because its proponents did not understand that all changes in education, after they have been adopted by the central office of a local school district, must still be accepted by personnel who make decisions in school buildings and in individual classrooms. The three levels are interdependent but operate in such a way that each controls its own realm and has only nominal or, at best, only partial power over the realms controlled by the others. Each exerts its own controls and imposes its own sanctions. Each has its own territory, its own prerogatives, its own traditions. Each is much more autonomous than either folklorists, researchers, or the participants themselves recognize. The fact remains that teachers and principals—not higher-ranking officials—make the decisions that determine whether a reform will be successfully implemented.[45]

Lowi, an eminent political scientist, has argued that the national government has allowed far too many of its programs to be shaped by unaccountable local governments and local nongovernmental groups, and that interest group liberalism insists on overdoing the notion of representation at points where it is inappropriate. This confuses representation with administration, and in so doing makes it impossible for the government to give firm definition to policy at the top.[46]

44. Ibid., p. 119.
45. William Wayson, "ESEA: Decennial Views of the Revolution, II. The Negative Side," *Phi Delta Kappan* 57 (November 1975): 153.
46. Theodore J. Lowi, *The End of Liberalism* (New York: W. W. Norton & Co., 1969).

For better or worse then, from a variety of points of view, educational professionals and the newly activated citizen-consumers in local school districts must now learn to function in an ever-evolving and contentious federal structure of governance. What would be the actual and appropriate leverage points for exerting influence in their respective spheres? This question has engaged a number of analysts seeking ways to make the schools more responsive to the needs and preferences of their clienteles. Porter has recently developed a model of intergovernmental transactions (fig. 2) that is useful for its comprehensiveness and its differentiation of professional and lay channels of influence.

According to Porter, the model indicates that public education receives funds from at least three levels of government, in roughly the proportions indicated in the figure. These funds come from substantially different tax bases. Although the citizen-consumer pays into education through each of the taxes, he is part of a very different constituency at each level. Only at the local level is there a direct relationship between the tax and the service provided. The citizen-consumer has limited control over the resources received by the producer, even at the local level. As the level of funding moves to higher levels of government, the citizen-consumer is less able to influence the amount of money a specific school building or school district may receive. The producer, on the other hand, is able to use these institutional arrangements to its advantage. The opportunities for multipocket budgeting are enhanced with the number of income sources. The ability of any one resource supplier to hold the producer accountable for its operations declines with the increase in revenue sources. And the more remote the supplier of funds (for example, the state and federal levels), the more freedom producers will have to pursue internally generated goals.

Perhaps most important, the citizen-consumer transfers no funds directly to the ultimate producer of education services, the school building and teachers. The consumers must rely almost entirely on persuasion to get adjustments or changes in the school program as it relates to their children. Direct complaints to the school board or central administration may bring relief in selected situations, but those institutions are not designed to monitor the delivery of spe-

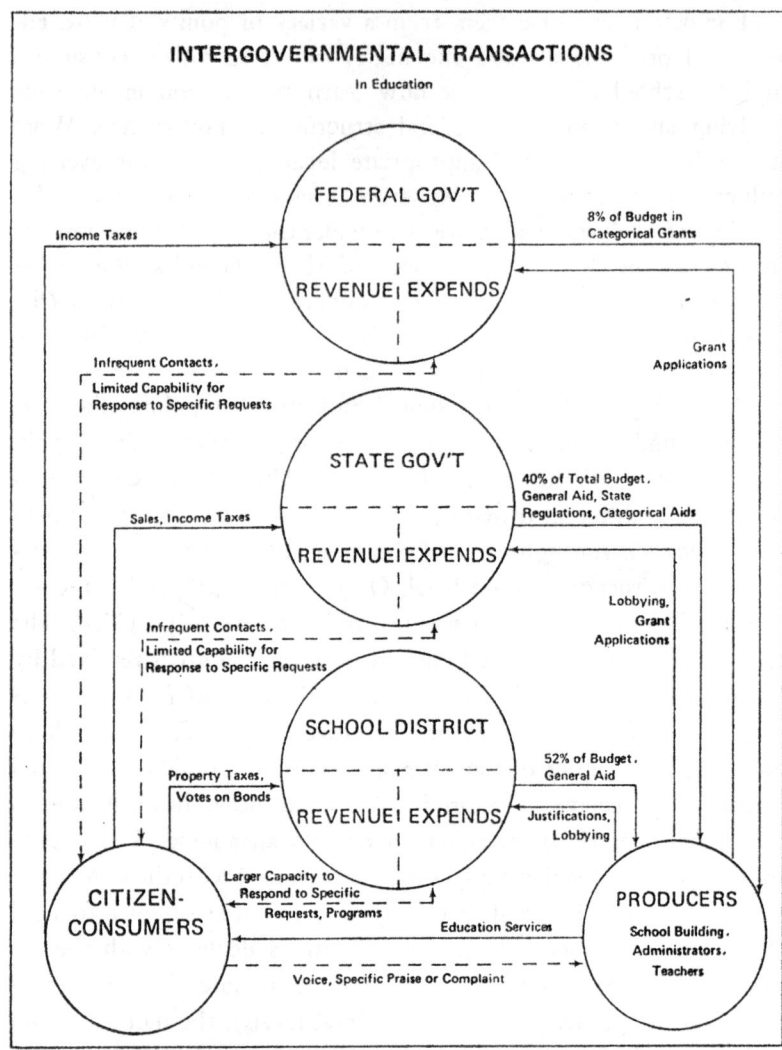

FIG. 2. Intergovernmental transactions in education
SOURCE: David O. Porter, "Responsiveness to Citizen Consumers in a Federal System," *Publius* 5 (Fall 1975): 68.

cific services to individuals.[47]

Porter's model exemplifies the current application to the public sector of private market concepts of consumer sovereignty. They

47. David O. Porter, "Responsiveness to Citizen Consumers in a Federal System," *Publius* 5 (Fall 1975): 68–69.

provide the rationale for proposals by Porter and others that parents receive from tax revenues vouchers which they may use to purchase preferred educational services, public or private. Presumably, principals and teachers would then become more responsive to their clienteles.

Campbell points out, however, that criteria derived entirely from either economics or political science do not provide consistent guidance for assigning functions among the levels of government. He suggests that reference to the criterion of equity makes it possible to combine disparate disciplinary approaches. By equity, he means that public sector benefits should be more directly based on need rather than on what each individual's pocketbook permits him to acquire. The amount of any public service received, including education, should relate to the need for the service, and to both interpersonal and interjurisdictional distribution of services.[48]

The wide disparities in provision of educational services within and between states and localities have recently made questions of equity a major research and political concern of the courts, the legislatures, and the citizenry. Prescriptions to ameliorate the inequities have called for the creation of larger-scale local governments whose economic bases would encompass both growing and declining subunits and which could support the diversity of educational services required to accommodate a range of consumer needs and preferences. Other reform proposals suggest that the flow of governmental aid should be in the direction of jurisdictions with weak tax bases and substantial needs and that, to overcome disparities, it may be necessary to transfer some functions, including education, to upper reaches of the governmental system. The adoption of such reforms would intrude upon cherished values of localism and make intergovernmental relations more complex. In short, within the evolving federal system of education, it appears that the problem of responding to the preferences of citizen-consumers must no longer be that of devising appropriate modes of representation and negotiation at the grassroots level. It will increasingly become a factor in efforts by governments of larger jurisdiction to accomplish broader social aims.

48. Alan K. Campbell, "Functions in Flux," in *American Federalism: Toward a More Effective Partnership* (Washington, D.C.: Advisory Committee on Intergovernmental Relations, 1975), pp. 37-38.

CHAPTER V

Two Models of the Supreme Court in School Politics

TYLL VAN GEEL

Introduction

Judges do not make law; they only discover preexisting rules and principles and apply them to the controversy at hand. In this conception judges are oracles in touch with that mysterious presence, "the law," which has an independent existence and about which we may know very little except as revealed to us by these black-robed intermediaries.

The ancient but now discarded understanding captured in these sentences has been replaced by the "legal realist" school of thought that today remains dominant.[1] In this understanding of the judicial process, judges make law even though they are bound by written constitutions and statutes. In a sermon before George I in 1717 Bishop Hoadley expressed the point thus: "Whoever hath an absolute authority to interpret written or spoken words, it is he who is truly the lawgiver to all intents and purposes and not the person who wrote or spoke them."[2] And in using this power to interpret the laws, legal realists insist that how a judge rules in the cases brought before him is determined only by his own policy preferences.

It is no refutation of the legal realists to argue that their theory needs amplification to bring out in greater detail the factors that

---

1. For a short account of the legal realist movement, see Alexander M. Bickel, *The Supreme Court and the Idea of Progress* (New York: Harper & Row, Torchbooks, 1970), pp. 11-42; Karl Llewellyn, "Some Realism about Realism—Responding to Dean Pound," *Harvard Law Review* 44 (June 1931): 1222-64.

2. Quoted in Learned Hand, *The Bill of Rights* (New York: Atheneum Publishers, 1972), p. 8.

influence how judges rule in specific cases. For reasons that ultimately may be rooted in personal psychology or self-interest, enlightened or not, we may reasonably hypothesize that a judge is also influenced by a variety of factors, including his theory of the Constitution, his theory of politics, his theory of society, and his assessment of the costs and benefits of judicial review. It is hypothesized here that all these factors are combined by the judge to form a personal judgment on the proper role of the court in which he presides. This notion of the court's institutional role in turn affects and is affected by the judge's social policy preferences relevant to the case at hand. There is a mutual resonance between his policy preferences and his conception of the role of his court. Thus, predicting a judge's position on a given case cannot be accomplished by simply gaining sufficient information about his social policy preferences. For example, the justice of the Supreme Court who favors judicial deference to legislative judgments on economic policy because he believes the Court lacks the expertise to enter this arena may be forced to vote to uphold statutes substantially curtailing the freedom of business to operate, despite his belief in a laissez-faire economic policy. More generally, whether a judge is receptive to a logically constructed legal argument based on premises he accepts depends on more than the logic of the argument; it depends also upon the implications that argument holds for the institutional role of the court in which he presides.

But it is one thing to hypothesize that justices are influenced by their conception of the role of the Supreme Court, and another thing to specify with more precision those conceptions of the Court's role that have held sway in chambers. A starting point for developing clearly distinguishable conceptions of the Supreme Court's role is found in a seminal book by Rawls, who develops three concepts that he calls perfect, imperfect, and pure procedural justice.[3] Perfect procedural justice obtains when there is an independent criterion for determining the acceptability of the outcome of a process and when a process exists that is sure to achieve the desired outcome. For example, if a cake is to be divided

3. John Rawls, *A Theory of Justice* (Cambridge, Mass.: Harvard University Press, 1971).

equally (the independent criterion), a procedure sure to achieve this result is to make the person who cuts the cake choose the last piece.[4] Imperfect procedural justice obtains when there is an independent criterion for determining the acceptability of an outcome, but no procedure that can assure such a result each time the procedure is used. Imperfect procedural justice is illustrated by the criminal trial: the desired outcome is that only the guilty are convicted, but there is no procedure that can be established to assure such a result in all cases.[5] Pure procedural justice obtains when there is no independent criterion for the right result as, for example, with a game of chance. In such cases, whatever the distribution of winnings and losses, the result must be deemed fair if the procedure was fair and fairly carried out.[6]

Using Rawls's conception of imperfect procedural justice we can say that our federal and state constitutions establish Congress and the state legislatures as imperfect procedural devices designed to produce legislation that satisfies the principles of right and justice catalogued in the state and federal constitutions. Thus, there exist independent criteria for assessing the acceptability of the outcome of the legislative process. But because the legislative process is one of imperfect procedural justice, from time to time the criteria of acceptability arguably will be violated; hence there is a need for a court of review to settle the question if and when it arises.

There are, roughly speaking, two judicial strategies that a supreme court of review, such as our Supreme Court, as well as judges sitting in the lower courts, might follow: a strategy of restraint and a strategy of activism. Following a discussion of these two strategies, we shall turn to an assessment of the work of the Supreme Court during the tenure of Chief Justices Warren and Burger in light of the two strategies. Specific reference is made to cases bearing on education. In the final section a hypothetical law suit filed against a local school board is discussed to reveal in a dif-

4. Ibid., p. 85.
5. Ibid.
6. Ibid., p. 86.

ferent way the relevance of the two strategies for understanding the role of the courts in educational politics.

The Model of Restraint

The advice that the Supreme Court act with restraint applies first of all to the question of jurisdiction, or more precisely, to the question, "To which outcomes of the political and policy-making processes should judicial oversight extend."[7] Under this model jurisdiction is limited to those controversies that are deemed to be justiciable. Thus, questions of taxation are ruled as beyond the Court's jurisdiction, since decisions as to what should and should not be taxed are matters of how best to promote the general welfare and as such tend to involve certain kinds of facts that the Court lacks the institutional capacity to ascertain. Such questions tend also to involve decisions as to what constitutes the good life—matters not addressed by or determinable in light of the

---

7. In this and subsequent sections of the chapter the author draws upon the following: Alexander M. Bickel, *The Least Dangerous Branch* (Indianapolis, Ind.: Bobbs-Merrill Co., 1962); idem, *The Supreme Court and the Idea of Progress:* idem, *The Morality of Consent* (New Haven, Conn.: Yale University Press, 1975); Charles L. Black, Jr., *The People and the Court* (Englewood Cliffs, N.J.: Prentice-Hall, 1960); Edmund Cahn, ed., *Supreme Court and Supreme Law* (New York: Simon & Schuster, Clarion Books, 1954); Archibald Cox, *The Warren Court* (Cambridge, Mass.: Harvard University Press, 1968); Jan G. Deutsch, "Neutrality, Legitimacy, and the Supreme Court: Some Intersections between Law and Political Science," *Stanford Law Review* 20 (January 1968): 169-281; Ronald Dworkin, "Hard Cases," *Harvard Law Review* 88 (April 1975): 1057-1109; Kent Greenwalt, "Discretion and Judicial Decision: The Elusive Quest for the Fetters That Bind Judges," *Columbia Law Review* 75 (March 1975): 359-99; Hand, *The Bill of Rights;* Robert H. Jackson, *The Supreme Court in the American System of Government* (New York: Harper & Row, 1955); Philip B. Kurland, *Politics, the Constitution, and the Warren Court* (Chicago: University of Chicago Press, 1970); Robert G. McCloskey, *The Modern Supreme Court* (Cambridge, Mass.: Harvard University Press, 1972); Henry P. Monaghan, "Constitutional Adjudication: The Who and When," *Yale Law Journal* 82 (June 1973): 1363-97; Eugene V. Rostow, "The Democratic Character of Judicial Review," *Harvard Law Review* 66 (December 1952): 193-224; Fritz W. Scharpf, "Judicial Review and the Political Question: A Functional Analysis," *Yale Law Journal* 75 (March 1966): 517-97; Martin Shapiro, *Law and Politics in the Supreme Court* (New York: Free Press of Glencoe, 1964); Harry H. Wellington, "Common Law Rules and Constitutional Double Standards: Some Notes on Adjudication," *Yale Law Journal* 83 (December 1973): 221-311; J. Skelly Wright, "Professor Bickel, the Scholarly Tradition, and the Supreme Court," *Harvard Law Review* 84 (February 1971): 769-805.

principles in the Constitution. Similarly, a Court adhering to this model believes that governmental choices as to which social programs to mount or not to mount, and how those programs are to be designed, are issues beyond the capacity of the Court to determine. Of course, when the legislature has clearly abused its powers and invaded the rights of individuals, then judicial examination of the policy is warranted with regard to this one point.

Even when such an encroachment on individual rights has occurred, arguably a Court acting consistently with the model of restraint will put off as long as possible giving its consent to review the extent and justifications for the encroachment to let the full implications of the governmental action come sharply into focus. In this way the Court will have "before it and will be able to use, both in forming and in supporting its judgment, the full rather than merely the initial impact of the statute or executive measure whose constitutionality is in question."[8] "A sound judicial instinct will generally favor deflecting the problem in one or more initial cases, for there is much to be gained from letting it simmer, so that a mounting number of incidents exemplifying it may have a cumulative effect on the judicial mind as well as on public and professional opinion."[9] Thus, under the doctrine of ripeness a Court acting with restraint will avoid issuing an advisory opinion that some official action would be unconstitutional if undertaken, but will only decide the case if in fact some official action has been taken and someone has in fact been injured. A statute will not be reviewed by such a Court unless and until it has been enforced against someone and that person has suffered an injury.

Just as the doctrine of ripeness discussed in the previous paragraph imposes a time lag between legislative action and court review, so does the notion of "standing" as used in the model of restraint. Under this version of the doctrine only those who have been materially and substantially injured by legislative action are permitted to seek review in the Court; thus until the governmental action produces such an impact the legislation must go unreviewed. It is thought that only those who have so suffered will press the

8. Bickel, *The Least Dangerous Branch*, p. 124.
9. Ibid., p. 176.

suit with sufficient attention to every possible basis upon which the government's action might be attacked, to assist the Court in rendering the most knowledgeable decision.

In addition to creating the likelihood of a time lag, this requirement excludes from access to the courts a wide range of potential litigants: those who may possibly suffer material harm at a future date; those who are ideologically offended by the legislation; those who are merely curious as to the constitutionality of the legislation; those who would find the advice of the Court on this issue useful; those who have a mere subjective fear they may be injured by the legislation; and those who may have suffered an injury that cannot be deemed to be sufficiently "material." By thus narrowing the range of people who are permitted to challenge the statute the Court diminishes the chances that there will be any Court review.

Once having accepted a case for review, a majority on the Court being guided by the model of restraint will condition the exercise of its discretion by taking to heart several propositions and admonishments. Such a majority recurringly reminds itself of its belief that the principles compiled in the Constitution only loosely specify the relationship of rights to other values. Thus the legislature constitutionally is left with a generous degree of discretion to make those trade-offs between rights and values it votes as socially advantageous.[10] Historically rooted and widely acknowledged rights found explicitly or implicitly in the Constitution are in this approach to be enlarged with one eye on the original understanding of their meaning; and new rights may be derived only

10. The Constitution functions to establish the relationship of rights to other values. One way these relationships might be expressed is contained in the following propositions: Rights are to be enjoyed as such and may be infringed upon by government, traded off only for some other values that are important or even compelling. Thus, only in compelling circumstances may the loss of a right to an individual be justified or offset by gains for others. Further, one's rights may not be infringed upon even if the individual is given some kind of compensating payment, unless perhaps the compensation is in the form of ultimately greater security for that right, or some other specific and limited compensating advantage. Finally, an individual's entitlement to a right may not be conditioned on the payment of a fee or the meeting of just any conditions government might decide upon. The individual must enjoy his right without having to buy somebody off—be it the government itself or other individuals—in order to enjoy his right. These propositions were adapted from Laurence H. Tribe, "Policy Science: Analysis or Ideology," *Philosophy and Public Affairs* 2 (Fall 1972): 66-110.

by means of a limited number of acceptable techniques.[11] The sources to which the justices may turn to aid in the parsing of the Constitution must be sharply limited. Not every piece of philosophizing, no matter how widely read and appreciated, may be a basis for choosing among plausible alternative interpretations of the Constitution. And adherents to the model of restraint insist the Court should be chary in doubting the legislature's claim that it has accurately and completely ascertained the facts upon which it premised its actions. Finally, even though doubts may undermine judicial confidence that the other branch of government has acted justifiably, if a *state* legislature or other state agency is involved, a justice sticking to the model of restraint will restrain his inclination to strike the action down by reminding himself that ours is a federal system of government under which states and their agencies should in their sphere be allowed the greatest possible scope of action, short of destruction of the notion that the states as well as the national government are bound by the Constitution. In short, justices working within this model of review constrain their discretion by entering into the reviewing process on the assumption, or rather with the rebuttable presumption, that the actions of the other agencies of government, national or local, are consistent with the Constitution.[12]

11. The Supreme Court has used a variety of techniques to develop new constitutional rights. It has used a form of instrumental analysis. For example, the right of association, which is not explicitly found in the Constitution, may be read into it since the formation of associations is instrumentally so important in the furthering of free speech activities. *NAACP v. Alabama*, 357 U.S. 449 (1958); *NAACP v. Button*, 371 U.S. 415 (1963). The right of privacy has been found in the penumbras of various provisions of the Bill of Rights. *Griswold v. Connecticut*, 381 U.S. 479 (1965). And it is suggested by Justice Marshall in dissent that a person may enjoy a right to obtain such public services as education, the closer the nexus between that service and a right such as that of free speech, which is expressly protected by the Constitution. *San Antonio Independent School District v. Rodriguez*, 411 U.S. 1 (1973) (Marshall dissenting). Another technique that is available is to imply an affirmative duty from a negative prohibition on government. Thus, if government may not discriminate on the basis of race, perhaps it also has the affirmative duty to provide an integrated education, and the individual student has a right to obtain such an education. *Keyes v. School District No. 1*, 413 U.S. 189 (1973) (Powell concurring in part and dissenting in part).

12. These presumptions are stated in what have also been termed standards of review. A classic article arguing for a strong presumption of constitu-

If despite the presumption of constitutionality these justices find themselves compelled to strike the action down, their inclination toward restraint leads them, when a choice is available, to favor basing their decision on those reasons that foreclose the fewest options for future action by the other agency of government.

Those adhering to the model of restraint are likely to stress that a ruling from the Supreme Court, while final between the parties, is not "law for the society in any full sense" unless the legislative and executive branches cooperate in establishing it. For that to occur the ruling must be compatible with the general principles to which society has given its consent. And the rulings must not be rigid, but must allow a wide range of outcomes from the political process.[13] Thus, to an important extent those justices adhering to the model of restraint confine the decrees they issue to society's present understanding of the Constitution; these justices do not gamble on imposing rulings society may at some future date come to embrace.

On those occasions when a majority on the Court working within the model of restraint do strike down an action of another branch of the government, the question of the fitting remedy raises yet another opportunity to choose between restraint and activism. An instinct to act with restraint leads justices to sanction only the minimal remedy that can be justified without rendering a decision that gives the complainant a victory in form but not in substance. Thus, the government may be asked to cease forthwith its improper activity, but it may not be asked to provide restitution for the

---

tionality is James Bradley Thayer, "The Origin and Scope of the American Doctrine of Constitutional Law," *Harvard Law Review* 7 (October 1873): 129-56. Thayer said a statute could be struck down as unconstitutional only when the legislature has made such a clear mistake it is not open to rational question. In equal protection cases the Supreme Court has fomulated what has been termed the "rational basis" test in the following terms: "The constitutional safeguard is offended only if the classification rests on grounds wholly irrelevant to the achievement of the State's objective. State legislatures are presumed to have acted within their constitutional power despite the fact that in practice their laws result in some inequality. A statutory discrimination will not be set aside if any state of facts reasonably may be conceived to justify it." *McGowan v. Maryland*, 366 U.S. 420, 425-26 (1961).

13. Robert H. Bork, "A Remembrance of Alex Bickel," *New Republic* 173 (18 October 1975): 21-22.

damage already inflicted.[14] A mere negative prohibition of this sort leaves the other branch of the government with more discretion than would be the imposition of an affirmative duty. Furthermore, justices acting with restraint keep in mind that each remedy—especially those requiring affirmative action—while serving to realize the rights of the complaining individual(s), may impose significant other costs upon government and society, costs which, if they become substantial, may warrant a reduction in the remedial demands being made even at the price of reducing the worth of the rights newly won in the case.

In sum, a majority of the Supreme Court acting with restraint will adhere to the notions of ripeness and standing as outlined earlier in deciding whether to exert jurisdiction over the case in the first place. Upon taking the case this majority will, for the reasons suggested earlier, work with the rebuttable presumption that the actions of the other agencies of government are consistent with the Constitution. Any decision to strike the action down will be based on as narrow grounds as possible and on the basis of principles already accepted by society. Similarly, the remedy imposed will be narrowly defined so as to minimize intrusion on the other branches of government.

The Model of Activism

There exists a different kind of Supreme Court justice who in

---

14. The Supreme Court faced this problem in the aftermath of its decision in *Brown* v. *Board of Education*, 374 U.S. 483 (1954). In the second *Brown* decision, *Brown* v. *Board of Education*, 349 U.S. 294 (1955) the Court said school districts had an obligation to implement in good faith the governing constitutional principles. For a time it was not clear whether this meant school districts merely had to stop assigning children to schools on the basis of race, or whether school districts had an affirmative obligation to go further, to bring about an integrated education. The question was answered in *Green* v. *County School Board* 391 U.S. 430 (1968) in which the Court struck down a freedom of choice plan that did not result in the transition to a unitary, nonracial system of education. Subsequently in *Swann* v. *Charlotte-Mecklenburg Board of Education*, 402 U.S. 1 (1971), the Court spelled out those affirmative requirements the lower federal district court could impose upon school districts. Thus it is now clear that in the segregation area school districts have an affirmative obligation to undo what they have done. Some have argued that the obligation imposed by the Court in fact goes further than original injury created by the school districts. Mark Yudof, "Equal Educational Opportunity and the Courts," *Texas Law Review* 51 (March 1973): 411-504.

comparison to those just described appears positively adventuresome. While such a justice does not disagree that only justiciable subjects should be accepted by the Court for review, his concept of the notion of justiciability is more expansive than that of those jurists who heed the counsel of restraint. Where the more cautious justice who is confronted with a case involving alleged violations of individual rights in the context of a state taxing and spending policy would be disposed to abstain from reviewing the case, the more active judge would take the case for review, experiencing minimal anxiety over his competence to give the individual his due without at the same time ignorantly and clumsily frustrating the legislature's policy. Furthermore, the activist justice finds his inclinations buttressed by the belief that the principles compiled in the Constitution, while not determinative of social policy writ large, are determinative of abuses of even the taxing and spending powers of the legislature.

The wariness found in the behavior of the justice working within the model of restraint is reflected in his strong attachment to the epigram that "ripeness is all." The more activist judge might counter with "justice delayed is justice denied." That is, every day the Court waits to let the full impact of the government's policy emerge is one more day the aggrieved individual must suffer the government's abuse. In any event, because the more activist justice begins his inquiry into the case with the belief that the principles of the Constitution specify with some precision the relationship of individual rights to other values, the multiplicity of specific details made available to the Court by delaying intervention, which the less active justice says he needs to assess the right-value trade-offs made by the legislature, are of lesser importance to the activist justice. In the view of the activist judge one does not need as many factual details to render a decision on the constitutionality of the legislature's right-value trade-off because the Constitution is reasonably clear in specifying the narrow range of permissible trade-offs at the expense of individual rights. One needs only a record rich in details if the Constitution speaks in few absolutist terms, leaving the justifiability of the invasion of individual rights an open question that can only be settled within the particular circumstances of each case.

In keeping with this more absolutist view of the Constitution the activist justice shows less hesitancy about issuing broad and general rulings, the limits to which are not sharply defined and which foreshadow his response to problems not yet brought before him. In other words, this justice is willing to engage, within limits, in a form of prospective overruling of those legislative actions that exist only in the realm of an imagined future. Here is a more aggressive attempt to guide the evolution of social policy, rather than leaving that task wholly to the legislature subject to a judicial response after the fact. Here the Court is less a tribunal of review and more the partner of the legislature, or a school board.

The likelihood of the Court being an active partner is further enhanced in this model by the use of a notion of standing, which extends the range of people who may gain access to the Court. The Court's attention may be obtained by those who may only possibly suffer material harm in the future, by those who have a subjective fear they may be injured by the legislation, and by those whose injury may not be "material" but who nevertheless have suffered in less material ways.[15] The tendency is to open the door to the ideological plaintiff whose only interest in the government's action is that it has contravened his conception of what the Constitution permits. Winning the suit would mean to this individual that the operations of government that did not affect him other than as a citizen had been set straight. Clearly, the more this kind of plaintiff is permitted before the Court, the more the Court is likely to become actively involved in judging and guiding the actions of the other parts of the government.

In the activist model the issuing of broad general rulings is coupled with the opening of the Court to many new kinds of plaintiffs and the more frequent and liberal acceptance of class actions that speed up the impact of the Court's rulings. This speeding up occurs because in class actions the group of people

15. Although the Supreme Court in *Sierra Club* v. *Morton*, 405 U.S. 727 (1972), denied standing to the conservation group to challenge governmental policy, the Court did suggest standing might have been available if the group had alleged that its members used the affected area. Thus the Court seemed to recognize that a new sort of injury to the individual, that resulting from damage to the public park used by the public, could provide a basis for standing in the Courts.

for whom the Court's ruling is binding is so large that the ruling will have an immediate and wide-ranging effect. Class actions reduce the necessity of spreading the influence of the Court's ruling through the slow process of case-by-case adjudication as individual litigants seek to vindicate their newly defined rights.[16] The class action changes the scope of judicial interference with the political process.[17]

Unlike their less interventionist brethren, activist justices recurrently remind themselves upon taking a case that the principles compiled in the Constitution state with discernible precision the relationship of rights to other values, in a way that limits the discretion of the legislature to make trade-offs between individual rights and other values. These activist justices do not disagree that the extension of widely acknowledged rights explicitly or implicitly found in the Constitution are to be understood in light of their historical origins, but, at the same time, they say the Constitution must be seen as a living document, the meaning of which changes as society changes. The law must inevitably grow as humankind's understanding of itself and relations with others changes. New rights must be fashioned that take into account the recognition that only part of the pain and pleasure and profit of life lies in physical things. New rights must also be fashioned to take into account that, as the society becomes economically and technologically more complex, goods and services that once were luxuries become indispensable to even a minimal existence. So that they may fully and sensitively comprehend the ever more swiftly changing cultural, political, and economic aspects of the society, the justices must turn to wide-ranging sources to aid in their explication of the Constitution. Adherents to the model of activism also view with at least a mild skepticism the legislature's willingness and capacity accurately and completely to ascertain the social facts upon which it premises its actions. At the same time, these justices exhibit a certain faith in themselves to cope soundly and intelligently with such factual questions. Finally, in the view of the more activist justice, the doctrine of federalism must not stand in the way

16. Henry P. Monaghan, "Constitutional Adjudication: The Who and When," p. 1383.

17. Ibid.

of the full protection of the rights of individuals; thus deference to the actions of state legislatures and agencies is less. In short, the justices who exhibit more activist tendencies more frequently enter into the reviewing process with the rebuttable presumption that the actions of the other agencies of government, national or local, are not consistent with the Constitution.[18]

As for the understanding of the Court's remedial powers, the activist justice shows a greater willingness to impose affirmative obligations on the other branches of government, even to the point of requiring them to rectify and undo the damage resulting from their illegal actions. There is found here a lesser concern with the social and governmental costs that might accompany implementation of the remedy: the individual who has lost his rights at the hands of the legislature should not find that once again full realization of his rights is put off for the sake of the advantage of others.

Finally, justices following the activist model are willing to engage in a risk their more restrained brethren avoid. While the more cautious justice limits his decrees to those that fall within the range of results permitted by society's present understanding of the Constitution, the activist justice is on occasion willing to venture a ruling that, while not acceptable now, may yet win the future. Such a justice gambles that his persuasive powers exercised in his opinion are potent enough to win to his side a sufficiently large proportion of the populace so as to bring the institutions of government into compliance with his ruling. This justice, of course, may lose his bet on the future and find that his decree has been relegated to the anthologies of historical anomalies.

It should be noted that each of these two models captures a range of judicial behavior. For example, under the model of restraint we might locate some justices who at times resemble more the justices adhering to the model of activism than do their

18. In equal protection cases the Supreme Court has said a presumption of unconstitutionality is created if the state's action touches upon a fundamental interest, for example, the right to vote, and/or inferior treatment is afforded a suspect class, which is usually defined in terms of race, alienage, or nationality. When this has happened the burden of proof shifts to the state and it must show that a compelling state interest is being served that cannot be satisfied by less onerous alternative means. *Shapiro* v. *Thomson*, 394 U.S. 618, 634 (1969); see also "Developments in the Law: Equal Protection," *Harvard Law Review* 82 (March 1969): 1083.

brethren whom we have placed in the restraint category. There thus exists a continuum of judicial behavior ranging from the most restrained and least active to the most active and least restrained. Talking as though there were in reality only two conceptually distinct models is but a convenience to aid the understanding.

Restraint and the Minimization of Costs

The grasp we have of the two models of judicial behavior will be strengthened if we move beyond their descriptions to their rationales. Both models grow out of a theory that stresses the establishment by the Constitution of a system of individual rights that imposes constraints on government and both models are designed to achieve similar benefits. But justices whose behavior conforms to the model of restraint do so because of the belief that this behavior, while assuring realization of the benefits, will avoid the costs they associate with the model of activism. The first cost of the model of activism they see is that it tends to weaken democracy; that is, the more judicial review is available for use and the more vigorously it is exercised, the more a demand for its use will be stimulated. And as individuals and groups are encouraged to rely on the Court they lessen their desire to develop their own political resources—skill, knowledge, money, political contacts—with which to defend their own interests and the spirit of liberty. "[In] a society which evades its responsibility by thrusting upon the courts the nurture of that spirit, that spirit will in the end perish."[19]

Second, active judicial review distorts the distribution of political power: advocates of restraint assert that in the normal political process every active and legitimate group can have an effective voice at some point in the decision-making process.[20] Thus, there is less need for an active Court to protect groups than adherents to the model of activism suppose. In any event, by enlisting an

---

19. Learned Hand, "The Contribution of an Independent Judiciary to Civilization," in *The Spirit of Liberty*, ed. Irving Dillard (New York: Alfred A. Knopf, 1953), p. 181.

20. Bickel, *The Supreme Court and the Idea of Progress*, p. 37. Bickel's conception of the political process is the classic pluralist conception most importantly set forth in Robert A. Dahl, *A Preface to Democratic Theory* (Chicago: University of Chicago Press, 1956), pp. 137-38.

active Court on the side of some groups one gives those groups an advantage in the political struggle not enjoyed by other groups. A political process that once consisted of the give and take between relatively equal groups now becomes a struggle the outcome of which is tilted in favor of those groups given special judicial solicitude. And when it is found that political victory is so easily won in the courtroom, the specially protected groups will increasingly resort to the Court without there being, under the model of activism, any natural restraints on the use of this method of gaining political advantages; severe distortions will continue to accumulate. Restrained review, on the other hand, attempts to minimize these distortions while at the same time protecting those minorities who truly are powerless if and when those groups clearly suffer abuse at the hands of the winning coalition.

Third, too active judicial review can contribute to the deterioration of the coherence, peace, and stability of the society. Ours is a nation pieced together from many factions, interests, sections, ethnic groups, and classes, like a patchwork quilt that is rendible. These elements are held together by the uneasy compromises and suspicious agreements struck in the marketplace of politics. A too active Court can easily cause these arrangements to pull apart. That is, harsh absolutist rulings imposed on the nonconsenting society will be bitterly resented. Perhaps one or two sweeping rulings can be absorbed, but there is a limit to the number of such rulings that can be issued without undermining coherence, peace, and stability. Further, since the Court cannot compel compliance with its rulings, as it lacks an armed force under its control, organized and even semiofficial resistance to its rulings can bring its work to naught, embittering those who won in Court to the further aggravation of the divisions within the society. Indeed, those whose expectations had been raised by the Court's decision may ultimately be the most embittered by the experience. Thus the Court should move more slowly and circumspectly and within the range of actions implicitly tolerated by the principles to which society through its own processes has given its consent.

Fourth, the active Court can impose a costly and ineffective social policy while wrecking the more carefully laid plans of the legislature and executive. Either the Court leads or lags too much;

it rarely is in step with the country. This feature of the Court's activity creates problems of the sort referred to immediately above. Besides, the Court lacks the institutional capacity to collect the kind of information needed to make wise social policy. The Court cannot run experiments to settle disputes of social science; it cannot run experiments to test the likely consequences of its rulings; and it is severely limited in the sources of factual information to which it can turn outside the record of the case before it—a record that was tailored to the best interests of the contending parties and not with a view to the best interests of the country. And, unlike the legislature, the Court cannot take immediate steps to compensate or rectify the unforeseen and undesirable consequences of its rulings. Thus the Court should be cautious in the number and kinds of cases it accepts for review. And, finally, an active Court can impose so many binding requirements that the costs of operating governmental programs are driven up with the result that the programs become less cost-effective.

Fifth, the activist Court runs the danger of destroying whatever theoretical justification there is for the institution of judicial review. Judicial review runs so fundamentally counter to the theory that social preferences should be determined solely by majority vote, that if there is any justification for the institution of judicial review by an appointed Court it must be because such an institution contributes something different to the policy-making process than an elected legislature contributes. Presumably that contribution is the assessment of policy in light of the principles of political and moral theory as adumbrated in the Constitution. The activist Court, however, tends to neglect reliance on principle; it makes policy in a way little different from the legislature. That is, it promulgates opinions that draw lines and establish classifications as arbitrary and ultimately as unprincipled as those the legislature draws. While an element of arbitrariness is permissible in legislative behavior, it is unacceptable when it comes from the Court. And for the Court to behave like the legislature means it contributes nothing to the policy-making process that a legislature has not already contributed, and thus there is no justification for the Court's continued existence. The Court should restrain itself until an adequately general principle is in hand as a basis for justifying its intervention.[21] Such restraint is also warranted by the fact that the public expects the Court to act from general principle, not personal predilection. Failure to base opinions on the solid foundation of general principles occasions disillusionment with the Court as a court of law and invites the ultimate repudiation of the Court as nothing but a brood of willful autocrats. And this will be no impotent disillusionment as it can be transmuted into action that can mutilate the Court. Not merely can the Court's commands be ignored, but through congressional action the appropriations for the Court can be curtailed. The lower federal courts—the arms of the Supreme Court—can be abolished. The remedial powers of the Supreme Court can be constricted and even the appellate jurisdiction of the Supreme Court itself eliminated.[22] And the possibility exists that all this may be done without deeply felt opposition, since those who have benefited from the Court's protection may come to feel that the Court has proven itself an ineffective ally not worth spending considerable political capital on to save. In short, only through the exercise of restraint can the Court assure its position in our system of government. In the phrase of Bickel, the court can better suffer not going forward than visibly retreating.[23]

Activism and the Maximization of Benefits

Like the arguments in support of the model of restraint, those

---

21. The argument that the Supreme Court should act only on the basis of "neutral principles" was first set forth in Herbert Wechsler, *Principles, Politics, and Fundamental Law* (Cambridge, Mass.: Harvard University Press, 1961), p. 5. The argument generated an enormous debate among legal scholars both over what Wechsler meant and over the wisdom of what he said, assuming it could be understood. See Bickel, *The Least Dangerous Branch* and Shapiro, *Law and Politics in the Supreme Court*.

22. It may surprise some that Congress does have this sort of power over the federal court system as well as the Supreme Court, but the fact is that only the Supreme Court itself is assured of an existence by the Constitution. As for the Supreme Court, there is a strong argument to be made that only its original and not its appellate jurisdiction is free from congressional regulation. Henry Hart, "The Power of Congress to Limit the Jurisdiction of Federal Courts: An Exercise in Dialectic," *Harvard Law Review* 66 (June 1953): 1362-402; "The Nixon Busing Bills and Congressional Power," *Yale Law Journal* 81 (July 1972): 1542-73.

23. Bickel, *The Supreme Court and the Idea of Progress*, p. 95.

in support of the model of activism consist of an attack on the opposing model as well as a positive case. First, it is argued, only by means of active review will the rights and values adumbrated in the Constitution be given sufficient protection. It frequently happens that legislatures refuse to act or are politically stalemated and incapable of acting to rectify obvious injustices. But even when the legislatures do act the legislative process is characterized by a concern with achieving material ends, the appeasing of pressure groups, and responding to crises. Accordingly, in the press of legislative business the rights and values of the Constitution tend to be neglected. The Court was established to act as the advocate on behalf of those rights and values, and it can only fulfill its mission by being a sufficiently active advocate. Put differently, the justices "are inevitably teachers in a vital national seminar." [24] Further, if the Court delays too long its review of the legislature's handiwork, the Court may be faced with a fait accompli that has become so much an established part of the institutional structure of the nation that the Court cannot and dare not overturn the legislation despite its inconsistency with the Constitution as the Court understands the Constitution. As a consequence the Constitution will have been effectively amended without resort to the amending process and without judicial approval in the real sense of the word.

Second, an active Court strengthens democracy and the spirit of liberty. The availability of an active Court raises the hopes of those groups that tend to be discriminated against in the political process, provides a safety valve for pent-up frustrations, and thus makes the political system tolerable and viable for those groups. The Court arms those same individuals and groups with the support of basic principle with which to go inveighing. And it is highly doubtful that an active Court invites excessive use of its powers, since there are many natural restraints on resorting to judicial action: suits are costly and use up valuable resources that might be deployed elsewhere more effectively; there is no guarantee that the victory in Court will not prove hollow, since obtaining compliance with the decree still remains to be obtained; individuals

24. Rostow, "The Democratic Character of Judicial Review," 208.

and groups who go to Court are visible, hence vulnerable to discreet retaliation; resort to the Court is risky since the Court may conclude by adding its imprimatur to what the government has done.

Third, active judicial review serves to protect insular and powerless minorities who traditionally have suffered under discriminatory policies of the majority. In the normal political process even active and legitimate groups, if they are an insular minority, rarely have an opportunity to have an effective voice in the decision-making process. Indeed such groups have frequently been the victims of "we-they" thinking in the legislatures. An active Court can provide these powerless political minorities with a modicum of protection that hardly represents a distortion of the political process, but instead a corrective to a pattern of neglect and abuse. In any event, the majority lives on to fight another day, as regards the implementation of the Court's decree and the reversal of that decree through amendments to the Constitution and the selection of new appointees to the Court.

Fourth, an active Court helps to secure the peace and stability of the society. To argue that the Court causes social conflict is to mistake the means for resolving conflict for the pervasive social conditions that are the true factor conditioning the nature, depth, extent, and violence of social conflict. The Court's opinions and decrees may at most make more articulate and visible the principles over which the conflict is occurring, thus contributing to a more rational approach to its solution.

Fifth, in an age of positive government when the possibilities of abuse of governmental power have multiplied, an active Court is needed to make sure that we have a good government. An active Court can correct the arbitrary exclusion of individuals from the benefits of governmental programs, which those excluded may need in order to have a minimally meaningful life. And as government augments its capacity to invade the private lives of its citizens, the necessity increases for the Court to become more watchful. These kinds of corrective activities hardly amount to the making of social policy in the true sense of the phrase, but in any event the Court is not without certain advantages *vis-à-vis* legislatures in formulating policy. Working after the fact, the

Court has the opportunity to evaluate the full and actual impact of the legislature's work. The Court can examine the legislation at a more leisurely pace than the exigencies of the moment permit the legislature. And the Court is immune from the kind of direct political pressure that can distort and confuse the judgment of the legislature. As for collecting facts, the Court usually obtains enormous assistance from the parties to the case. Also, interested groups file *amicus curiae* briefs that enrich the Court's understanding of the case. And the device of judicial notice allows, within bounds, for the rendering of a decision in which reliance is placed upon facts that are not officially part of the record. And the case may always be remanded to the lower courts for further development of the record. Besides, the legislative process itself is not without its flaws as a procedure for making policy. Debates are often shallow or off the point, directed to the "folks back home" rather than to the substantive issues on the floor. The legislative record itself is often incomplete and inaccurate, being the product of partisan and self-interested lobbying. As noted, enormous political pressures can muddle and deflect the thinking of the legislators. Finally, in most legislative bodies there are so many organizational and procedural devices available for a willful minority to impose its will and extract its price that the policy to emerge may hardly be a model of rationality or fairness.

Sixth, only if the Court is active will it gain in the appreciation of the public. An inactive Court that exercises its powers sparingly serves no useful function in our age of positive government and will be viewed with indifference, if not contempt and scorn. It is the prestige of the Court that makes its word effective, and prestige will only come with the vigorous and effective exercise of its powers. Further, the argument in support of the model of restraint grossly overestimates the extent to which the Court is merely tolerated. Since the founding of the republic, Congress after Congress has reaffirmed support of the Court and never once has the populace attempted, through a constitutional amendment, to abolish the Court. Besides, the Court was designed to be able to withstand a substantial amount of public criticism—its members are appointed for life, and the salary of a justice during his tenure may not be reduced by Congress. To underestimate the strength of the Court's support is to invite a serious miscalculation as to how vigorously the Court should use its powers, which is potentially fatal for the protection of the rights and values of the Constitution.

Last, only by being active can the Court develop those principles with which it is to review legislative policy in order to fulfill its role in the scheme of government. It is true that the activist Court does not delay reaching decisions until there comes to hand a full-blown general principle that can be neutrally applied in all imagined future cases of a similar nature. It does, however, move step by step toward the forging of such principles. Since time immemorial the case-by-case evolution of principle has been the way of the Courts. And if a sensible and workable principle is to be developed it requires judicial examination of a series of concrete cases, which can only be done by means of judicial activism. A quiescent Court would not gain the experience needed to hammer out practical principles. Additionally, if the Court, despite a deeply felt intuition that an injustice has been perpetrated, frequently refuses to give the complaining individual his due until in a flash of brilliant moral theorizing a general and workable principle comes to mind to explain the original intuition, obvious injustices will go uncorrected and the rights and values of the Constitution undefended.

The Model of Activism and the Warren Court

From 1937 to 1953 the majorities that ruled in the Supreme Court showed a remarkable degree of restraint and deference to the activities of the legislatures of the country. All this changed with the appointment of Earl Warren as Chief Justice in 1953. There began then a fifteen-year period during which the Supreme Court came to be known as the "Warren Court." Strictly speaking, the Warren Court consisted only of the dominant majority that shaped the Court's behavior and doctrinal direction. That majority consisted of the Chief Justice and Justices Black, Douglas, Brennan, Goldberg, Fortas, and Marshall. Allegiance to the majority was not unwavering, especially on the part of Justice Black. On the other hand, on occasion this majority could attract to its ranks additional support in the persons of Justices Stewart or

White. In regular opposition at different points during this period were Justices Reed, Frankfurter, Jackson, Burton, Clark, Minton, Harlan, and Whittaker.

The dominant majority between 1953 and 1968 has been identified as such because, as we shall see, it manifested a consistent set of behaviors and evolved a reasonably consistent body of doctrine. Of course, no group of people who "wreck themselves upon the world" in a public career always behaves the same way or leaves behind "a wholly coherent and self-consistent philosophy of law and politics, or of the Constitution, or even of a single large subject of constitutional adjudication." [25] Bickel notes that the men on the Supreme Court were not engaged in a life of system building but of action, and any attempt to draw from such lives a coherent, self-consistent pattern of behavior and philosophy inevitably distorts. "But we infer what we can from the evidence taken as a whole from the work of such men. It is, as it must be, an exercise in judgment and is not infallible." [26]

To begin, the Warren Court, perhaps more than any other Court, exemplifies the activist model of behavior. The majority overrode precedent to broaden the Court's jurisdiction to include issues that had previously been excluded as "political questions." [27] The doctrine of standing was liberalized so that the day might have come when the purely ideological plaintiff might have access to the Court.[28] Strong presumptions in favor of the complaining party were erected.[29] New groups of people were extended the

---

25. The phrase "wreck themselves upon the world" is from Justice Holmes and is quoted by Bickel in the sentence from Bickel partially quoted in the text. Bickel, *The Morality of Consent*, p. 10.

26. Ibid., p. 11.

27. *Baker v. Carr*, 369 U.S. 186 (1962).

28. *Flast v. Cohen*, 392 U.S. 83 (1968). That case involved a challenge based on the establishment clause of the First Amendment to the Constitution; hence its implications may be limited to challenges based on that clause. Nevertheless, the Flast case and others have opened the door to the possibility that the ideological plaintiff could constitutionally gain access to the Courts. See Louis Jaffee, "The Citizen as Litigant in Public Actions: The Non-Hafeldian or Ideological Plaintiff," *University of Pennsylvania Law Review* 116 (April 1968): 1033-47. As noted below, the Court has recently further developed the law of standing.

29. See note 18.

protection of the Constitution.[30] New rights not explicitly in the Constitution were recognized, and new sources of materials were relied upon to develop sweeping rules and principles that considerably narrowed the discretion of the other branches of government.[31] The Court established a closely weighted set of values, which tended to confine the directions that legislatively adopted social policy could take.[32] And the Court exercised its remedial powers with increasing vehemence.[33]

The willingness of the Warren Court to change the institutional role of the Supreme Court so as to insert the Court more frequently and with wider effects into the political affairs of the nation is closely associated with the Warren Court's conception of its substantive mission as protector of discreet and insular minorities that traditionally have suffered discriminatory treatment at the hands of the majority. The Court's protection of defenseless and powerless individuals and groups extended into such areas as race relations,[34] free speech,[35] criminal procedure,[36] and reapportion-

30. In *Tinker v. Des Moines Independent Community School District*, 393 U.S. 503 (1969), the students were extended the protection of the free speech clause of the First Amendment in a way that opened the door to student protests and criticism of the school itself.

31. *Griswold v. Connecticut*, 381 U.S. 479 (1965), (right of privacy recognized). In the famous footnote 11 in *Brown v. Board of Education*, 347 U.S. 483 (1954), the Court referred to a body of social science research in a way that left open the distinct impression that this research did have some influence on the Court's ruling. And in the reapportionment cases the Court seems to consult writings on the concept of democracy that did not reflect anything explicitly to be found in the Constitution itself, with the result that the well-known rule of one person, one vote was established and imposed. *Baker v. Carr*, 369 U.S. 186 (1962); *Gray v. Sanders*, 372 U.S. 368 (1963); *Reynolds v. Simms*, 377 US 533 (1964).

32. The desegregation and reapportionment cases are most important in this respect.

33. *Green v. County School Board*, 391 U.S. 430 (1968).

34. *Brown v. Board of Education*, 347 U.S. 483 (1954)

35. *Tinker v. Des Moines Independent Community School District*, 393 U.S. 503 (1969); *Cox v. Louisiana*, 379 U.S. 536 (1965); *Cox v. Louisiana*, 379 U.S. 559 (1965); *Brown v. Louisiana*, 383 U.S. 131 (1966); but see *Adderly v. Florida*, 383 U.S. 39 (1966). And see *Yates v. United States*, 354 U.S. 298 (1957).

36. *Griffin v. Illinois*, 351 U.S. 12 (1956); *Gideon v. Wainwright*, 372 U.S. 335 (1963); *Douglas v. California*, 372 US. 353 (1963).

ment.[37] The groups that received special judicial solicitude included not only the blacks but also the poor urban majorities that had been effectively denied their proper influence in state government, and dissident political minorities espousing unpopular viewpoints.

Because of the Warren Court's acceptance of an activist role for the Supreme Court in our system of government and politics, it was openly receptive to suggested constitutional doctrines that had the consequence of injecting the Court deeply into political affairs. Most importantly, the efforts to get the Court to promulgate the doctrine of equal opportunity, whether it be in voting, speaking out, criminal procedure, or in education, met with considerable success. It is here the mutual resonance between the conception of role and doctrine can easily be seen.

This mutual reinforcement of role and doctrine was most clearly illustrated in the various opinions touching the public schools. In the reapportionment and free speech cases the Warren Court agreed there must be equality of opportunity to be involved in the political process of the running of the public schools. The resulting reapportionment of the state legislatures meant that no longer would such issues as the financing of education be controlled exclusively by rural interests that resisted adequate funding of the larger urban school districts. Even local school districts were soon to come under the one person, one vote rule so that local school board elections could not be rigged to establish a bias in favor of one group or another.[38] Restrictions on who could vote in school board elections were also struck down, preventing efforts to bias the election results in favor of some groups over others.[39] In short, the basic mechanisms for affecting the outcome of school politics were opened to new groups of people.

In the area of free speech, once again the thrust of the Court's

---

37. See cases cited in note 32.

38. *Avery v. Midland County*, 390 U.S. 474 (1968), extended the rule of one person, one vote to local government, including school districts. In *Sailors v. Board of Education*, 387 U.S. 105 (1967), the rule was not applied because the county school board in question was deemed to be a nonlegislative body whose members were chosen by an appointment process.

39. *Kramer v. Union Free School District No. 15*, 395 U.S. 621 (1969).

work was to open the political process to dissidents with minority viewpoints so that their voices could now be heard by the legislature and school board. Teachers were given protection to enable them to speak out on public educational issues.[40] Free speech rights were extended to students so that they could now openly criticize their own school administration.[41] Demonstrators protesting government policy were extended rights to carry their message to the seat of government.[42] Teachers were given protection against governmental harassment because of the political views they held or because of the organizations to which they belonged.[43]

As for the content of the school program, the Court laid down significant constraints on the state legislatures and school boards. Religion and more specifically prayers could no longer be part of the school program except as it was a subject of objective study like any other subject.[44] Legislatures could no longer exclude the study of evolution from the public schools.[45] And the school itself was to be operated as a "market place of ideas" in which not merely what was orthodox and approved by the school officials was to be heard.[46]

Precedent was issued that laid the foundation for the recent constitutional attacks on the traditional systems of educational finance.[47] A foundation was laid for attacks on school fees for

40. *Pickering* v. *Board of Education*, 391 U.S. 563 (1968).

41. See note 31. *Scoville* v. *Board of Education*, 425 F.2d 10 (7th Circuit, 1970).

42. See note 35.

43. *Keyishian* v. *Board of Regents*, 385 U.S. 589 (1967); *Sweezy* v. *New Hampshire*, 354 U.S. 234 (1967); *Shelton* v. *Tucker*, 364 U.S. 479 (1960).

44. *Engle* v. *Vitale*, 370 U.S. 421 (1962); *School Districts of Abington* v. *Schempp*, 374 U.S. 203 (1963).

45. *Epperson* v. *Arkansas*, 393 U.S. 97 (1968).

46. *Keyishian* v. *Board of Regents*, 385 U.S. 589 (1967); *Tinker* v. *Des Moines Independent School District*, 393 U.S. 503 (1969).

47. The most notable attempt to formulate a justiciable case on the basis of the Warren Court precedent is to be found in John E. Coons, William H. Clune, and Stephen D. Sugarman, *Private Wealth and Public Education* (Cambridge, Mass.: Harvard University Press, 1970). The argument for the unconstitutionality of traditional systems of educational finance had an early victory in *Serrano* v. *Priest*, 5 Cal. 3d 584, 487 P.2d 1241, 96 Cal. Rptr. 601

such things as textbooks, and a basis was laid for all educational practices that lead to the absolute exclusion of certain categories of students from the public schools.[48] Indeed, doctrinal foundations were laid for an attack on the functional exclusion of students from the public schools and upon school tracking and ability grouping systems.[49]

The most important work of the Court was in the area of school segregation. Not only was de jure discrimination as practiced in the South struck down, but a basis was laid for assaulting de jure school segregation wherever it was found, including interclassroom segregation in individual school buildings.[50] The Court's reasoning in the *Brown* case even went so far as to suggest that schools may have an obligation to assure equal achievement; that is, the Court hinted that schools may have to sever the correlation between low achievement scores and race. But while such a reading of the case is only an interpretation, the Court signaled more clearly that the racial policy it was moving toward was one of total integration of the society, that regardless of the causes of racial separation in the schools, school boards had an affirmative duty to bring about integration.[51] A significant implication of such a duty would be that it would become almost impossible to maintain the existence of local school districts as we now know them. The governing system of education would have to become a sys-

---

(1971). But while the argument may retain vitality as an accurate interpretation of state constitutions, it has been rejected by the U.S. Supreme Court. *San Antonio Independent School District* v. *Rodriguez*, 411 U.S. 1 (1973).

48. For a discussion of the lower court decisions that pick up where the Supreme Court left off, see David Kirp, William Buss, and Peter Kuriloff, "Legal Reform of Special Education: Empirical Studies and Procedural Proposals," *California Law Review* 62 (January 1974): 40-155.

49. For a discussion of these developments see Tyll van Geel, "The Right to Be Taught Standard English: Exploring the Implications of *Lau* v. *Nichols* for Black Americans," *Syracuse Law Review* 25 (Fall 1974): 863-910; David Kirp, "Schools as Sorters: The Constitutional and Policy Implications of Student Classification," *University of Pennsylvania Law Review* 121 (April 1973): 705-97.

50. *Brown* v. *Board of Education*, 347 U.S. 483 (1954); *Keyes* v. *School District No. 1*, 413 U.S. 189 (1973); David Kirp, *op. cit.*

51. *Green* v. *County School Board*, 391 U.S. 430 (1968).

tem of even larger school districts than now and with more centralized government.[52]

But perhaps the most startling aspect of the Warren Court's work was its perceptible movement toward transmuting the Constitution from a document imposing only negative restraints on government to one imposing affirmative duties. The affirmative duty to integrate, which seemed about to emerge from the Court at its end, is but one example. The Court's precedent also lent itself to an interpretation that the Constitution established a right on the part of individuals to certain basic minimal services that colld be claimed from the government, for example, compensatory education to assure a minimally adequate education. And if this implied promise of the Warren Court were to have been fulfilled, the Court would have become one of the chief educational policy-making agencies. No more direct impact upon state and local educational politics could be imagined.

The Model of Restraint and the Burger Court

The Warren Court left a legacy of significant intervention into school politics and a doctrinal foundation that could, with the application of a little logical thinking, result in significant new rules and principles, thrusting the Court even more deeply into school politics. With the retirement of Chief Justice Warren, however, these potentialities would not be realized. The doctrinal paths pointed out by the precedent of the Warren Court would not be taken, largely because there came to dominance a different conception of the role of the Court.

With the appointment of Chief Justice Burger the activist majority of the preceding fifteen years entered upon a period of attrition that permitted the appearance of a new majority, sometimes called the "Nixon Court" because it was President Richard Nixon who appointed the new men to the Court, and sometimes called the "Burger Court." Between 1968 and 1975 such liberal justices as Chief Justice Warren and Justices Black, Douglas, Fortas, and Goldberg left the Court to be replaced by Chief Justice Burger and Justices Blackmun, Powell, Rehnquist, and Stevens.

52. For a discussion of the implications of the desegregation decisions see Bickel, *The Supreme Court and the Idea of Progress*, chap. 4.

Since 1968 the Court's behavior has not been entirely consistent with either of the two models. (This fact can only be partially explained by the contingent nature of the Burger majority, since in some of the most activist opinions it has been a member from the Burger majority who wrote the majority opinion, as when Justice Blackmun wrote the majority opinion in the cases striking down state antiabortion legislation.)[53] Despite these out of character departures, the prevailing majority has manifested greater restraint than the Warren Court. It is important to realize, however, that the restraint of the Burger Court has not led to the repeal of the work of the Warren Court but instead only to a refusal to follow to their logical ends the principles laid down by the Warren Court. As a result the restraint of the Burger Court is qualitatively different from the restraint exhibited by the Court during the period 1937–1953. Reliance upon even a narrow construction of the precedents from the Warren Court continues the injection of the Court into the political life of the country to a greater extent than had been the case prior to 1953.[54]

The Burger Court's narrow interpretation of the precedent of the Warren Court occurs in a number of areas. The Burger Court has shied away from reviewing closely state systems of educational finance since these systems include taxing and spending powers of state legislatures;[55] it has stepped back from allowing into Court the purely ideological plaintiff;[56] it has raised procedural barriers to the bringing of class action suits;[57] it has said the Courts lack the remedial power to force the consolidation of urban and suburban school districts to bring about a better racial balance in city schools when the suburban districts were not implicated in the de jure segregation to be remedied in the city; and it has said the lower federal courts lack the power to require local districts

53. *Roe v. Wade*, 410 U.S. 113 (1973); *Roe v. Bolton*, 410 U.S. 179 (1973).

54. For a discussion of a portion of this period, see McCloskey, *The Modern Supreme Court*.

55. *San Antonio Independent School District v. Rodriguez*, 411 U.S. 1 (1973).

56. *Schlesinger v. Reservists Comm. to Stop the War*, 418 U.S. 208 (1974); *United States v. Richardson*, 418 U.S. 166 (1974).

57. *Zahn v. International Paper Co.*, 414 U.S. 291 (1973).

to make annual readjustments in their attendance patterns in order to assure a racial balance in all schools in the face of demographic changes once the district has implemented a racially neutral attendance pattern to remedy the segregation brought about by the district's original unconstitutional actions.[58]

Furthermore, the Burger Court has shown a strong desire to move away from the heavy reliance of the Warren Court on presumptions against the constitutionality of state actions. Instead, the Burger Court, while not abolishing the use of such presumptions, has moved to an approach that relies less on presumptions either in favor of the complaining individual or the state and more on a method of analysis in which the risk of failing to persuade the Court falls fairly evenly on both parties.[59] In this respect the Burger Court shows it has not reverted atavistically to the posture of excessive deference to legislative judgment that characterized the Court in the years 1937 to 1953.

In this modified role the Burger Court has not abandoned the Warren Court's concern with equality and the protection of politically powerless groups, but instead has modified this theme in several respects. The standards for identifying those groups that will receive special judicial solicitude have been tightened so that, for example, children who happen to live in property-poor school districts, and thereby have less money spent on their education, do not receive special protection.[60] At the same time the Court has adopted the position that when people are afforded different treatment by government because of their sex, the Court will examine

---

58. *Milliken* v. *Bradley*, 418 U.S. 717 (1974); *Pasadena City Board of Education* v. *Spangler*, 44 U.S.L.W. 5114 (June 28, 1976).

59. Several articles have analyzed the emergence of yet another standard of review different from both the old and the new tests used in equal protection cases. See notes 12 and 18. Gerald Gunther, "Foreward: In Search of Evolving Doctrine on a Changing Court: A Model for a Newer Equal Protection," *Harvard Law Review* 86 (November 1972): 1-48; John E. Nowak, "Realigning the Standards of Review under the Equal Protection Guarantee—Prohibited, Neutral, and Permissive Classifications," *Georgetown Law Journal* 62 (March 1974): 1071-122; Kenneth M. Davidson, "Welfare Cases and the 'New Majority': Constitutional Theory and Practice," *Harvard Civil Rights, Civil Liberties Law Review* 10 (Summer 1975): 513-674.

60. *San Antonio Independent School District* v. *Rodriguez*, 411 U.S. 1 (1973).

such state action with extra care.⁶¹ Thus, the door has been opened for constitutional attacks on sex discrimination in the public schools—a door that has vast implications for the operation of public schools.⁶² In the area of reapportionment, while the Court has softened the Warren Court's insistence on virtual mathematical equality in the size of voting districts, it has gone on to say that the Court may design voting districts to maximize, for example, black voting power, if it has been shown that historically blacks in the area had been effectively excluded from access to the informal political processes of the area, making it impossible for black communities to elect black officials.⁶³ This ruling has obvious implications for the structuring of school board elections, as does the decision striking down one-year durational residence requirements in order to be eligible to vote.⁶⁴ And groups representing minority viewpoints continued to receive protection from the Court under the First Amendment when the Court said colleges could not arbitrarily refuse to recognize radical student organizations or suppress radical newspapers even when they contain material that is indecent but not pornographic.⁶⁵

When it came to attacks on existing systems for financing public schools—systems that permit and almost require that there be wide disparities among school districts in the amount of money spent per pupil—the Burger majority backed away.⁶⁶ Here perhaps more than in any other case the Court followed the model of restraint in refusing to extend the precedent of the Warren Court

---

61. *Weinberger* v. *Wiesenfeld*, 420 U.S. 636 (1975); *Schlesinger* v. *Ballard*, 416 U.S. 351 (1975); *Taylor* v. *Louisiana*, 419 U.S. 522 (1975); *Forntiero* v. *Richardson*, 411 U.S. 677 (1973); *Reed* v. *Reed*, 404 U.S. 71 (1971); but cf. *Kahn* v. *Shevin*, 416 U.S. 351 (1974).

62. Note also that Title IX of the Education Amendments of 1972 prohibits certain forms of sex discrimination. 20 U.S.C. § 1681–86.

63. *White* v. *Regester*, 412 U.S. 755 (1973).

64. *Dunn* v. *Blumstein*, 405 U.S. 330 (1972). A fifty-day durational residence requirement has been upheld. *Burns* v. *Forston*, 410 U.S. 686 (1973) (per curiam); *Marston* v. *Lewis*, 410 U.S. 678 (1973) (per curiam).

65. *Healy* v. *James*, 408 U.S. 169 (1972); *Papish* v. *Board of Curators of University of Missouri*, 410 U.S. 667 (1973) (per curiam).

66. *San Antonio Independent School District* v. *Rodriguez*, 411 U.S. 1 (1973).

and in refusing to second guess the state legislature's preference for local control over the raising and spending of money at the expense of greater equality in the level of expenditures among school districts. That "some inequality" existed in the amount of money spent from district to district and in the actual fiscal capacity of local districts to choose their own taxing and spending patterns was insufficient to cause the system to be unconstitutional. This was an area, the Burger majority said, that it was best to refrain from reviewing closely despite the fact that these systems were "chaotic and unjust." The Court, said Justice Powell, speaking for a majority of five, simply was not equipped to handle the dispute over social science data involved in the case, or to predict accurately the legal, economic, social, and political consequences of the sort of ruling asked for by the plaintiffs.

Despite the Court's unwillingness to protect children from the accident of residence in economically poor school districts, the Court did extend the protection of the due process clause to students, so that now suspensions of up to ten days must be preceded by notice of the grounds for suspension and an opportunity for the student to explain his conduct to the disciplining officials.[67] What process was due for suspensions greater than ten days the Court did not say. Students whose presence in the school, however, poses a continuing danger to persons or property, or an ongoing threat of disrupting the academic process may be suspended forthwith without these procedures. (Probationary teachers were also offered certain procedural protections before dismissal if they enjoyed an "expectancy of reemployment." And mandatory maternity leave requirements that forced teachers out of the schools in the fifth month of pregnancy were done away with.)[68] The Court interpreted 42 U.S.C. 1983 to bar a claim of immunity by school boards from a suit for money damages by students if the board knew or reasonably should have known that its actions would violate a student's clearly established constitutional rights.[69]

---

67. *Goss v. Lopez*, 419 U.S. 565 (1975).

68. *Board of Regents v. Roth*, 408 U.S. 564 (1972); *Perry v. Sinderman*, 408 U.S. 593 (1972); *Cleveland Board of Education v. La Fleur*, 414 U.S. 632 (1974).

69. *Wood v. Strickland*, 420 U.S. 308 (1975).

As for school segregation, the Court continued the march begun by the Warren Court toward the conclusion that even de facto segregation was not permissible. Like the Warren Court, the Burger Court has interpreted, with the major limitation noted above, the Court's remedial powers generously. Thus, school districts that have been found to practice de jure segregation may be forced to abandon the neighborhood school and to use such devices for promoting integration as pairing and busing.[70] And language minority students were given special protection when the Court upheld an interpretation of the Civil Rights Act of 1964 by the U.S. Department of Health, Education, and Welfare to the effect that those students who are effectively excluded from the all-English school program because they are non-English speaking must be given special instruction to learn English.[71]

The Models and Local School Politics

While the models have utility in coming to an understanding of past judicial behavior, it remains to be seen whether they at least can serve as a starting point for developing a prediction of the judicial response in a pending suit that has the potential of deeply involving the Court in local school politics. Obvious practical constraints preclude the running of a genuine experiment to test the predictive powers of the models. I shall therefore resort to inventing a suit and then discuss how two different majorities on the Supreme Court might handle the case. The problem I have chosen involves a highly controversial subject that is at the heart of the mission of the public schools.

All public elementary and secondary schools in the country mount programs in political education, usually with the purpose of building a generalized attachment on the part of the students to the government and the people of the nation. In my hypothetical case, a rock-ribbed Republican-dominated local board has gone further and required all students to take a highly indoctrinating

---

70. *Swann* v. *Charlotte-Mecklenburg Board of Education,* 402 U.S. 1 (1971).

71. *Lau* v. *Nichols,* 414 J.S. 563 (1974).

course in the benefits of the free enterprise system.[72] The parents of Jane Jones on behalf of their child bring a suit that seeks to force the local district to modify the content of the course by requiring that a range of opposing political and economic viewpoints be presented. The gist of their argument is that the First Amendment of the Constitution imposes upon the public schools a rule that requires schools to offer courses in political education (for example, courses in American history, civics, problems of democracy, and the like) that present political materials objectively and fairly so that all major viewpoints on a given issue are given at least roughly equal treatment.[73] If such a "rule of fairness" is not adhered to, argue the parents, the First Amendment rights of their daughter would be unjustifiably violated.

The Jones parents present several arguments in support of their "rule of fairness." As a practical matter, they argue, if there were no constitutionally based protection against a deliberate bias in the political education courses of the public schools, the country would be faced with the situation that government, having created a virtual monopoly over elementary and secondary education, would now be able to impose its own officially adopted viewpoint upon a captive audience, that is, those children forced by economic circumstances into the public schools. Further, dissenting taxpayers would be forced to support the propagation of a political viewpoint with

72. The example is realistic. The Arizona legislature has required all public schools to give instruction on the "essentials and benefits of the free enterprise system." " 'Free enterprise' means an economic system characterized by private or corporate ownership of capital goods, by investments that are determined by private decision rather than by state control, and by prices, production, and the distribution of goods that are determined in a free manner." A.R.S. sec. 15-1025.

73. In order to be workable, the rule argued for in this hypothetical case would have to be refined in a number of respects. For example, it would have to be decided if the rule applies to each class session, to a semester's work, or only to the year's work. We would have to know if the rule applied only to issues explicitly raised or also to those implicitly raised in class. A decision would have to be made as to whether the rule applied not simply to those issues currently being debated in the media and in legislatures, but also to those of a more "academic" or "theoretical" nature. Some criteria would have to be developed for deciding what are "major viewpoints" and what "roughly equal treatment" is. These matters are not insurmountable, however; a complete and workable statement of such a rule could be developed. See Tyll van Geel, "Constitutional and Philosophical Perspectives on Political Education in the Public Schools," unpublished manuscript, 1975.

which they disagreed. And public school parents who disagreed with the official line would be forced to counterinstruct their children, thus imposing on these parents a double payment for the education of their child: in taxes to support the school and in the time taken at home to provide an opposing viewpoint. Any parent who was not sufficiently aware of what was going on in the public schools would run the risk of a child forming political beliefs inconsistent with those of the parents.

In shortened form the legal argument of the parents in support of the "rule of fairness" begins with the proposition that students enjoy a constitutional right to hear *vis-à-vis* the public schools, just as the general public enjoys such a right *vis-à-vis* the electronic media.[74] This right to hear is especially important when government has a virtual monopoly over a crucially important means of communication, as in the case of the public schools. Without such a right vested in students, maintenance of the schools as a marketplace of ideas—as the Supreme Court has said on several occasions the schools should be—becomes difficult and increasingly less probable. In any event, the implication of a right to hear can take either of two forms: either it leads to the conclusion that students alone have the right to determine what shall be in the curriculum, or to the conclusion that the schools must follow some sort of principle like the rule of fairness. Since government has an interest in providing an education that is informed by opinions other than just those of the students, and since operations of the public schools would become virtually impossible if only students controlled the political curriculum, a rule placing the control of the school's political program in the hands of students should not be accepted by the courts as a requirement of the Constitution. Instead, the courts should adopt the rule of fairness as the best way of realizing the right to hear without converting the schools into a "common carrier" obliged to carry every crackpot viewpoint. School officials would still act as a sort of "editor," selecting what goes into the political education program, but that editorial discretion would be guided by the rule of fairness.

Such a suit as the one just sketched clearly invites the Court

---

74. Ibid.; *Red Lion Broadcasting Co. v. FCC*, 395 U.S. 37 (1969).

to become involved in an area fraught with controversy and touching upon one of the most important of the discretionary powers of local school boards, the authority to control the school curriculum. This is an area courts historically have tended to avoid, and it may very well be that the legal arguments in support of the rule of fairness ultimately may prove to be unavailing. But of interest here is not so much the logical soundness of those arguments themselves as the question of how each of the models of judicial behavior and their supporting rationales would condition the response of the Supreme Court to the substantive argument just outlined.

Justices inspired by the model of activism would most certainly have fewer problems with this suit than those of a more restrained bent. That an opinion in favor of Jane Jones would require the recognition of a new constitutional right, the right to hear on the part of students, would not unsettle the activist justice. It would be entirely in keeping with his approach to conclude such a right was necessary in light of the enormous growth in the power of government to control the education of children. Without such a right, this power to educate politically might simply go unchecked. More important, the special role the rule of fairness would impose upon the Court would not be troubling to the activist Court. That is, the rule would involve the Court, to some extent, in shaping the content of the school program. The best analogy to this role is that played by the Federal Communications Commission (FCC) *vis-à-vis* the electronic media.[75] In general terms, it is the task of the FCC to review the reasonableness of the decisions of the media with regard to the content of their broadcasts in light of a loose standard of review termed the "fairness doctrine."[76] In this reviewing capacity the FCC exerts a rather

---

75. The Federal Communications Commission was established by the Federal Communications Act of 1934 to oversee the radio industry, and later the television industry. The FCC has the power to grant and revoke broadcast licenses and to impose regulations upon the electronic media with regard to the kind of programming broadcast. 47 U.S.C. 301 *et seq.*

76. The fairness doctrine as developed by the FCC imposes a two-fold duty on broadcasters. They must give adequate coverage to public issues, and coverage must be fair in that it accurately reflects the opposing views. Other corollary duties are related to this basic duty. It is widely accepted that the fairness doctrine has statutory support in 47 U.S.C. 315(a) (1970),

lenient form of review that leaves the broadcasters with considerable discretion, but nevertheless keeps them within certain loosely defined bounds. In this way, in theory, the FCC neither abdicates control of the content of programs to the broadcaster nor consistently substitutes its judgment for that of the broadcaster. The aim of this supervisory arrangement is to check abuse of the power of broadcasters to communicate effectively while leaving a significant degree of editorial discretion in their hands. Similarly, the purpose of the rule of fairness in our case would be to interject the Court into the operation of the school system just far enough to prevent abuse by the schools of their power, but not so far as to make the Court a national school board. While there are likely to be disputes surrounding the Court's decisions under the rule of fairness, as one side or the other claims the Court either abused its powers or abdicated to the schools, this sort of controversial role would not be troubling to an activist Court already inured to controversy in its capacity as supervisor of desegregation plans. The price for intervention would be worth it to the activist Court.

But even if the activist Court found difficult the role it was forcing upon itself under the rule of fairness, it would still, in all likelihood, proceed to promulgate the rule, it is predicted here, because it would be clear that the political process in this case would not correct itself in the near term. And, as unpopular as the rule of fairness might be at first, the activist Court might be willing to run the risk of issuing the ruling, betting that ultimately the fairness of the rule of fairness would be appreciated and along with it the new role of the Court as supervisor of the political education programs of the public schools. Most people realize, the activist justice might further conclude, that controversy over the school program can reach extremes in bitterness and divisiveness. To interject the Court into these matters will help to ease the damage done to the social fabric as a result of these disputes.

---

and apparently its imposition upon the private electronic media is not inconsistent with the First Amendment. *Red Lion Broadcasting Co. v. FCC*, 395 U.S. 367 (1969). There are many articles discussing the FCC's fairness doctrine. One good recent article is "The Regulation of Competing First Amendment Rights: A New Fairness Doctrine Balance after CBS?" *University of Pennsylvania Law Review* 122 (May 1974): 1283-329.

And in quelling the controversies the Court would serve to carry out one of its most important duties, the protection of political minorities subject to tyrannical majorities.

In striking contrast to the activist justice's willingness at least to entertain the possibility that the argument of Jane Jones is legally sound, those justices whose behavior is more restrained would be averse to accepting the argument despite its logic. These justices would conclude the subject was nonjusticiable, not capable of resolution on a principled basis, and quite beyond the expertise of the Court. These justices would ask their more active brethren if they really believe they will be able, in case after case, to determine if fair and equal treatment has been afforded all major viewpoints on a given political question. The question would imply its own answer, in the view of these skeptical jurists. These justices would also argue that as the Court issues dubious decision after dubious decision, its credibility in the eyes of the public would steadily fall, provoking a strong adverse reaction to a Court that persists in meddling in matters that usually are left to local discretion. Indeed, not to leave this sort of matter to the local political process runs several risks. It runs the risk of converting the Court into nothing more than a branch of the state department of education. It runs the risk of undermining local political processes. It runs the risk of stimulating more controversy since the rule sought by the plaintiffs hardly resolves any problems but only frames the issues and encourages disputes. It runs the risk of trivializing the Constitution as petty dispute after petty dispute is brought up under the rule for a full constitutional hearing and decision.

By way of response the activist justice might argue that the Court would be fulfilling its destiny as propounder of principle with the issuance of the rule of fairness. Nothing could be less trivial than restraining the now unfettered discretion of public officials who have monopoly power over the political education of the overwhelming majority of children in the country. Further, the case-by-case determination of issues in light of the rule of fairness would largely be left to the federal district courts; and appeals from those decisions need not be accepted by the Supreme Court itself. Hence, the Supreme Court need not become another division in a state department of education.

The rejoinder to this argument might be that the rule remains ultimately unenforceable. It would be asked, "How can even the locally situated federal district courts enforce an order to local boards of education to be 'fair'?" If unenforceable orders are to be avoided the district courts would have to engage in drawing up the daily lesson plans for each course challenged under the rule of fairness. If that does not amount to the trivialization of the Constitution or the making over of the federal courts into a local school board, nothing does. And the fact that it would be the local district courts that would be on the line day after day implementing these lesson plans would not make the Supreme Court immune to criticism and attack; everybody would know it was the Supreme that forced the district courts into this new role as local school board for political education. Thus the more restrained justice would argue that, despite the logic of the plaintiff's argument, the principles sought by the plaintiff would lead the Court into a role in our governing system of education that it cannot and should not play save at great cost.

Conclusions

Legal realists are more accurate in their description of judicial behavior than the almost magical view of the law expressed at the beginning of this chapter, but what the legal realists fail to say is that the way justices of the Supreme Court rule in particular cases is determined not only by their personal policy preferences but also by their theory of the proper role of the Court. This proposition was explored first in connection with the legacy of the Warren Court where the interrelationship of role and substantive doctrine was probed. In brief, it was shown how an activist conception of the Court made the Court amenable to constitutional doctrine stressing equality of opportunity. With the coming of the Burger Court there was some reduction in the activism of the Court, which in turn had an effect upon constitutional doctrine itself. This point was most clearly demonstrated in the Texas educational finance case. While the Warren Court had established precedent that logically could have been extended in such a way as to strike down most present systems for financing public education, the Burger Court refused to undertake such an extension despite the objections of the remnants of the Warren Court majority. Justice Powell in his majority opinion made quite clear that the refusal to follow where logic might have led the Court was based upon a conception of the role of the Court in the system of government—a conception that stressed the Court's inability to handle matters of taxation and of spending, to wrestle with the social science data involved in the case, and to project accurately enough the practical implications of the ruling being sought from the Court, as well as a strong belief in the independence the states in our federal system should enjoy from the control of an agency of the federal government.

To test further the hypothesis that role conception affects doctrinal development, a mental experiment was run demonstrating how adherents to different models of judicial behavior would respond to a law suit seeking to impose upon the public schools a rule of fairness in the presentation of political materials. There again we saw that a logical argument based on Court precedent might not be accepted by a Court adhering to counsels of restraint.

While it might at first seem irrational not to let logic take a Court where it will, the concern with the judicial role is no trivial matter. As the arguments in support of each of the two models show, the determination of the proper role for the Court touches upon fundamental political issues and problems: the peace and stability of the society, the protection of individual rights, democratic theory, and the survival of the Court itself. Strict adherence to the logical extension of principle can severely unsettle a society, may result in the abandonment of the principle itself in practice if not also in professed allegiance, and may result in the crippling of the institution that promulgated and imposed those extensions. Yet failure to adhere to logic opens the door to charges of unconscionable compromise and to the abandonment of principle by the organ of government chosen to promote principle in our political affairs. Thus, on the one hand we cannot be a good society without principle, and on the other hand we cannot be "principle ridden." Both principle and expediency must exist in an uneasy relationship, with principle guiding expediency and expediency dulling the harsh edge of principle.[77]

77. Bickel, *The Least Dangerous Branch*, p. 64.

This dilemma is most acutely felt in the desegregation of the public schools. It is unthinkable to believe that desegregation of the races in the public schools is not sanctioned by principle, yet to pursue the principle of integration of the races with unbending rectitude can and does produce conflict and even violence. The two views of the role of the Court, then, importantly reflect different responses to this dilemma. The activist justice believes a vigorous Court is the best way to assure that our politics are not unprincipled, hence not shameful, shameless, and intolerable.[78] The more restrained justice sees the potential for conflict and chaos from an unyielding insistence upon principle. Both justices are caught up in this American dilemma that pervades our entire politics because we are a country founded on principles of right and justice.

78. Bickel, *The Morality of Consent*, p. 24.

CHAPTER VI

School Policy Culture and State Decentralization*

FREDERICK M. WIRT

The role of the state in shaping school policy has been central to American education because the U.S. Constitution reserves authority over education to the states and because Dillon's Rule still lives. (Dillon's Rule refers to a nineteenth century judicial opinion that characterizes the basic tie between state and local governments. In essence, the state can create and destroy all local units and it can grant or withhold authority for them to act.) Yet, how one approaches the study of the role of the state for analytical purposes is not so clear. In the last fifty years, political scientists have studied the state's role in policy making from such perspectives as the legal basis of authority, the institutionalization of that authority, the group pressure matrix within which policy is made, the impact of environmental and structural aspects of states upon their policy outcomes, and, most recently, state policy within an intergovernmental web of relations.

This chapter departs in two ways from these analytical approaches and from the traditional data on the analysis of school policy. First, it explores the extent of differences among the fifty states in the degree of centralization of control over local school policy by the state government. This is an "output" rarely developed except in case study fashion,[1] even though the *authoritative distribution of authority* would seem a significant variable shaping

---

* The author wishes to express appreciation to the University of Illinois Research Board for research funding, to David Fanta for assistance in processing the data, and to Professor Stephen Seitz for assistance in preparing the data and in programming.

1. Edgar Fuller and Jim B. Pearson, eds., *Education in the States*, 2 vols. (Washington, D.C.: National Education Association, 1969). Vol. 1 is a cross-state, topical analysis of the subject since 1900, while vol. 2 is a state-by-state analysis.

the distribution of policy outcomes. Second, the chapter presents a first examination of a massive content analysis of items related to schooling in constitutions, statutes, regulations, and court decisions in the fifty states. To focus this massive set of data and its accompanying conceptual framework of the allocation of authority, regional variations among these output measures will be sought.

The Setting of the State's Role

The background of this research is the expanding role of the American state in local schooling. Regardless of whether one examines educational function, structure, finance, or instruction, it is clear that the states have expanded their writ over the last century.[2] The one-room school of storied tradition is as remote from the contemporary scene as the steam locomotive whose haunting whistle once moaned through the school windows. The success of the Progressive reformation of school structure, starting at the end of the last century, depended upon the state to impose centralizing reforms upon decentralized urban schools.[3] Later, after World War I, an enormous consolidation drive shook down the myriad school districts into a much smaller number of much larger units. After World War II the drive was stepped up, and in the 1960s state law was wiping out three districts a day between breakfast and the morning coffee break.[4] Where nine school districts had stood in the early 1930s only one now exists.[5]

State action to reduce these units was accompanied by state action to improve the quality of instruction and administration. Schools of education, linked symbiotically to the legislature and to the state department of education, became the gatekeepers that certified such quality in teachers and administrators. The measure was simple—passing of specified numbers of courses or specified

---

2. Ibid.

3. Lawrence A. Cremin, *The Transformation of the School: Progressivism in American Education, 1876–1957* (New York: Alfred A. Knopf, 1961); Joseph M. Cronin, *The Control of Urban Schools* (New York: Free Press, 1973).

4. Carolyn M. Mullins, "School District Consolidation: Odds Are 2 to 1 It'll Get You," *American School Board Journal* 160 (November 1973): 23.

5. Fuller and Pearson, *Education in the States*. See section on consolidation.

courses. The would-be principal, superintendent, or teacher needed certificates to work their professions, and those without them, except in emergency conditions, could not work. Similarly, the details of local schooling set forth under state regulations became more extensive and intensive in the matter of finances. Financial accountability to state requirements in such matters as budgets, reporting systems, minimums, mandates, tax and bond uses and constraints became an ever-pressing condition of the local life of schools. Further, the teaching profession itself imposed more constraints by its standards of quality in the textbook, subject matter, and pedagogy. These professional criteria could be applied more effectively with the backing of state authority, so concepts of curriculum were reinforced by that authority—concepts relating to the classic curriculum, the vocational curriculum, Americanization, hygiene, and so forth.[6]

Yet somehow, this state centralization was ignored in the continuing rhetoric about local control of schools. The social and political value of local control was praised highly, even in textbooks for school administrators, which otherwise instructed them how to impose their own values upon local systems. Parents and taxpayers, on the relatively few occasions when they became exercised enough about school matters to mobilize for political action, led with the slogan "local control" emblazoned on their banners. But the reality was that they were objecting to state-imposed laws, over whose administration local officials and voters might have little authority, as long as Dillon's Rule had effect—as it did and still does have.[7] We shall return to this point later.

Yet, within the ambit of the local district, it was not only the state law that reached in to challenge any rhetoric about local autonomy. Other external forces had the same effect. National currents sweeping through professional school circles were borne to the local scene by local professionals—ideas about sex education,

---

6. Frederick M. Wirt and Michael Kirst, *Political and Social Foundations of American Education* (Berkeley, Calif.: McCutchan Publishing Corp., 1975). See chap. 10 on the politics of decision making in curriculum matters.

7. Frederick M. Wirt, "State Politics of Education," in *Politics in the American States*, ed. Herbert Jacob and Kenneth Vines. 2d ed. (Boston, Mass.: Little, Brown & Co., 1976). See chap. 8 for a review.

curriculum, management, finances, and so forth.[8] Federal agencies intervened by actions of the Congress (for example, passage of the Elementary and Secondary Education Act of 1965); by actions of federal administrators in the enforcement of laws (for example, the Civil Rights Act of 1964); and by court decisions (for example, *Brown* v. *Board of Education of Topeka* on school desegregation and *Tinker* v. *Des Moines Independent Community School District* on student rights).[9] Perturbations in the national economy or excitement over perceived national events had the same penetrating effects as when the growth in local financing was linked to the Sputnik crisis and the economic boom of the early 1960s, and decline was linked to the inflation arising from the Vietnam War and the oil crisis of the early 1970s.

A Paradigm for Comparative Research

This sketch of the role of the state in relation to the local education authority (LEA) suggests the contradictions between events and values in the issue of the control of educational policy in a democratic system. This chapter directs attention to a basic interrelationship in this picture, namely, the legal distribution of authority over school policy between state and LEA. While we have a number of case studies of that interrelationship,[10] there has never been a systematic investigation of these linkages for all states under comparable conditions. Yet knowledge of these relationships seems a basic requisite to policy making at the national level and to scholarship, either in comparative studies or in case studies. The larger view is necessary if one is to understand either national patterns in this matter or the significance of a single study.

8. See, for example, James Hottois and Neal A. Milner, *The Sex Education Controversy* (Lexington, Mass.: D. C. Heath & Co., 1974).

9. For a review of the role of the courts, see John C. Hogan, *The Schools, the Courts, and the Public Interest* (Lexington, Mass.: D. C. Heath & Co., 1974).

10. Stephen K. Bailey et al., *Schoolmen and Politics* (Syracuse, N.Y.: Syracuse University Press, 1962); Nicholas Masters et al., *State Politics and the Public Schools* (New York: Alfred A. Knopf, 1964); Joel S. Berke and Michael W. Kirst, eds., *Federal Aid to Education: Who Benefits? Who Governs?* (Lexington, Mass.: D. C. Heath & Co., 1973); and Jerome T. Murphy, *State Education Agencies and Discretionary Funds* (Lexington, Mass.: D. C. Heath & Co., 1974).

The paradigm that incorporates this distribution of authority is an expanded version of the familiar Eastonian model for the analysis of political systems. If we are to understand fully what differences the states make in policy operations, we need information to fill in components of the paradigm formally sketched in figure 1. Some of these are familiar, particularly the Input–Spending–Outcome linkage, so often studied in the recent macroanalyses of policy. But there are implicitly two other factors that hypothetically could intervene in this traditional analysis.

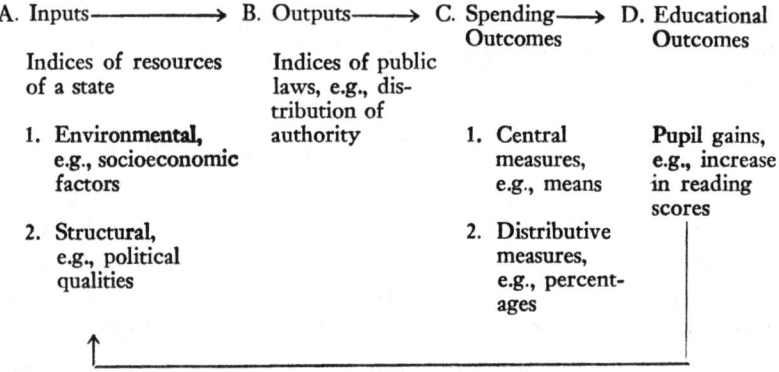

Fig. 1. Paradigm of state policy culture

First, such research ignores the possibility that the way in which a state distributes its authority to subordinate administrative and political agencies could condition the kinds of outcomes achieved. As an illustration drawn from limited cases, full state assumption of the policy service may necessitate different fiscal requirements than when the service is totally the responsibility of the subordinate agency. If so, then measures of outcomes focusing upon spending patterns, whether using central or distributive measures,[11] may have missed the key conceptual variable accounting for those outcomes.

A second linkage in the paradigm (although rarely studied and certainly not in studies of educational policy) is the difference made in the quality of service received by the client if outputs

11. Brian R. Fry and Richard F. Winters, "The Politics of Redistribution," *American Political Science Review* 64 (June 1970): 508-22.

vary with the distribution of authority. That is, are there more and better educational gains for pupils if states have more centralized or more decentralized systems for governing education? Does this ultimate outcome—what happens to the child—depend more upon input conditions, such as the financial resources or the characteristics of political structures of the state, than it does upon the state's distribution of local school authority? Or, how is this most socially significant dependent variable—pupil gains—differentially affected by this set of variables?

Clearly, not all these questions can be addressed substantially here. Rather, this chapter will analyze one aspect of the paradigm never set forth before—the patterns of distribution of authority between state and local agencies among the fifty states. This is the true output measure in the paradigm shown in figure 1. Dealing directly with this ignored variable will enable us to clear away some empirical underbrush by determining the answers to two questions. First, is there significant variation among the states in this state-local interrelation, hereafter termed *centralization*? Second, is there evidence of interstate variations that might be traced to regional influence?

These questions about patterns of centralization and their regional qualities are important both empirically and conceptually. Empirically, the answers will enable us to determine whether the variety of American federalism so familiar in many fields operates in educational matters too, or whether the charge of critics is true that the profession of education has standardized and institutionalized this service. Conceptually, in dealing with the question of regionalism we are reviewing one of the major historical influences upon the lives of citizens. A sizable literature provides theoretical guides to this research. Finally, with a firmer grasp upon the reality of the experiences of American states with authority and power in school policy, we are better prepared to deal with the intriguing theoretical questions implicit in the paradigm of figure 1 and to move to a firmer base for evaluating national policy for public education.

Research Design

The central measure of this study is one of centralization of authority over educational policy. Centralization is conceptualized as a variable that ranges from full state decentralization at one end of a continuum to full state centralization at the other end. There are seven logical categories of centralization on which a given school policy might be judged, as follows:

0. *Absence of State Authority.* The state constitution, laws, and regulations contain no reference to an exercise of authority on a given policy matter. Conceptually, this means that the local school is free to act or not—the epitome of local autonomy unfettered by any state influence. For example, the local school decides whether to treat the birthday of Martin Luther King, Jr., in any special way.

1. *Permissive Local Autonomy.* Policy is devised and administered by the local educational authority (LEA) without reference to state goals or supervision and the LEA need do nothing. The state is permissive about the goal of policy and about providing assistance to implement that goal. The key word in state authorization is *may* (what the LEA "may" do). For example, "love of country" is indicated as a desirable curriculum goal but nothing more is said about its meaning or state support of it.

2. *Required Local Autonomy.* The specifications are the same as in Permissive Local Autonomy, but the district must do *something* about the policy. For example, the LEA must provide some kind of unspecified course in civic training.

3. *Extensive Local Option under State Mandated Requirements.* The state sets broad guidelines for service or assistance that permit the LEAs a considerable number of options. The state sets the goal of policy but lets the LEA implement it with but few constraints. For example, a particular curriculum goal may be met by selecting one of five kinds of civics courses.

4. *Limited Local Option under State Mandated Requirements.* The state sets extensive and detailed guidelines for service or assistance, which the LEAs must administer with little option. The state uses the LEA to administer the state goal within tight (but not absolute) control. For example, the length of the school year will be from 160 to 170 days.

5. *No Local Option under State Mandated Requirements.* The LEA "must," "shall," or "will" (key words in law) provide a service or meet state requirements with *no* variation. There is no

leeway for the LEA to do anything other than what is mandated. For example, the number of years of service before a teacher is eligible for tenure is specified.

6. *Total State Assumption.* The state exercises full control over provision of policy service, with no LEA involvement in providing money, service, veto, or representation. In short, the state undertakes the educational service in its entirety. For example, the state provides schools for the blind.

Such a scale of centralization does not permit fine calibration. It does not, for example, indicate beforehand the exact line between "limited" and "extensive" local option (points 3 and 4 on the continuum). Rather, it permits only a rough categorization of any law or set of policy requirements. Some refinement is possible, however, by training those who will classify these legal instruments to make sharper discriminations between "limited" and "extensive." While precision in instrumentation is always desirable, it is clear that such a requirement constrains the instrument and hence the data that one can employ in social science research. Such has been the case in policy macroanalysis, where insistence upon such precision has constricted research to the budgetary context of policy services. But what an agency spends does not tell us much about why it does so, the goals it pursues, and the constraints of law within which budgets are devised and administered. The procedure outlined above, while much more roughly hewn, enables us to begin to examine the larger implications of budgetary activities. Moreover, it directs our attention to the basic focus of political science, that is, the distribution of authority within political systems.

The Data for Analysis

The heart of the research lies in a massive content analysis of the laws of the fifty states in thirty-six areas of educational policy. The analysis was performed during 1972-73 by the Lawyers' Committee for Civil Rights under Law under a grant from the National Institute of Education. Content analyses were made of the statements of legal authority over schools in the policy areas, covering each state's constitution, status, court decisions, and administrative regulations. The results were digested in brief statements of one or more pages for each area, describing what agency had authority, what policy goal was to be pursued, and the criteria of performance. The process resulted in a 300-page set of condensed statements concerning state authority over schooling in the fifty states.[12]

The data were reviewed by the author and an assistant for their applicability to a scale of centralization, and a preliminary scale was modified to arrive at the seven-point scale described in the previous section. A group of students then categorized the data in terms of this scale. Each state was reviewed by a two-person team, each person categorizing each legal datum independently, and the team then deciding upon a single designation for it. Differences of judgment were referred to the author and an assistant, but there were few such referrals. The data for each of the thirty-six areas could then be summarized by state and region. A School Centralization Score (SCS) ranging from 0.00 to 6.00 could be assigned for each policy area for each state. Summing procedures made possible a total SCS for each state or for sets of states and a SCS for each area for all states or for sets of states. In subsequent analysis, the total for each state constitutes a variable for use in the interactions set forth in the paradigm shown in figure 1 under the heading "Output."

Distribution of Centralization among the States

A first task is to describe the distribution of the SCSs of the fifty states on the centralization scale. The data for this task are shown in tables 1 and 2. There is considerable variation among the states, ranging from a SCS of 1.86 for Wyoming to a SCS of 6.00 for Hawaii. But there are patterns within this range. For example, two-thirds of the states cluster between point 3 (Extensive Local Option) and point 4 (Limited Local Option) on the scale. Yet eight lie below and seven above the range of one standard deviation for the distribution (standard deviation = .56). Table 2 shows large clusters of states close to these outer margins (thirteen

12. Appreciation is expressed for the assistance of the Lawyers' Committee for Civil Rights under Law (especially Hannah Geffert) in securing these state reports. For a summary of some of these provisions, see Lawyers' Committee for Civil Rights under Law, *A Study of State Legal Standards for the Provisions of Public Education* (Washington, D.C.: National Institute of Education, U.S. Department of Health, Education, and Welfare, 1974).

TABLE 1
School Centralization Scores, by States, 1972

State	SCS	State	SCS	State	SCS
Alabama	4.67	Louisiana	3.19	Ohio	3.65
Alaska	3.38	Maine	3.09	Oklahoma	4.91
Arizona	2.91	Maryland	3.56	Oregon	4.30
Arkansas	3.57	Massachusetts	2.73	Pennsylvania	3.75
California	3.65	Michigan	3.85	Rhode Island	3.21
Colorado	3.79	Minnesota	4.10	South Carolina	4.61
Connecticut	2.68	Mississippi	3.93	South Dakota	3.08
Delaware	3.15	Missouri	2.84	Tennessee	3.48
Florida	4.19	Montana	3.47	Texas	2.88
Georgia	3.24	Nebraska	3.81	Utah	3.42
Hawaii	6.00*	Nevada	2.84	Vermont	3.17
Idaho	3.26	New Hampshire	3.13	Virginia	3.88
Illinois	3.32	New Jersey	3.87	Washington	4.37
Indiana	3.90	New Mexico	3.79	West Virginia	3.94
Iowa	3.80	New York	3.63	Wisconsin	3.62
Kansas	3.38	North Carolina	3.80	Wyoming	1.86
Kentucky	3.90	North Dakota	2.89		

Mean = 3.59; Standard deviation = .56

* Out of Hawaii's royal heritage, all authority is centralized. There are no local districts.

TABLE 2
States with Centralization Scores within Specified Intervals

SCS Interval	States[a]
5.00 +	Hawaii (6.00)
4.50-4.99	Oklahoma (4.91), Alabama, South Carolina
4.00-4.49	Washington (4.37), Oregon, Florida, Minnesota
3.75-3.99	West Virginia (3.94), Mississippi, Indiana, Kentucky, Virginia, New Jersey, Michigan, Nebraska, Iowa, North Carolina, Colorado, New Mexico, Pennsylvania
3.50-3.74	California (3.65), Ohio, New York, Wisconsin, Arkansas, Maryland
3.25-3.49	Tennessee (3.48), Montana, Utah, Kansas, Alaska, Illinois, Idaho
3.00-3.24	Georgia (3.24), Rhode Island, Louisiana, Vermont, Delaware, New Hampshire, Maine, South Dakota
2.50-2.99	Arizona (2.91), North Dakota, Texas, Missouri, Nevada, Massachusetts, Connecticut
Under 2.50	Wyoming (1.86)

[a] For each interval the highest SCS is given in parentheses and the other states are listed in descending order within that set.

states with SCSs between 3.75 and 3.99 and eight states with scores between 3.00 and 3.24). In short, the mean for the fifty states (3.59) on this seven-point centralization scale is a deceptive measure.

As figure 2 clearly shows, the reality is better described as a bimodal distribution, with some outlying cases at the extremes. A rough picture emerges, then, of three broad patterns of state centralization in school policy: (a) the intermediates (nineteen states with SCSs in the first half standard deviation above or below the mean—scores from 3.31 to 3.87); (b) moderately centralized or decentralized (sixteen states in the second half standard deviation above or below the mean—scores from 3.87 to 4.15 or from 3.03 to 3.31; and (c) the most centralized or most decentralized (fifteen states with SCSs more than one standard deviation above or below the mean).

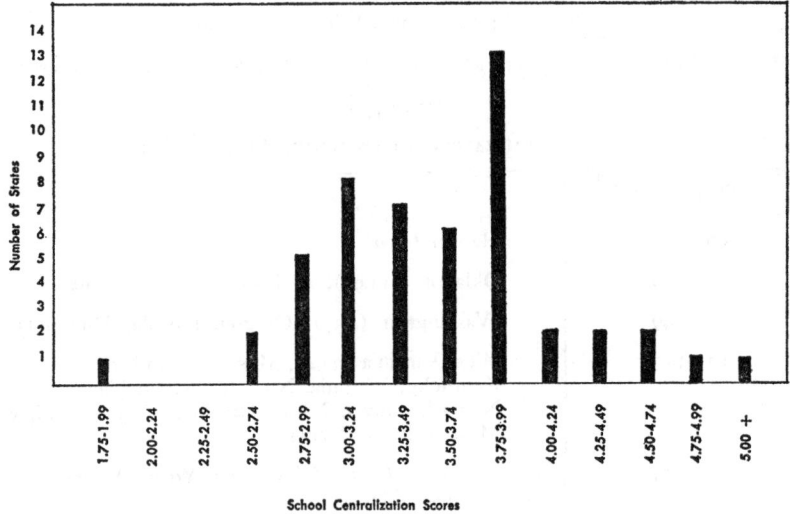

Fig. 2. Distribution of school centralization scores, by states, 1972

These findings are an important corrective to two kinds of distorted perspectives on American public education. There is little balm in these data for those who believe that the system is characterized by extreme uniformity. This "establishment" model of American education does not account for the presence of real diversity in what schools are mandated, permitted, or set free to do. On the other hand, those who claim that there is so much diversity ("This place is different from every other place") underestimate the rough patterning of state authorization that is revealed here. As shown in table 2, the range is from 1.86 to 6.00 but is concentrated overwhelmingly between points 3 and 4 on the centralization scale.

A similar finding emerges from an examination of the frequency distributions for each of the thirty-six policy areas among the fifty states. Histograms prepared for each area show some policies for which there is near uniformity, whether of centralization or decentralization. For example, in regard to certification, thirty-three states have an SCS of 6 and fourteen have an SCS of 5, revealing great centralization. Near uniformity was also found on decentralization, sometimes reflecting the absence of state law on the subject. For example, thirty-five states have no state provisions regarding standards for promotion. Many policies reflect a U-shaped distribution. For example, twenty-two states have no provisions for the evaluation of education, while the state assumes the function totally in sixteen states; in twenty-one states there are no provisions relating to accounting procedures, while in eighteen states there is total state regulation of those procedures; and in eighteen states there are no state provisions regarding equal educational opportunity programs as opposed to seventeen states in which those programs are totally a state function.

Hence, while there is nothing approaching uniformity among the states in these data, neither is it the case that each state is different from the others. Rather, there is evidence of clusters of states having a similar policy mix. Among these clusters it could be hypothesized that there exists a policy *culture* about education, a related set of beliefs that produce authorizations embodied in public law. If that is so, there must be some identity in this policy culture that is amenable to empirical analysis. Judging from the literature cited previously on state case studies on the politics of education, it is clear that educational constituencies *within* a state tend to share common viewpoints and engage in common actions, suggestive of the concept of culture. In 1962, Bailey and his colleagues noted such shared attributes *between* states of the Northeast.[13]

13. Bailey et al., *Schoolmen and Politics*.

The School Policy Cultures of American Regions

If we are to validate the concept of policy culture, we need evidence of common beliefs and behavior among a group of actors. In the absence of survey research that could furnish attitudinal data, which is a direct and important next step, we are restricted to legal data. In turning to the content of legal instruments of school policy, we are not presuming that actors will do what the law requires of them. Another necessary next step in research in this larger analytical field is the devising of a set of *reactional* biographies of the politics of education among American states of the kind that Bailey, Masters, and later Berke and Kirst essayed.[14] But in drawing out the empirical referents in such school politics one cannot ignore the constraints that arise from the allocation of resources by the state government and from the values that such allocations reflect. As this is still a nation of laws, political authorities of the school systems must work within these mandates and permissions, not outside or against then in any regular way. Hence, what the state requires, permits, encourages, or ignores becomes a vital element of the behavior of school policy actors. One can interpret *Hamlet* in a surprising number of ways, but he cannot ignore the lines that Shakespeare wrote, even when editing or performing them.

One indicator of the existence of policy culture would be distinctive ways in which like-minded states are grouped. We leave to another time the examination of the bases for such groupings in social, economic, political, or other indicators via multivariate analysis. But before we move to such sophisticated methods, we would do well to search the nearby familiar ground of scholarship for an explanation of these clusters. Among these explanations is the influence of regionalism.

The role of regionalism in American history is a familiar one, needing no explication here. But politically, most battles of parties in our past were rooted in regional differences over the major questions of national life. As Holcombe noted, that stimulus altered during this century to emphasize class and status as the generators

---

14. Ibid.; Masters et al., *State Politics and the Public Schools;* Berke and Kirst, *Federal Aid to Education;* Murphy, *State Education Agencies and Discretionary Funds.*

of party conflict.[15] In our own time though, regionalism can still be seen as a differentiating factor in the form of local government,[16] in political cultures,[17] in fiscal policies,[18] in attitudes about justice, liberty, and equality,[19] and in a surprising array of moral preferences and visions of America.[20] This neighborhood evidence of such an influence requires us to explore its potential explanatory power as an indicator of school policy culture.

THE THREE POLITICAL CULTURES

Elazar has delineated the concept of political culture, distinguishing three distinctive patterns of value and practice found among the states.[21] In the *moralistic* type, government is seen as a means for achieving the good community, or "commonwealth," through positive action. While nongovernmental action is preferred to this end, social and economic regulations are legitimate and to be pursued, while the bureaucrats who administer such policy are viewed positively if they are politically neutral. Second, the *individualistic* state culture is characterized by a view of government as a "marketplace" that responds to demands, favors economic development, and links directly to the political party as the vehicle for satisfying individual needs, hence a heavy emphasis upon partisanship. Third, the *traditionalistic* culture conceives of government's main function as maintaining traditional patterns, being responsive to a governing elite, with partisanship subordinated to personal ties.

Elazar has drawn no relationship between these types and educational policy, but it seems a fair extension of the concept to expect

15. Arthur Holcombe, *The New Party Politics* (New York: Harcourt, Brace & Co., 1933).

16. This distinction is drawn in all texts on state and local government.

17. Daniel J. Elazar, *American Federalism*, 2d. ed. (New York: Thomas Y. Crowell Co., 1972), chaps. 4 and 5.

18. Ira Sharkansky, *Regionalism in American Politics* (Indianapolis, Ind.: Bobbs-Merrill Co., 1969).

19. These attitudes are evident in most national polls. See those regularly assembled for *Public Opinion Quarterly* by Hazel Erskine.

20. See especially Norval D. Glenn and J. L. Simmons, "Are Regional Cultural Differences Diminishing?" *Public Opinion Quarterly* 31 (Summer 1967): 176-93.

21. Elazar, *American Federalism*, chap. 4.

different kinds of school policy among them. All have a view of government acting positively, whether for community, individual, or elite interests. But one would expect states sharing the moralistic culture to exercise state authority to construct schools whose benefit to the whole society is so obvious. Similarly, traditionalistic cultures, with their elite orientation, should not find as much use of authority to benefit the larger numbers who lack social and economic resources to provide their own schooling. Finally, if pursuit of personal interests is maximized in individualistic cultures, we should find them using the state to spread educational benefits to as many individuals as possible.

None of these logical extensions of the political culture concept holds up well in light of our centralization measure. Table 3 summarizes these scores by Elazar's types. The most centralized school

TABLE 3
SCHOOL CENTRALIZATION SCORES BY POLITICAL CULTURE, 1972

Political Culture Type	Mean SCS	Number of States
Individualistic	3.49	9
Individualistic-Moralistic[a]	2.94	6
Individualistic-Traditionalistic	4.42	2
Total	3.23	17
Moralistic	3.58	9
Moralistic-Individualistic	3.52	8
Total	3.55	17
Traditionalistic	3.82	8
Traditionalistic-Individualistic	3.94	6
Traditionalistic-Moralistic	3.36	2
Total	3.81	16

[a] In each pair, the first type predominates.
Source: Daniel J. Elazar, *American Federalism*, 2nd ed. (New York: Thomas Y. Crowell Co., 1972), p. 117.

systems are not moralistic but traditionalistic, heavily southern; therefore, an alternative inference is that in such hierarchical systems state control of education is centralized as an attribute of elite control. Moreover, the individualistic cultures, however combined, are the least (not the most) centralized, as far below the mean for all states as the traditionalistic are above it. This is particularly surprising, for the use of the political party to secure benefits from the political system for members leads us to expect that such states would provide more schooling laws, their reallocative benefits protected by imposing tighter state control over them. Finally, the moralistic culture is not excessive in securing the benefits of schooling through use of state power; rather, these states hover about the mean for all states, between the other two types.

What is suggested here is that there is a structural dimension of political culture not yet tapped in the research, namely, differing answers to the question of the territorial distribution of authority within the state. Our data support the inference that the distribution of authority is related to these Elazar types. The individualistic states resolve this question with a preference for decentralization, the traditionalistic prefer much more centralization, while the moralistic are intermediate because of wide variation on the matter (from Wyoming's SCS of 1.86 to Indiana's 3.91).

This structural question is not unimportant in the ideological conflict over federalism. Much of that conflict has centered around the relationships between state and nation, providing a debate continuous throughout our history about the nature of the federal compact entered into in 1789. But within the state, there has also been a running skirmish between the capitol and the home folks about what the former should do to the latter. It may be as Shields observed in an ignored but important analysis two decades ago.[22] That is, we may have approached the question of within-state centralization on a very pragmatic, empirical basis, letting problems be handled first privately. But if that did not meet the needs, then Americans have moved to governmental power, preferably on the lowest level feasible, but always willing to go to a higher level if their needs were unmet. Whatever the validity of Shield's observation—and it is supported by much history—it is clear that one element of the political culture concept is this debate over centralization. It needs considerably more research.

THE HISTORICAL REGIONS

There is, however, another analytical view of regions, a view that is rooted in history. These are the traditional regions, marked by a rich past and portrayed decennially in federal census figures.

22. Currin Shields, "The American Tradition of Empirical Collectivism," *American Political Science Review* 46 (March 1952): 104-20.

These collectivities of states share a common history as well as a common territorial location, with all the attendant commonalities of climate, land quality, and geographical features. On these multiple bases of region many political battles have been fought, while economic conflict has been generated both then and now. One attribute of these separated commonalities of region could well be practices of structuring the delivery of policy services. We know this was the case for some forms of governance. For example, the wider spaces of the feudal plantation economy of the Old South generated a county commission form of government, while the cramped proximity of small farmers in New England generated the town form. The question is whether region serves as a useful basis for distinguishing school policy cultures of the fifty states.

Table 4 summarizes the data on School Centralization Scores for the major regions and subregions for the thirty-six policy areas. The complete set of data is presented in table 5. Among the four major regions, the Midwest and West cluster around the mean SCS

TABLE 4

SUMMARY OF SCHOOL CENTRALIZATION SCORES BY REGIONS AND SUBREGIONS, 1972

AREA	MEAN SCS	NUMBER OF STATES	NUMBER OF POLICIES		NUMBER OF POLICIES SIGNIFICANTLY DIFFERENT[c]		
			More Centralized[a]	More Decentralized[b]	Centralized	Decentralized	Total
All states	3.59	50	—	—	—	—	—
Northeast	3.27	11	9	18	—	7	7
New England	3.00	6	2	24	1	7	8
Mid-Atlantic	3.59	5	18	11	7	3	10
Southeast	3.87	12	23	6	13	—	13
Midwest	3.52	12	13	14	3	5	8
Great Lakes	3.67	5	18	14	6	4	10
Plains	3.41	7	13	14	3	3	6
West	3.65	15	13	14	2	4	6
Southwest	3.65	4	18	15	8	1	9
Mountain	3.16	5	8	18	2	5	7
Far West	3.79	4	21	11	7	1	8
Pacific	4.69	2	17	7	9	—	9
All states vs. four regions			58	52	18	16	34
All states vs. subregions			138	128	58	29	87

[a] More than 0.20 greater than mean for all other states.
[b] More than 0.20 less than mean for all other states.
[c] "t" less than .15.

for all states, while the older states in the Northeast and Southeast demonstrate more divergent patterns of decentralization and centralization. Yet these aggregates are too large to show much, particularly in the middle regions. The subregion SCSs, however, reveal much more diversity within all regions. New England shares much with the Mountain states in its decentralization, although their neighboring regions (the Mid-Atlantic and Far West states, respectively) are much different.

The columns of table 4, showing the number of variables on which these areas were more or less centralized provide support for beliefs both about the uniform and the idiosyncratic nature of state school systems. On the one hand, among the subregions one could find differences on the thirty-six policy variables fairly often. For example, the states in the Southwest were more centralized than the rest of the nation on eighteen variables and more decentralized on another fifteen. Yet, when we ask how many of these were significantly different, much of this variation washes out. As the last columns of table 4 show, no subregion differed significantly on as many as a third of these thirty-six policy variables. Indeed, the Plains states differed significantly from the other states on only six variables.

These significant variables trace a somewhat different contour of highs and lows in SCSs across the nation. The South and West evidence high centralization in a great S-curve sweeping up from the old Confederacy through the Southwest along the Pacific shore and out to Hawaii. Great decentralization, however, is found only in New England and the Mountain states. Elsewhere, across the middle band of the continent from the Appalachians to the Rockies, the north central region hovers close to the mean for all states.

The reasons for these regional distinctions are not clear at this time, but history plays some part. For example, it is believed that New England has fostered local control of schools as a continuing suspicion against centralized power that stems from the colonial era. That attitude, it is thought, was translated into institutions and augmented by socialization through the generations. On the other hand, in the South, particularly in those states hit hardest by the Civil War, there is a history of centralization. This pattern, it is thought, stems in part from the gutting of local government

TABLE 5

School Centralization Scores on Thirty-six Variables, by Regions and Subregions

Variable	Northeast	New England	Mid-Atlantic	Southeast	Midwest	Great Lakes	Plains	West	Southwest	Mountain	Far West	Mean for All States
Accreditation	-3.90	4.74	-2.90*	+5.70*	4.58	-4.07	+4.94	-3.92	+5.13	-4.30	-2.81	4.50
School calendar	4.21	4.09	+4.35	-3.91	+4.38	4.20	+4.51*	-3.90	-3.68	-3.28	+4.37	4.09
Certification	-4.80*	-4.44	5.24	+5.73*	5.55	+5.76	5.41	+5.77*	+5.82*	5.67	+5.74	5.49
In-service training	-1.63	-1.67	-1.60	+2.59	-1.74	+2.37	-1.29	+2.31	+3.00	2.00	+3.18	2.09
Salary schedule	-3.14	-2.92	3.40	+4.32*	-2.70	+4.59*	-1.36*	-3.06	-3.00	-2.60	+4.00	3.29
Personnel policies	4.24	+4.59*	-3.82	-3.86	+4.44	+4.61	+4.32	4.13	+4.84*	+4.56	-3.95	4.17
School plant	+3.71	3.51	+3.95*	+4.18*	-2.46*	-2.96	-2.10*	-3.16	-2.08	3.34	+4.84*	3.36
School construction and equipment	+4.09	-3.57	+4.71*	-3.33	+3.92	3.78	+4.02	3.75	-2.00*	+5.63*	3.77	3.76
Safety and health standards	4.23	-3.92*	+4.59	+4.92*	4.35	-3.60	+4.89*	-4.04	+4.98*	4.52	-3.21	4.37
Grade organization	+3.81	-3.08	+4.68*	+4.01*	3.37	+3.93	-2.96	-2.57*	-2.65	-1.55*	+5.06*	3.38
Promotion requirements	-0.50*	-0.00*	1.10	+1.45	1.32	+1.96	-0.86	+1.47	+2.25	-0.20*	+1.50	1.21
Course or credit load	+2.89	-1.55	+4.50*	-1.89	-1.87	-0.60*	2.79	+3.83*	+5.50*	-2.40	+3.25	2.69
Pupil records	3.80	-3.11	+4.63*	3.83	-3.16	-3.01	-3.26	+4.00	-2.46	+3.95	+5.07*	3.71
Textbooks	-3.91	-3.52	4.38	+5.03*	-3.78*	-3.52*	-3.97	+4.57	+5.09*	-4.00	+4.69	4.35
Curriculum	-3.97	4.44	-3.40	+4.78*	4.32	-4.22	4.38	4.50	-3.70	4.45	+4.70	4.41
Extra curricular activities	-1.45*	-1.58	-1.30*	+2.66	+3.34*	+3.60	+3.15	2.46	2.45	+2.92	-1.89	2.50
Library	3.59	3.47	+3.73	-3.06	+4.40*	+4.29*	+4.48*	-3.08	-3.00	+3.99	3.57	3.51
Guidance and Counseling	-2.60	-2.52	-2.70	3.14	+3.65	+3.54	+3.73	3.16	-2.87	+3.73	-2.95	3.15
Vocational education	+5.09	+5.12	5.04	+5.49*	-4.40*	-3.77*	4.84	-4.65	5.01	-4.12	-4.40	4.89

Adult education	3.73	3.58	+3.90	+4.34*	-2.86*	-2.62	-3.03	3.61	+4.23	-2.45*	+4.25*	3.63
Special education	4.97	4.93	5.01	+5.38*	-4.82*	-4.63*	4.96	5.14	+5.28*	5.23	4.99	5.09
Experimental programs	+2.50	-1.83	+3.30	+3.54*	-1.72	+3.73	-0.28*	-1.43*	-0.95	-1.32	+2.75	2.24
Pupil-teacher ratio	3.08	-2.87	+3.33	+3.67	+3.92*	+3.64	+4.12	-2.02*	-1.25	-2.10	+3.69	3.11
Attendance requirements	-4.16	-3.51*	+4.94	+4.98*	-4.33	-4.66	-4.30	+4.95	-4.04	4.67	+5.68*	4.64
Admission requirements	-3.15	-2.31*	+4.15	+4.34	+4.03	+5.12*	-3.25	3.73	+4.11	2.87	+4.04	3.82
Graduation requirements	-3.87	-3.46	+4.37	4.20	-3.67	-3.80	-3.58	+4.40*	+4.80*	-3.06	+5.37*	4.06
School district organization	-2.19*	2.12	-2.26	+4.17	+3.81	+4.03	3.66	+3.93	+4.00	-2.00	+5.25*	3.58
Equal educational opportunity	-2.37*	-1.90*	-2.93	3.70	+3.53	+5.27*	-2.29	+3.60	-2.61	-1.90	+5.63*	3.34
Objectives	-2.14*	-2.58	-1.60*	+3.67	+4.21	+5.30*	3.43	3.50	+4.25	3.50	-3.00	3.41
Pupil transportation	-4.17	-3.96	4.42	4.44	-4.12	4.20	-4.06	+4.56	-3.45	+4.67	+4.91	4.34
Financial records	3.60	-2.61*	+4.79	+4.77	-4.00	-3.30	+4.50	+4.55	+5.34*	+4.93*	4.15	4.26
Accountability	+3.37	3.22	+3.53	+4.02	3.10	3.11	3.10	-2.30	+4.25	-1.20*	-1.37	3.14
Evaluation	+3.21	-2.00	+4.67*	-2.81	+3.51	+3.20	3.73	-2.56	+4.25	-1.20	-2.34	2.99
Per pupil expenditure	-1.44*	-1.71	-1.12	2.44	+3.08	+3.19	+3.01	+2.71	+4.22	2.34	-1.50	2.45
Bonds	+1.07	-0.00*	+2.35*	0.50	0.64	-0.00*	+1.09	-0.17*	0.65	-0.00*	-0.00*	0.56
Revenue	-3.12	3.53	-2.62	+4.31	3.62	+4.18	+2.26	-3.28	-3.19	-3.08	+4.44	3.57
Mean	3.27	3.00	3.59	3.87	3.52	3.67	3.41	3.47	3.62	3.16	3.79	3.59

Notes: The scores for the Pacific region are omitted from this table because of the unusual deviation of Hawaii, one state of a two-state set. The scores for the region are included, however, in all reports of means for all states.

- = less than mean SCS for all states by 0.20
+ = more than SCS for all states by 0.20
* indicates a "t" value significant at less than .15.

resources by the Civil War effort, requiring state governments to step in to provide vital services, including education.

A necessary but not sufficient test of these two historical explanations is possible. Table 4 shows how widely disparate these two subregions are, providing the largest difference of any two regions in the set. An even better test is possible by isolating the six states where most of the battles of the Civil War were fought, ostensibly the areas most destroyed by these struggles—Virginia, Tennessee, Mississippi, Alabama, Georgia, and South Carolina. When these six are matched against the six in the New England set, stark differences emerge. The six states of the Confederacy show more centralization on twenty-four policy variables, and less on four. This pattern is reversed in New England, where there is more centralization on two policy variables and less on twenty-four. The Southern set is significantly more centralized than the nation on eleven policies but the New England set on only one, while on seven others New England is more decentralized. The summary SCSs for the two tell the story simply—3.97 as compared with 3.00. Of course, there are limits to the utility of aggregate data as evidence of attitudes about political systems; at best, such data can be only suggestive or supportive, not definitive. Yet, we think these regional data support the existence of a policy culture in some surprisingly large sections of the nation.

Because the concept of regionalism always carries attitudinal components, as well as deposits of historical experiences to which values adhere, the regionalism portrayed in this chapter suggests several inferences about school policy culture. First, one should look to the past for the events, persons, and ideas that founded a state's school system. There is much inertia in policy operations, those "standard operating procedures" that carry a policy system through crises as well as routines. Therefore, what we see today of policy may be but the tip of the historical iceberg, as recent research points out when showing the high correlation between current year expenditures and those of decades earlier. For example, the ranking of the forty-eight states on state support of local school costs in 1900 and in 1966 revealed a rank order coefficient of .605; and on average instructional salaries in 1960 and in 1973 the rank order coefficient was .90.[23] Such signs of system stability, despite the enormous events affecting American education over these time periods, suggest that in examining state and regional patterns we must look first to history. We are badly in need of political histories of state educational systems incorporating on a comparative basis the historical forces of events, persons, and ideas.[24]

Local Consequences of State Centralization

No consideration of the political aspects of education should conclude without reference to the consequences for the life of the school and particularly for the effects on that ultimate client, the pupil. What this chapter suggests has several sides, all centered on the concept of policy culture.

First, "culture" always implies some uniformities of thinking and acting, and school policy culture has been shown here to contain these commonalities. As a result, any examination of the individual school or classroom, particularly if restricted to no more than the local education authority or even to the state, loses much of its explanatory power by such narrow focus. This is the old problem of the singular case study, bound to time or place for its generalizations. This chapter has indicated how states, even clusters of states, act in rather regular ways to structure the delivery of school services.

It follows that what and how much is delivered at the local level, possibly even how it is delivered, are sharply influenced, if not constrained, by state mandate. If so, then the uniformity or variation one experiences at the microlevel of classroom or school site may well be a function of this external factor—the state role. It clearly follows that any effort at generalization about American education based upon a study of the microschool system—classroom, school site, local education agency, and even a state—ignores the differentiation of patterns among all the states.

Second, and more precisely, much of what the local site does

23. Wirt, "State Politics of Education," p. 326.

24. The two volumes by Pearson and Fuller come closest, but they deal only with the twentieth century. For a statement of research needs, see Frederick M. Wirt, "Reassessment Needs in the Study of the Politics of Education." *Teachers College Record*, in press.

educationally may not be capable of effect by local factors. This chapter shows that even among the most decentralized of states or regions (for example, New England), the state still maintains rigid control over major gatekeeping functions, such as accreditation, certification, and attendance requirements. On matters of personnel, administration, and finances, as we have argued elsewhere,[25] the locals may do very little on their own. Local control is hard to distinguish in the data presented in this chapter. In that case, the efforts of parents and educators to improve the quality of their local schools, to influence what goes on in the classroom, may be buffered by the existence of state mandates and minimums, laws, and regulations.

Third, if much of the product that is delivered to the ultimate client, both quantitatively and qualitatively, is shaped by history and by an ongoing state structure of policy, reform efforts directed locally may be misguided. Local policy services are manifestations of state structures for allocating resources and values; trying to move the former without affecting the latter is like throwing an elephant by grabbing first the end of his trunk. Successful systemic reform of state schools has come only through change at the top, whether in the adoption of the professional model of school governance over the political party model, or in the consolidation movement that began after World War I.

If the locus of reform is the district or school site, efforts at reform, even if successful, win only a skirmish; the massive structure beyond it remains unengaged or unaffected. Consequently, much of the local politics of education tends to be episodic.[26] The victories are not always permanent, and the frustration potential for educators and parents seeking better classroom teaching is very high. Too often, then, local politics is a *marginal politics*, a struggle over things at the fringe, with the major decisions about how children will be taught having already been made elsewhere and therefore almost untouchable locally. That may well be the norm in a

25. Wirt and Kirst, *Political and Social Foundations of American Education*, chap. 5.

26. Roscoe C. Martin, *Government and the Suburban School* (Syracuse, N.Y.: Syracuse University Press, 1962); Wirt and Kirst, *Political and Social Foundations of American Education*, chaps. 3-6.

federal system where Dillon's Rule still prevails, and in a decade when the states are growing ever stronger in their efforts to deal with major social problems.

Yet those who believe that participation is the essence of democratic life should note that significant changes are indeed possible in these state policy cultures. Our data do not permit measuring any change, of course, but we know from other observations that states do alter school policy in significant ways. In recent years, states have made major alterations in their financial support, in equal educational opportunities, in students' rights, in teachers' bargaining position, and even in parental participation in local school affairs.[27] Also, because Americans are highly mobile, they are not locked into a particular school system for the lives of their children, and may well move once or twice a decade and thus experience different, maybe even better, local conditions. Certainly there is a surprising variety of state policy cultures in this respect. Sometimes it means no more than moving from New York (SCS = 3.63) to Connecticut (SCS = 2.68).

This picture of uniformities and differences among the states, based upon analysis of legal requirements, should not be confused with the picture of how these requirements are effectuated. The operational picture may be different from that set out here. But again, given the high professionalism of educational services, one would not expect much deviation. Professionalism, after all, is writ large in many of these laws, so that the service provided locally in response to a state mandate reflects what the private profession deems important or necessary. That is also a highly centralizing force in public education, one that should little alter the picture developed here. Indeed, the professional factor may represent a horizontal influence, working across the states, that accomplishes far more centralization of schooling than has been found in this study.

27. For evidence at the state level, see Wirt, "State Politics of Education": for evidence at the local level, see Frederick M. Wirt, "Political Turbulence and Administrative Authority in Schools," in *The New Urban Politics,* ed. Louis Masotti and Robert Lineberry (Boston, Mass.: Ballinger Publishing Co., 1976).

CHAPTER VII

Education and Politics in Large Cities, 1950-1970

NORMAN DRACHLER

Introduction

While the literature of politics and education is the work of a small group of political scientists and educators, the reality of the politics of education in urban areas is obvious to legislators and citizens alike. We are indebted to those scholars who have helped us understand the turmoil of the cities. This chapter seeks to enrich the understanding they have provided by introducing the observations of an administrator who has tried to reflect on his experiences.

Political scientists have noted a series of conditions and practices that limit the school's effectiveness in gaining public support. Among these are: (a) schoolmen pretend that they are not engaged in politics and often deny their involvement, but Bailey reminds them that "invisible politics is rarely good politics";[1] (b) Salisbury attributes some of the school's political and financial difficulties to the insulation of urban school leaders from the world of politics;[2] (c) Mann points out that under the cover of "professionalism" school officials behave in an autonomous manner and do not respond to the democratic rights of the community.[3]

As we assess the above views, two conditions become obvious: (a) a communication gap between political scientists and prac-

---

1. Stephen K. Bailey et al., *Schoolmen and Politics: A Study of State Aid to Education in the Northeast* (Syracuse, N.Y.: Syracuse University Press, 1962, pp. ix-x.

2. Robert H. Salisbury, "Schools and Politics in the Big City," *Harvard Educational Review* 37 (Summer 1967): 409-10.

3. Dale Mann, "Democratic Theory and Public Participation in Educational Policy Decision Making," in *The Polity of the Schools*, ed. Frederick M. Wirt (Lexington, Mass.: D. C. Heath & Co., 1975), p. 9.

titioners, and (b) the failure or reluctance of school practitioners to reflect publicly upon their political involvement.

Iannaccone, an educator who has contributed much to the literature of the politics of education, comments on this gap and expresses concern about those on the outside who are *"in* but not *of* education, safely based outside the public schools, and without the responsibility of action."[4] Kottmeyer, a former St. Louis superintendent, expressed his concern thus:

> A musky college prof flew in.
> (His teaching load was light.)
> "I haven't time to stick around.
> My schedule is awf'fly tight.
> The schools here *must* be obsolete.
> I'll depart and start to write!"[5]

Interviews and questionnaires, although useful, are insufficient to provide insights that fully reflect the issues involved. A scholar using a questionnaire to study community participation, without being enmeshed in the stormy sessions that often occur or in the issues raised, may resemble a groom kissing his bride through a veil—he misses much. Yet, with the growing number of sociopolitical issues, the practitioner needs the expertise of the political scientist.

On the other hand, school administrators who claim that scholars do not recognize the complexities of school governance have contributed little to the literature of educational politics. If practitioners have a theoretical basis for their political behavior, or for an assessment of their political experiences, they have not revealed it.

As a former practitioner, the author seeks to identify some of the political determinants in cities and to relate these to the concerns expressed by the above political scientists. Although the chief focus is upon Detroit, Michigan, other cities will also be examined. In

---

4. Laurence Iannaccone, "Increasing Irresponsibility in Education: A Growing Gap between Policy Planning and Operational Groups," in *State, School, and Politics: Research Directions*, ed. Michael W. Kirst (Lexington, Mass.: D. C. Heath & Co., 1972), p. 194.

5. William Kottmeyer, "Assessing the Establishment," *St. Louis Scorecard* (St. Louis, Mo.: St. Louis Board of Education, 1969), section 6/1.

regard to the findings of the political scientists, these premises are offered:

1. School administrators disclaim partisan involvement, but recognize the realities of political forces. The presence of school lobbyists in state and federal capitals is evidence of this fact. Whether this style of politics will be adequate merits serious exploration.
2. During the 1960s, the historically insulated urban school became the neighborhood city hall for redress of general grievances. Schools became involved in political issues from which politicians fled.
3. The school's history on citizen participation leaves much to be desired. Within the past ten years, however, city schools have involved citizens more than any traditional governmental agency.

A review of the politics of education in cities between 1950 and 1970 must take into account major new social forces and the conditions that brought them into being. Social, economic, political, and educational inequities that had been dormant for decades converged in the cities. This new heterogeneity led to confrontation and conflict and produced new forces that had to be orchestrated for effective educational impact. The encounter of old and new forces shaped the politics of urban education. Schools, the most accessible segment of the establishment, were regarded by the new populace as *the* most critical institution for eradicating their historic injustices. Educators were called upon to compensate for their *own* and *society's* shortcomings.

Whether the school understood its limitations is now a moot question. With divided school boards and staff, and lacking an overall strategy for the challenge ahead, the urban school entered, or was pushed into, the educational-political arena without allies or power. It was a task for which the school was not prepared. But as a democratic institution, it could not resist.

The incapability of the urban school to respond adequately to the challenges of the 1960s was partly due to the major and rapid changes that took place in large cities between 1950 and 1970. The school and city population changed. The new educational needs called for new approaches and programs, and the political power structure was being transformed. Let us examine (a) the demographic changes, (b) the educational needs and responses, and (c) the new politics of education.

Demographic Transformations in Large Cities

The large city of the early 1970s had more unemployment and poverty, more problems of health, housing, and crime, more needs for special services for its old and young residents, more children in school, but *less* political power than did the city of 1950. Those with the greatest needs had fewer economic and political resources to help their children and themselves.

Between 1950 and 1970 the large cities of the nation experienced several major demographic transformations that had significant political implications.

1. The exodus of the young but established middle-class white families and the in-migration of poor families from rural areas, Puerto Rico, Mexico, or the South diminished the city's political influence.
2. Due to the burgeoning population growth of the suburbs, the proportion of cities to their metropolitan areas dropped from 58.5 percent in 1950, to 44.6 percent by 1970.[6] This proportional shift of the population, coupled with the "one man, one vote" principle established during the 1960s, further reduced the political capability of cities.[7] Detroit's representation in the Michigan House of Representatives dropped from twenty-six members in 1960 to twenty-one by 1970, and the Senate seats declined from nine to seven.
3. Blacks in cities increased from 6.6 million in 1950 to 13.1 million by 1970, a growth of 99 percent, whereas the white population during this same period grew by only 5.5 percent, from 46.7 million to 49.4 million.[8] Most of the white growth was in the South and Southwest. Whites in Detroit declined from 83.6 per-

6. Raymond C. Hummel and John M. Nagle, *Urban Education in America* (New York: Oxford University Press, 1973), p. 61.

7. See *New York Times*, 20 June 1970, p. 54, and 12 April 1971, p. 1. See also, Robert A. Goldwin, ed., *Representation and Misrepresentation* (Chicago: Rand McNally & Co., 1968), p. 74.

8. Hummel and Nagle, *Urban Education in America*, p. 75.

cent in 1950 to 55.5 percent by 1970.[9] Detroit's growing black population represented over 65 percent of the schools' enrollment by 1970, but a large portion was poor, constantly moving, and required time before it could begin to assert its political influence. Schools lacked cohorts to exercise power in the political arena.

4. Between 1960 and 1970 the rate of increase of black youth between ages fifteen and twenty-four in cities was generally double the growth rate in the state for the same age group. Thus, black youth in New York City in that age group increased by 105 percent whereas the increase for the state of New York was 45 percent. The corresponding figures for Detroit and the state of Michigan were 121 percent and 56 percent respectively.[10]

5. Another factor affecting schools was the increase in the number of citizens sixty-five and over in cities. In 1970 nearly 15 million of the nation's 20 million citizens sixty-five and over resided in cities.[11] They were largely white, their children and grandchildren lived in the suburbs, and their personal concerns such as low taxes, medical services, and safety outweighed their interest in supporting schools. Detroit's populace sixty-five and over grew from 5.4 percent of the total in 1950 to 17.5 percent by 1970.[12] These senior citizens, a majority of whom were white, became a political force by 1970.

6. The decline of employment began in the 1950s and increased during the next decade.[13] Welfare needs and aid to dependent children competed with educational needs.[14]

7. Most indicators of poor health, such as premature birth (the

9. U.S. Department of Commerce, Bureau of the Census, *General Demographic Trends for Metropolitan Areas, 1960-1970* (Washington, D.C.: U.S. Government Printing Office, 1971).

10. Ibid.

11. Ibid.

12. Ibid.

13. Raymond Vernon. *The Changing Economic Functions of the Central City* (New York: Committee for Economic Development, 1959), pp. 30-31.

14. August C. Bolino, *Manpower in the City* (Cambridge, Mass.: Shenkman Publishing Co., 1969), pp. 30-31.

prime cause of mental retardation),[15] maternal and infant mortality,[16] deaths due to tuberculosis,[17] and defective housing,[18] were higher in cities than in the nation.

8. Between 1959 and 1964 ten of the fourteen largest cities reported that their tax base per pupil had declined.[19] With the tax rate yielding less than in previous years, the city's political activities at the local and state level increased. Although the tax rate had remained the same, Detroit schools lost over $40 million between 1960 and 1966.[20]

The admonitions of Conant and others in the early 1960s about the "social dynamite" in our cities were not heeded by society, and between 1965 and 1968 Watts, Newark, Detroit, and other cities exploded. The author recorded on transparencies several of Detroit's vital statistics for the year 1968: the areas with the highest incidence of infant mortality, of deaths due to tuberculosis, and of homicides, and the areas with lowest educational achievement and income. When the transparencies were placed one on top of the other, they overlapped at the exact geographic area that was the site of Detroit's 1967 riot.[21]

The demographic transformation of the city brought about a poorer and more divided population. The city had more needs, less funds, and too much conflict over priorities to reach agreement. Contrasting sets of values permeated the city's dwellers. The white

15. Welfare Administration, U.S. Department of Health, Education, and Welfare, *Cities in Crisis* (Washington, D.C.: U.S. Government Printing Office, 1967), p. 32.

16. Herbert C. Birch and Joan D. Gussow, *Disadvantaged Children* (New York: Harcourt Brace & World, 1970), p. 40; Department of Health, City of Detroit, *City Data Book, 1972* (Detroit, Mich.: City of Detroit, 1972), p. 28.

17. *City Data Book, 1972*, p. 58.

18. *Cities in Crisis*, p. 11.

19. Research Council of the Great Cities, *The Challenge of Financing Public Schools in Great Cities* (Chicago: Research Council of the Great Cities, 1964).

20. *Annual Financial Report of the Detroit Board of Education of the City of Detroit, 1970* (Detroit, Mich.: Detroit Board of Education, 1970), p. 5.

21. Norman Drachler, in *Hearings before the Select Committee on Equal Educational Opportunity of the U.S. Senate*, 92nd Congress, 2nd Session (Washington, D.C.: U.S. Government Printing Office, 1971), pp. 9681-86.

community felt that too much was being allocated for the blacks; the blacks were discouraged about their children's education; and the aged believed both that the schools could do with less and that they had already completed their obligation to the schools. The divisions were along racial, economic, and age needs, which often transcended political alignments. Leaders of the United Auto Workers Union, an ally of the Detroit schools in all tax campaigns, confirmed the opposition of its retirees to increased school taxes.

Educational Implications in an Age of Anxiety

The decades following World War II were years of unrest and anxiety in education. It was the era of Sputnik with its stress on science and the "new" mathematics, phonics, and "why Johnny can't read." Then the social-educational issues followed: the *Brown* decision and the neighborhood school, equal educational opportunity and *Serrano*, and compensatory education accompanied by accountability, performance contracts, and vouchers. The books of the period reflected the ferment and often implied the approach of an apocalyptic age: *The Transformation of the School, Slums and Suburbs, Death at an Early Age, How Children Fail, Crisis in the Classroom*, and *De-schooling Society*. Schools everywhere were affected by an avalanche of criticism—but urban schools became the major target. In the city, where the criticism was most poignant, the political activities around the school and educational issues became more intense.

Public school enrollment. Although public school enrollment in recent years has been declining, the school population in fifteen cities increased from 2.7 million in 1950 to 4.1 million by 1965. The enrollments in Houston schools grew during this period by 133.7 percent and in Los Angeles by 103 percent. In 1970, fifteen cities accounted for 10 percent of the nation's public schools, with New York City having 2.5 percent of the country's school population. Thirty cities had over 40 percent minority children in their schools by 1970, and Washington, D.C. had a black enrollment of 96 percent.[22]

22. Hummel and Nagle, *Urban Education in America;* Research Council of the Great Cities, *The Challenge of Financing Public Schools in Great Cities;* Recruitment Leadership and Training Institute, *Minorities in Policymaking Positions in Public Education* (Philadelphia, Pa.: Temple University, 1974).

School personnel. Throughout the 1960s substandard teaching certificates were held by 80,000 to 100,000 teachers, many of whom were in cities.[23] But the city had other unique personnel concerns: the hiring of minority applicants for teaching and other positions; the development of policies that would enable young, particularly minority teachers, to move up more quickly in the school bureaucracy; the integration of staff, which called for challenging the seniority system; and designing programs that would improve understanding, skills, and attitudes toward the new clientele. Although cities increased minority staff members by 1970, the discrepancy, particularly in the case of Hispanic educators, between the percent of minority students and the percent of minority staff, especially in key administrative positions, still prevailed.[24]

Student mobility. During periods of unemployment, the city's children, particularly its poor, move a great deal into, out of, and within the city. They have little feeling of belonging or stability. In 1969 the rate of pupils entering elementary schools after the fall enrollment was 10 percent for the nation and 21 percent for cities.[25] New York, Baltimore, and other cities reported annually tens of thousands of pupils moving in and out of the schools between 1950 and 1970.[26] Detroit, with nearly 300,000 students in 1969-70, reported a mobility rate of 40 percent, and each year its Attendance Department made approximately 130,000 inquiries about absence, poverty, and health.[27] Transiency was hardest upon the children

---

23. Richard H. Barr and Betty J. Foster, *Statistics of Public Elementary and Secondary Day Schools* (Washington, D.C.: U.S. Government Printing Office, 1969) p. 12.

24. Recruitment Leadership and Training Institute, *Minorities in Policy-making Positions in Public Education*, p. 41.

25. National Center for Educational Statistics, *Pupil Mobility in Public Schools during the 1969-70 School Year* (Washington, D.C.: U.S. Government Printing Office, 1973), p. 8.

26. Joseph Justman and Lucy A. Brancato, "Pupil Migration in the New York City Schools, 1955-56 to 1964-65," Report no. EPRS-PUB-264 (Brooklyn, N.Y.: New York City Board of Education, 1965), ED 018 485; *One Hundred and Twenty-eighth Report of School Commissioners of Baltimore City to the Mayor and City Council* (Baltimore, Md.: Board of School Commissioners, 1968).

27. Drachler, *Hearings,* pp. 9691-93.

and teachers, but it also impeded efforts in school-community relations.

Special education. The schools' new clientele had a greater need for special educational services. Six cities in New York State, with 40 percent of the state's public school enrollment, accounted for 54 percent of the state's handicapped children, 73 percent of pupils from poverty families, 83 percent of the state's pupils receiving aid for dependent children, and 90 percent of the state's full-time vocational students.[28] A similar condition was reported for Rhode Island.[29] In 1969-70, if Detroit were to have provided for each child in need of special services, an additional $34 million would have been required for that year.[30]

School housing. The city's growing enrollment, obsolescent buildings, and mobility exacerbated the problem of school space. Shifts in boundaries or in transporting students, with integration as a criterion, aggravated already strained relationships. Costs for buildings escalated and the task of convincing white middle-class citizens, who had become increasingly insecure, to vote for new funds became increasingly difficult. The cost per acre for land in the fourteen largest cities between 1958 and 1963 ranged from $5,692 in Houston to $197,841 in New York City. The average cost per acre for nonurban schools where these fourteen cities were located was $3,074.[31]

Educational achievement. Due to the impact of federal aid, the city school of the 1960s had more experimental programs and services than in any previous decade. Yet, reading scores continued to drop among the poor. The Froomkin study reported that in 1970, 17 percent of the nation's children and 20 percent of the city's

---

28. *Conference of Large City Boards of Education,* Louis A. Cerulli, chairman (Albany, N.Y., 1968), p. 4.

29. Charles S. Benson and James A. Kelly, *Consultants' Review and Report on the Rhode Island Comprehensive Foundation and Enhancement State Aid Program for Education* (Providence, R.I.: Rhode Island Special Commission to Study the Entire Field of Education, December 1966).

30. Norman Drachler, "The Large-City School System: It Costs More To Do the Same," in *Equity for Cities in School Finance Reform* (Washington D.C.: Potomac Institute, 1973), p. 36.

31. Research Council of the Great Cities, *The Challenge of Financing Public Schools in Great Cities.*

youngsters had reading problems.[32] This decade witnessed a succession of programs: for the culturally *deprived* and later (as we became more sensitive) for the culturally *different*, Head Start, Schools without Walls, and others. Detroit reported fifty-seven research projects in 1960-61.[33] Yet, in 1969, the U.S. Commissioner of Education established the Right to Read program as a tragic reminder that the challenge had not been met. Right to Read was an educational program with the overtones of a political manifesto. Its educational and political outcomes were demands for accountability, more minority teachers, cultural pluralism in the curriculum, bilingual education, vouchers, and competency-based teacher certification.

Cremin credits the public schools with contributing to the nation's development, despite our heterogeneity. But he points out that when the school succeeded, it was due to other complementary institutions. In regard to cities he states:

> When the configuration has disintegrated, however, as it has from time to time in our large cities, and when the centrifugal forces of heterogeneity have overbalanced the centrifugal forces of community, the public school has been less successful. My assertion is not the powerlessness of public schooling—far from it—but rather the limitations of public schooling. And the moral is simple: The public school ought never to take the entire credit for the educational accomplishments of the public, and it ought never be assigned the entire blame.[34]

Although the author shares Cremin's views and recognizes the accomplishments of many teachers and administrators who labor under very difficult conditions, he believes that, historically, the educational profession has not measured up to its full obligations. For example,

1. The school has not within its own structure, nor within the com-

---

32. Joseph Froomkin, J. R. Endriss, and Robert W. Stump, *Estimates and Projections of Special Target Group Populations in Elementary and Secondary Public Schools: A Report to the President's Commission on School Finance* (Washington, D.C.: Joseph Froomkin, Inc., 1972), p. 3.

33. S. M. Brownell, *The Pursuit of Excellence* (Detroit, Mich.: Detroit Board of Education, 1966).

34. Lawrence A. Cremin, "Public Education and the Education of the Public," *Teachers College Record* 77 (September 1975): 7.

munity, engaged in an ongoing dialogue on the goals of education.
2. Research, planning and policy, and staff development have not been given the priority that society's changes demanded.
3. Recently there have been initiatives to involve teachers, principals, and parents in educational planning, but the process still lacks depth and widespread acceptance. If parents are apathetic, possibly our past practices have contributed to this condition.
4. Although next to children, teachers and administrators suffer most from incompetent staff, the profession has not developed objective instruments to measure the effectiveness of its staff.
5. Teaching, as it presently functions, is not an adequate preparation for today's adult relationships. Teachers are fairly autonomous and loners. Reorganization of the teaching experience to involve teachers with their colleagues and other adults is essential.
6. A major deficit of education has been its historic disregard of our pluralistic society. We trained teachers who are insensitive to our clients' culture and produced texts that distorted their past.
7. Thus, when schools encountered an adversary society, we faltered in our efforts. Schools were not alone in this failing, for other professions shared this condition, but we had an obligation to be better prepared since the school has a limited or fixed time-space, and since education is compulsory.

The above concerns apply, of course, to schools everywhere. The city's crisis was more imminent and called for more immediate and effective response.

The demographic changes and their educational demands called for extraordinary political leadership to meet the city's needs. By 1970 the city's schools were a far cry from those of 1965: efforts for integration increased, more minority staff (over 40 percent in Detroit) existed, some sensitivity to pluralism appeared, advisory and concerned parent councils appeared at board meetings, and even reading scores improved slightly. But progress was not quick enough nor sufficient to stem the tide of discontent. There were some governmental and educational leaders who sought to chart new courses for the city, but as one student of urban life observed, they "found themselves overwhelmed and swept aside by forces over which they had no control."[35]

It was a period when current grievances mingled with historic injustices and appeared as one. Politically the city had to respond to the present and to history.

Political Implications

Nearly a century ago, Josiah Strong observed that "the city is the nerve center of our civilization. It is also the storm center." The accumulated discontent and frustration of decades surfaced in the cities during the 1960s. The black and brown newcomers were not the docile immigrants of earlier generations. Buttressed by congressional acts and court decisions that underscored their plight due to discrimination and frustrated by the apathy or racism of society, they vigorously asserted their constitutional rights. Equal educational opportunity was no longer a textbook slogan; it became the people's platform for social, economic, and political reform. Riis's prediction of 1902 that "the whole battle with the slum is to be fought out in and around the public school" came alive in the 1960s.[36] The neighborhood school became the people's "city hall."

Many of the new immigrants who came to the cities after World War II had fled from poverty, discrimination, and educational deprivation. They arrived with high hopes. However, as the previous pages have indicated, they found unemployment, poor living conditions, and inadequate educational services. The continued flight to the suburbs by business and the middle class further exacerbated the city's plight.

Abandoned and alienated, the new city dwellers focused upon schools as a means for improving their way of life. First integration and then decentralization became drives for better education. To achieve these goals political power was essential.

In the new politics, precedent was no longer a guide. Educational leaders had to acquire new antennas in order to be sensitive to the political climate that was evolving. Decision or indecision on an

---

35. Robert Conot, *American Odyssey* (New York: William Morrow & Co., 1974), p. 616.

36. Jacob Riis, *The Battle with the Slum* (New York: Macmillan Co., 1902), p. 404.

issue could stir up a storm. Compromise, the art of politics, did not operate as polarization increased. Whenever a board of education in a large city voted four to three upon a major issue, one could anticipate that at least a quarter of a million citizens would be dissatisfied.

The politics of education in large cities during the late 1960s and early 1970s was different from that of the decade immediately following World War II. Yet the decade from 1945 to 1955 paved the way for the educational politics in the decades that followed. The early 1950s were concerned with basic education, the controversy over phonics in the reading program, and the influence of progressive education upon American schools. The attacks upon American education came generally from citizens with more conservative ideologies. The citizens advisory committees that developed during the 1950s involved parents in education on a scale larger than ever before—and probably served as a transition to the politics of education in the 1960s and 1970s. Let us examine this earlier period and trace its impact upon the decades that followed.

CITIZENS ADVISORY COMMITTEES

As cities began to change in the post-World War II period, some boards of education and superintendents recognized that closer contacts with the various power groups in the school district would help to identify educational concerns and needs. The answer was the citizens advisory committee and the model was the National Citizens Commission for the Public Schools of the early 1950s. The Commission defended the schools against charges of subversive teaching and against accusations that the schools were engaging in unwarranted practices in the name of progressive education. It also became a friendly agent for involving citizens in the improvement of schools.[37] Over a period of fifteen years, committees were formed in Atlanta, Boston, New York, Los Angeles, Denver, San Francisco, Philadelphia, Detroit, and elsewhere.[38] Let us look at Detroit.

Between 1957 and 1968 the Detroit Board of Education initiated

---

37. See Association for Supervision and Curriculum Development, *Forces Affecting American Education: 1953 Yearbook* (Washington, D.C.: National Educational Association, 1953).

38. Luvern L. Cunningham and Raphael O. Nystrand, *Citizen Participation in School Affairs* (Washington, D.C.: Urban Coalition, 1969).

and appointed three major citizens committees to examine the schools and make recommendations to the board for educational changes. The first, in 1957, was influenced by Hunter's then recent study on decision makers and included members from industry, labor, the Parent-Teacher Association, the League of Women Voters, the National Association for the Advancement of Colored People, and others.[39] There were also regional committees. Few challenged the membership on the city-wide committee of some who lived outside the city.

A review of the three committees indicates that (a) more residents, particularly blacks, were included in later committees; (b) the staff was wary of citizens being involved in professional matters; (c) the first committee "thanked" the board for being involved and the third declared that it would not disband until its recommendations were implemented; and (d) each committee felt at first that not all of its recommendations were fully implemented, but at a later date noted some progress due to its efforts.

Some of the effects of the work of the committees were: the focus by media upon school issues; changes in school organization, top-level staff, and programs; utilization by parents and staff of the committee recommendations to support their demands; the passage of the only Detroit bond issue and a major tax election victory; and policy changes affecting minorities.

Generally, where the membership of the committee was representative and its independence preserved, the impact was positive. School boards that were prepared "to open the books," able "to stand the heat," and wise enough not "to jump the gun" with recommendations of their own while the committee was still at work, gained from the process. Cunningham and his associates, in their studies of citizen participation in thirteen cities, found some shortcomings but judged the experience important and valuable.[40]

As the 1960s drew to a close, the aura of a city-wide committee faded. Parents were no longer impressed with a blue ribbon com-

---

39. Floyd Hunter, *Community Power Structure: A Study of Decision Makers* (Chapel Hill, N.C.: University of North Carolina Press, 1953).

40. Cunningham and Nystrand, *Citizen Participation in School Affairs.*

mittee report. The new climate called for the resolution of problems at the local school level. The earlier citizens advisory committee had made its contribution to the children of the city—it may still be applicable for macro issues affecting education—but the issues affecting individual schools could not be decided on the basis of a general city-wide polity, and the local school became an active partner. A new trend in urban politics appeared.

BOARDS OF EDUCATION AND URBAN LEADERSHIP

The transformation of the city altered its leadership. In 1961 the *Harvard Business Review* published the results of a survey in which it was found that only 27 percent of the business executives who worked in the ten largest cities lived in those cities. The article concluded that the larger the city "the smaller the proportion of executives responding who work and live in that city."[41] Professionals also moved from the city and a new leadership had to be formed.

Large cities that are often the home base of major industrial institutions generally find that these corporations regard themselves as national or international institutions and have little involvement with the city's cultural or educational concerns. They are *in* but not *of* the city. There are few cultural landmarks that represent their presence. A man from Mars visiting Detroit would not know that this was the center of the auto industry, except for a few schools named Ford, Chrysler, and Kettering, or a music hall named Ford Auditorium.

It took the riot of 1967 to create the New Detroit Committee, when for the first time in the city's history the chairmen of General Motors, Ford, and Chrysler, and the heads of utilities, the head of the United Auto Workers, the school superintendent, and several leaders from the inner city sat together in the same room to assess the city's needs.

These changes in leadership also affected boards of education. In cities with appointed boards, membership was no longer a reward for a distinguished citizen. Regardless of the method of appoint-

41. George Sternlieb, "Is Business Abandoning the Big City?" *Harvard Business Review* 39 (January-February 1961): 8.

ment, boards became more representative of the city's pluralistic composition.[42]

In cities where elections took place, a change also occurred. Competition became more spirited as labor, ethnics, teacher groups, and others supported candidates or slates. A newspaper endorsement no longer carried its former power. The new breed of board member was generally not close to the top business or political power structure. Black membership, although still underrepresented, increased between 1968 and 1971.[43]

During this period, the white Protestant homogeneity of the board disappeared, as blacks, Jews, Catholics, and labor representatives were elected. No longer did a board leave major policies to the superintendent, whose former professional role was altered. The new board reflected the divisiveness of the city. Differences over integration, church and state, collective bargaining, and allocations for school construction became obvious. A resolution against a company that allegedly discriminated against labor split the board and antagonized the press. A decision not to renew a Title I contract with the city symphony became a stormy public issue, when a board member pointed out that the absence of minority artists in the orchestra was a breach of the board's affirmative action policy.

Board members became aware that they were ignored by top governmental officials. There were public meetings where the mayor or governor acknowledged or introduced elected officials from drain commissioner to senator, but ignored elected board members. These acts, although minor, stiffened board members' independence and caused them to suspect and resent some government officials. In turn, they began to assert themselves more vigorously at meetings and to the media. On occasions board members suggested the services of a press relations bureau for the board and superintendent. One Detroit board member initiated an annual dinner in which *he* reported to the people on educational issues.

42. See Joseph M. Cronin, *The Control of Urban Schools* (New York: Free Press, 1973) and National School Boards Association, *Survey of Public Education in Big Cities* (Evanston, Ill.: National School Boards Association, 1968 and 1972).

43. National School Boards Association, *Survey of Public Education in Big Cities, 1972*, pp. 32-39.

The school superintendent of Detroit was evidently regarded by political leaders as either impartial or barren politically. When the two major gubernatorial candidates in Michigan agreed to a public debate, it probably was no accident that the Detroit superintendent was invited to chair the debate.

COLLECTIVE BARGAINING

The advent of collective bargaining affected both the leadership and the politics of the school. In the early stages, when competing teacher groups were vying for power, contenders had to outdo one another to assure their constituents that they would be formidable opponents when confronting management. If one said the superintendent was a "rascal," the competing group had to say, "yes, and his father was too." Most large cities had from ten to twenty bargaining groups.

When negotiations began, teachers and management had to assure their respective publics that each was acting in the public interest. Accusations flew back and forth, while the real problem was a shortage of funds. When a strike occurred, polarization was inevitable. Students and parents voiced their views along with the media and others. When schools were reopened, wounds and scars resulting from the encounter required time for healing. Principals had to be retrained to deal legally and effectively with teachers' building representatives. Collective bargaining also occurred in smaller districts, but the conflict in cities received wide attention and escalated the city's problems in the eyes of the public.

There were other political factors that entered into collective bargaining. Large cities have many labor unions that in the past supported schools in tax elections and at the state legislature. Alienation could mean the loss of support and the refusal of other unions to cross picket lines with deliveries or repairs. Then there were those who demanded tough action and reprisals against strikers. Former political coalitions could be lost during a strike. The school board and the superintendent were tossed between Scylla and Charybdis.

The section on school tax elections that follows reflects the political difficulties faced by an independent school district. By 1963 attitudes on the part of the white population that had formerly supported schools changed. A belief was expressed by many white voters that "everything went to them" (the "them" meaning blacks and poor). The poor and the black continued to support the schools but they were not politically effective to overcome the resistance of the white middle class.

SCHOOL TAX ELECTIONS

Students of school tax elections generally relate their failure or success to campaign strategy, the satisfaction or dissatisfaction of voters with schools, or the public's reaction to collective bargaining. We lack data to assess the impact of collective bargaining since it is new. We do know that tax elections were lost long before negotiations appeared on the school agenda.

The Gallup Poll on school tax elections offers little comfort to cities. It predicts that the poorer the voter, the less education he has, the more voters over fifty years of age with no children in school, and the larger the attendance in parochial schools, the more likely a "no" vote.[44]

There are other factors that need to be considered. Until 1963 the Detroit white middle class and blacks, particularly in the inner city, supported school tax elections. An exception was northeast Detroit with its many private schools and aged people. In 1963, however, the northwest section of the city stopped its support. Whether this change on the part of white voters was due to dissatisfaction with the schools, the growing racial tensions, or both, was not clear, but the trend continued.

Starting in 1963, we noted the phenomenon that voters in areas where there were schools with high educational achievement voted "no," whereas voters in areas where schools showed low achievement voted "yes." The black and white poor, the "yes" voters, had their complaints, but their support continued.

Table 1 shows the voting patterns in two school tax referendums in Detroit, in 1966 when the referendum won and in 1968 when it lost.[45] The voting pattern is broken down by high school constel-

44. Stanley Elam, ed., *The Gallup Polls of Attitudes toward Education, 1969-1973* (Bloomington, Ind.: Phi Delta Kappa, 1973).

45. Detroit Public Schools, *Report of Vote, November 8, 1968, with Comparative Figures for November 8, 1966* (Detroit, Mich.: Detroit Public Schools, 1969).

TABLE 1
Vote in Millage Referendums of 1966 and 1968 in Detroit, Michigan (in percent)

November 3, 1966				November 5, 1968			
High School Constellation	Votes Cast[1]	Yes Votes	Blank Votes[2]	High School Constellation	Votes Cast[1]	Yes Votes	Blank Votes[2]
Up to 25 percent Negro				Up to 25 percent Negro			
Cody	65.2	41.6	14.1	Cody	80.5	23.1	14.6
Denby[3]	65.8	36.4	13.6	Denby	82.3	21.6	14.6
Finney	62.6	46.0	16.4	Ford	80.5	29.8	11.4
Ford[3]	65.4	50.6	11.7	Redford	80.2	30.0	11.3
Osborn	66.1	34.6	15.5				
Redford[3]	63.3	50.6	11.1				
25 to 75 percent Negro				25 to 75 percent Negro			
Chadsey	65.5	46.4	30.3	Chadsey	81.6	32.1	35.4
Cooley	64.8	48.6	13.7	Cooley	79.3	32.3	16.8
Mackenzie	60.7	55.6	23.0	Finney	80.0	31.3	27.3
Murray-Wright	49.4	72.5	41.7	Murray-Wright	68.9	63.2	52.3
Pershing	66.9	17.5	28.0	Osborn	82.2	21.0	21.8
Southeastern	56.1	56.3	32.8	Pershing	81.3	31.5	30.5
Southwestern	60.5	56.9	33.6	Southeastern	72.2	42.8	38.4
Western	57.3	56.1	38.5	Southwestern	78.9	38.1	39.5
				Western	76.0	40.7	46.1
75 percent Negro and over				75 percent Negro and over			
Central	59.9	79.3	37.7	Central	78.9	66.0	47.4
Kettering	60.1	55.9	35.8	Kettering	77.7	42.8	45.6
King	59.7	74.3	41.8	King	77.6	63.7	48.1
Mumford	64.2	66.5	24.3	Mackenzie	76.9	41.9	32.4
Northeastern	58.3	62.8	49.5	Mumford	78.3	50.3	32.0
Northern	58.5	80.6	46.0	Northeastern	75.5	52.2	56.8
Northwestern	60.3	80.0	42.0	Northern	76.2	67.8	54.2
				Northwestern	80.6	66.0	55.0
Total	61.9	54.0	26.6	Total	78.8	37.5	32.3

Source: Detroit Public Schools

[1] Percent of registered voters who came to the polls. There was a presidential election in 1968.

[2] Blank votes represent the percent of voters who entered the booth but did not record a vote on the school issue. Generally, the poorer the area, the higher the blank vote.

[3] Negro enrollment in these areas was primarily due to an open enrollment policy and not to residence.

lations, with the percent of black students generally reflecting the racial distribution of the voters in those constellations.

The voting patterns of Detroit and St. Louis do not bear out the national predictions of Gallup nor the rationale of political scientists.[46] Several general facets of school tax elections need to be related to cities.

1. Americans, as other nationals, dislike paying taxes and distrust the tax disburser.
2. The school tax is the one major tax bill that citizens can accept or reject. It is difficult to determine whether one opposes schools or additional taxes. To date Congress has not asked the people to approve an increase in income tax. We lack comparisons.
3. In theory, a school tax election is desirable since it provides a forum for accountability. In practice, nearly half of the eligible voters do not come to the polls; a large segment of the active voters are primarily concerned with keeping taxes down; and the issues of quality are replaced with rumors and charges of extravagance or threats by school officials to cut services.
4. In a heterogeneous city, with racial divisions and high concentrations of senior citizens, a school tax victory is more difficult.
5. The large city is burdened by higher overall tax rates than its suburbs. In 1973-74, the total municipal tax rate for Detroit was 88.83 mills, of which 22.5 were for school operation. In the surrounding thirteen highest-achieving school districts, the total tax ranged from 47 to 56 mills, with a low of 26 mills and a high of 32 mills for school operation.[47]
6. A school tax election must be examined for what it is, a pocketbook concern. In 1972 Detroit lost three tax elections. In desperation, the state legislature gave the Detroit Board of Education the right to impose a one percent income tax *without* a vote of the people. With income tax, individual taxpayers bear a greater burden of the tax; with property tax, industry bears the greater burden. For a fourth time the Board of Education placed the formerly defeated request for an increase in the property tax on the ballot. It assured the city that if the tax proposal passed, the income tax would not be levied, and each property owner would save approximately $35. The property tax increase passed

46. Kottmeyer, "Assessing the Establishment," section 1.

47. Detroit Public Schools, Office of Research, Planning, and Evaluation, *Comparison of Ability to Tax, Per Pupil Expenditures, and Educational Impact for Detroit, Other Michigan Districts over 25,000 Pupils* (Detroit, Mich.: Detroit Public Schools, 1975).

by a very large margin. A school strike was taking place during the election.[48]

7. The most economical car produced in Detroit has more concern for the consumer than does the voting machine. The auto informs its user whether he needs gas or oil, or if his handbrake is on. But a voter accustomed to a paper ballot is bewildered by the complexity of the machine. There is no electronic device to alert him as to whether he has voted on all candidates and issues. Thousands of voters, primarily the poor, leave the voting booth thinking that they have completed voting. In 1963, 20 percent of Detroit's voters failed to register a vote on the adoption of the new state constitution. On the school tax issue 26.6 percent in 1966 and 32.3 percent in 1968 failed to record their vote. The latter election, in a presidential year, with many more candidates and issues on the ballot, had a blank vote that totaled 197,000 out of a vote of 610,000.[49] In this election the blank vote was not large enough to alter the outcome, but in others the result would have turned the defeat into a victory since most of the blank votes were in areas where school support was high.

8. A study of the 1972 school tax elections revealed that the support for the Detroit schools in black affluent areas was decreasing.[50]

After completing a series of studies on school finance in large cities, H. Thomas James announced what he thought was the "most significant generalization" to come out of those studies:

> That generalization was that local property tax-paying ability was the major determinant of the social policy for public education and that unless we could reverse that relationship and let social policy determine what should be spent for education, we would have deep trouble in our schools.[51]

48. *Proceedings of the Board of Education of the City of Detroit*, September 25, 1973, p. 159.

49. Detroit Public Schools, *Report of Vote, November 8, 1968*.

50. School Finance Task Force, *Detroit: An Urban School System in Crisis* (Syracuse, N.Y.: Syracuse University Research Corp., 1973).

51. Quoted by Joel S. Berke, Alan K. Campbell, and Robert J. Goettel, *Financing Equal Educational Opportunity: Alternatives for State Finance* (Berkeley, Calif: McCutchan Publishing Corp., 1972), p. 7.

James's warning about the future of school finance is evident in such cases as *Serrano* and *Rodriguez*, which confirm his conclusion.

The author has participated in school tax elections for nearly thirty years, in periods of recession and prosperity. As far as he can recall, there never was a year when community leaders said to the board of education, "This is a good year to ask for a tax increase."

DESEGREGATION AND DECENTRALIZATION

Desegregation and decentralization, the two most politicized and publicized issues in urban education, are direct outcomes of the transformation of the city and its educational concerns. The *Brown* decision did not stem the trend toward segregation, particularly in northern cities. Efforts such as open enrollment, the Princeton Plan, magnet schools, and educational parks failed with the flight of the white families from the cities.

The setback in desegregation was followed by the war against poverty of the 1960s with its thrust by the federal government to improve the quality of life, particularly education, among the poor. Despite the floundering by schools in the early years of the Elementary School Education Act and some mismanagement by federal agencies, the effect upon educational achievement after several years was positive, although limited. By 1975 Model City schools in Detroit were informed that their compensatory aid stipend would be less due to the educational progress made.[52]

There were yet more significant gains from the war against poverty. Citizen participation by the poor in various educational and other governmental agencies helped to shape and arouse a politically conscious, organized, and assertive citizenry. With growing frustration over continued poverty, segregation, and slow educational progress, demands for decentralization increased. The quest for community control had educational, economic, and political motivations.

Detroit's similarity to New York City, where decentralization was approved by the state legislature in 1969, the growing participation by blacks in Detroit and Michigan politics, and the historic

52. *Detroit News*, 6 October 1975.

rural distrust of bigness in the state legislature eased the passage of decentralization for Detroit in 1969. The 1967 citizens advisory committee had recommended to the board that parent advisory committees be established for each region, but board members lacked confidence in local advisory groups and could not agree upon any plan submitted by the superintendent's staff. Instead the board supported the superintendent's ongoing plan for administrative decentralization.

In 1969 the Michigan legislature enacted, without any major dissent, a decentralization bill for the Detroit schools. The author of the bill had consulted with the Detroit Board of Education and the Detroit Teachers' Union. He included provisions requested by the union and left the development of the regional guidelines to the board, which consisted then of four white members and three blacks. The Detroit board did not support or oppose the bill.

The majority of the Detroit board agreed upon three criteria: (a) to abide by the guidelines for establishing regions; (b) to observe the principle of one man, one vote; and (c) to establish, insofar as possible, integrated regions. The latter two criteria were adopted by the board majority and were not in the original bill. After a series of public hearings the board faced the task of forming the regions. Meanwhile one member, an influential black, became seriously ill, leaving the board with six members. During the deliberations, two white members supported compact white and black regions, since this viewpoint was supported by the majority of black and white spokesmen at the hearings. Three members, two white and one black, were committed to integrated regions, and the sixth board member, a black who supported community control concepts, stated that he would like to support an integrated plan, but only if it produced integrated schools within the regions. If this could not be achieved, he would vote with the two members who supported segregated regions. The superintendent and staff then developed a plan that integrated a number of high schools and the fourth vote was won.

On April 7, 1970, when the board officially approved the plan by a four to two vote, the vast majority of nearly forty speakers opposed the plan. Only one black was among those who were in opposition. Support for the board majority came from the Michigan

Civil Rights Commission, the American Civil Liberties Union, the NAACP, the PTA Council, the Detroit Urban League, and some other groups.[53]

Although the integration plan involved only about 3,000 white and black high school students per year, out of a high school enrollment of 54,000, it aroused greater opposition in the white community than had been anticipated by the staff or board. The combined forces of protesting white citizens and white students, the sudden appearance of racist literature in the city, and the political sensitivity of legislators running for office that year threatened the decision of the board. Citizens started a recall movement against the four members who had supported the plan, students in white high schools demonstrated against the decision, and incidents of violence between white and black students occurred.

On Thursday, April 9, *only two days after the board's decision*, the Michigan House of Representatives, by a vote of sixty-eight to thirty-one, passed a bill that required the Board of Education to submit any decentralization plan to the city's voters. The Michigan Senate *repealed* the original decentralization bill for Detroit by Friday, April 10. On July 19, both houses agreed on a bill, creating eight regions and delaying the integration plan until January 1, 1971, when the newly elected board members assumed office. On August 4, 1970, in a primary election with less than 40 percent of the registered voters at the polls, the four members who had voted for the integration plan were overwhelmingly recalled.[54]

There are several observations about the Detroit decentralization-integration effort that apply to the politics of education at this time. First, the distinction in the early 1950s between "de facto" and "de jure" segregation in northern cities resulted in a faulty stance by educational leaders. The emphasis was on not doing anything to further segregation—"from now on"—rather than on affirming integration as a desirable measure for educational and democratic reasons. We waited, and feelings and emotions became polarized.

Second, although it is doubtful whether any evidence would have made a difference to white parents, schools nevertheless lacked

---

53. *Proceedings of the Board of Education of the City of Detroit* (April 7, 1970), pp. 497-555.

54. *Detroit News*, 5 August 1970.

convincing reasons to persuade white parents that integration was vital to all.[55]

Third, in their zeal to correct injustices to blacks, some schools neglected the white ethnic with his real or imagined grievances. We reacted, rather than developing ties with our total clientele. This was also true later in our relationships with the Hispanic community and with women.

Fourth, when regional and central board elections in Detroit took place in November, 1970, white voters generally supported white separatist candidates. In predominantly black areas, the black separatists had a slate headed by one of the best known blacks in Detroit, but few blacks were elected and not one candidate on the black separatist slate won. Only one of the recalled members, a black, ran and was elected. It is difficult to determine who speaks for the community.

Fifth, an election year, when legislators run for office, is not the time to attempt an integration plan. Legislative moves and threats blocked all efforts for communication with parents. Why listen or compromise when a legislator promises to stop the proposed plan?

Sixth, the Detroit board members who were committed to integration were looking to the courts for support. By 1974, when the Detroit case came before the U.S. Supreme Court, the composition of the court had changed. A recent federal court decision ordered an integration plan for Detroit by January 1976, a plan estimated to include about 30,000 children.[56]

Seventh, a review of the agendas of the Detroit Board of Education for the past thirty years reveals a decided increase of citizen participation in school affairs during the past ten to fifteen years. Since the beginning of decentralization in 1971, participation has been shifted from the central to the regional boards. A glance under "Hearings" in the Index of *Board Proceedings of the Detroit Board of Education* illustrates this fact.[57] In addition to advisory councils a series of "concerned parent groups" and "concerned students of

---

55. David J. Kirby et al., *Political Strategies in Northern School Desegregation* (Lexington, Mass.: D. C. Health & Co., 1973), p. 158.

56. *Detroit Free Press*, 19 August 1975.

57. See *Proceedings of the Board of Education of the City of Detroit* (1950-1975) under "Hearings."

X High School" appeared periodically. Advisory councils occasionally complained that administrators sought to manipulate them, and officials contended that council members wanted to assume the role of administrators, but that is a normal condition in the process of power-sharing. Generally, where confidence and trust were developed betwen parents and educators, the role of each was resolved without too much difficulty.

Proponents of citizen participation, who frequently romanticize the concept of community control, would be helpful if they clarified their views on how this change in power should be implemented. Greater clarity is needed on the role of parents, teachers and administrators, and citizens in general. We must also clarify the role of the elected board of education. Alienation in large cities points to the need for greater participation and involvement by parents—but guidelines are essential. The claim that in small districts or in wealthier areas citizens play a greater role in school decision making than in cities is not supported by facts and only irritates city staff. After all, many teachers come from small communities or live there and know the facts. The call to "give the schools back to the people" is misleading since it suggests that parents formerly played a greater role in educational decision making.

As pointed out earlier, city schools have changed. A recent study of nine cities by Warren, Rose, and Burgunder states that "the school ranked *higher* on *responsiveness* and *innovation* than did the other traditional city agencies studied."[58] Only agencies specifically established for community participation, such as community action agencies and Model Cities, ranked higher than schools, the former on innovation and the latter on responsiveness. The author believes that further studies will continue to support these findings.

Some Reflections About Education and Politics

At the outset of this chapter I listed some of the concerns expressed by political scientists about the politics of education. In the pages that followed I discussed some of the conditions in urban education as these affect the politics of education.

---

58. See William L. Boyd, "The Public, the Professionals, and Educational Policy Making: Who Governs?" (Paper read at the annual meeting of the American Educational Research Association, Washington, D.C., 1975), p. 37.

In 1965, a year after four new books appeared on education and politics, Goldhammer observed: "Political scientists, it seems, have suddenly discovered education, while specialists in education have discovered political science."[59] Five years later Kirst, after reviewing a number of studies on politics and education, described the entire field as being "in great transition" as new political actors appeared on the scene.[60] The author has been mindful of Goldhammer's admonition and has attempted to note some of Kirst's old and new actors and the forces that had to be orchestrated for effective urban leadership. A few additional observations seem to be necessary.

First, educators have historically been somewhat sanctimonious about their leadership role. That view, however, represents an era that is long gone. School officials today are not as naive or secretive about their political activities as some suggest. They probably are as involved in politics as their boards and constituents would tolerate.

Large cities have had lobbyists in state capitals for years. Detroit has had a registered lobbyist at the state capital for at least twenty years, and a lobbyist in Washington D.C. for about ten years. During the 1970s, the number of school lobbyists has grown in Michigan; recently they have organized as the School Alliance Political Action Committee and have issued a political handbook for principals, precinct delegates, and others.[61]

Schoolmen still restrict their political activities to issues that directly affect education. Their political influence is thus limited, partly because of the nonpartisan stance of schools, and partly because urban school officials do not have the full support of their city delegation in the state legislature and must depend upon interparty votes to gain fiscal support.

Second, boards of education and superintendents are, of course, influenced by power groups in their communities. On occasions, when their actions exceed the tolerance level of the active voters, as in Detroit in 1970, they are recalled. It is doubtful, however,

---

59. Keith Goldhammer, review essay in *Educational Administration Quarterly* 1 (Spring 1965): 63.

60. Kirst, *State, School, and Politics*, p. vi.

61. School Alliance Political Action Committee, *Political Action Handbook* (Okemos, Mich: School Alliance Political Action Committee, 1973).

whether a political machine would have altered the outcome on the issue of integration. One year later, in 1971, the defeat of a powerful political leader, running in Michigan for the U.S. Senate, had been attributed to a somewhat mild statement issued by the leadership of his party accepting busing as an "imperfect and temporary mechanism."[62] The defeated candidate was then the state's attorney general, a Democratic winner in a Republican gubernatorial victory, and yet he could not overcome the onus of integration.

Third, the proposal to place schools under city government, although rejected by school leaders some forty years ago, merits review today.[63] The limitations of local taxes and the energy and time expended by school officials upon financial campaigns make one ponder whether fiscal independence has the advantages that its defenders claim. The city's future is closely tied to its schools. There are many city agencies whose activities need to be coordinated with education. Possibly the city's needs could be served better under a united leadership. The experiences of fiscally dependent school systems do not seem to justify the fears that some educators express. The impact of *Seranno* and *Rodriguez* may lead to equalization of educational financing, but will this benefit cities? The evidence seems to suggest that unless social needs influence fiscal policy, cities will suffer. The alternatives for schools are not simple.

Fourth, proposals by some political scientists for greater political participation by school people in politics need exploration. Schools in cities are unable to tap the resources necessary for their current needs. Large cities were disliked when they were wealthy and helped to support the state; now that they are poor, their popularity has not increased. Priorities in our society are determined by political forces, and schoolmen must be in a position to influence the decision makers.

Another factor for consideration is, what influence would a political alliance have upon educational change? Elected officials, unlike civil servants as educators, have a limited time in which to

62. Patrick E. Shipstead, *New Perspectives on American Politics: A Report from Michigan on the Busing Issue*, Woodrow Wilson Association Monograph, Series in Public Affairs, no. 5 (Princeton, N.J.: Princeton University, 1973), p. 14.

63. Nelson B. Henry and Jerome G. Kerwin, *Schools and City Government* (Chicago: University of Chicago Press, 1938).

make an impact. Possibly under the pressure of political coalitions, educational reform, which traditionally has been slow, would begin to move at a faster pace.

There are, of course, limitations to political involvement: (a) Would Americans fear that this change would lead to political indoctrination in the classroom? Or do citizens regard schools as political institutions now? (b) Could political alignments lead to state-wide collective bargaining and would this be helpful to cities? London and Amsterdam, with national salary scales, lose many of their teachers to their suburbs, where costs of living are lower and tensions less. American city schools lack staff mobility but they have little turnover. (c) And finally, what are the political trade-offs that schools have to offer to elected officials? Unlike mayors and governors, school boards and superintendents have very few appointments to disperse. Today, even the naming of a school after a legislator would under most city regulations require that he first be dead. And dead legislators have little influence—at least in state capitals.

Broudy believes that the public regards educational administrators apart from executives of other social institutions as business leaders or politicians. "The public," he states, "will never quite permit the educational administrator the moral latitude that it affords some of its other servants." [64] Would this apply to partisan involvement by school officials?

Consideration of political alternatives in large cities will not be determined by professionals or boards of education. The decisions for political realignments will involve more participants than in previous decades. The growing black community with its increasing political power will look with suspicion upon plans that may dissipate its political gains.

The findings of political scientists are being updated and earlier conclusions are being challenged.[65] A similar trend is evident in

64. Quoted in Willard R. Lane, Ronald G. Corwin, and William G. Monahan, *Foundations of Educational Administration* (New York: Macmillan Co., 1967), p. 131.

65. Boyd, "The Public, the Professionals, and Educational Policy Making"; Paul E. Peterson, "The Politics of American Education," in *Review of Research in Education*, ed. Fred N. Kerlinger and John B. Carroll, vol. 2 (Itasca, Ill.: T. E. Peacock, 1974), pp. 348-89.

recent studies on urban life and politics.[66] We seem to be entering a stage where the thrust is not in seeking targets for blame but in clarifying the determinants of urban life and utilizing this understanding for new programs.

This chapter has focused upon some of the forces and constraints that have influenced and limited the political behavior of school board members and administrators. On some of the political issues confronting schools, school tax elections or integration, many voters listened to their neighbors rather than local or national leaders. The actions taken by the Detroit Board of Education on affirmative action, integration of classrooms, or curriculum antagonized a large proportion of voters. It would be unfair to say that board members were not in touch with the people—they were in disagreement. The position on integration taken by the majority of the Detroit Board of Education was praised by the NAACP, the U.S. Commissioner of Education, and the U.S. Civil Rights Commission—but the active voters recalled them. Public reaction to urban politics is more open to immediate public judgment than political activities on the national scene, but it is not as lasting. One of the board members recalled in 1970 subsequently became the president of the Detroit Central Board of Education.

The transformation of the city during the past thirty years has radically altered the politics of urban education. The growing hegemony of the suburbs, the economic decline of the city, the new political actors and forces in central cities, the state legal battle over inequality in school financing, and the growing numbers of minority board members and school administrators—all point to a new era in the politics of urban education.

66. Harlan Hahn, ed., *People and Politics in Urban Society*, vol. 6 (Beverly Hills, Calif.: Sage Publications, 1972), pp. 34-35.

CHAPTER VIII

Communication and Decision Making in American Public Education: A Longitudinal and Comparative Study*

HARMON ZEIGLER, HARVEY J. TUCKER, L. A. WILSON, II

Who Governs Public Schools?

The political influence of technological elites has captured the imagination of social scientists, and for good reason.[1] In a technological age, especially one in which the conservation of scarce resources replaces the distribution of abundant resources as a focus of policy, elected officials are frequently required to deal with issues containing components too sophisticated for them to comprehend. Thus, they turn to experts for information, and the experts' knowledge is easily transformed into a political resource for the acquisition of influence. Recognition of the growing importance of experts has caused social scientists to reevaluate their empirical and normative models of public policy formation.

Traditional democratic theory holds that political influence follows—and ought to follow—lines of legal authority. The public elects a representative legislative body (congress, city council, school board) to make policy. An executive body, with senior officials who are elected or appointed, is employed to administer policy. Administrators follow the instructions of legislators, who follow the instructions of their constituents. The major source of power is

---

* The study reported in this chapter was conducted as part of the research of the Center for Educational Policy and Management at the University of Oregon. The Center is funded under a contract with the National Institute of Education, U.S. Department of Health, Education, and Welfare. The authors wish to acknowledge the support of the Research and Development Division of the Center in the preparation of this report.

1. See, for example, Robert L. Heilbroner, *An Inquiry into the Human Prospect* (New York: W. W. Norton & Co., 1974) and Victor L. Ferkiss, *The Future of Technological Civilization* (New York: George Braziller, 1974).

popular electoral support, and the norm of policy decision making is responsiveness to public desires and preferences. The newer model, which might be called the technological model, sees the implementation of information systems and management science techniques causing a fundamental change in the governing process.[2] Problems and policy alternatives are now too complex for the public and its representatives to evaluate. Legislators solicit and follow the recommendations of professional administrators. The major source of power is information; the new norm of policy decision making is deference to expertise.[3]

Proponents of the technological model stress the importance of experts as the "new political actors." [4] However, in that portion of the political process concerned with educational policy making, experts are certainly not new. Although historical interpretations may vary, there is consensus that educational experts, the superintendent and his professional staff, had become influential, if not dominant, actors by the 1920s.[5] The increase in political influence of experts in education predated similar developments in other arenas of decision making. As a result, a major thrust of the educational policy literature has been to emphasize the uniqueness of educational decision making. Research has been undertaken with the implicit assumption that education is more vulnerable to expert dominance than are other areas of public policy. Consequently, very few studies have been undertaken that compare decision making in school dis-

---

2. The contradiction between concurrent demands for direct control of leaders on the one hand, and for increasing government initiative on policy development on the other hand, is well noted in Henry Jacoby, *The Bureaucratization of the World* (Berkeley, Calif.: University of California Press, 1973).

3. Don K. Price, "Knowledge and Power," in *Science and Policy Issues*, ed. Paul J. Piccard (Itasca, Ill.: F. E. Peacock, 1969). See also Guy Benveniste, *The Politics of Expertise* (Berkeley Calif.: Glendessary Press, 1972).

4. Allan W. Lerner, *Experts, Politicians, and Decision Making in the Technological Society* (Morristown, N.J.: General Learning Press, forthcoming).

5. David Tyack, *The One Best System* (Cambridge, Mass.: Harvard University Press, 1974), pp. 126-76. See also James W. Guthrie et al., "The Erosion of Lay Control," in National Commission for Citizens in Education, *Public Testimony on Public Schools* (Berkeley, Calif.: McCutchan Publishing Corp., 1975), pp. 92-101.

tricts with decision making in other units of local government.[6] In view of the paucity of evidence, we agree with Peterson, who offers the following admonition:

The literature on school politics may not be fundamentally incorrect in identifying a good deal of autonomy on the part of a small group of educational decision makers. The central role that superintendents and their staff play in the decision-making process is well documented. ... But the explanations and interpretations of this phenomenon depend heavily on the assumption that such influence relationships are peculiar to the field of education. Not only is such an assumption not demonstrated empirically, but it prevents scholars writing on the politics of education from seeing the broader implications of their field. ... If decision-making patterns in education are the rule, not the exception, interpretations of American politics need to give greater weight to the role of experts, professionals, and the directors of administrative structures than most political scientists generally have given.[7]

Ironically, while other social scientists were recognizing the wider applicability of the technological decision-making model employed in the literature on educational policy, some researchers were questioning the continued applicability of that model to educational policy making. The contention appeared in both popular and academic literature that the increasing politicization of education had changed the climate in which school officials must work to the extent that deference to expertise could no longer be the preponderant form of policy making.

On the surface, the turbulence of the 1960s certainly seemed to have contributed to a politicization of education. Popular accounts of highly publicized conflicts portrayed professionals as struggling vainly against a variety of powerful interest groups. Professionals themselves were active in promulgating the view of the "beleaguered superintendent."[8] One observer quoted from the ranks of the

6. R. J. Snow, "Local Experts: Their Roles as Conflict Managers in Municipal and Educational Government" (Ph.D. diss., Northwestern University, 1966) and Roland L. Warren et al., *The Structure of Urban Reform* (Lexington, Mass.: D. C. Heath & Co., 1974) are examples of such efforts.

7. Paul E. Peterson, "The Politics of American Education," in *Review of Research in Education*, ed. Fred N. Kerlinger, vol. 2 (Itasca, Ill.: F. E. Peacock, 1974), p. 365.

8. This apt phrase is found in William Boyd, "The Public, the Professionals, and Educational Policy Making: Who Governs?" (Paper presented at the annual meeting of the American Educational Research Association, Washington, D.C., 1975), p. 7.

beleaguered to support his contention that the world of the superintendent, as seen from the inside, is far more conflictual than the world as described by students of educational policy making:

> The American school superintendent, long the benevolent ruler whose word was law, has become a harried, embattled figure of waning authority. . . . Browbeaten by once subservient boards of education, [teachers' associations], and parents, the superintendent can hardly be blamed if he feels he has lost control of his destiny. . . . Administrative powerlessness is becoming one of the most pervasive realities of organizational life.[9]

While some might be inclined to dismiss such testimony as self-serving, the view has been to some extent echoed by scholars who argue that the model of professional dominance is no longer correct. In their study of fifty-one school districts in the Northeast and Midwest, for example, McCarty and Ramsey conclude:

> One can hardly avoid the view that today's educational administrator is engulfed in a pressure-packed set of constraints. . . . Individuals previously without power are rapidly becoming aware of the strength that can be marshalled if they work together. . . . The tensions so apparent throughout American society have galvanized [school] boards into the political arena with a vengeance.[10]

The upshot of this controversy is a renewed interest in the question, "Who governs schools?" There is clearly a need for further research into relations between school boards, superintendents, and the public in order to test the hypothesis that patterns of influence are changing.[11] There is also a growing concern that educational policy researchers should make greater use of research techniques employed by other social scientists. Proponents of both the democratic and technological models of educational decision making have relied almost exclusively on the case study approach. Their

9. Gene I. Maeroff, "Harried School Leaders See Their Role Waning," *New York Times* 5 March 1974, pp. 1, 29; Donald A. Erickson, "Moral Dilemmas of Administrative Powerlessness," *Administrator's Notebook* 20 (April 1972): 3-4.

10. Donald J. McCarty and Charles E. Ramsey, *The School Managers* (Westport, Conn.: Greenwood Publishing Co., 1971), pp. 153, 211, 213.

11. It should be noted that most proponents of the "beleaguered superintendent" position viewed threats to expertise as originating from outside the local community (court decisions, administrative regulations, and so forth) or from the increasing efforts of teacher organizations.

studies typically examine a small, unrepresentative sample of school districts and focus on major decisions in those districts. Consequently, the studies are not replicable and their findings are not generalizable. A study based on a national sample of school districts, systematically selected, which takes a comprehensive view of the decision-making process, is a desirable complement to the growing literature subsumed under the rubric "Politics of Education."

Zeigler undertook such a project in 1968 and published a portion of the results in 1974.[12] A brief synopsis of the findings indicates that, although the preponderance of evidence supports the view that professionals are the dominant actors, there are systematic variations from this mode of governance. With regard to community input through interest groups, the conclusions were:

1. *Most* districts do not receive much attention from formal organizations. However, *some* districts find themselves heavily involved in group politics. High levels of group activity are associated with (a) the size of the district and (b) the extent of public discontent with educational policy. Larger districts and districts with declining public support are more likely to experience high levels of interest group activity.

2. By far the most active groups are those directly linked to the governance structure (for example, PTAs and teacher groups).

Concerning the distribution of influence between the board and the superintendent, the following conclusions were offered:

1. In two-thirds of the districts, the superintendent was solely responsible for setting the agenda.

2. General opposition to the superintendent existed to varying degrees: no opposition was reported by 17 percent of the boards; 16 percent revealed less than one-fourth of the members in opposition; 32 percent indicated more than one-fourth but less than a majority in opposition; and 35 percent recorded more than half of their members in opposition.

3. When asked to estimate if school board opposition to a proposal by the superintendent would be "very likely" to result

12. L. Harmon Zeigler and M. Kent Jennings, with G. Wayne Peak, *Governing American Schools* (North Scituate, Mass.: Duxbury Press, 1974).

in a defeat of the proposal, the majority of members in slightly more than half of the boards said such a defeat was not very likely.

4. Board opposition to the superintendent and probability of victory are *not* significantly related, indicating that the factors associated with opposition are probably different from those associated with winning. Indeed, opposition to the superintendent was *highest* in metropolitan districts but the probability of victory was lowest. Opposition was lowest in nonmetropolitan districts, but the probability of victory was *highest*.

With regard to the interaction of community tension, articulation of community demands, and board constraint upon the superintendent, the findings were:

1. Community tension leads to opposition but *detracts* from the probability of board constraint.

2. The articulation of demands as a consequence of tension results in the same phenomena.

3. These relationships are not stable throughout all districts, but rather are most pronounced in metropolitan districts. In nonmetropolitan areas, tension and consequent demands strengthen the ability of the board to constrain the superintendent. In metropolitan areas, tension and demand articulation strengthen the position of the superintendent. The greater the complexities of the environment, the greater the value placed upon the expertise.

The overall conclusion, given the variations described here, was that superintendents, in spite of the rhetoric, are the dominant actors in educational decision making, and that their decisions are only occasionally made within a context of community participation through interest groups.

Unfortunately, that study, while enjoying the advantages of generalizability from a national sample, suffered the unavoidable limitations of survey research. Survey data are inevitably removed from reality, since surveys tap not events, but perceptions of events. The difficulty is magnified when respondents are asked to summarize many events or to recall events outside the immediate past. In the 1968 study, the attempt to describe the functioning of boards of education from the reports of participants faced three interrelated problems of survey research.

The first problem is familiar to all social scientists who employ the observations of participants: quite often their reports do not agree. For example, in the 1968 study there was substantial disagreement between the perceptions of superintendents and school board members on the probable result of board opposition to a policy recommendation from the superintendent. There was consensus in only 45 percent of the sample: 30 percent agreed that the superintendent would prevail, 15 percent agreed that the school board would prevail. In 21 percent the superintendent thought he would lose but the board believed he would win, and in 33 percent the superintendent believed he would win but the board thought he would lose. This lack of congruence between assessments of influence by boards and superintendents suggests that "the superintendent and school board operate in two different worlds of power, perhaps equally false."[13] Survey data alone cannot resolve the conflict in perceptions.

A second and more basic problem is that individuals often do not accurately recall and report their own behavior. Burns asked executives in a business organization to keep records of people with whom they talked and what they said.[14] He then asked them what they *thought* they did. Comparing observation with interview, Burns found sharp discrepancy between administrators' perceptions of what they were doing and the actual record. The probability of such discrepancy is increased as the period of recall is lengthened. For example, school board members asked to recall the incidence of conflict over an entire school year may base their reports not on the hundreds of decisions made, but on a smaller number of "important" issues. Clearly, individual recall provides an imperfect record of events.

13. Michael O. Boss, "The School Superintendent: Politician or Manager?" (unpublished manuscript). Boss died in 1975, leaving an incomplete, but brilliant analysis of these data. Boss's analysis followed our scheme of examining boards as units rather than by working with individual data. It is instructive, however, to note that 79 percent of the superintendents, as compared to 54 percent of the board members, estimated the probability of superintendent victory as very likely or fairly likely.

14. Tom Burns, "The Direction of Activity and Communication in a Departmental Executive Group: A Quantitative Study in a British Engineering Factory with a Self-recording Technique," Human Relations 7 (February 1954): 73-87.

The third problem is that discrepancy between reported and actual behavior is exacerbated when recollections involve interactions with others. Communications research has emphasized that how one views the content of a communication is related to how one views the source of a communication.[15] One's frame of reference significantly affects how one interprets a communication. Burns, for example, often found that when a superior claimed to give a subordinate an "instruction," the subordinate would note that he had been given "advice."[16] Similarly, a school board member's request for information from the superintendent may be variously interpreted as an incident of support, neutrality, or opposition by different observers. These subjective distortions are particularly troublesome if one's intent is to describe patterns of communication and influence.

The dilemma of the 1968 study is apparent. Survey research permits replication and generalization, but it sacrifices depth for breadth. Survey research makes it possible to learn what those who govern perceive as the distributions of influence, but does not indicate the accuracy of those perceptions. Because of these limitations the question, "Who says what to whom with what effect?" can be only partially answered by survey research.

A New Approach

Our attempt to resolve the problems of past research was to conduct longitudinal comparative research that incorporated both systematic observation of events and periodic recording of participants' perceptions.[17] During the nine-month 1974-75 academic year we collected data on the flow of communications and decisions in eleven public school districts in the United States and Canada. Our data set consists of three major elements:

15. See, for example, Carl I. Havland et al., *Communication and Persuasion* (New Haven, Conn.: Yale University Press, 1953), pp. 35-36.

16. Burns, "The Direction of Activity and Communication."

17. Our methodology was heavily influenced by Benjamin Walter, *Bureaucratic Communications: A Statistical Analysis of Influence* (Chapel Hill, N.C.: University of North Carolina, Institute for Research in Social Science, 1963) and by David Kovenock, "Influence in the U.S. House of Representatives: A Statistical Analysis of Communications" (unpublished manuscript, 1967).

1. Objective records of all statements and decisions made at central school board meetings, meetings of the superintendent and his administrative cabinet, and other formally constituted media of communication exchange (for example, regional board meetings, public hearings) were recorded by two trained observers in each school district.[18]

2. School board members, superintendents, and other senior administrators were interviewed regularly to record their perceptions of presentations made by members of the public at meetings and private communications about school policy from members of the public. Those who made presentations at public meetings were interviewed concerning their perceptions of how they had been received by school district officials at the meeting and of any other previous contacts.

3. An opinion survey on school policy was conducted among samples of the mass public, leaders of interest groups, and among the school board members and senior administrators in each school district.

While the sample of districts is small, the amount of information obtained is immense. We have information on unarticulated preferences of the mass public, private and public communications between school district officials and their constituents, and policy decisions made at school board and administrative cabinet meetings. We have both objective and perceptual data relevant to the query, "Who says what to whom with what effect?"

Our first departure from past research on educational decision making was to collect data on events as well as perceptions over a long period of time. Our second departure was to make the communication the central focus of our study. Social scientists typically concentrate on the behavior modification component of policy making. Given this interest, the decision or choice quite naturally becomes the unit of analysis. Unfortunately, this approach neglects the fact that much public business is dispatched without any attempt at closure: frequently "the decision" simply does not exist.

---

18. All data collection was constrained by precise rules. Observers were trained in the use of various protocols for recording of observations and interview data. These instruments insured that the information collected and recorded was consistent across districts.

It is entirely possible that a substantial proportion of the demands placed upon school districts can be satisfied without the modification of behavior or policies or a decision (for example, demands may require no more than the dissemination of readily available information). We believe that to focus exclusively on major decisions can be misleading because it ignores the overwhelming majority of routine public business.

Thus, we attempted as complete a description as possible of the pattern of communications in public school districts. We define communication as a set of premises transmitted from one unit to another. Our foci are: (a) the content of communication, (b) the source of communication, (c) the source of response, and (d) the content of response.

Given the decision to attempt a comprehensive description of communications, we could study only a limited number of school districts. Our sample is certainly too small to attempt statistical inferences applicable to all school districts. Furthermore, since our method of analysis required a sustained commitment on the part of a school district, we were constrained by access problems. Nevertheless, we attempted to select a sample of districts that would reflect, albeit incompletely, the variety of districts in America. We attempted to include school districts that fell across the range of possible demographic attributes, formal decision rules and informal decision processes, and expected degree of conflict during the observation period.

In this chapter we shall provide a comprehensive description of communications at public school board meetings. From the pattern of communications we shall draw some preliminary inferences about patterns of influence among school board members, school district administrators, and members of the public. These inferences will hopefully contribute to an evaluation of the relative status of responsiveness to the public and deference to expertise as norms of decision making. In order to simplify presentation and to meet space limitations, we have selected for consideration three districts, each with appreciably different demographic attributes, preponderant decision-making styles, and different levels of conflict.

The major demographic differences between the three school districts are portrayed in table 1. Leeville is located in the Northeast, Barwig Park in the Midwest, and Grahamdale in southwestern United States. All three are located in Standard Metropolitan Statistical Areas (SMSA) of comparable size and contain at least one sizable urban area. The Barwig Park and Leeville districts encompass only part of their SMSAs; the Grahamdale district includes an entire SMSA, and has about three times the enrollment of the

TABLE 1

School District Characteristics

District	Enrollment 1974	Per Pupil Expenditure 1974	Percent Negro and Spanish Heritage Pupils, 1970		Approximate Population of SMSA, 1972
			Below High School	High School	
Barwig Park	25,000	$1,139	17.4	14.4	350,000
Leeville	29,000	1,217	4.3	2.0	375,000
Grahamdale	83,000	838	43.5	39.1	360,000

other two. Grahamdale is the poorest district, as measured by expenditures per pupil; Barwig Park and Leeville are moderately wealthy school districts by that standard. Finally, Grahamdale has a very heterogeneous school population in terms of minority student enrollments; Barwig Park is slightly over the national average of minority enrollment, while Leeville has a very low minority enrollment.

In terms of formal decision rules, Barwig Park and Grahamdale have traditional lines of authority. The school board appoints the superintendent, and decisions are made formally at central board of education meetings. Both districts are financially and structurally independent of the other local government units. In Leeville, the superintendent is appointed by the board, but the mayor serves as chairman of both the school board and the city council. The school district is financially linked to city government: the school budget is part of the city budget. Both regular and capital expenditures must be approved by the city council. As a result, the school board chairman in Leeville is unusually powerful *vis-à-vis* the superintendent. Our assessment of informal decision-making structures in Barwig Park and Grahamdale was that the superintendent appeared to have wide latitude for decisions. In Leeville, the superintendent was more constrained by the district's formal relationship to city government and the existence of a powerful opponent. Our preliminary description of the preponderant mode of decision making was "hierarchical" in Barwig Park and Grahamdale and "bargaining" in Leeville.[19]

The three districts varied considerably in potential and actual conflict during our period of observation. Grahamdale experienced virtually no conflict. Although there were potential problems, such as an apparent misuse of federal funds that might jeopardize future grants, and dissatisfaction with the district's limited program of native language instruction, no conflict appeared. In Barwig Park, the acting superintendent was named superintendent at the beginning of the academic year. Dissatisfaction was voiced about the method of appointment—no other candidates were brought in for interviews. Potential for conflict also arose in connection with the superintendent's plan for funding of new buildings. He proposed to circumvent a public referendum on a bond issue by seeking necessary taxing authority from an agency of state government. The deliberate avoidance of an election generated some rather articulate demands for more responsive behavior, but not a popular controversy.

Leeville did experience substantial conflict on three issues during the observation period. The first conflict surrounded plans for construction of a new high school. The school had been urging the city council to authorize construction for years without success. Spurred by a threatened loss of accreditation, the city council authorized a bond issue. However, the threat of a reduction in state financial support caused the council to place a moratorium on "unnecessary" construction—including the school. This controversy spilled over into other budgetary matters. The discovery of a deficit in the current operating budget led the mayor to call for elimination of 100 teaching positions. The teachers' union re-

19. Our classification is taken from Robert A. Dahl and Charles E. Lindblom, *Politics, Economics, and Welfare: Planning and Politico-Economic Systems Resolved into Basic Social Processes* (New York: Harper & Row, 1953). Briefly, a hierarchical process of organization is one in which leaders exercise a very high degree of unilateral control whereas bargaining is a form of reciprocal control among leaders.

sponded that administrative positions should be eliminated. The budget was ultimately reduced without eliminating any positions. Finally, a school board decision to close several small neighborhood schools was met by sustained vocal opposition from parents in the affected areas. The board reversed its decision and created a citizens committee to study the problem and make recommendations.

These elements are summarized in table 2.

TABLE 2
Categorization of Three School Districts

District	Size	Wealth	Hetero-geneity	Formal Structure	Informal Structure	Conflict Potential	Conflict Articulation
Grahamdale	Large	Low	High	Traditional	Hierarchical	Moderate	Low
Barwig Park	Medium	Medium	Medium	Traditional	Hierarchical	High	Moderate
Leeville	Medium	Medium	Low	Unique	Bargaining	High	High

All three school districts hold bimonthly public school board meetings. The school boards meet as deliberative, decision-making bodies. However, the meetings also serve as media of communication between the school board, school administrators, and members of the public. Information and recommendations are solicited from all three groups in the contexts of both decision making and communications exchange. In all three districts formal arrangements and informal norms permit all to speak at public school board meetings.

Our descriptive analysis of communications at school board meetings will be organized by the following questions: (a) What is the agenda of school board meetings? (b) Who sets the agenda? (c) Who participates in discussion? (d) Does participation vary by topic of discussion? (e) Who proposes policy? and (f) Do boards defer to superintendents' recommendations?

What is the Agenda of School Board Meetings?

We define the agenda of school board meetings as all the communications that occur at the meetings. Our most basic unit of analysis is the oral statement. Observations in eleven school districts indicate that statements were only partially organized and bounded by the formal parliamentary agenda. The ideal sequence of events, that is, topic introduction, discussion, and resolution rarely occurred. A more typical pattern was topic introduction, discussion on a number of related topics, and resolution of *some* of the issues raised. Thus, our definition leads us to work with data that are more comprehensive but less organized than those found in agenda documents and reconstructed minutes of meetings.[20]

Our procedure was to record the substance of each statement, and to aggregate statements on the same topic at a single meeting into units called discussions. As table 3 shows, there was considera-

TABLE 3

PERCENT OF DISCUSSIONS, BY PURPOSE, RESOLUTION, AND MODE OF RESOLUTION

District	Purpose		Resolution of Discussions When Decision is Intended		Mode of Resolution	
	Decision Intended	Information Discussion	Decision	No Decision	Vote	Consensus
Barwig Park	96	4	58	42	86	14
Grahamdale	60	40	94	6	73	27
Leeville	97	3	94	6	90	10

ble variation across districts in the purpose and resolution of discussion. In Barwig Park and Leeville, over 90 percent of all discussions were introduced for the purpose of reaching some sort of decision. In Grahamdale, 40 percent of topics were introduced for the purpose of exchanging information with no decision intended. Of discussions intended for resolution, Grahamdale and Leeville reached some sort of explicit decision (for example, take action, gather information, table) over 90 percent of the time; in Barwig Park over 40 percent of these discussions terminated without a clear decision. Thus, the decision-making function dominated board meetings in Barwig Park and Leeville; in Grahamdale, the functions of decision making and communications exchange were more

---

20. Eugene R. Smoley, *Community Participation in Urban School Government* (Washington, D.C.: U.S. Office of Education Cooperative Research Project S-029, 1965). In Smoley's study, written records were used to reconstruct events at board meetings.

balanced. In all three districts most discussion on items for decision making resulted in an explicit decision. However, in Barwig Park, a sizable minority of discussions aimed at decisions did not meet that goal.

Finally, there is the method of resolution. In all three districts, over 70 percent of discussions intended for decision were resolved by means of a vote (either by voice or roll call). In each district a minority are resolved by consensus, that is, by agreement that no vote is necessary. Consensual decision making is highest in Grahamdale (27 percent) and lowest in Barwig Park (14 percent) and Leeville (10 percent). Thus, Grahamdale displayed the lowest proportion of decision-focused discussion, and the highest proportion of nonvoting decisions.

The agenda of school board meetings can also be described in terms of the substance of discussions. Our typology of topics discussed was developed from survey, interview, and observational data collected in eleven school districts. The distribution of discussion units among topics in three school districts is presented in Table 4.

In two of the three districts one topic was clearly more frequently discussed: in Barwig Park 30 percent of discussions concerned students, and in Grahamdale 43 percent of discussions centered on district operations. No single topic was as predominant in Leeville. Looking at the frequency of topics across districts, district operations received greater than average attention in all three districts; and students, curriculum, student services, and teachers were particularly important in two of the three districts. It is interesting to note that issues such as busing, affirmative action, and civil rights, were rarely discussed in all three districts—particularly since popular and scholarly literature emphasizes the importance of these issues for school districts. These data suggest that the alleged public and administrative outcry on these topics did not take place at school board meetings in these districts.

How similar are the distributions of discussion in the three school districts? Ordinary least squares regressions of the percentages in table 4 were undertaken to evaluate the null hypothesis that one or more pairs shared the same agenda. The null hypothesis would be supported if coefficients of determination approached 1.0

TABLE 4
Distribution of Topics Discussed at School Board Meetings, in Percent

Topic Categories	District		
	Barwig Park	Grahamdale	Leeville
Curriculum (general education programs; basic skills vocational education; bilingual education; sex education; topical education)	19	9	3
Student Services (athletics; guidance, counseling; special extra programs; programs for special students; transportation; food, health services; safety programs)	11	6	14
Parents (parental responsibilities; parent-teacher conferences; parental participation in decision making; relations with teachers)	4	0	2
Teachers (teacher values; teacher performance; teacher-staff unions; teacher support staff)	5	11	15
Administrators (principals; staff administrators; consultants; superintendent; administrative reports, research; administrative professional activities)	6	4	15
Local Schools (alternative schools; community schools; other innovative schools, methods)	0	4	4
Students (student values; student performance; student misbehavior; student records; enrollment, attendance)	30	6	5
School Board (school board evaluation; appointment, election of board members; board behavior)	2	5	9
Finance (appropriations, revenues; bond issues)	7	7	11
Discrimination (equality; busing; affirmative action)	0	0	1
Other Government (activities of federal government, state government, county government, municipal government; other educational institutions)	5	4	4
District Operation (maintenance; facilities; materials)	12	43	15

while slope and intercept terms approached 1.0 and 0 respectively. The results of that analysis summarized in table 5 indicate that the hypothesis of overall agenda similarity should be rejected.

TABLE 5

INTERDISTRICT AGENDA SIMILARITY

Pairing	Intercept	Slope	R^2
Barwig Park — Grahamdale	5.64	.31	.06
Grahamdale — Leeville	6.12	.25	.25
Barwig Park — Leeville	8.12	.01	.00

It is possible to describe the intensity of discussion across topics by turning attention to the number of statements made on each topic. Table 6 summarizes the distribution of statements among topics.

TABLE 6

DISTRIBUTION OF STATEMENTS AT SCHOOL BOARD MEETINGS, BY TOPIC

District	Curriculum	Student Services	Students	Parents	Teachers	Administrators	Local Schools	School Board	Finance	Discrimination	Other Government	District Operation
Barwig Park	19	11	30	4	5	6	0	2	7	0	5	12
Grahamdale	9	6	6	0	11	4	4	5	7	0	4	43
Leeville	3	14	5	2	15	15	4	9	11	1	4	15

In Barwig Park and Grahamdale the pattern of intensity of discussion was similar to the pattern of distribution: the most discussed topics remained students and district operation respectively, and the other topics retained their relative order of magnitude. It is interesting to note the dispersion of discussions on topics: generally speaking, the most frequently raised topics received fewer statements per discussion.[21] In Leeville, there was greater dispersion in the distribution of statements than in the distribution of topics. In terms of intensity, district operation in Leeville clearly emerged as the most important topic. Student services and administrators were still seen as particularly important topics, and the distribution of statements shows that the school board itself was a topic of intensive discussion, an intensity unequalled in the other districts.

Differences were evident between the distribution of discussion and intensity of discussion by topic in all three districts. An obvious question is, Which issues received disproportionate attention when raised? A simple way of addressing this question would be to compare proportions of discussion and statements presented in tables 4 and 6 for each topic. This method implies the expectation that each discussion of a topic will consist of the same number of statements. Our data collection experience suggests that another model is more appropriate. When a topic is first discussed there is a certain amount of expository discussion necessary for purposes of introduction. As the topic is discussed again and again, the number of introductory statements necessary decreases. As a result, a topic that is seldom discussed should receive a greater proportion of statements than its proportion of discussions. Conversely, a topic that is discussed throughout the school year can be expected to contain a smaller proportion of statements than discussions.

Linear regression is a statistical model that is isomorphic with this model of expected intensity of discussion. The independent variable is the proportion of times a topic is discussed and the dependent variable is the proportion of statements made on the topic. The intercept term, which represents the constant cost of introducing a topic, should be positive, and the slope term should be less than one to indicate that fewer statements per discussion occur as a topic is more frequently discussed. As table 7 indicates, the

---

21. As measured by the following standard deviations: Barwig Park, 8.69 (topics), 8.48 (statements); Grahamdale, 11.35 (topics), 9.34 (statements); Leeville, 5.59 (topics), 6.45 (statements).

TABLE 7
Correlations between Statements and Discussions

District	Intercept	Slope	R^2
Barwig Park	.63	.91	.90
Grahamdale	2.47	.79	.95
Leeville	.58	.95	.71

regression coefficients meet these expectations in all three districts. Furthermore, the level of statistical explanation indicates that the model is quite accurate for Barwig Park and Grahamdale, and less accurate, although satisfactory, for Leeville.

The extent of disproportionate discussion is represented by the residual of actual proportion of statements from the prediction of the model. These residuals are presented in table 8.

In each district there was at least one topic for which the intensity of discussion differed by more than 5 percent from the prediction of the model. "Finance" was overdiscussed in Barwig Park; "teachers" was overdiscussed in Grahamdale and underdiscussed in Leeville; and "district operation" was overdiscussed in Leeville. Linear regression of residuals shows that there was no consistent pattern of overdiscussion and underdiscussion over all three districts. (Pairwise, the values for R^2 were as follows: Barwig Park—Grahamdale, .14; Barwig Park—Leeville, .27; and Grahamdale—Leeville, .03.)

This brief description indicates that the three schools had quite different agendas. There were differences in both the purpose and substance of discussions in the three districts. A slightly different picture of the substance of the agendas results from looking at distributions of discussions and statements among topics. In each district there was variation in intensity of discussion on different topics, and there was no consistent pattern of overdiscussion and underdiscussion of topics across districts.

The Nature of Communication

Beyond an investigation of topics raised at school board meet-

TABLE 8

DISPROPORTIONATE INTENSITY OF DISCUSSIONS, EXPRESSED AS RESIDUALS FROM ANALYSIS SHOWN IN TABLE 6

DISTRICT	CURRICULUM	STUDENT SERVICES	STUDENTS	PARENTS	TEACHERS	ADMINISTRATORS
Barwig Park	1.20	−.62	−1.87	−2.26	1.83	−2.08
Grahamdale	1.41	−2.22	3.78	−2.67	5.37	−3.63
Leeville	−1.43	1.13	1.67	.52	−5.82	−2.82

	LOCAL SCHOOLS	SCHOOL BOARD	FINANCE	DISCRIMINATION	OTHER GOVERNMENTS	DISTRICT OPERATION
Barwig Park	—	−.45	6.01	−.89	−2.17	2.38
Grahamdale	2.37	−.43	.20	—	−3.63	−.52
Leeville	.62	3.88	−3.02	−1.53	−.38	7.18

ings, one should also be concerned with the nature of the discussion. We distinguish between communications characterized as substantive demands for specific action by the school board and simple informational exchanges.

To investigate the qualitative nature of the discussion at school board meetings, we have utilized a four-category typology. Statements have been characterized as demands in favor of some action, demands opposed to some action, requests for information, and supplying of information. Table 9 provides a summary of the communications by type in each of the three districts.

TABLE 9
Percent of Various Types of Communication

District	Demands in Favor	Demands Opposed	Requests Information	Supplies Information
Barwig Park	16	*	26	58
Grahamdale	4	2	19	75
Leeville	27	11	21	42

* Less than 1 percent.

As can be seen from the table, communications characterized as supplying information were most prominent in each of the districts. In two of the three districts, Barwig Park and Grahamdale, the next largest proportions were those that refer to the requesting of information. Interestingly, in Leeville the second highest proportion of communications was for those characterized as demands in favor. In all three districts, the lowest proportion of discrete communications was for those characterized as being demands opposed.

Our interest in the characterization of discrete communications during school board meetings extends beyond simply describing the nature of school board meeting discussion. Instead, both the proportion of total discussion characterized as demands in favor and demands opposed, as well as the relative proportion of demands in favor to demands opposed, are taken as indicators of the amount of conflict in a school district. This approach to the definition of district conflict is based upon the twin assumptions that (a) demands must be present in order to have district conflict and that (b) conflict is a function of competing demands in which some favor and some oppose specific action by the school district.

This conceptualization of school district conflict means that it is not simply the presence of demands that leads to conflict but rather the competition of demands for and against specific action that characterizes conflict. As a result, an investigation of school district conflict over specific topic areas means that one must look at both the total proportion of communications categorized as demands for and demands against as well as the relative proportion of demands for and demands against.

Table 10 shows the nature of communication by topic in each of the three districts. In terms of district conflict, Grahamdale scored very low in the proportion of total demands for and against specific action. The total percent of demands for (4 percent) and demands against (2 percent) as well as the number of demands for and against in specific topic areas were all very low. Even for

TABLE 10

NATURE OF COMMUNICATION BY TOPIC, IN PERCENT

District	Nature of Communication	Curriculum	Student Services	Students	Parents	Teachers	Administrative Cadre	Community Schools	School Board	Finance	Issues	Other Governments	District Operations	Totals
LEEVILLE	Demands in Favor	2 / 36	17 / 32	9 / 29	3 / 21	9 / 27	7 / 23	4 / 24	12 / 27	20 / 26	0 / 40	4 / 25	13 / 23	100 / 27
	Demands Opposed	2 / 13	15 / 11	7 / 9	1 / 4	12 / 14	4 / 4	4 / 9	17 / 15	23 / 11	0 / 0	3 / 7	11 / 8	100 / 10
	Requests Information	2 / 20	14 / 20	8 / 22	3 / 15	9 / 21	6 / 15	6 / 25	12 / 21	20 / 20	0 / 0	4 / 19	17 / 24	100 / 21
	Supplies Information	1 / 31	13 / 37	8 / 41	5 / 60	8 / 37	4 / 21	5 / 43	10 / 37	23 / 44	0 / 60	5 / 50	17 / 46	100 / 42
	Totals	2 / 100	15 / 100	8 / 100	4 / 100	9 / 100	6 / 100	5 / 100	12 / 100	21 / 100	0 / 100	4 / 100	15 / 100	100 / 100
BARWIG PARK	Demands in Favor	8 / 7	6 / 10	56 / 36	2 / 16	4 / 9	6 / 22	0 / 0	3 / 38	5 / 6	0 / 0	3 / 13	6 / 9	100 / 16
	Demands Opposed	57 / 1	14 / 1	0 / 0	0 / 0	0 / 0	0 / 0	0 / 0	14 / 5	0 / 0	0 / 0	0 / 0	14 / 0	100 / 1
	Requests Information	23 / 29	11 / 27	21 / 20	1 / 13	8 / 28	4 / 22	0 / 0	0 / 10	18 / 33	0 / 0	3 / 21	11 / 22	100 / 25
	Supplies Information	21 / 63	12 / 64	20 / 45	3 / 71	8 / 63	4 / 55	0 / 0	1 / 48	13 / 60	0 / 100	4 / 66	14 / 69	100 / 58
	Totals	19 / 100	11 / 100	26 / 100	2 / 100	7 / 100	5 / 100	0 / 100	1 / 100	13 / 100	0 / 100	3 / 100	12 / 100	100 / 100
GRAHAMDALE	Demands in Favor	15 / 6	9 / 8	6 / 2	0 / 0	12 / 5	1 / 1	1 / 0	11 / 9	9 / 5	0 / 0	4 / 7	32 / 4	100 / 4
	Demands Opposed	0 / 0	0 / 0	3 / 1	0 / 0	17 / 3	0 / 0	40 / 9	13 / 4	0 / 0	0 / 0	0 / 0	27 / 1	100 / 2
	Requests Information	14 / 24	5 / 16	7 / 11	0 / 0	10 / 16	3 / 23	6 / 14	3 / 11	13 / 26	0 / 0	2 / 16	36 / 18	100 / 18
	Supplies Information	10 / 70	5 / 76	13 / 86	0 / 100	11 / 76	2 / 76	8 / 76	5 / 75	8 / 69	0 / 0	2 / 77	36 / 77	100 / 76
	Totals	11 / 100	5 / 100	11 / 100	0 / 100	11 / 100	2 / 100	8 / 100	5 / 100	9 / 100	0 / 100	2 / 100	36 / 100	100 / 100

Note: The upper number in each pair of numbers is the row percentage (distribution of communications among topics) and the lower number is the column percentage (distribution of communications by nature of communication).

"district operation," in which 32 percent of all demands in favor and 27 percent of the demands opposed were found, these demands constituted only 4 percent (demands in favor) and 1 percent (demands opposed) of the total discussion of district operation. This distribution is consistent with the fact that the majority of Grahamdale's meetings were occupied with discussions with no resolution intended. If nothing is to be decided, why make demands?

Of the three districts, Barwig Park was the next least conflictual. While 16 percent of the total number of communications were characterized as demands in favor of specific action, much less than 1 percent of the communications were characterized as demands opposed to specific action by the district. Of all the topic areas, "students" received the greatest proportion of the demands for district action (56 percent) and demands in favor constituted 36 percent of the total discussion of that topic area. However, there were no demands opposed registered for that topic area and, as a result, school district conflict over the issues relating to students was judged to be very low. The only topic area that appeared to generate any district conflict had to do with the school board, where 38 percent of the total communication were demands in favor and 5 percent were demands opposed to specific district action. This topic area, however, constituted only 1 percent of the total discussions of all topic areas. Therefore, while there may have been conflict in the consideration of this area, the topic accounted for so little of total board discussion that, taken as a whole, Barwig Park must be judged to have had very little conflict.

Leeville presented an interesting contrast to both Grahamdale and Barwig Park. In this district, the proportions of demands in favor (27 percent) and demands opposed (10 percent) were relatively high. Unlike the other districts, the proportions of demands in favor and demands opposed were high for *all* topic areas. The idea that conflict is a function of both the amount of demands in favor and demands opposed as well as the relative proportion of each was demonstrated well by the example of the discussion of finance during two consecutive board meetings in Leeville occurring in late February and early March. During the discussion of this issue, 56 percent of all demands in favor of specific substantive action on finance (28 percent each meeting) and 58 percent of all demands opposed (29 percent each meeting) were articulated. Thus, conflict tended to be brief and explosive, rather than sustained. Overall, demands in favor varied from a high of 40 percent for "issues" to 21 percent for "parents" and demands opposed varied from a high of 15 percent for "school board" to a low of 4 percent for "parents."

In terms of the twin concerns for total proportion of demands in favor and demands opposed as well as the relative proportion of the one to the other, the topic area "curriculum" must be judged to have been the most conflictual, followed closely by "student services," "teachers," and "finance." The least conflict was noted for the topic area "parents," but even so the conflict in that area exceeded the conflict in either of the other two districts over any of the other topic areas. One is led to conclude, therefore, that Leeville was the most conflictual of our three districts and that this pattern of high conflict extended across all topic areas.

Who Sets the Agenda?

An important question about the governance of any political institution is, "Who sets the agenda?" The power to decide what will be discussed is important in both a positive and a negative sense. It is important in a negative sense because it presumably includes the power to decide what *will not* be discussed. In the absence of discussion, the status quo continues, and policy review, evaluation, and change are impossible. It is important in a positive sense because whoever decides what will be discussed also tends to establish the boundaries and the rules of discussion. The power to limit the topics and policy alternatives that will be entertained gives the controller of the agenda considerable power in determining what policies will be adopted.[22]

We define agenda setting in terms of introducing a topic for discussion. The superintendent is responsible for preparing the parliamentary agenda in almost all school districts, and in many districts responsibility for presenting agenda items is assigned to

22. As Schattschneider argues, "Whoever decides what the game is about also decides who can get into the game." Elmer E. Schattschneider, *The Semisovereign People: A Realist's View of Democracy in America* (New York: Holt, Rinehart & Winston, 1960), p. 105.

school board members and/or administrators. Our interest is not with who prepares the agenda document or who makes the introductory statement on a topic, but with who is responsible for the topic's being discussed at the board meeting. This responsibility could usually be established from the discussion of an issue at a meeting or from discussion at earlier recorded meetings. When there was doubt about the originator, the information was considered to be missing. Responsibility for a topic's being discussed was determined and recorded for 73 percent of the discussions in Barwig Park, 85 percent in Grahamdale, and 98 percent in Leeville.

We have divided participants at school board meetings into six general categories: school board members, superintendents, staff experts, line experts, members of the public, and representatives of other governments. Staff experts were associate superintendents and other cabinet level administrators. Line experts included principals, teachers, lower level administrators, and other employees of the school districts. Assignment to a category was made on the basis of the role assumed by the individual during his statement. Individuals could be—and were—assigned to different roles at different times. For example, a principal would be coded as a member of the public when he spoke as a little league coach, and as a line expert when he spoke in his professional capacity.

Before turning to the data, it may be helpful to reiterate that the agenda is defined in terms of the communications made at board meetings. Although it is reasonable to expect that superintendents and school board members, as the major actors, will control most of the agendas, it is possible for all actors to introduce agenda items by our definition. Members of the public can "control the agenda" by introducing topics of discussion during the portion of meetings set aside for that purpose, or by introducing a related topic of discussion during a discussion initiated by another actor.

Table 11 summarizes the proportion of discussion initiated by various actors in each school district. Barwig Park and Grahamdale showed similar patterns; in each district the superintendent introduced nearly three-fourths of all discussions, line experts and members of the public each introduced about 2 percent, and government officials accounted for virtually none of the discussions. In Barwig Park, the school board controlled about 8 percent and staff experts

TABLE 11

PROPORTION OF DISCUSSION INITIATED BY VARIOUS ACTORS

DISTRICT	ACTORS					
	School Board	Superintendent	Staff Experts	Line Experts	Public	Government Officials
Barwig Park	8	58	26	2	5	0
Grahamdale	5	76	15	3	1	0
Leeville	36	42	20	0	2	0

Note: Responsibility for initiation of discussions could be determined for 73 percent of the discussions in Barwig Park, 85 percent in Grahamdale, and 98 percent in Leeville.

controlled about 26 percent of introductions, while in Grahamdale, the corresponding figures were 5 and 15 percent.

In Leeville, control of the agenda was much more evenly divided among the school board, superintendent, and staff experts. This was largely due to Leeville's decentralized system of setting the parliamentary agenda. In Leeville, the preliminary formal agenda was set by all school officials submitting items for inclusion. In Barwig Park and Grahamdale, the superintendent drafted a preliminary agenda and other actors added to it; in Leeville, the superintendent made additions to items submitted by other actors. As a result, in Leeville, the school board was a major agenda setter, followed by the superintendent and then staff experts.

Aside from the superintendent, school board members, and major administrative officers of the three school districts, almost no one else placed items on the agenda for school board meetings. In each district government officials accounted for virtually none, the public for less than 5 percent, and line officials for zero to 3 percent of the agenda. Experts controlled a majority of the agenda in all three districts; furthermore, line experts, who had the greatest day-to-day contact with members of the community, had the least control.

These data clearly support the deference to expertise model. In all three districts the leadership role was assumed by administrators; in Barwig Park and Grahamdale, the school boards relied almost entirely on the superintendent to set the agenda, whereas in Leeville the superintendent shared responsibility for agenda setting with his staff.

Who Participates in School Board Meetings?

Our definition of participation in school board meetings is also made in terms of communication: a participant is one who speaks at meetings. Once a discussion has been initiated, virtually anyone can speak. In the three school districts considered here, some restrictions were placed on the point in the discussion at which a member of the audience could speak and on how long an individual could hold the floor. But, generally speaking, ample opportunity existed for speaking at school board meetings and the general public was actively encouraged to attend and participate.

As was the case with the agenda, it is possible to examine participation in two ways: distribution of participation and intensity of participation. In looking at the distribution of participation, our unit of analysis is the discussion and our query is, "In what proportion of all discussions does a given actor speak?" Conceivably, a representative of each category could have participated in 100 percent of the discussions. Table 12 presents participation in discussion for our six types of actors.

TABLE 12

PERCENT OF DISCUSSIONS IN WHICH VARIOUS ACTORS PARTICIPATE

District	Actors							
	School Board	Superintendent	Staff Experts	Line Experts	All Administrators	School Establishment	Public	Government Officials
Barwig Park	93	18	45	25	57	99	6	1
Grahamdale	84	57	63	14	88	100	10	2
Leeville	99	48	25	19	62	100	31	*

* Less than 1 percent.

In all three districts school board members spoke in virtually all discussions—not a startling finding. However, there was considerable variation in participation by other actors across the districts. The superintendent made comments in over half the discussions in Grahamdale and Leeville, but the Barwig Park superintendent participated in less than 20 percent of the discussions. Staff experts were heavy participants in Grahamdale, making statements in nearly two-thirds of discussions, while staff experts spoke 45 percent of the time in Barwig Park and 25 percent of the time in Leeville. There was greater stability of participation by line experts across districts: the participation rate was 14 to 25 percent.

When the categories of superintendent, staff experts, and line experts were combined (shown as "All Administrators" in table 12), a different pattern of participation by administrators emerged in the three districts. In Grahamdale, administrators spoke in 88 percent of all discussions, compared to 62 percent in Leeville and 57 percent in Barwig Park. Thus, it appears as though school board meetings could be characterized largely as discussions between school board members and administrators in all three districts.

Table 12 also shows the percent of discussions in which all members of the school establishment (school board, superintendent, staff experts, and line experts) participated. From the last two columns of table 12, which show participation by those outside the school establishment, it appears that government officials were infrequent participants in all three school districts. In Leeville, members of the public participated in 31 percent of all discussions. The figures were 10 and 6 percent for Grahamdale and Barwig Park, respectively. The residents of Leeville were clearly more active in presenting their views directly at school board meetings. When one considers that the vast majority of discussions at school board meetings concerned routine housekeeping matters, the participation rates on the order of 10 percent in Barwig Park and Grahamdale were not unimpressive.

In looking at intensity of participation our unit of analysis is the statement and our query is, "What proportion of all statements do actors of a given category make?" Table 13 presents the distribution of statements among types of actors for the three school districts. When participation is viewed in this way, the difference in school board patterns is accentuated. In Barwig Park and Leeville, school board members accounted for 60 percent of all statements. In Grahamdale, board members made less than 50 percent of all statements. The Grahamdale board members apparently were listening as much as speaking. The Leeville superintendent made 12 percent of all statements; his colleagues in Barwig Park and Grahamdale

TABLE 13

Intensity of Participation: Distribution of Statements among Various Actors, in Percent

District	Actors					
	School Board	Superintendent	Staff Experts	Line Experts	Public	Government Officials
Barwig Park	59	9	23	8	2	*
Grahamdale	47	9	30	7	6	1
Leeville	61	12	7	6	14	*

* Less than 1 percent.

each made 9 percent of the statements in their respective districts. Administrators in Grahamdale accounted for 46 percent of all statements at school board meetings, while their counterparts in Barwig Park and Leeville made 40 and 25 percent of all statements respectively. If control of the floor is synonymous with control of decision making, deference to expertise was unquestionably the keynote in Grahamdale.

In Barwig Park and Leeville, school board members made the majority of statements, and administrators accounted for about 40 and 30 percent of all statements. In Barwig Park and Grahamdale the superintendent let his staff and line people carry the burden of administrative comment; in Leeville, administrative comment was evenly divided between the superintendent and other officers. These data suggest a typology of differences in division of labor among administrators in the three districts: the burden was shared between superintendent and other administrators; staff and line administrators carried most of the burden. (We refer, of course, only to the labor of speaking at board meetings.)

The pattern of intensity of participation of actors outside the school establishment was essentially the same as their pattern of distribution of participation in the three school districts. Government officials accounted for 1 percent or less of statements made. Intensity of public participation was greatest in Leeville (14 percent), followed by Grahamdale (6 percent), and Barwig Park (2 percent). The public was heard at school board meetings in all three districts, but, at least in Barwig Park and Grahamdale, the public voice overall was not very loud. Perhaps members of the public—and other actors—concentrated their communications resources on a limited number of topics and, thus, increased their influence.

A logical extension of the question, "Who participates?" is an investigation of the pattern of participation across different substantive areas. Again, there are two queries: "Do actors specialize in certain topics?" and "Are topics dominated by different actors?" Table 14 presents data relevant to both questions.

Looking first at the proportion of statements on each topic accounted for by specific actors, we find that the actors who were most important overall were also most important on each topic. In Barwig Park and Leeville, school board members were the modal speakers on all topics. In Grahamdale, the school board was the modal participant on all topics except local schools, where staff experts made an equal proportion of statements.

Generally speaking, actors' proportion of statements on individual topics reflected their proportions of statements on all topics. There were, however, some interesting exceptions. In Barwig Park, both line experts and members of the public contributed a disproportionately large part of the statements on finance. In Grahamdale, line experts' statements on curriculum and public statements on local schools were disproportionately large. In Leeville, the public's proportion of statements on finance was substantially larger than their proportion of statements overall.

Turning to the question of the distribution of statements by actors across topics, we find that, although the topic that received the greatest attention from the superintendent and school board varied across districts, within each district the superintendent and school board members directed their greatest attention to the same topic. The topic area most discussed by both superintendent and school board members was "students" in Barwig Park, "district operation" in Grahamdale, and "finance" in Leeville. In Barwig Park and Grahamville, staff experts shared the emphasis of their superintendent and school board; in Leeville, "finance" and "student services" are the second most discussed topics by staff experts.

While the school board, superintendent, and staff experts were involved in the discussion of almost all topics, generally speaking,

248 COMMUNICATION AND DECISION MAKING

TABLE 14

STATEMENTS BY SOURCE AND TOPIC, IN PERCENT

District	Source of Statement	Curriculum	Student Services	Students	Parents	Teachers	Administrators	Local Community	School Board	Finance	Discrimination	Other Services	District Operation	Row Totals
Barwig Park	School Board	15 / 45	10 / 54	30 / 69	2 / 58	7 / 59	6 / 74	0 / 0	2 / 71	12 / 52	0 / 0	4 / 71	13 / 58	100
	Superintendent	19 / 9	11 / 9	22 / 8	3 / 11	10 / 12	2 / 4	0 / 0	1 / 4	19 / 13	0 / 0	2 / 6	11 / 7	100
	Staff Experts	23 / 26	16 / 34	22 / 10	2 / 20	8 / 24	4 / 21	0 / 0	0 / 4	12 / 20	0 / 0	2 / 15	12 / 21	100
	Line Experts	40 / 18	4 / 3	13 / 4	2 / 9	1 / 1	1 / 1	0 / 0	0 / 0	26 / 16	0 / 0	1 / 3	13 / 9	100
	Public	23 / 2	3 / 1	10 / 1	3 / 2	13 / 4	0 / 0	0 / 0	13 / 21	0 / 0	5 / 100	0 / 0	31 / 5	100
	Government Officials	40 / 1	0 / 0	0 / 0	0 / 0	0 / 0	0 / 0	0 / 0	0 / 0	0 / 0	0 / 0	60 / 5	0 / 0	100
	Column Totals	100	100	100	100	100	100	100	100	100	100	100	100	
Leeville	School Board	2 / 59	14 / 56	8 / 52	3 / 52	10 / 64	6 / 66	5 / 61	15 / 66	18 / 49	0 / 0	4 / 57	15 / 59	100
	Superintendent	2 / 20	9 / 9	10 / 17	4 / 18	9 / 16	7 / 19	7 / 18	9 / 11	23 / 16	0 / 0	3 / 12	16 / 16	100
	Staff Experts	0 / 2	16 / 9	14 / 13	2 / 4	5 / 4	6 / 8	1 / 2	13 / 8	15 / 1	0 / 0	7 / 14	20 / 11	100
	Line Experts	3 / 14	29 / 13	9 / 7	8 / 14	5 / 4	2 / 3	12 / 14	9 / 4	11 / 0	0 / 0	3 / 5	10 / 4	100
	Public	1 / 5	14 / 13	7 / 11	3 / 12	8 / 12	2 / 5	2 / 4	10 / 10	41 / 26	0 / 0	1 / 5	12 / 11	100
	Government Officials	0 / 0	15 / 1	0 / 0	0 / 0	0 / 0	0 / 0	0 / 0	0 / 0	0 / 0	0 / 0	69 / 8	8 / 0	100
	Column Totals	100	100	100	100	100	100	100	100	100	100	100	100	
Grahamdale	School Board	10 / 43	5 / 42	9 / 38	0 / 0	12 / 51	2 / 47	6 / 35	7 / 58	9 / 45	0 / 0	3 / 57	37 / 47	100
	Superintendent	14 / 12	8 / 15	10 / 9	0 / 0	15 / 13	4 / 17	4 / 5	6 / 11	9 / 10	0 / 0	3 / 14	24 / 6	100
	Staff Experts	3 / 9	3 / 17	13 / 34	0 / 0	10 / 27	3 / 36	9 / 35	3 / 15	9 / 31	0 / 0	1 / 19	45 / 37	100
	Line Experts	34 / 26	11 / 17	14 / 11	0 / 0	9 / 7	0 / 0	0 / 0	1 / 2	13 / 13	0 / 0	0 / 1	17 / 4	100
	Public	16 / 10	3 / 4	13 / 7	0 / 0	6 / 3	0 / 0	26 / 21	12 / 14	1 / 1	0 / 0	3 / 9	20 / 4	100
	Government Officials	0 / 0	18 / 4	0 / 0	0 / 0	0 / 0	0 / 0	29 / 4	0 / 0	0 / 0	0 / 0	0 / 0	53 / 2	100
	Column Totals	100	100	100	100	100	100	100	100	100	100	100	100	

Note: The upper number in each pair is the row percentage (distribution of actor's statements among topics). The lower number is the column percentage (distribution of statements on a topic among actors).

other actors were much more selective and issue-specific in their participation. These latter groups tended to concentrate on a small number of topics. In Barwig Park, line experts concentrated on curriculum and finance, the public concentrated on curriculum and district operation, and government officials concentrated on curriculum and other services. In Grahamdale, government officials and the public joined the school board and top administrators in concentrating on district organization. The public also concentrated its comments on local schools, and line experts focused on curriculum. In Leeville, the public followed the lead of senior officials by concentrating on finance, line experts focused on student services, and government officials concentrated on other services.

In summary, actors who dominated discussion overall also tended to dominate discussion on each topic. Line experts, members of the public, and government officials focused on a small number of topics, but there was little common focus of types of actors across districts. Rather, the foci of these actors coincided with those of their school board and top administrators.

Who Proposes Policy Decisions?

After the agenda has been set and discussion has been completed, some sort of decision is in order. We now turn to the question, "Who makes policy proposals at school board meetings?" Our unit of analysis is the discussion, and we will be focusing on how discussions in which decisions are intended are resolved. This question differs from that of agenda setting because the person who initiates discussion may or may not make a policy proposal. We define a proposer as the first person who articulates a proposal that is decided upon—favorably or negatively—by the school board. (See table 3 for how discussions are resolved.) The distribution of proposals among our six types of actors is summarized in table 15.

The pattern of proposals reflects the patterns of agenda setting and discussion in the three school districts. In Grahamdale, the superintendent made most policy proposals, while school board members made most proposals in Barwig Park and Leeville. Looking at the distribution of proposals among administrators, we see that line experts made virtually no proposals in Barwig Park and Grahamdale, and about 1 percent of the proposals in Leeville. The

TABLE 15

Who Makes Policy Proposals? Distribution of Proposals Made by Various Actors

District	Actors					
	School Board	Superintendent	Staff Experts	Line Experts	Public	Government Officials
Barwig Park	90	1	9	*	0	0
Grahamdale	34	57	9	*	0	0
Leeville	79	11	3	1	6	1

* Less than 1 percent.

Grahamdale superintendent carried the burden of administrative proposal making, while staff experts "outproposed" the Barwig Park superintendent, and staff experts more evenly shared proposal making with the superintendent.

In Barwig Park and Grahamdale, only school officials made policy proposals at school board meetings. In Leeville, nonschool officials made about 7 percent of all proposals. Thus, in all three districts, members of the public attended meetings and voiced opinions, but, in two of the three districts, they deferred to elected and professional school officials in the responsibility of proposing policy. In the third district, school officials made 93 percent of proposals. It is tempting to infer that the role played by those outside the school district establishment at school board meetings was that of spectator rather than participant.

Decisions

The final subject of this survey of communications at school board meetings is decisions. Our units of analysis are decisions reached by voting. As noted above, in all districts a majority of decisions were reached by means of a vote. The subset of decisions reached by votes was not a random sample of all decisions, but it probably contained the most important decisions made by the school board. Some votes were required by statute, some votes were taken to record the policy of a school board more officially, and some votes were due to conflict and a desire to articulate dissent.

Our analysis of voting behavior will focus on two familiar topics from the literature of educational policy making: the extent of conflict and consensus within the school board, and the extent to which the school board relies upon the superintendent in its policy decisions. The results are summarized in Table 16.

TABLE 16
Voting Behavior

District	Total Votes	Unanimous Votes	Superintendent's Position Known	Superintendent's Position Adopted
Barwig Park	154	149	128	128
Grahamdale	157	156	127	127
Leeville	268	173	124	116*

* One tie vote

During our observation period 154 votes were taken in Barwig Park, 157 in Grahamdale, and 268 in Leeville. Unanimous voting was the rule in two school districts: 97 percent unanimous in Barwig Park, 99 percent in Grahamdale. In Leeville, 65 percent of all votes were unanimous. The low incidence of conflict makes an analysis of voting blocs within each school board unwarranted.

The voting behavior of school board members was quite easily observed and recorded. The assessment of the superintendent's position was a somewhat more difficult task. The superintendent's position was recorded on the basis of his explicit policy recommendations, expressions of support or opposition during discussions at school board meetings, and statements made at administrative cabinet meetings prior to school board meetings. If there was doubt about a superintendent's position, the information was considered to be missing.

The superintendents in Barwig Park and Grahamdale made their policy preferences known to their school boards over 80 percent of the time; the Leeville superintendent stated a position on 46 percent of the votes. The pattern of school board adoption of superintendent recommendations is striking: 94 percent of the Leeville superintendent's preferences were enacted, and 100 percent of the preferences of the Barwig Park and Grahamdale superintendents were enacted. A total of eight votes in Leeville were "lost" by the superintendent. Despite varying degrees of conflict, public participation, administrative control of agenda, and discussion in the districts, all three superintendents enjoyed the support of their school boards when they made policy proposals. Regardless of how responsive school board members were to their constituents in the public, they were undeniably responsive to their senior expert, the superintendent.

Conclusions

In order to facilitate the assimilation of the information presented in the body of this chapter, a summary is provided in table 17.

Barwig Park emerged as a district striving to contain conflict, to achieve consensus. The superintendent, new to the job, kept a low profile. There was potential for conflict, but it did not achieve articulation. In keeping with his low key approach, the superintendent set the agenda, but allowed his staff to do more discussing and proposal making. The board also played a major role here. However, the superintendent, while content to share authority with the staff, set the agenda, made his position known, and won. Public input was apparently not a significant aspect of the process.

Grahamdale provided a more classic picture of superintendent dominance, and adherence to the administrative ideology of unity. Conflict was very low, and meetings served largely as a forum for information exchange. The superintendent dominated the board in agenda setting. He also appeared to dominate his own administrative staff. He made a majority of the proposals, took a position in almost all cases, and always won. Public input, while incrementally higher than that of Barwig Park, was not appreciable.

In contrast to these districts, Leeville was substantially more complicated. Two powerful antagonists, the mayor and the superintendent, engaged in protracted disputes. Although we can hardly do more than speculate, it appears that the interdependence of city and school district governance was crucial to the maintenance of such a bargaining process. To the extent that Leeville was "unreformed" (that is, not insulated from "normal" political processes), the ideology of the reform movement was empirically supported. The key to the conflictual nature of meetings, the relatively active

TABLE 17
Summary of Results

	Barwig Park	Grahamdale	Leeville
Purpose of Agenda	Decision	Information/Decision	Decision
Content of Agenda	(a) Students, (b) Curriculum, (c) Finance, (d) District Operation, (e) Student Services	(a) District Operation, (b) Curriculum, (c) Students, (d) Teachers.	(a) Finance, (b) District Operations, (c) Student Services, (d) School Board.
Level of Conflict	Controlled	Low	High
Agenda Setting	Superintendent	Superintendent	Board/Administration
Participation in Discussion	Board active, administrative staff more active than superintendent. Public passive.	Board active, administrative staff more active than superintendent. Public participation low to moderate.	Board active, superintendent and staff divide responsibility. Public participation relatively high.
Proposals for Action	Board dominant	Superintendent dominant	Board dominant
Votes	Superintendent usually takes a policy position and wins.	Superintendent usually takes a policy position and wins.	Superintendent less likely to take policy position, but wins when he does so.

board, and the higher involvement of the public may be the emergence of a legitimate challenge to the authority of the superintendent from within the elite strata of the community. The challenge to the authority of the superintendent may have a ripple effect, encouraging the board and certain portions of the public to become active. However, even with such a challenge, the superintendent still achieved success when he took a position. His reluctance, in contrast to other superintendents, to state a position may have been a consequence of his assessment of the probability of defeat. It is equally plausible to speculate that, in the presence of conflict, "expert" opinion is harder to justify. Also, since, unlike our other districts, the board was active in agenda setting, the superintendent may not have been able or expected to develop and present a recommendation. In any case, influence, although formidable, was not unchallenged.

Despite varieties in participation, the superintendent clearly emerged as the dominant actor. To this extent, the observational data and the survey data from the 1968 study are in agreement. It should be kept in mind that the present study is limited to public board meetings. The public may elect to communicate in other ways, either to the school board or to the superintendent. If this is true (and we will present evidence on this subject in the future), several possibilities occur. First, given the key role of the superintendent, it is possible that he, rather than the board, "represents" the active public. Preliminary analyses of our survey data do not support this assertion, but the findings are quite tentative. Even if representation by administrators is established, one wonders what range of opinion the superintendent represents. Is such representation an adequate alternative to a board reflecting constituent demands? This study suggests that boards serve this function poorly, and that the technological model of decision making is characteristic of education.

CHAPTER IX

Three Views of Change in Educational Politics

LAURENCE IANNACCONE

Introduction

The world of educational politics and change today teems with dilemmas. But as Getzels has pointed out, "dilemmas do not present themselves automatically as *problems* capable of resolution or even of profitable contemplation."[1] The purpose of this chapter is to describe the meaning and significance of political change in education and to explain it insofar as the research on educational politics allows. The approach taken rests on the belief that problem finding is the critical activity in the advancement of knowledge. In essence, the chapter consists of three answers in search of a question.

It is possible to view the research on change in educational governance as using three alternative orientations. The first of these orientations is the focus upon change in the service function of government, a function that refers to those processes that either produce or provide activities or resources that will meet socially perceived needs such as the need for education. A second orientation for research focuses upon the political function of government, the function of managing conflict and settling disputes between contesting coalitions over matters of public importance.[2] Public controversy lies at the heart of this function.

The conceptual separation of these two functions is particularly useful to professionals in a public service because the influence of expertise is different with respect to each of them. In the service

---

1. Jacob W. Getzels, "Problem Finding" (Address given at the 343rd Convocation of the University of Chicago, Chicago, Ill., March 16, 1973).

2. The distinction between the service and political functions of government is made in Edward C. Banfield and James Q. Wilson, *City Politics* (Cambridge, Mass.: Harvard University Press, 1963).

function the application of expertise is usually dominant in dealing with questions, but professional expertise is significantly less useful in the resolution of political disputes. Indeed, such disputes often challenge the validity of professional expertise. The distinction between the service and political functions of government becomes particularly important when public controversy about education increases.

A third orientation of the research on change in educational governance pays particular attention to a special type of political function. When public controversy arises over the ideological assumptions and organizational structures that have customarily managed conflict, governments are called upon to settle disputes over the system for settling disputes. Such conditions occurring in senior governments may produce a constitutional crisis. In junior governments with delegated powers, such as an educational government, this type of controversy often evokes the intervention of senior governments, which are the sources of delegated powers. If continued long enough, the intervention will take the form of restructuring the junior governments. The influence of technical expertise, which is dominant in the service function, is least relevant and least powerful in dealing with questions about the nature of the system for settling disputes.

Each of these three research orientations begins with a different question and hence with a different definition of the problem with which the research is concerned. The first orientation addresses the question, "What is the nature of the politics of educational change?" The second asks primarily, "What is the nature of political change in education?" And the third orientation asks, "What is the nature of change in the politics of education?"

Administrative Politics: The Politics of Educational Change

Research focusing on the service function provides insight on an administrative perspective that developed from municipal reforms that restructured educational government at the turn of the century. This administrative perspective centers upon the operational realities of educational policy and decision making, reflecting a theory of government that became dominant at that time. As Waldo points out in referring to public administration,

"In essence, this new theory or philosophy of government was a reinterpretation of the meaning of democracy for America, one for the new, urban America. . . . It sought to attain the values of equality and freedom for citizens by making government strong and efficient."[3] In commenting upon this development, Schattschneider writes: "While we were thinking about something else a new government was created in the United States, so easily and so quietly that most of us were wholly unaware of what was going on."[4]

The administrative-political system centered upon by the first research orientation was produced by a single reform program and it continues to be the dominant system for determining educational policy.[5] Decisions produced by this administrative-political system and the consequent changes in educational operations are the primary objects of inquiry in this research approach. The bulk of the day in, day out interactions between education and the political order fall within this category. The research pays attention, therefore, to the customary political processes in educational governments by which the demands and supports of organized publics (including professional ones) are routinely translated into incremental policy changes in educational operations. This kind of research has the virtue of centering attention upon the incremental character of policy making, a pattern that Lindblom found to be most common in the making of policy.[6] The research clarifies the routinization of decisions in educational policy making noted by Smoley.[7] It explains the function of changes in educational decisions, whether reactive or proactive, to maintain the policy system.

3. Dwight Waldo, *The Study of Public Administration* (New York: Random House, 1955), pp. 19-20.

4. E. E. Schattschneider, *The Semisovereign People* (New York: Holt, Rinehart & Winston, 1960), p. vii.

5. L. Harmon Zeigler and M. Kent Jennings, with the assistance of G. Wayne Peake, *Governing American Schools: Political Interaction in Local Districts* (North Scituate, Mass.: Duxbury Press, 1974).

6. Charles E. Lindblom, *The Policy-Making Process* (Englewood Cliffs, N.J.: Prentice-Hall, 1968).

7. Eugene R. Smoley, "Community Participation in Urban School Government" (Ph.D. diss., Johns Hopkins University, 1965).

This first research orientation has been particularly fruitful in answering the question, "Who governs in educational governments generally?"[8] It provides a useful insight into the meaning of the episodic political crises and ephemeral issues, described by Martin as the other side of the coin of routinization, and into the control of this political system by the educational establishment.[9] Willower's functional analysis of schools suggests that these petty political crises most often fill the vacuum produced by the absence of political mechanisms for facilitating public articulation of value choices, an absence that Iannaccone has characterized elsewhere as the lack of a loyal opposition.[10] Such findings are important for describing the essential character of educational politics for most of this century.

The customary politics of educational change has most often entailed adjustments among participating subunits of the administrative-political system for establishing school policy. The subunits have combined technical-professional and social elites that operate with consensual processes within nonpartisan political and governmental structures. As a result, educational policy making regarding the service functions of educational governments has been largely "privatized," to use Schattschneider's terminology.

Schattschneider offers a political theory useful for understanding the significance of the politics of an administrative-political policy system in contrast to a system of extended public controversy.[11] For him, the universal language of conflict is at the root of all politics and the extreme contagiousness of political conflict is the central political fact in a free society.[12] His theory contains two basic elements: (a) the few individuals who are actively en-

8. Laurence Iannaccone and Peter J. Cistone, *The Politics of Education* (Eugene, Oreg.: ERIC Clearinghouse on Educational Management, University of Oregon, 1974).

9. Roscoe C. Martin, *Government and the Suburban School* (Syracuse, N.Y.: Syracuse University Press, 1962).

10. Donald J. Willower, "Educational Change and Functional Equivalents," *Education and Urban Society* 2 (August 1970): 385-402; Laurence Iannaccone, *Politics in Education* (New York: Center for Applied Research in Education, 1967).

11. Schattschneider, *The Semisovereign People.*

12. Ibid., p. 2.

gaged in the center of a conflict, and (b) the much larger passive audience fascinated by the conflict who may enter it as contestants rather than remain as spectators. For Schattschneider, therefore, the central focus of political analysis is the relationship between the combatants and the audience. The audience is never truly neutral, it is overwhelmingly larger than the combatants, and its direct involvement in the conflict will not only determine the outcome but will likely change the organization of the combatants. Organization is the mobilization of bias for action, and changes in organization will change the values at issue. The spectators, therefore, are "a part of the calculus of all conflicts."[13] The extent to which otherwise passive citizens become involved in a political conflict determines the scope of its contagion. Hence his advice to the political analyst: "Watch the audience." More precisely, changes in the highly permeable boundary separating combatant from audience will indicate changes in at least two sorts of political phenomena. First, there are changes in the composition and organization of the contesting coalitions, including changes in their status and role characteristics. Second, the character of the issues that will then become significant for every combination of contestant and issue will involve the domination of some issues and the subordination of others.[14]

The customary administrative politics of education has displayed considerable consistency in the nature of its contesting coalitions for most of this century. It has also displayed consistent biases toward issues that have received most attention, as well as toward those that have been accorded only peripheral status. The kinds of issues that are dear to educational professionals have commanded center stage. They include (a) the mobilization of support for educational budgets, (b) the adjustment of state aid formulas to the disadvantage of large cities, (c) the political opposition to private schools, (d) district reorganization to achieve larger local districts, and (e) the increased certification requirements and protection of educational professionals. The broader issues of race, religion, and rights of clients (pupils and parents) have been held off stage.

13. Ibid., p. 66.
14. Ibid., p. 4.

The distinctive character of both sorts of issues and their on-stage or off-stage location are exactly what is to be expected of a privatized political system reflecting organized professional leadership for much of this century.

Schattschneider views the history of American politics as a perennial struggle between tendencies toward "privatizing conflict," which restrict its scope, and tendencies toward "socializing conflict," which enlarge its scope. Control of the scope of conflict has always been a prime instrument of political strategy. The tactics of privatizing and socializing political conflicts are influenced by the structure of the federal system, a structure that itself is the outcome of major strategic considerations for controlling the contagion of political conflict. One way to restrict the scope of conflict is to localize it. Thus, debates about the "religion" of localism in education, about local, state, and national relations, about community control, or about centralization or decentralization are in reality controversies about the scale of conflict. Schattschneider points out:

> One-party systems . . . have been notoriously useful instruments for the limitation of conflict and depression of political participation. This tends to be equally true of measures designed to set up nonpartisan government or measures designed to take important public business out of politics altogether.[15]

Privatization of conflict is exactly what the structures of educational government and the political ideology resulting from the reform at the turn of the century produced. The research focused upon policy making in the service function in educational government amply describes its activities. The politics of education has been characteristically the politics of interest groups, as contrasted with the politics of party, and has thus operated largely apart from the two-party structure. The politics of education has also found its chief points of focus and impact in the local school board and the state legislature. Here again the absence of the two-party mechanisms mediating between the voter and governmental offices is reflected. Furthermore, direct democracy implied in the focus on school board operations places a premium upon achieving a

---

15. Ibid., p. 12.

consensus in the legislative process. Consequently, the politics of education has traditionally been the low visibility politics of informal agreement and consensus building among educational interest groups. It has conferred special advantages on the insider:

> It is the politics of the sacred, rural rather than secular, urban community; a politics of the priesthood rather than the hustings. The two genres of politics are different in kind. The politics of the hustings are visible and thrive on conflict and its resolution. The colorful kaleidoscope and cacophonic calliope of the campaign is its milieu. They subsist on the informal development of consensus prior to public debate.[16]

The research focus on the service function has serious weaknesses that follow from its strength. This focus cannot easily surmount the governmental philosophy that produced it. Its data categories too readily accept the political ideology and organizational structures of the service function as fixed. As Lindblom has demonstrated, the normal policy process is one of incremental change, but incremental policy making depends upon general agreement about basic ideological principles.

> Any even loosely organized set of interlocking generalizations or principles about social organization—or more specifically about politico-economic organization—is of enormous help to policy analysis. . . . All policy analysis rests to a degree on ideology so defined. . . . In effect an ideology takes certain beliefs out of the gunfire of criticism. . . . These beliefs . . . can thereafter be introduced into policy analysis as though they were settled fact. . . . Even mistaken beliefs can serve . . . because we chose a common set of assumptions.[17]

Every policy system rests upon such beliefs or political myths.[18] Most often the beliefs or myths appear to reconcile the irreconcilable and competing values dear to a society by papering over a large number of unavowed conflicts and by managing tensions too fundamental for political controversy, usually by benignly neglecting them. Some examples of these tensions are the competing values

---

16. Laurence Iannaccone and Frank W. Lutz, "The Changing Politics of Education," *American Association of University Women Journal* 60 (May 1967): 160-62, 191

17. Lindblom, *The Policy-Making Process*, p. 23.

18. Robert M. MacIver, *The Web of Government*, rev. ed. (New York: Free Press, 1965).

of the lay public and of the organized profession that seek to influence educational decision making, the competition for power between teachers and administrators within the profession, and the differences in attitudes and values between the upper-middle and lower classes within the lay public. Currently, the issue of elite versus egalitarian education (including the competition between elite and egalitarian outcomes of education) is a persistent part of the agenda of public schooling. Such tensions may in the final analysis be fundamentally unresolvable except as they periodically become compromised and redefined within the assumptions of the dominant political doctrine of an era. "Some controversies must be subordinated by both parties because neither side could survive the ensuing struggles."[19] So also the research with an orientation toward the service function of educational government tends to use assumptions woven into its political ideology without seeing alternatives.

The research orientation that focuses on the administrative-political system has proved useful for describing and explaining the traditionally privatized politics of education. It is ill-suited, however, for grappling with the spread of political controversy and it also tends to place the school in the role of independent variable with its politics as a dependent variable.

Political Adjustment: Political Change in Education

The second research orientation, concentrating on the political function of educational governments, is more truly a political science orientation. As Wirt and Kirst have pointed out, "For political scientists . . . the essence of the political act is the struggle of men and groups to secure the authoritative support of government for their values."[20] It follows that the political function of educational governments is to manage or to channel conflict.

The research orientation that focuses on this political function takes as its point of departure the natural laws or regularities of political change in education as found largely in four governmental arenas—the typical local education authority, the urban school

---

19. Schattschneider, *The Semisovereign People*, p. 76.

20. Frederick M. Wirt and Michael W. Kirst, *The Political Web of American Schools* (Boston: Little, Brown & Co., 1972), p. 4.

district, the state, the nation. The vantage point of this orientation has the virtue of giving primary attention to the recent and increased spread of political conflicts in education. The research shows these conflicts to be theoretically explicable in part as lawful, periodic cycles of political change in education in each of these four areas of government. Thus a cycle of changes following elections in which incumbent school board members are defeated, with consequent changes in patterns of executive succession, appears significant in local school districts at specific times in their history.[21] A similar cyclical pattern is noted in urban educational politics, but with different political mechanisms.[22] Research of the past two decades on the state politics of education indicates a dramatic increase in fragmented influence structures upon state policy making.[23] The politics of education in the national government is a most sensitive indicator of the fundamental change underway in educational politics generally and perhaps in educational government itself. The educational politics of the White House, the Congress, the Supreme Court, the U.S. Office of Education, and the National Institute of Education are important indicators of basic changes. Research on the national politics of education has demonstrated basic changes in the use of federal funds to intervene in state and local educational politics.[24] It has also described

21. Richard O. Carlson, *Executive Succession and Organizational Change: Placebound and Career-bound Superintendents of Schools* (Chicago: Midwest Administration Center, University of Chicago, 1962); Laurence Iannaccone and Frank W. Lutz, *Politics, Power, and Policy: The Governing of Local School Districts* (Columbus, Ohio: Charles E. Merrill Publishing Co., 1970).

22. Laurence Iannaccone, *Problems of Financing Inner-City Schools* (Columbus, Ohio: Ohio State University Research Foundation, 1971); Laurence Iannaccone and David K. Wiles, "The Changing Politics of Urban Education," *Education and Urban Society* 3 (May 1971): 255-64; Theodore J. Lowi, *At the Pleasure of the Mayor* (New York: Free Press, 1964).

23. Stephen K. Bailey et al., *Schoolmen and Politics* (Syracuse, N.Y.: Syracuse University Press, 1962); Roald F. Campbell and Tim L. Mazzoni, *State Policy Making for Public Schools* (Berkeley, Calif.: McCutchan Publishing Corp., 1976); Iannaccone, *Politics in Education*; Nicholas A. Masters, Robert H. Salisbury, and Elliot H. Thomas, *State Politics and the Public Schools* (New York: Alfred A. Knopf, 1964); Mike Milstein and Robert E. Jennings, "Educational Interest Group Leaders and State Legislation: Perceptions of the Educational Policy-Making Process," *Educational Administration Quarterly* 9 (Winter 1972); 54-71.

24. Frank J. Meinger and Richard F. Fenno, Jr., *National Politics and Fed-*

the most significant planned restructuring of the U.S. Office of Education in this century.[25] At the same time, the research indicates some of the limitations upon the power of federal intervention.[26]

Even a cursory review of such studies, to say nothing of reports in news media, abundantly documents the fact of a dramatic increase in the politicization of education in every type of educational government and in general American governments as well. The strength of this research approach is that its attention is centered upon the political function of managing controversy. It deals with issues of the responsiveness of educational governments.[27] It appears to have made significant contributions to our understanding of what may be lawful patterns of adjustment to periodic conditions of imbalance between public demands and the privatized tendencies of the administrative-political systems of diverse educational governments.

But this research, like that concentrating on the service function, is primarily concerned with the management of controversy within present educational governments. Such a focus is too limited, since it is concerned with political controversy within existing educational governments and with the political and ideological assumptions embodied in those governments. It tends to ex-

---

eral Aid to Education (Syracuse, N.Y.: Syracuse University Press, 1962); Philip Meranto, *The Politics of Federal Aid to Education in 1965: A Study in Political Innovation* (Syracuse, N.Y., Syracuse University Press, 1967).

25. Stephen K. Bailey and Edith K. Mosher, *ESEA: The Office of Education Administers a Law* (Syracuse, N.Y.: Syracuse University Press, 1968).

26. Jerome T. Murphy, "Title I of ESEA: The Politics of Implementing Federal Education Reform," *Harvard Educational Review* 41 (February 1971): 35-63; idem, "Title V of ESEA: The Impact of Discretionary Funds on State Education Bureaucracies," *Harvard Educational Review* 43 (August 1973): 362-87; Gary Orfield, *The Reconstruction of Southern Education* (New York: Wiley Interscience, 1969); Robert L. Crain, *The Politics of Desegregation* (Chicago: Aldine Publishing Co., 1968); Robert L. Crain et al., *School Desegregation in New Orleans: A Comparative Study in the Failure of Social Control* (Chicago: National Opinion Research Center, 1966); John F. Hughes and Anne O. Hughes, *Equal Education: A New National Perspective* (Bloomington, Ind.: University of Indiana Press, 1972); Joel S. Berke and Michael W. Kirst, *Federal Aid to Education: Who Benefits? Who Governs?* (Lexington, Mass.: Lexington Books, D. C. Heath & Co., 1972); Iannaccone, *Problems of Financing Inner-City Schools;* David O. Porter et al., *The Politics of Budgeting Federal Aid* (Beverly Hills, Calif.: Sage Publications, 1973).

27. Zeigler and Jennings, *Governing American Schools.*

amine issues of citizenship and representation with the bias of concern for the responsiveness of educational governments as instruments for achieving order, efficiency, and uniformity rather than concern for the central issues of democracy itself. The spread of political conflict about education may therefore be misunderstood. The increased amount of political controversy around education noted in the research of the last two decades is not sufficiently explained. Neither is there adequate explanation for the marked increase in the rate of change of elected and appointed officeholders. Such changes could be merely a substitution of a new guard for the old, an exchange of positions between traditional "ins" for a customary group of "outs." These developments are not explained by the customary policy changes of incrementalism, in accordance with Lindblom's analysis of policy systems.[28] Such policy changes are more often than not seen as changes necessary simply to maintain the basic policy system in the midst of societal changes. Increased political conflict is seen only to vary in amount, but it also varies in kind, the latter variation being much more significant. If dealt with at all, variation in kind is handled indirectly as if it were only an aberration or a phase in the natural adjustment of the educational policy system. Furthermore, only some of that increased political controversy appears to be explicated by the natural laws of governmental adjustment through systemic periodic political crises in educational governments. Neither the examination of the research carried on under this orientation nor the explanations it offers for political change in various educational governments is likely to provide a sufficient explanation of the fundamental nature of the expansion of political conflict underway in education.

The research produced by this second orientation, which was taken by a recent publication in an ERIC state-of-the-knowledge series,[29] centers on the politics of education and political change in education. There are several arguments against taking this point of departure. While this research focus has produced most of the theoretically useful findings in the politics of education, it is in

28. Lindblom, *The Policy-Making Process*.
29. Iannaccone and Cistone, *The Politics of Education*.

its own way too narrow a view to grasp adequately the political revolution it reflects. Its strength is in its attempt to document and explain the political conflicts of education in the family of governments that are the heart of the American governmental structure. Precisely as it has fulfilled that necessary task, the research in educational politics of the last two decades has placed limitations upon itself. Explanations that depend for their primary variables upon the exclusiveness of educational politics, upon the lack of responsiveness of school systems, or upon the power of educational interests, however accurate in other respects, run the risk of misattributing causation. The approach tends to underestimate the extent to which we are encountering for the second time in this century a political revolution in education. Most important, even as data from this research have begun to indicate the presence of this revolution, its perspective tends to misattribute causation by failing to see how much the revolution is rooted in the larger political order.

While this second orientation toward research is expanding its understanding of the increased politicization of education in different types and levels of government, and to some extent of the interaction among these types and levels, the research tends to give superficial attention to a number of issues about the whole of American educational politics. The research, like the popular communication media, tends to miss the forest for the trees. In doing so it pays tribute to the basic ideological and structural biases built into the government of education by the municipal reform.

Recent events and research support Eulau's position on the relation between politics and education:

I think we have to think of politics, broadly conceived as including both government and societal happenings, as the independent variable and of education as the dependent variable.[30]

One implication of this assumption is that students of educational politics need to go beyond the parochial view that seeks to explain educational politics from the events and developments that occur in it alone. Education, educational politics, governments, and the

---

30. Heinz Eulau, "Political Science and Education: The Long View and the Short," in *State, School, and Politics,* ed. Michael W. Kirst (Lexington, Mass.: D. C. Heath & Co., 1972), p. 3.

political ideologies of educational politics are only a part, perhaps the smaller part, of the origin of the major changes underway. But an ethnocentric view of education tends to attribute causation to educators rather than to the political order of education. In contrast, recent research makes it increasingly clear that "the issue is misconceived when stated as 'Dare the school build a new social order?' . . . The question is, 'Dare the social order build a new school?' "[31] Again following Eulau:

> If the political order is sound, stable, legitimate, just, or whatever other criteria of "goodness" one wishes to apply, education and all that is implied by education, such as the creation of new knowledge or the transmission of traditional knowledge, flourishes. If the political order is in trouble, education is in trouble.[32]

Similarly, political conflicts in education around issues of community control, for example, have been too often seen purely as failures of educational governments. A broader perspective is necessary. As Elazar says,

> While we are concerned here with the demand for community control of schools, we must begin any inquiry into the meaning and likely consequences of that demand and its satisfaction or frustration by understanding that it is a part of a larger demand for community self-government.[33]

The focus upon the political function of governments of education makes these peculiar subsets of the federal system the units of observation, thereby missing some of the significance of the ability of the federal system to limit the spread of conflict.

Federalism is both the fundamental character of American government and the source of its pragmatic flexibility.[34] Federalism, with its structural distinctions and divisions of powers, is historically basic to the American system of educational government viewed both externally in its separation from general government

---

31. Iannaccone and Cistone, *The Politics of Education*, p. 62.

32. Eulau, "Political Science and Education," p. 2.

33. Daniel Elazar, "School Decentralization in the Context of Community Control: Some Neglected Consideration," in *State, School, and Politics*, ed. Michael W. Kirst, p. 180.

34. Morton Grodzins, *The American System*, ed. Daniel Elazar (Chicago: Rand McNally & Co., 1968).

and internally in its national, state, and local units. The nonhierarchical sharing pattern of the American system also is found in education. Because educational governance is shared by this family of governments, "each sphere of authority and responsibility tends to obscure the operational realities of educational policy making."[35] So, for example, a piecemeal view of the causes of the changing politics of education tends to highlight the closed system character of educational politics and the lack of responsiveness of schools, school systems, and particular units of educational government as the antecedent conditions for increased politicization of education.[36] Consequently, as a recent review of studies in the politics of education points out, "Even within the present domains of research we note the absence of studies that move across the range of federal, state, and local educational politics. Their relationships emerge piecemeal from present work."[37] These conclusions appear valid, but they leave unanswered the question of why we are experiencing the spread of conflict in all governments around educational issues at this time. Worse, they may not be able to ask the question well.

The second research orientation has not surmounted the conceptual limitations of a federal structural frame of reference. For this reason it has paid insufficient attention to the significance of the tendencies of the federal structure to blur social class conflicts, to insulate educational issues, and to mute regional controversies. So textbook issues rage in West Virginia. Accountability and sunshine laws are debated in Florida and ignored in some other states. In some states collective bargaining is given legal sanction and changes internal power relations of the local school district. Once again, we may find that while we are thinking about something else a new educational government is being created, so easily and quietly that most of us are wholly unaware of it. Despite the longitudinal studies produced by the research on political adjustment within educational governments, the approach falls short of an adequate historical grasp of the significance of its findings. A longer historical perspective provides awareness of other periods

35. Iannaccone and Cistone, *The Politics of Education,* p. 17.

36. Iannaccone, *Politics in Education;* Zeigler and Jennings, *Governing American Schools.*

37. Iannaccone and Cistone, *The Politics of Education,* p. 65.

that experienced an analogous spreading of political conflict about education. It highlights similarities in the sources of the problems fought over, the cast of characters, and the nature of the issues involved. Such a view helps strengthen understanding of the fundamental relations among political ideology, governmental structure, their political functions, and the educational outcomes of schools.[38] Without such understanding, contemporary political changes cannot be adequately comprehended. Finally, a historical orientation may even suggest in general outlines the future toward which the politics of education is moving.

As to analogous developments, the historical perspective suggests we may be at the end of one era in the government of education and on the threshold of another.[39] Historically, the spread of political conflict appears analogous to the upheavals in educational politics during the 1840s and 1890s. Katz and Callahan point out the significance of these decades in opening up the arena to a debate of fundamental issues.[40] Thus Katz notes the reemergence of issues about heredity and environment in the parallels he draws between 1840, 1891, and 1960.[41] For the second time within a century we are experiencing a revolution in the politics of education. In both cases the origins are to be found in the problems of the cities, problems which in both eras extend far beyond the spheres and competencies of education. The first of these revolutions, which took place around the turn of the century, restructured American educational government as municipal reform took control of urban school systems away from city political machines and their neighborhood subunits. The second, which has been developing for some two decades, displays a similar propensity and potential for transforming the structures of educational government again.

38. Michael B. Katz, *Class, Bureaucracy, and Schools: The Illusion of Educational Change in America* (New York: Praeger Publishers, 1975).

39. Raymond E. Callahan, "The American Board of Education, 1889-1960," in *Understanding School Boards*, ed. Peter J. Cistone (Lexington, Mass.: Lexington Books, D. C. Heath & Co., 1975) pp. 19-46; Katz, *Class Bureaucracy, and Schools;* David Tyack, *Turning Points in American Educational History* (Waltham, Mass.: Blaisdell Publishing Co., 1967).

40. Katz, *Class, Bureaucracy, and Schools;* Raymond E. Callahan, *Education and the Cult of Efficiency* (Chicago: University of Chicago Press, 1962).

41. Katz, *Class, Bureaucracy, and Schools.*

Neither the administrative politics nor the political adjustment approaches discussed above are adequate to cope with these historical parallels. Finally, even the research that has centered upon periodic political readjustments in the present system of educational government tends to underestimate the extent to which its own questions are limited by assumptions that rest upon political myth. Katz takes a historical perspective, especially in viewing the period when the present system developed, and points out that alternative basic assumptions exist: "If order, efficiency, and uniformity are preferred to responsiveness, variety, and flexibility, then, indeed, bureaucracy is inevitable."[42]

Research analyzing the changing politics within educational governments tends to ignore fundamental issues such as whether the service ought to be rendered. It reflects the prison of its data categories. Lindblom illustrates the point thus:

Whether children are to be educated by public authority is itself a big question. How they are to be educated raises many more questions. Not surprisingly, big questions like these are not turned over to any one policy maker but require cooperation in policy making among many persons including the ordinary citizen himself in a democratic society.[43]

In fact, such big questions seldom get raised. They fall between the cracks of policy-making organizations. They are precluded by the ideological assumptions that are treated as settled fact by the policy organization, thus taking them out of the gunfire of criticism. Only a longer historical view helps in the interpretation of the emergence of such assumptions as issues of political controversy. That view identifies these recent developments as a *reemergence* of basic issues. It reveals that these issues were set aside from the center stage of political controversy in education for about fifty years of this century. They were set aside partly by the structure of federalism that subdivided the political drama among many political theaters. They were also subordinated to other issues through the sharp separation of educational governments from the mainstream of the American political order. Lastly, the historical

---

42. Ibid., p. 108.
43. Lindblom, *The Policy-Making Process*, p. 32.

view suggests that the reemergence of such issues implies an end to one political era and the beginning of another. It points to the strong political challenges to the doctrines of the old period as indicators of a revolution in the politics of education, a revolution that has implications for restructuring the governments of education.

Political Ideology: The Key

The tendency toward privatization eventually leads to increases in conflict. In education that tendency had depended heavily on public faith in the technical expertise of school professionals, which is to say that the political myth of authority in educational government, for most of this century, has been interdependent with the techniques of that service area. By technique, we mean a way of knowing, compactly applied to the world of objects including persons, that is primarily a way of control. This is the sense in which knowledge is power. But technique, while interdependent with man's political myths, is never a substitute for the myth. The tendency toward privatization in government is a tendency toward that impossible substitution. To follow an analogy used by the seventeenth century English political philosopher, James Harrington, in *Oceana*, it cuts the cake of power more and more in favor of those who have the technique. For as Brogan says:

It is a dangerous and idle dream to think that the state can be ruled by philosophers turned kings or scientists turned commissars. For if philosophers become kings or scientists commissars, they become politicians and the powers given to the state are powers given to men who are rulers of states, men subject to all the limitations and temptations of their dangerous craft."[44]

The tendency toward privatization not only helps the advantaged but also further detaches their sphere of government from the rest of the political order. This drift leads to increased spread of conflict. The scope of conflict also expands because no system can remain isolated when the larger body politic is experiencing critical social changes. Privatization submerges basic value questions while social change raises them. In such situations even the best

44. D. W. Brogan, "Preface," in Bertrand de Jouvenel, *Power: The Natural History of Its Growth*, trans. J. F. Huntington (New York: Viking Press, 1949), p. xvi.

adjustment mechanisms may falter. Furthermore, as MacIver notes, it is especially true in privatized political systems that "established power is so tenacious of its prerogatives that rather than part with any of them it will often by blind resistance invite the loss of them all."[45] The research suggests both conditions. Empirical indicators of the revolutionary changes in educational politics may be seen in the bulk of the research on the politics of education reported in the last two decades as well as in the existence of that subfield of study itself.[46] The research notes an increase of all sorts of political conflicts in educational governments, state and local, urban and suburban. An even stronger indication of the significance of these conflicts is found in the increased politicization of educational issues in national, state, and municipal governments. In addition to changes in the political actors participating in the controversies, there are major changes in the issues at stake. Most of the important tenets of the municipal reform movement that terminated the political controversies at the turn of the century, having been the policy system assumptions of most of this century, are now increasingly under fire.

The central thesis of this chapter is that we are in the midst of a revolution in the politics of education that appears likely to lead to revolutionary change in the character of educational government itself. Precisely because the doctrines of that earlier reform have been visibly shattered in the last two decades, the necessary if not sufficient conditions for a restructuring of educational governments are present. The desertion of the intellectuals identified by Crane Brinton as a necessary precondition for revolution is present. Revolutions are first made in the minds of men. An unvarying forerunner of revolutions is not only the challenge to the ideology of a government but specifically an attack upon the belief in the authority of those who rule and upon the governmental structures in which they rule. Political ideology, especially authority, and institutions are challenged together because institutions do not treat all forms and issues of conflict impartially. As Schattschneider says, "All forms of political organization have a bias in

---

45. MacIver, *The Web of Government*, p. 287.
46. Iannaccone and Cistone, *The Politics of Education*.

favor of the exploitation of some kinds of conflict and suppression of others because *organization is the mobilization of bias.*"[47] As MacIver points out, "The guardians of the myth, no matter what its character, maintain focal agencies not only for the authoritative interpretations of its tenets but also for the authoritative control of those who reject or seek to evade its prescriptions."[48] Hence the ultimate political acts are the struggles over defining the public policy issues about which conflicts are fought and the structure of the institutions for channeling them.[49]

Schattschneider says, "The best way to manage conflict is before it starts."[50] Out of the incalculable number of potential conflicts in a modern society or community only a few become politically significant. Politics selects from the number of potential conflicts, placing some at center stage of public attention and subordinating others. In effect, conflicts compete with each other and people must choose among them. Indeed, "political conflicts are waged by coalitions of inferior interests held together by a dominant interest."[51] Because political cleavages around different issues are usually incompatible with each other, the development of one sort of issue is likely to suppress others. Further, the alignment of given persons or groups or organizations around one issue is likely to be different from the alignment around others. This is clearest when the usually passive audience enters the conflict. Thus the politics of issue selection or choice of conflicts influences the twin processes of unification and division—the ways in which people are brought together as well as the ways they are divided into political interests, associations, groups, and parties. As far back as the English Revolution of the seventeenth century, Harrington saw (in *Oceana*) the definition of alternatives and the choice of conflicts as the supreme instrument of power and the central issues of constitutional structure.

Precisely because institutions are not impartial with respect to

47. Schattschneider, *The Semisovereign People*, p. 71.
48. MacIver, *The Web of Government*, p. 42.
49. Schattschneider, *The Semisovereign People*, pp. 69-72.
50. Ibid., p. 15.
51. Ibid., p. 69.

all conflicts and issues, because governmental organization too is the mobilization of bias, a fundamental change in the nature of the issues in the politics of education (or any other political realm) will place an intolerable stress upon the old structures that channel conflicts. Either they must be restructured or the new conflicts must be displaced by ones compatible with the old structures. Further, since the development of cleavages over issues is a prime instrument of power, the party that is able to define the issues is likely to take over the government.[52] This is why Schattschneider says, "The substitution of conflicts is the most devastating kind of political strategy," or, we may add, social happening.[53] In sum, we suggest that a condition of mutual dependence exists between the nature of the issues around which political conflicts revolve, the coalitions of political actors engaged in those conflicts, and the structural features of the governments that channel such conflicts. Further, changes in one or two of these elements will, unless reversed, result in changes in the others. The process may be initiated by the displacement of traditional central issues by new ones or ones previously peripheral to political conflicts. Again, as Schattschneider says, "the new conflict can become dominant only if the old is subordinated, or obscured, or forgotten, or loses its capacity to excite the contestants, or becomes irrelevant."[54] A substitution of issues based on a set of assumptions different from those that previously characterized the policy system is the surest way to transmute political conflict and turn existing political alignments inside out. It is also bound to threaten the system that channels conflicts. As Schattschneider points out, "In politics the most catastrophic force in the world is the power of irrelevance which transmutes one conflict into another and turns all existing alignments inside out."[55] The process may be initiated by changes in the composition of contesting coalitions occupying central positions in the organization of political conflicts, especially when these changes result from a major shift in role from that of customary

52. Ibid., p. 76.
53. Ibid., p. 74.
54. Ibid., p. 65.
55. Ibid., p. 74.

spectators into that of political contestants. Above all, the privatized incremental policy system is in trouble when its assumptions, having removed from criticism beliefs that were later introduced into policy analysis as settled facts, are themselves under attack.

A Change in the Politics of Education

The third research orientation inquires into the nature of change in the politics of education. Its focus is upon public controversies over the system for managing public controversy in education itself. To comprehend this approach some explanatory political theory is needed. Account also has to be taken of the historical drift, which reveals that the spread of conflict exists in a variety of governmental units and these upheavals appear to be converging during one time period. The strength of this approach is that it moves us toward asking the right questions. Its weakness is that its empirical bases are weak. The strongest research in the politics of education was directed only to part of the problem. The educational historians whose works bear on the issue were not sufficiently guided by political theory. The political theorists whose concepts are most useful in attacking these questions have been little concerned with American education. Nevertheless, a beginning can be made. The focus needed is upon the doctrines under attack, their meaning in determining the present administrative policy system, and the significance of the challenges to them and to the system. The ideological focus is fundamental to this third approach because, as pointed out earlier, such ideology introduced as settled fact is the chief guide to policy analysis and its incremental development. It follows that the erosion of such an ideology is the best early indicator of a revolution in politics that can lead to a revolution in government.

Not accidentally, the problems that triggered the educational and political conflicts of the turn of the century, as well as those of the 1960s, are to be found in the cities. The 1890s saw a rapid increase in controversy. Joseph M. Rice's exposé of the schools in the 1890s shocked the people by its indictment of the lack of both quality and equality within the existing system. Previous formulas that balanced these issues were not working. Rice's analysis focused on problems resulting from the intervention of political machines in the schools and from the kind of individual who served on the multiple lay boards. His book was grist for the mill of reform ideology. The municipal reform movement was manned by financial and professional leaders including superintendents, who, as Hays has noted, "deplored the decentralized ward system in large part because it empowered members of the lower and lower-middle classes (many of whom were immigrants)."[56] Tyack makes the same point even more forcefully:

> Underlying much of the reform movement was an elitist assumption that prosperous, native born Protestant Anglo-Saxons were superior to other groups and thus should determine the curriculum and the allocation of jobs. It was the mission of schools to imbue children of the immigrants and the poor with uniformly WASP ideals.[57]

The municipal reform movement was not merely dreamed up. It was a response to basic social problems of the period. Callahan and Button, while describing the changing concepts of the chief school administrator as a reflection of the municipal reform movement of the early twentieth century, list a series of societal problems that placed schools under heavy stress during this period.[58] Among these conditions were the difficulties of the growing school population, often immigrant; the need for more schooling for educators because of the expanded high school; and the increasing financial needs in education. These changes occurred in a climate of suspicion about education and all government services, and it paralleled in time a developing tax-saving ideology. The preferred solutions of the politically moderate muckrakers to the problems they exposed was the application of modern business methods to public service. Within this context the mounting political conflict

---

56. Samuel P. Hays, "The Politics of Reform in Municipal Government in the Progressive Era," *Pacific Northwest Quarterly* 55 (October 1964): 163.

57. David B. Tyack, "Needed: The Reform of a Reform," in National School Boards Association, *New Dimensions of School Board Leadership* (Evanston, Ill.: National School Board Association, 1969), p. 35.

58. Raymond E. Callahan and Warren H. Button, "Historical Change of the Role of the Man in the Organization," in *Behavioral Science and Educational Administration*, Sixty-third Yearbook of the National Society for the Study of Education, Part II, ed. Daniel E. Griffiths (Chicago: University of Chicago Press, 1964), pp. 73-92.

around education tended to center attention upon the fundamental tensions of the very warp and woof of education in America.

The conflicts reflect intrinsically unresolvable issues about the nature of public education in America. They are unresolvable in education because they are fundamental tensions inherent in American society. They appear most dramatically in the social order of large cities. One such tension is that between the idea of education for all children and the desire of each family to assure the best education for its own children. Given the reality of political and economic advantages of elites, this tension becomes a struggle between elite and egalitarian educational goals. A second struggle is that between the few and the many in government, which was seen by Aristotle and most political theorists as the underlying powder keg of all societies. In education this tension is reflected in the conflicts between administration and teachers within the professional system. Among laymen concerned with schools it surfaces in the political conflicts between the neighborhood clients of the schools and school district lay elites, who influence boards and central office staff. A third fundamental source of tension, which cuts across the other two, arises over the issue of the relative power of professionals and lay citizens over educational decisions. Any continuous pursuit of these conflicts to their logical end would destroy the political order. Some controversies cannot be openly addressed because the political order could not survive continued debate about them.

The substitution of conflicts, replacing the most fundamental issues with less basic ones, is one of the remarkable achievements of the municipal reform. That displacement produced a political myth that appeared to resolve the recurrent issues in education. Operationally they were resolved for an era, which is the best one can ask of a political formula that removed essentially unresolvable issues from public debate. Municipal reform doctrines have become the ideology underlying fundamental policy assumptions in education, and these tenets have been the basis of educational policy analysis for much of this century.

THE APOLITICAL POLITICAL MYTH

In education the municipal reform's political myth rests upon three major doctrinal tenets with their operational corollaries. All three had the manifest function of destroying the impact on education of the corruption of the urban political machine and the boss system. Their latent consequences played no small part in the renewed spread of political controversy over education in the 1960s. Briefly the three major tenets are: the separation of public service from politics, the view of the community as unitary, and the belief in the neutral competency of professionals. The last tenet is especially germane to the ideology of the professional administrator.

The separation of politics and education. The separation of politics and education was seen as necessary for order, efficiency, and effectiveness in the delivery of educational services. The belief in the apolitical nature of education is tenaciously held to this day by many school people as well as other citizens. Political mechanisms were developed to operationalize this ideology. Since the machine's power base appeared strongest in urban ethnic neighborhood politics, the reform sought to eliminate or at least suppress those neighborhoods. Mechanisms used to separate education and politics included the reduction of the size of boards, the separation of local school district elections from other local elections, and the development of local districts that were deliberately drawn with boundary lines not coterminous with other local governments. The most important governmental mechanism designed to cut the roots of the machine was the selection of school board members in nonpartisan, at-large, and districtwide elections. This mechanism disadvantaged the neighborhood political base of the machine. In effect, the central tenet of the apolitical nature of educational governance was used to keep the "wrong" people out of educational politics. It was relatively successful until the 1960s. The conflicts around educational governments were privatized, especially at the local level.

Fashionable as it was to argue the need for reform in order to clean up the corruption of ethnic and Catholic machines in the cities, the evidence reveals a bias that goes far beyond a desire for honesty in government. Abuse of power was the visible target. The invisible agenda was the transfer of power from one class to another. Cubberley's text in educational administration, a work that dominated the field in the early twentieth century, is an example of class prejudice as much as prejudice against the urban ethnics.

The original text, published in 1905 and reprinted in 1916, uses a map to illustrate the benefits of structural reform as advocated by the reformers.[59] The map is not of an eastern city overwhelmed by immigrants. Instead it appears more like a midwestern or far western town influenced by the radical agricultural groups or the western federation of miners. There are nine wards, in three of which the best people live (according to Cubberley). Three others are comprised of lower-class groups, one of which contains a black neighborhood of shanties, and three are swing districts. The implications of a government run by representatives from these wards were clear. Cubberley's advocacy of the system of at-large elections was designed to take advantage of the social inequality in neighborhoods as a political device to disenfranchise the poor.[60] Reformers organized coalitions and groups to restructure the system in such a manner that access to decision-making centers was convenient only for individuals and interest groups inclined toward reform ideology because of their social class ideological outlook and education.

Schattschneider pointed out that privatized political systems open up politics to interest groups. Schools now became more vulnerable to economic and social elites within the district. The political weakness of the school because of its dependency on a local taxation process encouraged the district's dependence on business elites with tax-saving interests. The deep-seated norm of separating education from politics made school districts less vulnerable to the political machine. It created a new vulnerability. Upper middle-class social and economic interest groups filled the void. Nonpartisan, at-large municipal and school district elections insured the middle-class and professional domination of educational decision making.[61] When Counts examined the composition of school boards

---

59. Ellwood P. Cubberley, *Public School Administration: A Statement of the Fundamental Principles Underlying the Organization and Administration of Public Education* (Boston, Mass.: Houghton Mifflin Co., 1916), p. 95.

60. Ibid., pp. 93-97.

61. Robert H. Salisbury, "Schools and Politics in the Big City," in *The Politics of Education at the Local, State, and Federal Levels*, ed. Michael W. Kirst (Berkeley, Calif.: McCutchan Publishing Corp., 1970), pp. 17-33.

in 1927, after the reform was well-established, it was clear that the middle class had won. Those who led the reform movement sat on the boards.[62]

The fundamental character of educational politics was changed in another way as well. The weakening of the neighborhood had implications for the influence of parent-clients on the service and for the importance of microlevel and building-level political issues that tended to get lost in the centralized at-large board structure.

The unitary community. The unitary community doctrine was a necessary element in the apologia for the power of the few. It is second only to the separation of politics and education in importance to the ideology of the reformers. It argued that there existed a single unitary community. A proper city manifests no social or economic cleavages, or at least none should be allowed to surface politically, since it would threaten the tranquility of this idealized unitary community. All special interests, according to this perception, ought to be subordinated to this single community interest. Good men residing in the best neighborhoods should be able, with guidance from the professionals, to govern the schools successfully. Controversies, especially those involving single schools, were considered as "special interest" situations and unwarranted intrusions. Nonuniform handling of on-site conditions was believed to be antithetical to the pursuit of city-wide interests. Implications of a unitary direction were obvious in terms of educational output. Programs were to be devised that applied to all children and the melting pot philosophy became the dominant thrust in the curriculum. The reformer's mandate was to implement an elite educational system for all. The needs and values of ethnic or class neighborhoods different from the dominant ones were ignored. Indeed, they were considered to be hostile to good education. A concomitant effect of the unitary community and melting pot doctrines was to provide ideological support for a macro-district political orientation. Such an orientation encourages boards to focus on educational means at the general level rather than concerning themselves with educational ends as they relate to the individual pupil.

62. George S. Counts, *The Social Composition of Boards of Education* (Chicago: University of Chicago Press, 1927).

Little attention was paid to the loss of power by the clients of education. Few reformers would have been comfortable in declaring the intervention of local groups in policy making as inappropriate, especially since they promoted their image as increasing participation in the decision-making process. They did develop a system, though, that favored the participation of one set of actors over another. The reform also shifted the political center of gravity from the neighborhood and the school building to the central office. Neighborhood participation was reduced, making it difficult for parents and local community members to influence decisions about educational outputs.

The micropolitics of the site became a kind of political wasteland, eventually occupied by managed PTAs and noneducational groups that appeared during episodic upheavals. A separation of politics from education, combined with the unitary community view as espoused by the prevailing ideology, destroyed the micropolitics of the neighborhood as it took power from the working classes and poor in order to empower the native, white, upper middle-class, and professional elites.

Administrative neutral competency. The reform needed a new administrative doctrine. Writing in the 1950s, Kaufman noted that institutions of American administration generally have been organized and operated to pursue successive value orientations.[63] The quest for Jacksonian representationalism dominated most of the nineteenth century. That administrative value orientation supported the spoils system of the urban political machine. The new administrative doctrine was founded in the belief that administrators operating as professional experts in their public service area, make decisions that are value free and apolitical.

The twentieth century saw the rise of professional managers. Reformers themselves were educated people who represented a growing technical-managerial class. Municipal reform focused on the city manager type of government as the ideal. This government was to be directed by a trained nonpartisan manager who met high standards of expertise.

---

63. Herbert Kaufman, "Emerging Conflicts in the Doctrine of Public Administration," *American Political Science Review* 50 (December 1956): 1057-73.

Superintendents, who at the turn of the century were in contention with boards (often ward elected) for control of education, benefitted substantially from the reform movement. The belief in neutral competency favored professional influence over lay control. Professionals were now designated as the proper individuals to determine educational operations. As Callahan effectively documents, superintendents soon became extremely vocal advocates of this kind of professionalism.[64] Scientific management evolved as a buffer ideology against a variety of value systems. A scientific approach to problem solving assumed the validity of the results as long as the methodology was sound and the experts were qualified to interpret the data. Those who commanded technical knowledge under these circumstances controlled the system. Superintendents armored themselves with the technical expertise of the business manager and with the frame of reference of the time and motion study.

Clearly increasing reliance on expertise and professionalism also provided substantial support for the unitary city myth, the directions of its educational program, and the melting pot. It removed education from an arena with conflicting value systems and placed it in the realm of science. In doing so it changed the nature of the questions being asked. It further supported the separation of politics and education. A good school was the same for all and the expert was best able to determine what the nature of a good school is. Schools could and should be run independently of differing value systems, ethnic, or racial backgrounds. Issues discussed were technical, while questions of purpose were ignored. These consequences were inevitable, given the reformers' redistribution of power from neighborhood leadership to a coalition of upper middle-class board members and professional schoolmen, who were steeped in the ethos of neutral competency. An ideological commitment to professionalism in the operations of the service became a vehicle for the supremacy of the superintendent over lay boards.

By the 1920s the political revolution in education was in place. The present administrative policy system had been institutionalized by changes in governmental structures. Its political ideology was

---

64. Callahan, *Education and the Cult of Efficiency*.

the basis for policy analysis. Its administrative handmaiden, scientific management, was effectively embedded in the training of school personnel, and the changes became a permanent part of educational governance.[65] Obviously it did not eliminate or suppress politics in education. What it did was substitute a different, nonparty, elite interest group politics for that which had existed. It resolved the issue of the many versus the few in the wielding of political influence in educational government. Power was in the hands of the upper middle-class few. The municipal reform determined that politics of the local educational authority would be about general district macroissues of finance rather than about building site microissues such as teaching and learning. Obviously the myth is not apolitical. The reform doctrine is a thoroughgoing apologia for power of the strong administrative state, especially in its belief in the neutral competence of the professional. Given the doctrine of neutral competency and the increased training of educators, it was inevitable that school administrators would acquire greater control over the policy system. The extension of the myth to its logical extreme was a major factor in producing a second revolutionary spread of political controversy in education in this century.

THE NEW EDUCATIONAL POLITICS

The roots of a new educational politics are in the ideology of municipal reform. Given the political function of that ideology to close off discussions about basic and unresolvable tensions of the American political order by displacing them with other controversies, their eventual resurgence was inevitable. Three events may be seen as critical in challenging the major reform doctrines. These events demanded that the reform tenets be carried to their logical ends. They are the Supreme Court desegregation decision of 1954, the aftermath of Sputnik in education (1957), and the New York City teachers' strike of 1960.

By deciding that separate is not equal, the Court took a position consistent with the unitary community view. Indeed, that decision carried the doctrine to its inevitable conclusion. The political conflicts that followed desegregation efforts have often found the

---

65. Ibid.

supporters of that doctrine in opposition to its implications. The resulting ideological imbalance or cognitive dissonance, if continued, is likely to lead to the development of a new cognitive frame of reference. That would mean the demise of one of the crucial ideological tenets of the reform.

The post-Sputnik demand for quality education for all pupils further challenged the unitary community doctrine in its operational goal of an educational melting pot. The demand for more science and mathematics and for higher academic achievement may have produced its greatest effects in the stress it placed upon the system to standardize education. The consequent shift of policy evaluation to educational output considerations and the research evidence on continued inequality have challenged the belief in the system's capacity to deliver on its early reform promises. The combination of segregation and the dubious quality of outcome, especially for the poor, has cast serious doubt on whether the reform's promise of increased social equality through education is possible or even whether schools are designed for that purpose.

The 1960 strike and the continued growth of teacher organizations in conflict with administrators combines to react against the myth as it operationally developed, as well as to reaffirm it—but with a significant twist. The real outcome in power relations produced by the belief in neutral competency was the dominance of school administrators in the administrative policy systems of education. From one perspective, the developments in teacher organizations and collective bargaining are a reaction to the carrying out of the doctrine's logic for some fifty years. From another view, one ideological base of the teacher movement is consistent with the doctrine of neutral competency and its correlate of faith in technical expertise. The teacher groups are pitting their claim of instructional expertise against the administrative claim. The reform doctrines function as part of the apologia for teacher power.

During the 1960s the demand for community-based influence, the micro-political locus of educational politics, commanded attention. Its most strident cries were heard by then. The power of its appeal appears no less today. As noted earlier in this chapter, the community education demand goes beyond the educational governance issue. Its roots lie in the general political order.

These continuing controversies about education all challenge the tenets of the municipal reform. That challenge constitutes a persistent thread running throughout the increased political conflicts in and about education. These controversies are different in kind, not only in degree. Hence the answer to the question of whether or not this revolutionary era in educational politics will restructure educational government is to be found in developments not in education but in the larger political order.

Conclusion

This chapter has offered three views about politics and change in education that are based upon the existing research in the politics of education. If that research is used to understand and explain the routine workings of the administrative policy system in education it will answer questions about the nature and processes of incremental policy changes in educational services. If the findings and conclusions about periodic political adjustment within educational governments are the center of attention, the research answers questions concerned with the system's laws for managing political conflict. Finally, the focus upon how the ideological underpinnings of the system developed helps to answer questions about the meaning and significance of the increased spread of political controversies over education since 1960—the changing politics of education in America.

For the second time within a century we are experiencing a revolution in the politics of education. In both cases the origins of the revolution are to be found in the problems of the cities, problems that in both eras extend far beyond the spheres and competencies of education. The first of these revolutions restructured American educational government as the municipal reform took control of urban school systems away from city political machines and their neighborhood subunits. The second, which has been developing for some two decades, displays a similar propensity and potential for transforming the structures of educational government again. However, while major elements of the pattern of educational politics produced by the municipal reform, especially its doctrinal tenets, appear to have undergone erosion, it may be premature to announce the funeral. As Iannaccone and Cistone note:

Two decades of effort in the area of race, equality, and curricular revision with more federal input than impact speak loudly enough for those who will listen. Schools today are more like schools of twenty years ago than they are like anything else.[66]

66. Iannaccone and Cistone, *The Politics of Education*, p. 64.

CHAPTER X

Evaluation and Politics

GERALD E. SROUFE

The decision to include a chapter on the relationship between evaluation and politics in this yearbook is a bold one, representing a substantial departure from paradigms conventionally used by scholars in either of these fields.[1] The principal goal of this chapter, therefore, is to muster support for the contention that practitioners and scholars will profit from attending more directly to questions about the political aspects of evaluation.[2]

My own view on this question is unambiguous: formal evaluation is an inherently political process and in some instances it has even greater policy consequences than do board or bond elections. Significant decisions regarding evaluation (that is, what to evaluate, how, when, and by whom) are made on the basis of the political values and resources of those involved in any given system, including the evaluators themselves. The discussion that follows seeks to substantiate the position that politics and evaluation are intimately

1. Two recent publications, one in evaluation and one in politics, provide ample illustrations to show that politics is politics and evaluation is evaluation. Exceptions to this generalization, largely derived from experiences of evaluation in social action programs, are cited in this chapter. The two publications, each the work of established scholars, are Laurence Iannaccone and Peter J. Cistone, *The Politics of Education*, (Eugene, Oreg.: University of Oregon Press, 1974) and W. James Popham, ed., *Evaluation in Education* (Berkeley, Calif.: McCutchan Publishing Corp., 1974).

2. A few of the works that introduced this contention and therefore merit specific attention are David K. Cohen, "Politics and Research: Evaluation of Social Action Programs in Education," *Review of Educational Research* 40 (April 1970): 213-38; Ernest R. House, ed., *School Evaluation: The Politics and Process* (Berkeley, Calif: McCutchan Publishing Corp., 1973); and William L. Speizman, "Evaluation: An Evaluation from a Sociological Perspective," in *Uses of the Sociology of Education*, ed. C. Wayne Gordon, Seventy-third Yearbook of the National Society for the Study of Education, Part II (Chicago: University of Chicago Press, 1974), pp. 192-210.

related and to consider implications of this position with regard to the political life of the school.

Toward an Understanding of Politics and Evaluation

A principal reason that it is reasonable to address evaluation as a political phenomenon at this time is that both politics and evaluation have only recently been redefined. So long as politics was studied principally as government, and evaluation was considered a soft form of research, there was little basis, or interest, in forcing an examination of the relationship between the two. Indeed, it was inconceivable to do so under the older concepts of politics or evaluation.

THE EMERGING PARADIGM OF POLITICAL SCIENCE

Until relatively recently, the study of politics has followed the paradigm established by Aristotle, who was concerned about the merits of alternative structures of government. Political scientists have retained the focus on the structure and processes of formal government, but have broadened their focus to include the legislative process, voting, interest groups, and other phenomena of twentieth century industrial society.

The emerging paradigm is less closely tied to government. It encourages systematic examination of the politics of armies or police departments, school systems, and bureaucracy as well as the politics of the nation state.

Tullock describes the change in the study of national politics:

> Traditionally, national politics—which includes the activities of the President, the Congress, and the Supreme Court—has commanded much wider interest than, say, army politics, or any one of the other types alluded to above. Surely political activity, as such, is quantitatively far more significant in almost any of the major hierarchal structures that characterize large organizations than it is among the strictly limited group of individuals assumed to be engaged in national politics at any one time. Traditional political theory seems to have neglected, in a relative sense, this extremely important "politics of bureaucracy," or "politics at the lower level."[3]

3. Gordon Tullock, *The Politics of Bureaucracy* (Washington, D.C.: Public Affairs Press, 1965), p. 10. Seymour Lipset includes a similar example of paradigm shift in his *Political Man* (Garden City, N.Y.: Doubleday Anchor, 1963), p. 387.

Some benchmarks of the changing paradigm have been the introduction of concern for interest groups and group processes by Truman in 1951;[4] the introduction of the systems context of policy formulation by Easton in 1953;[5] and the study of political systems in underdeveloped societies (that is, politics independent of formal government) by Almond in 1960.[6] These theoretical studies have provided a foundation for conceptualizing political systems apart from government. One might say that theoretical formulations such as these encourage the development of a systematic or scientific study of politics.

Changes in the paradigm of political science are still emerging and within the discipline one continues to find a wide range of vigorously contested views about the meaning and scope of political science.[7] Nevertheless, it is possible now, as it was not possible in 1950, to contemplate studies of the politics of the schools, or of welfare, or of the television industry. It is reasonable now to consider the concept of micropolitics (for example, the study of small political systems such as schools of education or English departments), which appears to be an area rich in insights about the dynamics of our educational systems. Lasswell's formulation of politics as bounded only by influence and influentials appears to have

---

4. David B. Truman, *The Governmental Process* (New York: Alfred A. Knopf, 1951).

5. David Easton, *The Political System: An Inquiry into the State of Political Science* (New York: Alfred A. Knopf, 1953).

6. Gabriel A. Almond and James S. Coleman, eds., *The Politics of Developing Areas* (Princeton, N.J.: Princeton University Press, 1960). See especially the introductory chapter.

7. Political science is easily the most self-conscious of the behavioral sciences. A number of volumes document the continuing search for the core of the discipline. Charlesworth believed that Oliver Garceau's study of the American Medical Association and the study of the state politics of education made by Masters, Salisbury, and Eliot went beyond the traditional scope of political science. See James Charlesworth, ed., *A Design for Political Science: Scope, Objectives, and Methods* (Philadelphia, Pa.: American Academy of Political and Social Science, 1966), p. 16. See also Austin Ranney, ed., *Political Science and Public Policy* (Chicago: Markham Publishing Co., 1968); Albert Somit and Joseph Tanenhaus, *American Political Science* (New York: Atherton Press, 1968).

many more adherents today than when he published his *Politics: Who Gets What, When, How* in 1936.[8]

In keeping with the new paradigm, in this chapter we shall use the simplest and most basic definition of politics: politics has to do with the distribution of stakes within a society or group. "Stakes" means jobs, money, prestige, influence, status, or even acceptance of ideas. People care enough about such stakes to try actively to influence their distribution. To this end they develop and husband their influence, and seek to use it wisely to affect the distribution of stakes. "Politics ain't bean bag."

THE EMERGING PARADIGM OF EVALUATION

Evaluation, especially in education, has undergone even greater changes than political science. Evaluators have not so much modified the established paradigm carried over from models of educational research as they have sought to create a new discipline in which research methodology is but one component of a technical support system.

The degree of self-examination, model building and rebuilding, role defining, and self-criticism among evaluators of national stature is simply astounding. A recent observation that evaluators "have overlooked the self-conscious examination of their own goings-on" is simply incorrect.[9] We shall argue that the efforts of evaluators at self-examination have been distressingly apolitical, but there can be no gainsaying the amount of hard criticism characterizing major panels of the recently organized Division H (School Evaluation and Program Development) of the American Educational Research Association, or the high degree of criticism and self-reflection in the literature of educational evaluation.[10]

8. Harold D. Lasswell, *Politics: Who Gets What, When, How* (New York: McGraw-Hill Book Co., 1936).

9. Speizman, "Evaluation: An Evaluation from a Sociological Perspective," p. 192.

10. Criticism, including support, for Michael Scriven's championing of a "goal-free" evaluation model is indicative of the fervor within the field. See Michael Scriven, "Pros and Cons about Goal-free Evaluation," *Evaluation Comment* 3 (December 1972): 1-8. The discussion continues, with many recent publications characterized by criticism of various models, specific attention to the roles of evaluation and evaluators, and examination of appropriate training for evaluators. For example, see Malcolm Provus, *Discrepancy Evaluation* (Berkeley, Calif.: McCutchan Publishing Corp., 1971);

What are the characteristics of the new field of evaluation? Foremost among them is the distinction between evaluation and research in both purpose and methodology. Also, evaluation is oriented toward improved decision making, directly or indirectly, and evaluation is believed to be essential to effective administration of programs. Evaluation is rational, above all, and it is this dimension that creates the interest in the relationships between evaluation and politics: "rational man" and "political man" are seldom compatible for very long.

Stufflebeam and his colleagues provide one of the most definitive statements about the problem of the research model. They state that, "perhaps the greatest challenge facing the evaluator is overcoming the idea that evaluation methodology is identical to research methodology."[11] They make a number of distinctions between the two approaches, but emphasize the following: "the purpose of research is to provide new knowledge. . . . Evaluations are designed . . . to make possible judgments about some phenomena."[12] This distinction is echoed by Worthen and Sanders: "Research is the activity aimed at obtaining generalizable knowledge by contriving and testing claims about relationships among variables. . . . Evaluation is the determination of the worth of a thing."[13] Scriven's statement, representing the sentiments of many evaluators, provides an excellent introduction to the political basis of evaluation:

Evaluation is emerging as a discipline in its own right, and, as we look back on the very earliest attempts to grapple with or eliminate the distinction between evaluation and research, we realize that we have come a long way toward understanding evaluation. The distinction is not simply, mainly, or always one of generalizability, policy implications, or decision servicing. These factors permeate and affect

---

Daniel L. Stufflebeam et al., *Educational Evaluation and Decision Making* (Itasca, Ill.: F. E. Peacock, 1971); and Blaine Worthen and James R. Sanders, *Educational Evaluation: Theory and Practice* (Worthington, Ohio: Charles A. Jones Publishing Co., 1973).

11. Stufflebeam et al., *Educational Evaluation and Decision Making*, p. 22.

12. Ibid., p. 22.

13. Worthen and Sanders, *Educational Evaluation: Theory and Practice*, p. 19.

some of the methods of evaluation research, but the basic distinction seems to be that evaluation research must produce as a conclusion exactly the kind of statement that social scientists have for years been taught is illegitimate; a judgment of value, worth, or merit. That is the great scientific and philosophical significance of evaluation research.[14]

The importance of this distinction for the present discussion is that educational research can conceivably take place outside the political realm, but that evaluation, dealing as it does with the worth or merit of a phenomenon, carries in its basic formulation the necessity for approval or disapproval, continuation or discontinuation, praise or sanction, attention or inattention. These are things that educators value and it is no surprise that evaluation and evaluators become central to educators' efforts to influence the distribution of these stakes.

There is considerable disagreement about the degree of influence evaluators should seek to exercise over decision makers; there is little disagreement that evaluators are to provide useful, timely information for decision makers. A supplementary role is proposed by Stufflebeam: "The evaluator is viewed as an extension of the decision maker's mental process.... [He] seeks to aid the decision maker ... by working with him to delineate the information which is needed, by obtaining this information, and by helping the decision maker to use the information."[15] If this seems like an unusually intimate relationship between decision maker and evaluator it is nevertheless one that is shared by most scholars. Evaluators are urged to enter the picture early, establish close working relationships with all relevant parties, and to persevere in the face of irrational political forces.

Evaluators lament the fact that they are so few and that so much needs to be evaluated. They wish to be able to accomplish much more. Provus believes that his model will assist in the management of programs.[16] Stufflebeam asserts that the lack of trained

---

14. Michael Scriven, "Evaluation Perspectives and Procedures," in Popham, *Evaluation in Education*, p. 4. "Evaluation research" appears to be a term used to call attention to the systematic scholarly procedures used in serious evaluations. Since this is the only kind of evaluation worth discussing, the unadorned term "evaluation" has been used here.

15. Stufflebeam et al., *Educational Evaluation and Decision Making*, p. 93.

16. Provus, *Discrepancy Evaluation*, pp. 36-45.

personnel to carry out evaluations may be the biggest stumbling block of the profession.[17] Worthen and Sanders point to the serious need to train many persons directly for evaluation roles if the process of education is to be improved.[18] It is well to be reminded of the certitude accompanying research and evaluation in the happier time of Ellwood P. Cubberley:

> For the superintendent, standardized tests have meant nothing less than the ultimate changing of school administration from guess work to scientific accuracy. The mere personal opinion of school board members and the lay public, and even the old method of a comparison of school systems, have been in large part eliminated, and in their place has been substituted demonstrable proof as to the validity of a method or a procedure or the effectiveness of the administration of the supervision of a school system. The development of standardized tests has meant a vast improvement in our ability to evaluate educational procedures, and as great an advance toward scientific organization as did the introduction of the conception of an orderly psychological development in the [eighteen] sixties.[19]

Contemporary evaluators will smile at the self-deluding confidence expressed in this passage. Their faith in rational decision making, however, and their concomitant apolitical view of education are not really very different from that of Cubberley. In this instance, at least, evaluators have failed to discharge all the trappings of their previous apolitical research model.

A representative statement of the field is provided by Stufflebeam:

> Evaluation is a complex process. It is everyone's responsibility. Professional evaluators are needed, not to take over all evaluation responsibilities but to provide leadership and coordination in evaluation. The ultimate aim is to provide better information for decision making and thereby to make education a more rational process.[20]

The difficulty here, to be illustrated at some length in following sections, is that the statement ignores the fact that information

17. Stufflebeam et al., *Educational Evaluation and Decision Making*, p. 342.

18. Worthen and Sanders, *Educational Evaluation: Theory and Practice*, pp. 348-9.

19. Ellwood P. Cubberley, *Public Education in the United States*, rev. ed. (Cambridge, Mass.: Riverside Press, 1947), p. 698.

20. Stufflebeam et al., *Educational Evaluation and Decision Making*, p. 105.

is itself a political resource. Those actors in the programs to be evaluated do not passively seek out objective information. Rather, they actively seek to influence the nature of the information sought, the constituency, and the timing of an evaluation, to say nothing of the selection of the evaluators, the amount of money, staff, and facilities to be provided.

An Expanded Definition of the Politics of Education

The observation that politics has to do with distribution of stakes must be expanded if it is to be helpful as a focal point for an examination of the relationship between evaluation and politics in education. It is an essential understanding, freeing one from the unfortunate and constraining definitions in which politics is explicitly or implicitly bounded by political parties, voting, and legislative practices. "Stakes" is a shorthand expression, however, and requires specific explication in relation to education. As this entire yearbook is devoted to political aspects of education, the following effort to define the area will be brief, designed to lay the groundwork for the discussion about evaluation and politics that follows.

Easton's definition of politics "as the authoritative allocation of values" is, clearly, similar to the simpler notion of politics as the distribution of stakes.[21] In fact, however, Easton's definition means both more and less. His general political systems framework, which provides the context for this definition, involves the now familiar systems characteristics and concepts such as suprasystems and subsystems, feedback, gatekeepers, inputs, outputs, and withinputs. As a political subsystem of the suprasystem, education and educators must, by definition, seek to secure resources and authority from the larger system while simultaneously seeking protection from unwarranted intrusions by outside forces. It is in this context that the general understanding of the politics of education is most elegantly housed: education interest groups, bond and board elections, judicial decrees, and testimony before state and federal legislative committees may be clearly understood as the specific

---

21. David Easton, *A Framework for Political Analysis* (Englewood Cliffs, N.J.: Prentice-Hall, 1965).

procedures or vehicles whereby the educational subsystem continuously engages the political suprasystem.

But conceiving the politics of education as a subsystem of the larger governmental system overwhelms other equally significant political aspects of education. Easton's own illustrations continue to reflect an understanding of politics dominated by activities related to government. He provides a framework for increased understanding of education as a political system but little encouragement for the application of such a framework to the study of politics in education. Viewing education itself as a political system proves to be especially rewarding in insights about evaluation and politics.

A broad understanding of the politics of education is required in order to encompass the unique role of the educational system in political socialization for the society, the distribution of education itself as a stake, the micropolitical system of the school, and the notion of an educator as a "political man" (or woman).

The role of education in political socialization has little direct importance in our discussion of evaluation and politics and will be discussed, in passing, merely to flesh out the dimensions of educational politics. While there is room for debate on such matters as the importance of schools as compared with mass media and mass culture in the socialization of youth, the schools are the only institution for which political socialization is a legitimate and ascribed function and for which public resources are provided.[22] Clearly, the inculcation of values regarding the appropriate role of government and appropriate responses of citizens to government, is of unusual importance to the continuation of the political system. Because questions about appropriate relationships between men and government are irresolvable in nontotalitarian societies, education and educators will constantly be mustering influence in order to embrace or resist persons, groups, or institutions holding firm views about these questions. Often these struggles will culminate in an

---

22. "It is our conclusion from these data that the school stands out as the central, salient, and dominant force in the political socialization of the young child." Robert D. Hess and Judith V. Torney, *The Development of Political Attitudes in Children* (Chicago: Aldine Publishing Co., 1967), p. 219. The Hess and Torney study considered the impact of family and social class, but not the impact of television, in political socialization.

institution of government such as a court. For example, it is permissible for students to wear arm bands as a protest against particular governmental policies because the judicial system has determined that it is permissible to do so. More often, however, these issues are resolved outside the formal governmental bodies according to the relative influence of educators and advocates at a particular time. The issue of separation between church and state, as reflected in religious observances in public schools, has been resolved by the U.S. Supreme Court but not in the classrooms and principals' offices across the nation. At the local school level struggles to shape the political values of children are continuous.

Additional dimensions of the politics of education are more central to evaluation and politics. These dimensions are somewhat unique to education and are obscured by attention to formal institutions and processes of government. For example, education is itself a stake: almost all people in society care about the quantity and quality of education and, especially, how it is distributed. Of course, people care also about how automobiles are distributed. The distinction is that the auto manufacturers deal with the government in questions pertaining to the production of autos (tariffs, taxes, regulations) but not with the distribution of them. Distribution of autos is controlled by the money market and not, with some exceptions, by the manufacturer. Educators, however, almost alone control the distribution of education within schools and school systems. Like other stakes, there cannot be enough education to satisfy everyone (for example, not enough first-rate language teachers), so educators must make choices about who gets what of the resources available for education. Granted, educators are not autonomous in making these decisions; school boards, courts, or legislative bodies have enforced some stipulations (for example, with regard to integration, equalization of dollar expenditures) and these decisions were made in formal governmental arenas. However, equal dollar expenditure is not the end of the question. Distribution of education (for example, literacy) is controlled in large part by educators. In particular, within a given school system or school building, a micropolitical system exists that determines the distribution of education (teachers, curricula) to students and the struggle to gain influence with regard to these allocative decisions is constant. Because education is a stake, an evaluation depicting how, or how well, it is distributed is a politically salient undertaking.

It is a simple but important extension of the notion of education as a stake distributed through political processes to the discussion of education as an especially potent political symbol. Edelman explains that every political act that is controversial or regarded as really important serves in part as a condensation symbol: a symbol evoking emotions associated with the situation.[23] Educational procedures such as middle schools or modular scheduling—to say nothing of busing—can become intense political issues because they are condensation symbols. They represent all that is good or bad in the world as it pertains to parents' aspirations for themselves and their children. Certainly, the middle school controversy presently immobilizing the Broward County (Florida) Public Schools is not based on the pedagogical consequences of this particular arrangement for learning. Rather, it is based on the fact that the middle school has become a symbol for many dissatisfactions, among them integration, progressive education, increased drug usage, and new sexual mores of preadolescents. The point of this example, and others that the reader can provide from any educational system, is that one may not reasonably expect to engage in an evaluation of a condensation symbol, such as the middle school in Broward County, that does not become of immediate political relevance. Education seems to have more condensation symbols with which to contend than any other public institution, perhaps because it is an institution in which much of the public believes itself to have a stake.

The stakes involved are apparent, for example, in the activities of the Full Funding Committee in Washington, in the formulation of regulations regarding sex discrimination, or in teacher contracts being negotiated by a local board of education. If one applies the general political systems framework to "microsystems" of the political system, another dimension of the politics of education appears. Political struggles of this dimension seldom reach legislative bodies for formal policy determination. Yet distribution of the stakes of jobs (salary increase, status, prestige, and deference) often takes

---

23. Murray Edelman, *The Symbolic Uses of Politics* (Urbana, Ill.: University of Illinois Press, 1964), pp. 6-7.

place in the microsystem. In addition, distribution of money and authority often takes place within the microsystem.

The importance of the micropolitical systems is two-fold. First, it calls attention to the administrative or executive role in politics. The current discussion over whether sex regulations on discrimination have been made more stringent by the bureaucracy than the Congress intended is a ready example. Administrators serving in nonpolitical or nonpolicy positions often determine who gets what by their administrative decisions. These decisions are often the result of agency politics and become apparent only when one focuses on the microsystem of the agency or department. Second, microsystems are the arenas in which it is decided who will be provided a company car or parking space, a wooden or metal desk, a secretary or a "pool." These specific stakes may appear trivial, but they can readily be given significance when one considers the final aspect of the expanded notion of the politics of education: the educator as political man.

We say that the elected superintendent of schools is a "politician," but we know, also, that all administrators are politicians in terms of all the dimensions mentioned above. Furthermore, their major motivating force is to influence the distribution of stakes within their system and their major preoccupation is to increase, or maintain, as much influence within the microsystem of the school as possible. This is the nature of political man.

Is it not ironic that when we observe the behavior of men and women as far removed from a formal political system role as possible (clerics or artists, for example), we discover they are also political actors?[24] The mobilization of resources to influence the distribution of stakes, whether it be the curtailment of sin through a particular dogma or the acceptance of a style of artistic expression, is common to all who have not withdrawn from society. It is prevalent among educators, also, and especially among program or project directors, administrators, and creators of innovative programs—those most likely to be involved in an evaluation. Such

---

24. The intense political struggle between adherents of Lamarck (acquired characteristics) and the neo-Darwinians (change mutation, natural selection), portrayed in all its bitterness by Arthur Koestler in *The Case of the Midwife Toad* (New York: Random House, 1971), is but one compelling example of this phenomenon among scientists.

persons are not neutral about their endeavors in their field. They are in politics. They seek to influence those with whom they deal in specific directions and they use whatever influence they can muster —including the status symbols and otherwise innocuous prestige trappings mentioned above—to do so.

Blau has developed a full-blown political model based on social exchange among individuals.[25] From the efforts, allegorically at least, of two persons seeking to influence one another, Blau explains the cohesion, development, and continuation of formal political institutions such as political parties. To the extent that Blau's work and the common sense observations of the preceding paragraphs are valid, one must conclude that educators, and especially evaluators, who believe they work outside politics are engaged in a self-deception. We shall necessarily return to this theme later in this chapter.

Many political scientists have centered their discipline on the allocative processes of governmental bodies, a reasonable decision that provides loose boundaries to their discipline. But educators and evaluators can ill afford to operate according to this narrow paradigm. For their activities it is necessary to consider the expanded definition of the politics of education involving education itself as a stake to be distributed, the special importance of symbolic issues within education, the importance of micropolitical systems, and the gentle reminder that the model of rational man must be supplemented with the observation that rationality assumes self-interest and politics assumes the acting out of self-interest.

Evaluation and Politics

Evaluation is a political resource that can be used to influence the distribution of stakes in education. As shown in the preceding sections, one reaches this conclusion by reflecting on the meaning of evaluation as expressed by leading practitioners, by adopting a broad definition of politics, and by attending to the specific dimensions of education as a political phenomenon. It remains to demonstrate that it is not only feasible but useful to understand the inherently political nature of educational evaluation. We shall ac-

25. Peter M. Blau, *Exchange and Power in Social Life* (New York: John Wiley & Sons, 1967).

complish this demonstration through vignettes and citations from the growing literature on evaluation of social action programs and demonstration projects. Educational evaluation is certainly broader than program evaluation, but program evaluation offers the best vehicle for the examination of the political nature of evaluation. Much of what follows is applicable to any evaluation.[26]

Many social scientists have commented about the political aspects of evaluation. Several substantial texts have grown from efforts to evaluate programs of the Great Society. Sjoberg provides extensive analyses of the ethical and political aspects of social research.[27] Rossi reviews pertinent studies of social action programs for the purpose of improving the theory and practice of evaluation.[28] Rivlin has generalized from her experiences with the evaluation of several action programs to the end of encouraging procedures resulting in more useful and timely policy information.[29]

House, an educational evaluator, has examined the relationship between evaluation and politics and has reached a conclusion similar to my own:

The major theme of the book is the political nature of evaluation. Contrary to common belief, evaluation is not the ultimate arbiter, delivered from pure objectivity and accepted as the final judgment. Evaluation is always derived from biased origins. When someone wants to defend something or to attack something, he often evaluates it. Evaluation is a motivated behavior. Likewise, the way in which the results of an evaluation are accepted depends on whether they help or hinder the person receiving them. Evaluation is an integral part of the political processes of our society.

At its simplest, evaluation is the process of applying a set of standards to a program, making judgments using the standards, and justifying

26. There are certainly important distinctions between summative and formative, process and product, large-scale and small-scale program evaluations. The discussion does not apply to all evaluation equally, but it is applicable to all evaluations in which genuine stakes are involved.

27. Gideon Sjoberg, ed., *Ethics, Politics, and Social Research* (Cambridge, Mass.: Schenkman Publishing Co., 1967).

28. Peter Rossi and Walter Williams, eds., *Evaluating Social Programs: Theory, Practice, and Politics* (New York: Seminar Press, 1972).

29. Alice M. Rivlin, *Systematic Thinking for Social Action* (Washington, D.C.: Brookings Institution, 1971).

the standards and their application. But there are many standards, especially in a pluralistic society: which to apply? There are many ways of using the standards. Often the initiator of the evaluation determines the standards: if a school superintendent wants to defend a program, he usually chooses the ground on which it is evaluated; if a school critic wishes to attack the program, he chooses different standards. Whichever side the results favor will use them to gain political advantage. Evaluation becomes a tool in the process of who gets what in the society.[30]

The politics of evaluation has more facets, and is more interesting than even House suggests. Certainly, as he states, a decision to evaluate something or someone is a political decision primarily because it is intended to modify the distribution of stakes, or, at least to modify the influence available to some persons to press for a new distribution or to maintain the status quo. The decision to evaluate is itself a political decision, one determined by the relative influence of pertinent actors at any point in time. Moreover, a decision to evaluate is not the final political decision: those to be evaluated are not without political influence and they always use it to insure, to the best of their ability, that an evaluation does not reflect badly on their efforts. The political nature of evaluation is readily apparent through examination of tactics used in offensive evaluation (that is, evaluation undertaken to alter the existing or anticipated distribution of stakes) and defensive evaluation (that is, evaluation or tactics designed to thwart an offensive evaluation).

OFFENSIVE EVALUATION

One of the tactics of offensive evaluation is simply to bring reasonably credible information to a setting devoid of "hard" information. Breslin captures the notion in a passage from a book quite outside the professional literature of educational evaluation:

> A copy of the book was placed on the desk of each Congressman; a loaded gun for use in a duel. When Tip O'Neill came in, he picked up his copy, thumbed it, turned to the last page, saw to his surprise that it was 718 pages long, and announced, "Peter did a hell of a job."
>
> He walked out onto the floor of the House. "Did you see the book Peter put together? Isn't that some job he did? Geez, that Peter is something. What a job he did. Did you see it?"

30. House, *School Evaluation: The Politics and Process*, p. 3.

"I have it in my office, Tip."

"Well, geez, you ought to read it. Peter did the best research on impeachment that's ever been, they tell me. You ought to see the calls I've been getting . . ."

"It's that good, Tip?"

"Hey, there's Peter now. What a job he did. I want to go over and congratulate him."

There was now a book on impeachment. It wasn't an undefinable topic any more. Now it was right there, in a book, that Congressmen could lift and feel and thumb through. And on the cover it said, "Impeachment." It was 718 pages long. Jeee-zus! Goddam big book! Seven hundred and eighteen pages long. Keeerist! This is gettin' to be important business now.

Nobody read a line of the book, but everybody held it and looked at the last page to see that it was 718 pages long.[31]

A somewhat less obvious illustration of offensive evaluation, and one in which evaluation is used more nearly as discussed in this chapter, may be seen in the staffing and procedures of congressional investigations and hearings. The staff of the U.S. National Advisory Commission on Civil Disorders was recruited primarily from among civil rights activists in the various government agencies.[32] Once the staffing decisions were made there could be little doubt about the nature of the ultimate report. Of course, decisions regarding appointment of staff directors, resources to be made available, and access to be provided are reached always on the basis of the relative influence of contending parties.

House demonstrates that extensive evaluations of PLATO (Programmed Logic for Automated Teaching Operations) and of the Illinois Program for the Gifted were undertaken as offensive political tactics. With regard to the program for the gifted, in which he became a principal evaluator, House reports:

When the program was threatened with extinction after five years of operation, it undertook a unique and extensive evaluation to justify its existence. The results were reported to the legislature and top govern-

31. Jimmy Breslin, *How the Good Guys Finally Won* (New York: Viking Press, 1975), pp. 71-2.

32. For an interesting treatment of this topic see Michael Lipsky and David J. Olson, "On the Politics of the Presidential Riot Commission" (Paper presented at the annual meeting of the American Political Science Association, Washington, D.C., 1968).

ment officials, giving the program renewed life and an extra million dollars in funds.[33]

Offensive evaluations can be created to curtail or eliminate programs, as well as to support them. Those involved in the Westinghouse study of Head Start decry the intentional misuse of their evaluation report. Nevertheless, offensive evaluation could not be more clearly illustrated than in the use of that report as a basis for then President Nixon's message on economic opportunity in 1969: "The long-term effect of Head Start appears to be extremely weak."[34] The interesting point here is that while the principal evaluators claim to have been objective and to have used the best evaluative procedures possible under the circumstances, their report predictably became a part of a political battle between a conservative President and a liberal Congress.

The politics involved in reaching a decision to evaluate and the tactics appropriate to offensive evaluation are only half of the story. The reluctant agency or decision maker also has tactics available that are designed to preserve influence or minimize status loss related to an evaluation.

DEFENSIVE EVALUATION

Tactics of defensive evaluation are utilized when there is a presumption that the evaluation will produce negative results. For a variety of reasons, this is a prevalent expectation on the part of those to be evaluated. Ferman attributes this negative orientation to the common understanding that much time will be required, that the evaluators will be insensitive to the political realities of the situation (and therefore draw inappropriate or silly conclusions), that those to be evaluated already know what is lacking in their program, and that the evaluator's concern with the program effects will jeopardize the very existence of the program and, with it,

---

33. Ernest R. House, *The Politics of Educational Innovation* (Berkeley, Calif.: McCutchan Publishing Corp., 1974), p. 201.

34. For a thorough discussion of the Head Start evaluation controversy, see Walter Williams and John W. Evans, "The Politics of Evaluation: The Case of Head Start," in *Evaluating the War on Poverty*, ed. Louis A. Ferman, *Annals of the American Academy of Political and Social Science* 385 (September 1969): 118-32.

accompanying jobs and statuses.[35] Drawing on his experiences in evaluating social welfare programs, Ferman states the negative orientation of administrators and agency staff as follows:

> A common perspective is that "no good can come of it" or "you can only be hurt" because evaluation is organized fault-finding, usually without adequate understanding or explanation of why the faults exist. There are strong feelings among the staff that the evaluator is concerned with negatives, neglects the positives, and gives little credit to the program for operating in the first place. At the core of these perspectives is a deep resentment at having one's behavior studied and judged by an outsider—a feeling that is common in American life.[36]

Certainly, educators have been known to be unenthusiastic about plans to evaluate their endeavors.

Feeling this way about a proposed evaluation carries with it an obvious tactic: prevent the evaluation. The *Washington Post* carried a story about a plan to evaluate principals in the school system of the District of Columbia:

> School Superintendent Hugh J. Scott's proposal that committees of students, parents, and teachers help evaluate the work of principals was greeted yesterday by the principals with shouts of "no" and a warning that such a move would turn them into "political eunuchs." . . .
>
> Washington Teachers Union president William Simons called Scott's proposal "a move in the right direction." Opposition from the principals is ironic, he added, since it is the school principal who is the evaluator of teachers.[37]

Ironic, indeed. Using political resources available to them in the context of the school system bureaucracy, the principals succeeded in having the plan dropped.

Efforts to evaluate social action programs and educational innovations have produced a wealth of rationalizations that can be used by an agency to reduce or obliterate the impact of a critical evaluation. Reports of evaluations conducted in the fields of criminology, mental health, poverty, compensatory education, and state

---

35. Louis A. Ferman, "Evaluating Social Welfare Programs," in *Evaluating the War on Poverty*, ed. Louis A. Ferman, *Annals of the American Academy of Political and Social Science* 385 (September 1969): 147-8.

36. Ibid., p. 147.

37. *Washington Post*, 26 May 1972.

assessment all carry anecdotes depicting the resourcefulness of agencies and individuals to sustain themselves in the face of evaluation-created adversity. Borgatta lists ten rationalizations that he has observed to be useful in avoiding evaluation or in mediating negative findings.[38] Tactics include challenging the conceptualization of the evaluation, its methodology, the time frame utilized, and even the statistical techniques employed. The importance of these defensive tactics lies not in their correctness, but in their utility as vehicles for carrying on the political struggle. Methodological esoterica are useful political resources in countering the impact of a negative finding. Williams has stated the situation well, drawing on his painful experiences as an evaluator of Head Start:

> As the controversy developed, the principal weapons in the battle were the esoteric paraphernalia of modern statistics. One cannot help but find some irony in the spectacle of one academic person accusing another of the mortal sin of an unrepresentative sample, not in the cloistered halls of some professional meeting but on page 1 of the *New York Times*.
>
> But far more important than the barbs in methodological raiment was that the limitations of current methodological capability structured much of the debate.... It is a near certainty that a competent methodologist can call into question such things as the test used, the drawing of the sample, the comparability of the control group. In short, no evaluation can be expected to be unassailable in terms of its methodological and field development. And these deficiencies open up the debate so that ideological or political concerns can be pursued in a methodological framework.[39]

Consequently, even the procedures of evaluation become political resources or liabilities in the struggle over the stakes of education.

ADMINISTRATORS AND EVALUATORS

Evaluators have sought repeatedly to define correct relationships between themselves and decision makers. We have argued above that the consensus seems to be that evaluators should work closely

---

38. Edgar Borgatta, "Research Problems in Evaluation of Health Services Demonstration," *Milbank Memorial Fund Quarterly* 44, Part 2 (October 1966): 186-87.

39. Walter Williams, *Social Policy Research and Analysis: The Experience of the Federal Agencies* (New York: American Elsevier, 1971), pp. 103-4.

with the decision maker who, as Speizman points out, is more often than not their employer, but that they should try to maintain a neutral or apolitical posture.[40] Students of administration prescribe a role for administrators that renders such a posture impossible. Erlandson depicts the proper role of the administrator in the following terms:

> If the administrator expects to maintain a central role in the school organization, he must maintain a central role in the evaluative process. He cannot let himself be frightened or intimidated.
>
> ... The administrator can, and often should, call in outside experts to help him with his evaluation but, in doing so, cannot afford to abdicate his central role in the process. He needs to know specifically what he wants of the evaluation. He should realize that not all evaluation specialists are the same. His decision to call in a particular expert should be based upon that expert's particular competence.
>
> ... The administrator should tell the expert: "This is what I want. Can you get it for me? If you can, how do you propose to do it? If not, I'll shop around. . . ."[41]

If the administrators or decision makers undertake to control an evaluation to this extent, how can evaluators remain outside the politics of the setting?

Suchman draws on his experiences in evaluating mental health programs to describe the uses (he refers to "abuses") to which an administrator who is in control can turn evaluation:

1. *Eye-wash*—an attempt to justify a weak or bad program by deliberately selecting only those aspects that "look good." The objective of the evaluation is limited to those parts of the program that appear successful.
2. *White-wash*—an attempt to cover up program failure or errors by avoiding any objective appraisal. A favorite device here is to solicit "testimonials" which divert attention from the failure.
3. *Submarine*—an attempt to "torpedo" or destroy a program regardless of its worth in order to get rid of it. This often occurs in

---

40. Speizman, "Evaluation: An Evaluation from a Sociological Perspective," p. 204.

41. David A. Erlandson, "Evaluation and an Administrator's Autonomy," in House, *School Evaluation: The Politics and Process*, pp. 21-22.

administrative clashes over power or prestige when opponents are "sunk" along with their programs.
4. *Posture*—an attempt to use evaluation as a "gesture" of objectivity and to assume the pose of "scientific" research. This "looks good" to the public and is a sign of "professional" status.
5. *Postponement*—an attempt to delay needed action by pretending to seek the "facts." Evaluative research takes time and, hopefully, the storm will blow over by the time the study is completed.
6. *Substitution*—an attempt to "cloud over" or disguise failure in an essential part of the program by shifting attention to some less relevant, but defensible, aspect of the program.[42]

Evaluators are not unmindful of such administrator or agency "abuses." Scriven has proposed procedures that approach the status of ethical canons for assuring the independence of the evaluator from his project.[43] Stufflebeam has described seven sociopolitical problems confronted by evaluators and has provided an extended discussion of the need for meta-evaluation—evaluation of evaluations—as a means of assuring that each problem is treated appropriately.[44]

The problem is that, even when the bias of the evaluators is controlled, evaluation remains a political resource of tremendous potential for altering the status of education and educators. As will be seen below, even an evaluation in which measures to assure independence of the evaluators are attempted, evaluation remains an essentially political phenomenon.

Politics of Evaluators and Evaluation Agencies

Educational evaluators have attended scarcely at all to the political aspects of their work or of their agencies and when they have tried to do so they have, by and large, demonstrated little understanding of the politics of education. Other evaluators, especially sociologists, have provided an alternative literature that allows

42. Edward A. Suchman, *Evaluative Research* (New York: Russell Sage Foundation, 1967), p. 143.

43. Michael Scriven, "Evaluation Bias and Its Control," Occasional Paper no. 4, mimeographed (Kalamazoo, Mich.: Evaluation Center of the College of Education, Western Michigan University, 1975).

44. Daniel L. Stufflebeam, "Meta-evaluation," Occasional Paper no. 3, mimeographed (Kalamazoo, Mich.: Evaluation Center of the College of Education, Western Michigan University, n.d.).

one to raise some appropriate questions about the politics of evaluators and the politics of agencies for evaluation.

POLITICS OF EVALUATORS

Popham states that the current fervor within the field of evaluation has emerged within the decade.[45] The literature reviewed in the preparation of this chapter corroborates his observation. Consequently, because of the recency of the movement, merely pointing out that evaluators have neglected the political facet of their world is more an observation than a criticism. Sociologists, who now have the luxury of confessing to methodological and political sins committed when they were younger, provide a dimension of evaluation that generally is lacking in the work of educational evaluators.

In Hammond's book *Sociologists at Work*,[46] for example, a dozen sociologists report on misgivings, wrong turns, methodological errors, self-aggrandizement, and frustration that now lie buried and otherwise unknowable on the cutting room floor of classic studies such as *Union Democracy*, *The Adolescent Society*, and the *Dynamics of Bureaucracy*. Throughout these accounts runs the common theme that the evaluators (in most cases, but not all, these were "researchers") made a great many choices on the basis of their political persuasion, including the decision of whether or not to undertake a study in the first place. Questions of economic rewards and status-building opportunities (including publication potential) are discussed quite matter-of-factly. No doubt, such considerations also occur to educational evaluators and also help determine their methodology, level of commitment to an evaluation project, and the construction of their final reports.

One set of interesting questions, then, about the politics of evaluators has to do with their own values—their stakes—and the relation of their stakes to the work they seek or accept, and the way they go about completing their work. Evaluators necessarily have an interest in satisfying funding sources, in securing or maintaining the respect of their peers, as well as being true to themselves. Re-

---

45. Popham, *Evaluation in Education*, preface.

46. Phillip E. Hammond, ed., *Sociologists at Work: Essays on the Craft of Social Research* (New York: Basic Books, 1964).

ports describing evaluators' responses to the dilemmas created by mutually exclusive goals exist within the literature of evaluating social action programs. They are not included, generally, in the set of questions educational evaluators ask about their profession.

Benveniste depicts the shrewd aggressiveness required on the part of experts seeking to gain access to a decision maker or to cinch their access by warding off competitors.[47] Without evidence in his experience to the contrary, Benveniste assumes that experts seek access to decision makers in order to influence policy. He describes the political resourcefulness, exquisite timing, skill, energy, commitments, and compromise necessary to achieve this end. The experts Benveniste analyzes are not educational evaluators, but there are intriguing parallels between the two. One parallel is that both offer tangible expertise to the decision makers. For neither, however, is their bona fide expertise alone sufficient to gain and hold the attention of the decision maker. Expertise is plentiful. Benveniste has described the political tactics of experts but, thus far, none has addressed himself to the question of competition among evaluators to secure and maintain positions of maximum influence.

House is the only educational evaluator to demonstrate sensitivity about the politics of evaluators along the lines described here. He asserts, for example, that he would not have expended the time necessary to evaluate the Illinois Program for the Gifted if he were a neutral observer and he points to the effect of his values on the manner in which he carried out his responsibilities.[48] Moreover, House implores evaluators to accept responsibility for putting their reports in a "context of persuasion," [49] and acknowledges that most evaluations are sponsored by groups who are seeking to alter the distribution of stakes of education.[50]

Throughout this chapter we have implied that evaluators have ignored the politics of evaluation and evaluators. An example is called for and fortunately *Phi Delta Kappan* has presented us with

---

47. Guy Benveniste, *The Politics of Expertise* (Berkeley, Calif.: Glendessary Press, 1972).

48. House, *School Evaluation: The Politics and Process*, p. 132.

49. Ibid., p. 135.

50. Ibid., p. 128.

a report on the now controversial evaluation of the Michigan Accountability Program.[51] Equally fortunate for rhetorical purposes, the evaluators of the Michigan Accountability Program are leaders in the field, including House, whose work in the politics of evaluation has already been noted.

House, Rivers, and Stufflebeam agreed to conduct an evaluation of the Michigan Accountability Program at the request of the Michigan Education Association and the National Education Association. They did so, and subsequently agreed to have the report, which was critical, published in the *Phi Delta Kappan*. Several months later, representatives from the Michigan State Department of Education responded,[52] and the evaluators provided a rejoinder to the response.[53]

There is much in the criticism of the Michigan Accountability System that is compelling; certainly, the methods and procedures of the evaluation epitomize the professional standards of the field. But there are a number of special features of the evaluation that are so blatantly political that they simply cannot be swept under the worn carpet of professional objectivity.

First, accountability is an ideal example of a condensation symbol in education. An evaluation report of any accountability system will become a political resource if not handled with extreme care. This report was drop-kicked from Lansing, Michigan, to Bloomington, Indiana.

Second, it was no secret that there were contending views about the merit of the accountability system introduced in Michigan. The teachers did not like it. They caused an evaluation to be made. The evaluators contend that the agreement negotiated with the MEA-NEA, which established the evaluators' complete independence in conducting, writing, and disseminating the study, is regarded as a

---

51. Ernest R. House, Wendell Rivers, and Daniel L. Stufflebeam, "An Assessment of the Michigan Accountability System," *Phi Delta Kappan* 55 (June 1974): 663-69.

52. C. Philip Kearney, David L. Donovan, and Thomas H. Fisher, "In Defense of Michigan's Accountability Program," *Phi Delta Kappan* 56 (September 1974): 14-19.

53. Ernest R. House, Wendell Rivers, and Daniel L. Stufflebeam, "A Counter-response to Kearney, Donovan, and Fisher," *Phi Delta Kappan* 56 (September 1974): 19.

model for others to follow.[54] Perhaps so. We trust, however, that the preceding sections of this paper have demonstrated that the funding agency generally knows what it hopes to gain by an evaluation and that it seeks out evaluators accordingly. We know, for example, that House was not a neutral evaluator in the Illinois Program for the Gifted. Is it not simply reasonable to assume that he and his associates held strong beliefs about, say, the desirability of evaluating teachers through the performance of students, and that they welcomed an opportunity to conduct an evaluation that would influence others with regard to this value?

Murphy and Cohen, writing about the Michigan accountability plan in *Public Interest*, also call attention to the crucial importance of selecting the right evaluators. They state:

The panel was chosen after a "nationwide search" for individuals with "competencies that we [MEA-NEA] believe essential to an evaluation" of accountability. Indeed. House has attacked the basic ideas behind accountability, and last summer he helped NEA develop its antiaccountability platform; Rivers has written about the evils of culturally biased tests; and Stufflebeam is an expert on evaluation and a stickler for research design.

We are sure that these experts' conclusions were not "dictated" by their employer. But the MEA did not choose experts with other views.[55]

The three evaluators quite properly point out that government agencies choose the evaluators they wish. And, certainly, teachers should have the same right (a point to be discussed further below). They ask, rhetorically, "Why, now that teacher organizations have hired a panel of experts, do charges of bias arise?"[56] The charge of bias is patently obvious: an evaluation conducted by a team selected by John Porter, Michigan's Chief State School Officer and a

---

54. The full contract drawn up between the evaluators and the MEA-NEA is discussed at length by Daniel Stufflebeam, "A Response to the Michigan Education Department's Defense of Their Accountability System," mimeographed (Klamazoo, Mich.: Evaluation Center of the College of Education, Western University, 1974). The contract stipulated that the evaluation team would be "solely in charge of developing and editing its final report."

55. Jerome T. Murphy and David K. Cohen, "Accountability in Education: The Michigan Experience," *The Public Interest*, no. 36 (Summer 1974): 66.

56. House, Rivers, and Stufflebeam, "A Counter-response," p. 19.

prominent advocate of the Accountability Program, would not have provided the same report. Especially, such a team would not have provided a report focusing on teacher concerns. It is humorous to note that one of the "failures" of the Michigan effort observed by the evaluators was that the four teachers who helped develop and review objectives "felt their involvement was cursory and too much a formality."[57] This finding represents an inconsequential, but not very subtle, tilt in the direction of the MEA-NEA values.

Finally, publishing or permitting someone else to publish an evaluation report in a major educational journal must be viewed as a strategem for increasing the influence of one group at the expense of another. Publishing the evaluation in a national educational journal suggests that the stakes the evaluators hope to influence are national stakes. In the response to the Michigan State Department of Education reply, the evaluators offer their own ideology, previously unstated:

We strongly support local school curricula that are diverse and responsive to individual needs; the Michigan Department of Education in its talk of objectives that transcend local districts clearly does not. If state objectives and state tests prevail now, can state curricula really be far behind?[58]

This is a surprisingly conservative ideology, but the important point is that it is an ideology. The evaluators have a stake in the Michigan accountability system, and their stake is very close to that of the MEA-NEA.

Clearly, evaluators occupy influential positions in the politics of education. They have access to critical, politically potent information and their expertise has currency sufficient to gain the attention of the media and decision makers. This has not always been true, and may not be true in the future, but for the moment

57. House, Rivers, and Stufflebeam, "An Assessment of the Michigan Accountability System," p. 666. It is not surprising that this question was addressed. "Involvement of teachers in developing both objectives and tests" was a specific question to be investigated. See Stufflebeam, "A Response to the Michigan Education Department's Defense of Their Accountability System," p. 9.

58. House, Rivers, and Stufflebeam, A Counter-response," p. 19.

it must simply be acknowledged. A set of questions helpful in examining the values of evaluators properly should be introduced.

POLITICS OF EVALUATION AGENCIES

Even less attention has been given to the politics of evaluation agencies than to the politics of evaluators. Rodriguez provided a free-swinging, muckraking political perspective on the Educational Testing Service.[59] Rossi has introduced the concept of "Robin Hooding" within research organizations such as the National Opinion Research Center, as well as the topic of the political relationships of such centers to the university and to faculty scholars.[60] Both Williams and Speizman support the contention that little is known about the politics of evaluation agencies, although they choose different expressions to do so. Williams states: "Little effort has been expended to study systematically the social science research community—no one has researched the researchers."[61] Speizman charges that no one has evaluated the evaluators.[62]

Evaluation agencies and research institutes have been shown to come under rather heavy-handed political constraints. Record reports three instances in her personal experience in which evaluative reports offensive to persons with influence over the agency were modified, delayed, or simply never released.[63] The offended agencies were able to influence the institute by threatening curtailment of funding or curtailment of future access. In a fourth case, the research institute refused to conduct a study because it became apparent that only certain findings would be acceptable to the government agency contracting the study. While Record initiates consideration of the political resources and liabilities of an agency

59. Eric Rodriguez, "Inside the Educational Testing Service," *Washington Monthly* 6 (July-August 1974): 5-12.

60. Peter Rossi, "Observations on the Organization of Social Research," in Rossi and Williams, *Evaluating Social Programs*, pp. 267-286.

61. Walter Williams, "The Capacity of Social Science Organizations to Perform Large-scale Evaluative Research," in Rossi and Williams, *Evaluating Social Programs*, p. 293.

62. Speizman, "Evaluation: An Evaluation from a Sociological Perspective."

63. Jane Cassels Record, "The Research Institute and the Pressure Group," in Sjoberg, *Ethics, Politics, and Social Research*, pp. 25-50.

for withstanding aberrant influence on its evaluations and research, little has been done to explore this question.

Firestone presents an enlightening report about work patterns and productivity associated with a "contract shop"—Abt Associates.[64] He touches on only one of the political aspects of evaluation agencies: the responsiveness of the agency to the needs of its clients. According to Firestone, one of the fears of researchers or evaluators working in the field is that of incurring the displeasure of a client: "Although monitoring within Abt Associates has not been extensive, signs of serious discontent on the part of the client agencies for other projects have elicited actions from higher levels that ranged from extensive supervision of report writing to removal of the project director and other staff reassignments."[65]

In the absence of descriptive information about the politics of evaluation agencies we may at the least assume that they are similar to the politics of other micropolitical systems, such as schools of education. Certainly, evaluation agencies must develop mechanisms for influencing the external world, if not to gain at least to keep; certainly, difficult questions that are resolved within the micropolitical system, must arise regarding trade-offs between evaluation opportunities and institutional integrity.

Prognosis for the Politics of Evaluation

We have provided a general framework appropriate for considering the topic of evaluation and politics in education, and we have illustrated some of the dimensions of this relationship. While politics and evaluation are themselves timeless concepts, we have imposed a narrow time frame on our examination (most citations and examples have been drawn from the period between 1965 and the present) in order to encompass adequately the emerging paradigms of the disciplines of political science and educational evaluation. While it is clear that our discussion differs from one that would have been undertaken twenty years ago, assuming anyone would have grouped the words politics, evaluation, and education in a single title, it is not clear that a similar effort conducted ten years

64. William Firestone, "Education Field Research in a 'Contract Shop'," *The Generator* 5 (Spring 1975): 3-16.

65. Ibid., p. 9.

from now will take the same form as ours. It is, perhaps, worthwhile to try to imagine future developments in the politics of evaluation.

Ten years hence, one trying to think about this topic might want to follow three lines of inquiry. First, a foundation has already been laid here for an investigation of the general level of understanding or attention to the politics of evaluation in education. A second line of inquiry might involve examination of methodological changes in the process of evaluation that reflect adequate understanding of the political function of evaluation. A third line of inquiry might focus on the dynamics within the field as it seeks to maintain its credibility in the face of increasing cynicsm about the politics of evaluation.

I believe one can be sanguine about development of a more comprehensive understanding of the politics of evaluation. We may anticipate that questions raised throughout our discussion will have been answered by systematic examination within ten years. The politics of evaluation agencies, for example, will have been the subject of investigation. Some of the political functions of evaluation in education will have been fully explored, perhaps in terms of a typology already introduced by Iannaccone.[66] Finally, one may anticipate that more sophisticated understandings of the politics of evaluation will have replaced present notions that politics should not be allowed to "interfere" with one's work or the equally inadequate notion that politics is a necessary burden that must somehow be finessed.[67]

66. Iannaccone, for example, has already proposed formal research on the basis of a typology comprised of four dimensions: (a) participants (for example, schoolmen, research types, social action types); (b) who initiates? (for example, outsiders, insiders); (c) who conducts? (for example, outsiders, insiders); and (d) career effects (that is, potential effects of particular study on the career of the evaluator). See Laurence Iannaccone, "Increasing Irresponsibility in Education: A Growing Gap between Policy Planning and Operational Groups," in Michael Kirst, ed., *State, School, and Politics* (Lexington, Mass.: Lexington Books, 1972), pp. 198-203.

67. Under the index listing "negative impact of politics of evaluation" in the *Encyclopedia of Educational Evaluation* one finds this admonition: "Since the politics of evaluation may thus be seen as a potential obstacle to conducting evaluations, those concerned with evaluation must perforce be concerned with political factors and prepared to deal with them." Scarvia Anderson et al., *Encyclopedia of Educational Evaluation* (San Francisco, Calif.: Jossey-Bass, 1975), p. 238.

This is to say that the discussion of evaluation and politics provided here will be superfluous within a decade. I am reasonably confident that this will be the case because I believe that the emerging paradigm of the politics of education, symbolized by a concern for the distribution of stakes within microsystems, will become pervasive in education. More importantly, evaluators themselves, once they have established their new discipline, will no longer have to husband their intellectual energy. Given time, the vigorous examination of methods and models that now characterizes the field will shift to other questions, including those of the politics of evaluation.

It is for the evaluators themselves to investigate methodological approaches that reflect an understanding of the politics of evaluation. However, three methodological approaches are already on the horizon and can be mentioned by way of illustration.

One modification, suggested indirectly by Stufflebeam,[68] involves the creation of evaluation designs in accord with a more comprehensive understanding of the stakes involved for various levels or segments of a program. Understanding the potential effects of an evaluation on the staff of an agency, for example, should be useful in anticipating and accommodating various forms of resistance to the evaluation, and in insuring that all relevant persons or groups are included in the evaluation.

Another procedure that may accommodate greater understanding of the political function of evaluation is the advocate/adversary model of evaluation put forward by Stake[69] and elaborated more recently by Scriven.[70] In essence, such procedures can minimize the importance of the evaluators' values by balancing them with a competing set of values, or by requiring that one evaluator be an

68. In a discussion of appropriate training for school evaluators, Stufflebeam et al. suggest that knowledge of political science can enhance the design of an evaluation by providing a more thorough identification of decision makers involved. Stufflebeam et al., *Educational Evaluation and Decision Making*, p. 307.

69. Robert Stake and Craig Gjerde, *An Evaluation of T City: The Twin City Institute for Talented Youth* (Urbana, Ill.: Center for Instructional Research and Curriculum Evaluation, University of Illinois, 1971).

70. Michael Scriven, *Evaluation: A Study Guide for School Administrators* (Fort Lauderdale, Fla.: Nova University Press, 1974), pp. 52-53.

advocate, the other an adversary of the program under review. These procedures would seem to increase the information available to the decision makers, and also to reduce the degree of "stonewalling" that will otherwise be encountered in the conduct of an evaluation. Ideally, the procedure would allow the evaluator to maximize his value position and still leave the ultimate responsibility for decision with the appropriate decision maker.

Wilensky believes that advocacy proceedings are essential devices for administrative truth finding, and that they have been throughout history. He states:

> In the popular view, science is a more distinterested and, therefore, better institution for uncovering truth. But major advances in scientific theory often come from men insisting on opposing models of physical or social nature. They are often polemical; their debate is sometimes carried on in the spirit of armies at war, as Priestley's holding action against Lavoisier's theory of chemical elements, Marx's invective about German idealism, and Weber's insistence on the role of religious ethics in economic life all illustrate.[71]

The appealing character of the advocate/adversary procedure is considerably diminished by noting that two evaluations will cost about twice as much as one, and that there are more than two sides, or two value positions, on many educational issues.

Reporting of findings is the area of evaluation that is most likely to be modified as the consequence of a broader understanding of evaluation and politics. Full understanding that many educational programs become politically rich condensation symbols and that evaluation information is valuable information in the politics of education will make responsible evaluators more cautious. More attention will be given to stating exactly what was studied, how, and at whose request. Explicit attention will be given to conclusions that may *not* be drawn from an evaluation. The recent RAND survey of education is representative of this approach.[72] Sophisticated reporting can only be accomplished, of course, if the evaluator is fully cognizant of the politics of that which has been evaluated.

71. Harold L. Wilensky, *Organizational Intelligence: Knowledge and Policy in Government and Industry* (New York: Basic Books, 1967), p. 153.

72. Harvey A. Averch et al., *How Effective is Schooling?* (Englewood Cliffs. N.J.: Education Technology Publications, 1975).

Those who have been evaluated—the evaluatees—are very sensitive to the political functions of evaluation. Case studies from the literature of social action programs indicate that claims for the significance of evaluation in other than political terms will be met with cynicism. It will be interesting to observe how evaluators seek to accommodate increased understanding of the political functions of evaluation without incurring even greater cynicism and without suffering a loss in credibility.

CHAPTER XI

If Schools Are for Learning, the Study of the Politics of Education Is Just Beginning

WILLIS D. HAWLEY

Some forty years ago, Lasswell, one of the nation's most esteemed political scientists, observed: "Students of politics are expected to have something pertinent to offer about the probable effects of adoption of one form of government or another, or one policy or another relating to power."[1] Judging by the published literature, however, such expectations are apparently not held by most scholars who study politics. Moreover, from the paucity of political scientists who play important roles in government or as counselors to those who govern, one might also infer that the notion that political scientists have something to say to policy makers is not widely shared by those with political power.

Political scientists have been known to argue to exhaustion about the proper concerns of their "discipline." While countless definitions of politics have emerged from such debates, the formulation that appears to have both the greatest currency and the greatest staying power is Lasswell's. Politics, he says, is "who gets what, when and how."[2] Whether one accepts Lasswell's definition or other such widely held and related conceptions that politics involves the authoritative allocation of resources and values,[3] my point is the same—political scientists have been more interested in studying the political *processes* than they have been in studying who receives what benefits from the political process.

---

1. Harold D. Lasswell, *Politics: Who Gets What, When, and How* (Cleveland, Ohio: Meridian Books, 1958), p. 187.

2. Ibid.

3. See David Easton, *A Systems Analysis of Political Life* (New York: John Wiley & Sons, 1965).

Of course, much of value can be learned without concerning oneself with the empirical consequences of political action and this brief essay is not meant to be a critique of what most political scientists have done. This chapter, however, does seek to encourage greater attention by those who study politics—and, more particularly, the politics of education—to issues that go beyond questions of who governs and how governors behave to the straightforward question, "So what?"

There are at least two reasons why it seems important to begin a more concerted effort to document and understand the linkages between political processes and political outcomes. First, even if one is not interested in who benefits from politics, the relative neglect of the consequences of political processes and political behavior places significant limits on our explanations of why these processes and behaviors take the forms they do. Thus, political theories are less robust and more fragile than they could be. Second, inattention to political outcomes limits importantly the contributions political scientists can make to the development of a more just society, whatever one's definition might be of justice. And, if systematic scholarship has little to say to those who would bring about change, then a potentially significant source of political power, namely knowledge, is in effect neutralized. Under these circumstances, the justifications for academic political inquiry are defined —conveniently, some would say—by criteria determined by scholars themselves. The measures of "good" research and scholarship take on a technical quality that to many outside the *profession* seem esoteric and arcane.

Many of those who are familiar with the titles of recent books and articles by political scientists will surely suspect that I at least overstate the argument. For example, what about the newfound interest of political science in public policy? It does seem increasingly hard to find one of us who does not make some claim that what he or she does is policy-revelant. But in most cases a closer look will show old wine in new bottles. Although there is a growing number of studies that deal with particular public policies, it is invariably the policy *process* that is under investigation. Moreover, with some exceptions, it is that part of the policy process that occurs in the absence of those who are the recipients or targets of public services. In schools, for example, little attention is given to what goes on in classrooms and why.

Policy Studies and the Field of American Political Inquiry

One way to clarify the point is to suggest that one can think of recent research on public policy as falling into four general categories: (1) studies of policy formulation, (2) studies of policy outputs, (3) studies of implementation, and (4) studies of policy impact. We have quite a number of studies in the first and second categories, some in the third, and very few in the fourth. Our understanding of politics could be substantially enriched if we had more research that dealt with the linkages among these various dimensions of politics. Among the studies that deal with three or more of the categories are Lipsky's *Protest in City Politics*,[4] Allison's *Essence of Decision*,[5] Greenstone and Peterson's *Race and Authority in Urban Politics*,[6] Keech's *The Impact of Negro Voting*,[7] Lowi's *The End of Liberalism*,[8] Wirt's *The Politics of Southern Equality*,[9] and some reports of the "Oakland Project."[10] But this work does not have much company.[11] It seems that the point I am making can

---

4. Michael Lipsky, *Protest in City Politics: Rent Strikes, Housing, and the Power of the Poor* (Chicago: Rand McNally & Co., 1969).

5. Graham Allison, *Essence of Decision: Explaining the Cuban Missile Crisis* (Boston, Mass.: Little, Brown & Co., 1971).

6. J. David Greenstone and Paul Peterson, *Race and Authority in Urban Politics: Community Participation and the War on Poverty* (New York: Russell Sage Foundation, 1973).

7. William R. Keech, *The Impact of Negro Voting: The Role of the Vote in the Quest for Equality* (Chicago: Rand McNally & Co., 1968).

8. Theodore Lowi, *The End of Liberalism: Ideology, Policy, and the Crisis of Public Authority* (New York: W. W. Norton & Co., 1969).

9. Frederick M. Wirt, *The Politics of Southern Equality: Law and Social Change in a Mississippi County* (Chicago: Aldine Publishing Co., 1971).

10. See, for example, Frank S. Levy, Arnold J. Meltsner, and Aaron Wildavsky, *Urban Outcomes* (Berkeley, Calif.: University of California Press, 1974).

11. This assertion is admittedly difficult to test, since the universe of relevant studies is ill-defined and what makes them "political" is a matter of debate. However, one of the most distinguished commentators on the profession of political science, has written a major assessment of the field of American politics. See Heinz Eulau, "Understanding Political Life in America," *Social Science Quarterly* 57 (June 1976): 112-53. Eulau cites forty-one works as

too readily be dismissed by pointing to the large body of research that deals with some aspect of public policy. Thus, at the considerable risk of losing my audience to less pedantic writing, let me try to clarify the boundaries of these four types of policy-related research so as to illustrate that the fourth type, policy impacts or outcomes, remains largely uncharted territory.

POLICY FORMULATION

Studies of policy formulation deal with legislative or executive processes that have public policies as their products. The policies themselves may be dealt with but they are not the focus of the research and there is little concern for the effects of the legislation or administrative orders involved. Many political scientists have toiled in these fields. Among the better recent examples of such work are Price's *Who Makes the Laws?*,[12] Fritschler's *Smoking and Politics*,[13] and Sundquist's *Making Federalism Work*.[14] However, to know what a policy looks like when it is passed by a legislature or ordered by a high level executive officer is not to know what that policy looks like to its putative beneficiaries. A policy approved is not a policy implemented.

POLICY OUTPUTS

A second type of policy study focuses on variations in formal policies, almost always in terms of taxation or expenditure levels

---

"landmarks." Only one of these, *The Political Character of Adolescence: The Influence of Families and Schools*, by M. Kent Jennings and Richard G. Niemi (Princeton, N.J.: Princeton University Press, 1974), deals with policy implementation and outcomes, although the study treats policy formulation implicitly and measures implementation through the eyes of children rather than directly. The reader is invited to apply my "three out of four" test to a number of issues of any major political science journal. My effort to do this for the *American Political Science Review* for June 1975 to July 1976 failed to discover one article that met the test.

12. David E. Price, *Who Makes the Laws? Creativity and Power in Senate Committees* (Cambridge, Mass.: Schenkman Publishing Co., 1972).

13. A. Lee Fritschler, *Smoking and Politics: Policy Making and the Federal Bureaucracy* (New York: Appleton-Century-Crofts, 1969).

14. James L. Sundquist, *Making Federalism Work: A Study of Program Coordination at the Community Level* (Washington, D.C.: Brookings Institution, 1969).

in a number of different communities, states, or countries.[15] These studies, which we can call output research,[16] examine the correlation between various social and political characteristics of particular jurisdictions and the expenditures of taxation politics pursued by these governments. Much has been written about the usefulness of such research and there is no need to review that debate here.[17] It is enough to note that (a) almost all of this work fails to take into account important aspects of the political process and (b) it is "policies" that are being examined, frequently in terms that actually aggregate diverse policies, rather than the effects the policies have on people.[18] For example, to know how much a government spends on recreation is not to know where such services are located, who participates in them, or what impact these services have on the lives of people. Similarly, to know that a given school system spends more than another is not to know whether such variations in spending result in variations in the benefits children receive from school.

IMPLEMENTATION

A third class of policy-related research deals with how legislative and administrative policies are modified and even negated, while new policy is being formulated, by those charged with policy implementation.

---

15. See, for example, Thomas R. Dye, *Politics, Economics, and Public Policy: Outcomes in the American States* (Chicago: Rand McNally & Co., 1966); Richard E. Dawson and James A. Robinson, "Interparty Competition, Economic Variables, and Welfare Policies in the American States," *Journal of Politics* 25 (May 1963): 265-89; and Richard I. Hofferbert, "The Relation between Public Policy and Some Structural and Environmental Variables in the American States," *American Political Science Review* 60 (March 1966): 73-82.

16. See Levy, Meltsner, and Wildavsky, *Urban Outcomes*, chap. 1.

17. For a recent critique of these studies see J. M. Munns, "The Environment, Politics and Policy Literature: A Critique and Reformulation," *Western Political Quarterly* 28 (December 1975): 646-67.

18. One might argue that studies focusing on taxing policies rather than spending policies speak directly to policy outcomes, since there is a direct effect on individuals (no discretionary implementation is required in most cases) that can be assessed. However, these multijurisdictional studies generally do not deal adequately with how variations in the political process might be linked to variations in individual or group tax burdens. See, for example, Ira Sharkansky, *The Politics of Taxing and Spending* (Indianapolis, Ind.: Bobbs-Merrill Co., 1969).

The new emphasis on "implementation," as exemplified by the work of Pressman and Wildavsky,[19] and the insights into the importance of bureaucratic processes gained from analyses in the work of Herbert Kaufman, David Rogers, Samuel Halperin, Harold Seidman, and others provide substantial evidence of the capacity of "administrators" and civil servants at all levels of the hierarchy to shape public policy. These and similar studies should contribute significantly to the sophistication with which political analysis is undertaken and they help us understand why the study of expenditures or other legislative action does not tell us enough about public policy to answer the question, "So what?" This type of research focuses on the making of public policy and seldom on how the policies involved affect those they are alleged to serve or regulate, or whether different patterns of decision making would have had different consequences.

POLICY IMPACT

A fourth type of policy study is concerned directly with the impact of political actions on potential beneficiaries. Here, again, we might make some further distinctions between impact on the level of goods, services, and privileges received and the impact that these actually have on the quality of life people experience. I shall call the first of these "allocation" studies and reserve the notion of outcomes for the second. Most of the impact research falls into the allocation category. Allocation studies deal with what are initially considered means to higher ends but often (although not always) come to be thought of as ends in themselves. For example, the distribution of education, health, and welfare expenditures is of concern regardless of their consequences, as is racial balance in the schools, the level of police services, clean streets, and the like.

Allocation studies differ from output studies in that the latter focus on what governments do rather than on what people receive. In some cases, this distinction is a matter of the degree of specificity given to labeling the recipients. And as one begins to identify variations in services delivered by neighborhood, social class, race, and

---

19. Jeffrey Pressman and Aaron Wildavsky, *Implementation* (Berkeley, Calif., University of California Press, 1974).

the like, the possibilities of linking such variations to political events and activity is enhanced. Let me emphasize, however, that a concern for allocations, or outcomes for that matter, cannot provide answers to the "So what?" question if the political process itself is not well specified.

In some cases, the distinction between allocation and outcomes is difficult to sustain either because the linkage between a service and an outcome is so close, such as the provision of certain services like street paving or the fluoridation of water,[20] or because the means to achieve a given end becomes as important as the end itself, such as the elimination of de jure school desegregation without overt racial conflict[21] or the protection of certain rights.[22]

This effort to distinguish between types of policy studies seeks to clarify the point that even among the minority of political scientists who do directly consider the policy question, only a handful deal with the impact of public policies and most of these deal with the allocation of resources and privileges rather than the outcomes such allocations have for the quality of life experienced by different groups or individuals.

In short, few political scientists have linked the political process to policy outcomes. A few examples from major areas of research in political science may suffice to suggest where future research might go if one finds the argument I've been making at all persuasive:

1. We know a fair amount about voting behavior or turnout but almost nothing about whether variations in behavior or turnout affect the substance and impact of public policy.

2. We know something about the socialization of party activists and legislators and we can classify legislators by the dominant roles they play but we cannot say much about whether that socialization or these roles make any difference in terms of the policies they support or to the people the legislators allegedly serve.

20. See Robert Crain, Elihu Katz, and Donald B. Rosenthal, *The Politics of Community Conflict* (Indianapolis, Ind.: Bobbs-Merrill Co., 1969).

21. See David Kirby et al., *Political Strategies in Northern School Desegregation* (Lexington, Mass.: Lexington Books, D. C. Heath & Co., 1973).

22. See Francis Fox Piven and Richard A. Cloward, *Regulating the Poor: The Function of Public Welfare* (New York: Pantheon Books, 1971).

3. In thinking of the countless articles by political scientists on such topics as decentralization, metropolitan government, government reorganization, community power, party organizations, and judicial reform, it is hard to identify more than a handful that speak in other than speculative terms to the quality of life experienced by the citizenry.

4. How many studies of the President or of the Office of President (one can substitute governor, or mayor, or city manager) give any guidance to those who seek hard evidence on the "So what?" question?

Research on the Politics of Education

What are the implications of all this for those who are concerned with the politics of education? It is not my goal to debunk or devalue the work of the growing number of persons who have decided that schooling is a worthy subject for political analysis. It is instead to urge that we take seriously the notion that the purposes of politics are to resolve conflict and to alter or sustain the conditions that make up the life experiences that people value. If that is the purpose of politics, its study must go beyond processes and formal policies to examine the linkage between how political actors (both public officials and other citizens) behave and the factors shaping such behavior to studies of the consequences of the delivery of public services for those the services are meant to affect.

All of this implies the inevitable agenda for future research. While the objective of this chapter is not to undertake a comprehensive critique of the literature dealing with the politics of education, one can scarcely urge a redirection of such research without illustrating how important areas of political inquiry dealing with education fall short of meeting the "So what?" test. Thus, I wish to take three general topics about which much has been written and try to indicate why the previous research seldom helps one know and explain policy outcomes and what types of questions deserve, therefore, to be addressed more extensively.

THE STRUCTURE OF SCHOOL GOVERNANCE

Not surprisingly, political scientists studying education have given considerable attention to issues related to the structure of political institutions and formal decision making. The research reflects concern for such matters as voter turnout and electoral competition; the pros and cons of partisanship, at-large versus district elections, and "community control"; fiscal and political autonomy of schools with respect to other agencies of local government; the role conceptions of board members and school officials; and, especially, the relative influence of school boards and key administrators in decision making.[23]

Clearly, these and other questions dealing with the structure of school governance are important but almost none of this research deals with the impact of different institutions and actors on the quality of life in public schools. How do variations in electoral conflict affect the adaptiveness of schools to student needs? Does community control or greater parental involvement affect the values children hold or their attitude toward school and achievement? Are school systems where policy formulation is dominated by the superintendent any more effective than those in which major initiatives come from the elected officials? There appear to be some journalistic case studies that seek to deal with such questions but few scholars examine the impact of school politics on the learning environments children experience, much less the effects such political activity has on what children learn.[24]

ORGANIZATIONAL CHANGE AND INNOVATION

In recent years educational reform has become a growth industry and some scholars have devoted their energy to studying the "politics of innovation." The focus of most of this research has been on how the adoption of new programs and policies are affected by

23. The most important recent research in this general area is that of L. Harmon Zeigler and M. Kent Jennings, with G. Wayne Peak, *Governing American Schools: Political Interaction in Local School Districts* (North Scituate, Mass.: Duxbury Press, 1974). See also chapter 9 in this volume for a report of further work by Zeigler and his colleagues. For an overview of much of the literature see Frederick M. Wirt and Michael Kirst, *Political and Social Foundations of Education* (Berkeley, Calif.: McCutchan Publishing Corp., 1975).

24. One could say that studies such as that by Robert L. Crain and James Vanecko do address some of the issues raised here, but the consequence being measured in this case is the adoption of school desegregation plans, not the impact of the plans on children. See Crain's report of this research in *The Politics of School Desegregation* (New York: Doubleday Anchor, 1969). See also Kirby et al., *Political Strategies in Northern School Desegregation.*

either (a) certain structural characteristics of communities or school systems or (b) characteristics of formal leaders.

There is considerable evidence that teachers can and often do significantly alter the "innovations" formally adopted by boards and key administrators. Thus, the programs students experience are very different from those developed by the formal political process.[25] But these conclusions are not derived from research that has a fundamental interest in how political considerations shape teacher behavior.[26]

It seems ironic that while research on the politics of education has done much to illuminate the importance of professionals in setting agendas and formulating policies, little of the research on the politics of innovation actually examines how, or if, these programs and policies are implemented. And there is apparently no evidence at all that the political processes linked to efforts at educational change actually have any effect on children.

Is it not possible that conventional politics is unrelated to adaptiveness in schools because the linkages between the formal political process and the teacher are so attenuated that there is no significant relationship between what we usually think of as political events and the experiences students have in school? Given the centrality of teachers in the change process and the substantial power they will invariably have to frustrate or reward efforts at shaping student behavior, it would seem that efforts to understand how politics might be related to change in schools might begin with an analysis of the conditions that foster adaptiveness at the classroom level. Most political scientists do not approach problem solving by looking back from the point of impact to examine alternative explanations for political outcomes. Perhaps this is because they tend to see political activity most clearly when it is focused on or encompassed by institutions that are nominally political. Or perhaps it is because they have a commitment to setting priorities and changing things

---

25. An exception to this generalization is Ernest House's *The Politics of Educational Innovation* (Berkeley, Calif.: McCutchan Publishing Corp., 1974).

26. For a brief review of this research see Willis D. Hawley, "Horses before Carts: Developing Adaptive Schools and the Limits of Innovation," in *Political Science and School Politics: The Princes and the Pundits*, ed. Samuel Gove and Frederick M. Wirt (Lexington, Mass.: D. C. Heath & Co., 1976).

through the formal political process, a notion that is invested with the considerable majesty of democratic theory.

One may compare Seymour Sarason's observation that "in education, the more things change the more they remain the same" with the considerable preoccupation of educators and politicians at all levels of government with new programs and reform. Such a comparison might lead one to wonder how much of the politics of education is "symbolic" in the sense that political activity itself (voting, legislative policy making, government investigations, and so forth), rather than social change (or its absence), is used by those with power as evidence that the political system is "working" in a democratic way.

POLITICAL LEARNING

The one area of scholarly research dealing with the politics of education that is concerned with outcomes is the investigation of children's acquisition of certain norms, values, and attitudes presumably related to the way people play political roles, that is, the study of political socialization. However, one will not find in this voluminous literature much research on the effects of those socialization processes that we might actually change through public policies.[27] The impact of teachers and school environments on political learning is not well understood despite the fact that outside academia decisions related to such effects are hotly debated and involve the expenditure of enormous financial and human resources.

Among the questions to which we have no clear answers from the research on political socialization are these: (a) Are textbooks important sources of political values? (b) Do variations in teaching approaches (for example, "open" versus "self-contained" classrooms) affect students' dispositions toward such notions as freedom of expression, tolerance of others, and political participation? (c) Does the school-wide climate affect the influence of classroom teachers

---

27. Among the most significant works of this sort are Jennings and Niemi, *The Political Character of Adolescence* and Sara F. Liebschutz and Richard G. Niemi, "Political Attitudes among Black Children," in *The Politics of Future Citizens*, ed. Richard G. Niemi (San Francisco, Calif.: Jossey-Bass, 1974), pp. 83-102. For a critical review on the role of schools in political learning, see Willis D. Hawley, "The Implicit Civics Curriculum: Teacher Behavior and Political Learning" (Working paper of the Institute of Policy Sciences and Public Affairs, Duke University, August 1976).

and classmates? (d) Does school desegregation increase interracial tolerance and understanding? (e) How does the political learning that goes on in school affect the later behavior of adults? (f) Does the behavior of teachers, aside from the substance of what they teach, affect political learning? (g) What is the impact of students of protests over curricula or books, court-ordered school desegregation, teacher strikes, and other instances of community conflict?

OTHER ISSUES

The three broad areas of inquiry on the politics of education discussed briefly above are meant to illustrate the general point of this chapter rather than to identify definitively the shortcomings of research in the policies of education. One could raise similar questions about a range of other topics that have intrigued political scientists interested in education. Examination of the available scholarly research tells one very little about such important issues as (a) the effects of program evaluation on the behavior of professionals (other than they try to avoid it);[28] (b) the consequences of intergovernmental conflict or cooperation in shaping the behavior of educators and the quality of education; (c) whether decentralization or local autonomy accounts for differences in school level programs and in educational outcomes for children; (d) the effects of individual parent involvement in school affairs on school climate, teacher behavior, and student learning; (e) whether the great school controversies of recent years, many of which (such as those relating to prayer restrictions, financial equity, desegregation, and the like) were brought on by court action, make much difference in benefits children receive from attending school;[29] (f) what ac-

---

28. One recent effort related to this issue is Milbrey Walling McLaughlin's *Evaluation and Reform* (Cambridge, Mass.: Ballinger Publishing Co., 1975).

29. The importance of educational resources that money can buy was seriously called into doubt by the Coleman Report. See James S. Coleman, *Equality of Educational Opportunity* (Washington, D.C.: U.S. Government Printing Office, 1966). Other research seems to give more support to the idea that money matters. See James Guthrie et al., *Schools and Inequality* (Cambridge, Mass.: M.I.T. Press, 1971). But the evidence is mixed. The only major study I know that links aspects of the political system with the availability of resources, and resources with outcomes for children, is that of Robert L. Crain et al., *Southern Schools: An Evaluation of the Effects of the Emergency School Assistance Program and of School Desegregation*, 2 vols. (Chicago: National Opinion Research Center, University of Chicago, 1973).

counts for different patterns and styles of leadership at the school level and whether such differences themselves account for significant variations in policies and educational outcomes. One could go on.

I am not arguing that nothing can be derived from the extant literature regarding these issues and those noted earlier. The point is that most of these are very important questions to educational policy makers and/or to many parents and that the vast bulk of the research on the politics of education only hints at answers. Moreover, where there is some research on outcomes, such as on expenditures and desegregation (although almost none of the latter is the work of political scientists), the results are conflicting or ambiguous.

ARE SCHOOLS FOR CHILDREN?

Sweeping critiques of whole fields of scholarly inquiry often overstate their case and perhaps this one has also. Examples, although they will be few in number, can be cited that contradict the thesis. Moreover, many will feel that my insistence on raising the question "Who benefits?" asks too much of a single discipline. And one may argue that the education of children is not the only reason for schools nor the only issue to which school politics should be addressed.

Of course, children's learning may be only one consequence of the politics of education that people may value. There is status to be had, authority to be allocated, financial costs to be avoided, curricula to be adopted (thus allocating resources, recognition, and privileges), standards to be set, taxes to be assessed, rights to be assured, conflict to be avoided, and a series of other outcomes that are often valued as ends in themselves by people interested in schools. Nonetheless, it seems reasonable to argue that the fundamental purpose for schools, most generally stated, is to create environments that foster student learning.

Whatever a given community or family wants its children to learn in school, it is clear that the crucial determinant of the impact of schools is what teachers do. To be sure, parental values, student intelligence, and peers all shape the willingness and capacity of individuals to learn, but the contributions schools can make to student development are within the power of teachers to shape in significant ways. It is, in short, how children are affected by what goes on in schools and classrooms that should be of primary concern to students of educational politics. Knowing about the legislative dynamics involved in the passage of major educational bills or developing an understanding of judicial behavior is interesting, but these are not enough in the long run to fully justify political research. Unlike the study of literature, art, or music, the study of political behavior, processes, and institutions cannot rest on its intrinsic value.

WHY THIS STATE OF AFFAIRS?

Why is it that political scientists devote so much attention to the political processes themselves rather than to the question "Who gets what?" from those processes? Three general answers come to mind.

First, and most obviously, to engage the question "So what?" is to take on a whole set of assessment problems, the answers to which may require patience, energy, and skills many of us do not have. There are two kinds of problems here. One is that we not only need to identify policies that emanate from the formal political process but to trace such policies through to their targets so that the policy making undertaken by bureaucrats is taken into account. Another problem, once we know what services, regulations, and the like have been delivered to or imposed on whom, is to know what the effects of these governmental actions are. Determining the effects of policies is very difficult indeed, even for those better trained in psychological and social measurement than are most political scientists. One answer to this problem is interdisciplinary collaboration. Another is interdisciplinary training. Both of these are costly and sometimes threatening. Further, even if we could solve the measurement problems, the best studies of impact will be longitudinal and therefore costly in terms of money and commitment. Whether universities provide incentives for such risky and long-term research is questioned by many scholars.[30]

A second general problem is that most of us, while we recognize that important political decisions are made outside formal political institutions, including some decisions about what shall be decided through our institutions, feel uncomfortable and uncertain in trying

---

30. See Robert L. Crain, "Why Academic Research Fails to Be Useful," in *School Desegregation: Shadow and Substance*, ed. Florence H. Levinsohn and Benjamin D. Wright (Chicago: University of Chicago Press, 1976), pp. 31-45.

to identify these decisions, much less in assessing their consequences. Once we acknowledge such complexities and accept the difficulty of studying "nonpublic politics" and "nondecisions," the logic of confining our research to the workings of formal political processes and those political actors who participate in such processes becomes persuasive.[31]

Third, and more speculatively, "modern" political science is rooted in earlier commitments to research and writing that sought to compare what is, at least implicitly, to what should be with the prescriptions derived from normative political and organization theory. Thus, we have seen ourselves dealing with the "big" questions of democratic political philosophy such as leadership, political participation, alternative governmental forms, the role of parties, and so forth, often without questioning the assumptions we tacitly make about consequences of these phenomena. This disposition allows us to deal with political issues in language that speaks to enduring questions and in work, therefore, that is *significant*. Thus, for example, within the discipline, the subfield of voting behavior has been substantially more prestigious than research on the delivery of urban services.

Final Comment

Despite all of the above I do not want to be understood as arguing that all political inquiry need be justified in terms of whether, in Lasswell's words, we "have something pertinent to offer about the probable effects of adopting one form of government over another, or one policy or another." But surely the inability of political science research and writing to offer something pertinent should be a cause of concern not only to political scientists but those who support them. Justifications for research and writing about politics that are couched in such terms as "contributions to the

---

31. One of the most perceptive analyses of the difficulty of doing such research is found in Frederick W. Frey, "Comment: On Issues and Non-issues in the Study of Power," *American Political Science Review* 65 (December 1971): 1081-1101. A significant effort to study "nonpublic politics" is Karen Orren's study of the role of private institutions in shaping housing opportunities. See Karen Orren, "Corporate Power and the Slums: Is Big Business a Paper Tiger?" in *Theoretical Perspectives on Urban Politics*, ed. Willis D. Hawley and Michael Lipsky (Englewood Cliffs, N.J.: Prentice-Hall, 1976), pp. 45-66.

discipline" or, "theoretical or methodological rigor," while they have some place, might be compared more often to criteria like the extent to which we advance the probability that greater numbers of people will experience justice, social equality, opportunities for self-expression or self-actualization, or a higher standard of living.

Index

Academia, forces of, contributing to emergence of a politics of education, 12
Activism and the maximization of benefits, 140-44
Activist court: protection of minorities by decisions of, 142; public appreciation of, 143-44
Activist judges, views of, 135-36
Administrative neutral competency, doctrine of, 287-88
Administrative politics: issues of, 259-60; politics of educational change in relation to, 256-62
Administrative state, characteristics of the constituency of, 78-79
Administrator, relation of, to evaluator, 305-7
Advisory Commission on Intergovernmental Relations, 113
Age of anxiety: educational achievement in, 196-197; educational implications in, 194-99; school enrollment in, 194-95; school personnel in, 195-96
Agger, Robert, 53
Allison, Graham, 321
Almond, Gabriel, 27, 42, 63, 289
American Association of School Administrators, publication of, quoted, 31
American education, model of policy-making system of (fig.), 99
American Medical Association, nature of influence of, 37-38
Apolitical myth of education, reasons for persistence of, 4-5
Apolitical political myth, nature of, 277-83
Averch, Harvey A. et al., quoted, 86-87
Azzarelli, Joseph J., 25

Bachrach, Peter, 37, 92
Bailey, F. G., 50, 51
Bailey, Stephen K., 18, 19, 175, 176, 188; quoted, 5, 14

Banfield, Edward C., 24, 48, 49, 50, 55
Baratz, Morton S., 37, 92
Becker, Howard P., 47
Behavioralism, rise of, in relation to politics of education, 8
Bendix, Reinhard, 46
Bensman, Joseph, 32
Benveniste, Guy, 309
Berke, Joel S., 176
Bertalanffy, Ludwig von, 41, 42, 63
Bickell, Alexander M., 140, 145
Blau, Peter M., 299
Bloland, Harley, 56
Borgatta, Edgar, 305
Boyd, William L., study by Warren, Rose, and Burgunder quoted by, 213
Breslin, Jimmy, quoted, 301-2
Bridge, R. Gary, 74
Brinton, Crane, 272
Brogan, D. W., quoted, 271
Brown v. *Board of Education of Topeka*, 9, 149, 167
Burger Court: conception of role of Court by, 150-52; difficulties of position of, 152-53; narrow interpretation of Warren Court decisions by, 151-52; partial exemplification of model of restraint by, 150-55
Burns, Tom, 224
Button, Warren H., 276

Callahan, Raymond E., 76, 269, 276, 282
Campbell, Alan K., 123
Campbell, Roald F., 18, 19, 20, 27, 28
Carter, Richard F., 52, 53; quoted (with Savard), 52
Centralization: degree of, among the states, 172-75; tendencies toward, in government, 171-72
Centralization patterns and their regional qualities: data for analysis

in study of, 171-72; paradigm for, 167-69; research design for study of, 169-71
Centralizing federalism, discussion of, 106-8
Cistone, Peter J., 21, 58, 285; quoted (with Iannaccone), 286
Citizen-consumers, responsiveness of, in federal system of educational governance, 119-23
Class power models: class polyarchy model, 45-46; discussion of types of, as represented by the power-elite model, 43-44, and social class model, 44-45; use of, in study of educational politics, 43-46
Cohen, David K., quoted (with Murphy), 311
Collective bargaining, effect of, on leadership and politics, 204-5
Communication: decision making in relation to, 218-54; nature of, in school board meetings, 239
Communications and decisions, approach to study of flow of, 225-30
Community power structures, studies of, 15-16
Comparative analysis methods, use of, in research on political systems, 40-41
Comparative-descriptive models, use of, in study of educational politics, 58-61
Conant, James B., 193
Conflict, concept of, associated with politics, 25
Constituencies, responsiveness of, 82-83
Control: factors in, 76-77; future of, 90-93; position of school administrator in regard to, 87; voting and voters in relation to, 73-76
Conway, James A., 34
Cooperative federalism: effect of New Deal on, 108-10; features of, 109-10
Cooperative Program in Educational Administration (CPEA), support of Kellogg Foundation of, 12
Counts, George S., 279
Court's remedial power, activist judges in relation to, 136
Crain, Robert L., 26
Creative federalism, Presidents Kennedy and Johnson in relation to, 111-12
Cremin, Lawrence A., quoted, 197
Cronin, Joseph M., 17, 24; quoted, 4
Cubberley, Ellwood P., 278, 279; quoted, 293
Cunningham, Luvern L., 16, 19, 201

Dahl, Robert L., 32, 36, 47, 66, 90; quoted, 31
Daley, Richard J., failure of, to restore educational funds, 59
Decentralization, issue of, in urban education, 209-13
Decision making: Claremont studies in, 17-18; communication in relation to, 218-54; participation, representation, and control factors in, 67; Stanford studies in, 16-17
Defensive evaluation, definition and illustration of, 303-5
Demographic change, political implications of, 199-216
Descriptive representation, nature of, 79
Desegregation, issue of, in urban centers, 209-17
Dillon's Rule, 164, 166
Doctrine of restraint, behavior of judges working under, 130-32. See also Model of restraint
Dyck, Harold J., 17
Dye, Thomas R., 28

Easton, David, 25, 27, 42, 63, 85, 168, 289, 294, 295
Easton model, nature and use of, 42
Education, evaluation and politics in relation to, 299-307. See also Schools
Educational change, politics of, 256-62
Educational effectiveness, criticisms of, 12-13
Educational government: agencies participating in (table), 104-5; architecture of federal system of, 102-9; centralizing federalism in relation to, 106-8; creative federalism in relation to, 111-12; early, local, sectional, and state influences on, 102-9; federal system of, in perspective, 102-9; federalism basic to, 267-68; New Deal and cooperative federalism in relation to, 109-11; new federalism in relation to, 112-

INDEX

18. *See also* Governance of education
Educational policy making; federal government in relation to, 19-20; relation of politics to, 30-31. *See also* Decision making
Educational politics: advent of, 9-21; changes in, 275-85; content of field of, 26-27; description of field of, 21-22; early studies of, 13-21; forces in rise of, 1-13; new factors in, 283-85; revolutions in, 269-71; specter of, 2-5; theoretical approaches to, 27-29; views on changes in, 255-85
Education and politics, reflections on, 113-17
Efficiency, reformers' borrowing from industry's theories of, 3-4
Elazar, Daniel J., 177, 178, 179; quoted, 267
Elementary and Secondary Education Act (ESEA), 10, 19, 113, 115, 167
Eliot, Thomas H., quoted, 13, 14, 18
Erlandson, David A., quoted, 306
Etzioni, Amitai, 44
Eulau, Heinz, 266; quoted, 267
Evaluation: emerging paradigm of, 290-94; politics in relation to, 287-318; prognosis for the politics of, 314-18; understanding of politics in relation to, 288-94
Evaluation and politics, discussion of, 299-307
Evaluators: politics of, 308-13; relation of, to administrator, 300-307

Federal Communications Commission (FCC), 158, 159
Federal government, effect of greater involvement of, in education, 10-11. *See also* Government
Fenno, Richard V., 15
Ferman, Louis A., 303; quoted, 304
Firestone, William, 314
Ford, Gerald R., 112, 116; leadership of, 111
Formalistic representation, nature of, 79
Fritschler, A. Lee, 322
Froomkin, Joseph, 196

Galbraith, John Kenneth, 93
Gallup Poll, 206; report on tax elections by, 205
Garms, Walter I., 17
General systems models, application of, in studies of politics and education, 41-43
Getzels, Jacob W., quoted, 255
Goldhammer, Keith, 13; quoted, 214
Governance of education: criticisms of, 78; new approach to study of, 225-30; power and politics in relation to, 32-33; research on changes in, 255-56. *See also* Educational government
Government, education in context of, 94-97. *See also* Federal government
Graunt, John, use of demographic data by, 33
Graves, Thomas J., quoted, 112
Greenstone, J. David, 321
Gregg, Russell T., 18
Gross, Neal, 13
Gusfield, Joseph, 57
Guthrie, James E., 60

Hall, John Stuart, 52, 72
Halperin, Samuel, 324
Hammond, Phillip E., 308
Harrington, James, 271, 273
Hays, Samuel P., quoted, 276
Holcombe, Arthur, 176
Hollingshead, August B., 32
Homans, George C., 42
House, Ernest R., 309, 310, 311; quoted, 300-301, 302-3
Hunter, Floyd, 47, 201; quoted, 37; Regional City study by, 35

Iannaccone, Laurence, 20, 21, 33, 34, 38, 43, 47, 51, 55, 58, 64, 71, 189, 258, 284, 285, 315; quoted, 117-18, (with Lutz), 261, (with Cistone), 286
Ideal typical models: discussion of types of, 46-52; uses of, in studies of educational politics, 44-52
Intergovernmental transactions in education (fig.), 122
Isolationist politics, adherence of educators to, 101
Issue analysis: importance of selecting issues for, 37-38; nature and use of, in study of the power structure, 35-38

Jacobson, Lenore, 74

INDEX

James, H. Thomas, 17, 209; quoted, 208
Jennings, M. Kent, 24, 47, 75, 82, 83, 84, 88, 98, 222; quoted (with Zeigler), 30, 55, 81, 83-84; 96-97, 98
Jennings, Robert E., 34
Johns, Roe L., 16
Johnson, Lyndon B., 112, 114; leadership of, 111
Judgments: effect on, of adherence to model of activism, 134-35; factors influential in making of, 125-26
Junker, Buford, 39

Kahl, Joseph A., 44
Kaplan, Harold D., 24
Katz, Michael B., 269, 270
Kaufman, Herbert, 107, 118, 281, 324; quoted, 98, 99-100
Keech, William R., 321
Kelly, James A., 17
Kelly, Stanley, Jr., 38
Kennedy, John F., leadership of, 111
Kennedy, Robert, origin of evaluation mandate of Title I attributed to, 119
Kerr, Norman D., 85
Kimbrough, Ralph B., 15, 16, 34, 47, 53
Kirst, Michael W., 20, 21, 28, 42, 52, 178, 214; quoted (with Wirt), 262
Knutson, Jeanne N., 61
Koerner, J. D., quoted, 85
Kottmeyer, William, 189

Lane, Willard R., Broudy quoted by, 216
Large cities: demographic transformation in, 181-94; determinants of politics in, 189-91; education and politics in, 188-217. *See also* Urban areas, Urban patterns
Lasswell, Harold D., 24, 289, 319
Lawyers Committee for Civil Rights under Law, analysis of laws by, 171-72
Layton, Donald M., 18
Lazarsfeld, Paul, 53
Lindblom, Charles E., 257, quoted, 261, 270
Lipham, James M., 18
Lipset, Seymour Martin, 45
Lipsky, Michael, 321

Local school politics, models in relation to, 155-61
Lonsdale, Richard, 56
Loomis, Charles C., 42
Lowi, Theodore J., 120, 321
Lutz, Frank W., 25, 33, 34, 38, 40, 43, 47, 50, 55, 56; quoted (with Iannaccone) 261
Lyke, Robert F., 84
Lynd, Robert S. and Helen Merrell, 32

McCall, George J., 39
McCarty, Donald J., 13, 16, 25; quoted (with Ramsey), 221
McClelland, Charles A., 41, 42
MacIver, Robert M., 272
McLaughlin, Milbrey Wallin, 119; quoted, 120
McPhee, Roderick F., 19
Maeroff, Gene I., quoted, 221
Mann, Dale, 26, 74, 87, 188
Mann, Horace, reformist impulse or, 106
March, James G., 24
Martin, Roscoe C., 14, 15, 258
Marx, Karl, 32
Masotti, Louis, 18
Masters, Nicholas A., 18, 176
Mazzoni, Tim L., Jr., 27, 28
Meranto, Philip, 19
Michels, Robert, "Iron Law of Oligarchy" of, 32, 36, 64
Miller, Delbert C., 36, 45
Mills, C. Wright, 43, 44, 45
Milstein, Mike M., 34
Minar, David W., 16, 28
Model of activism: behavior of judges working under, 133-34; discussion of, 132-37; range of judicial behavior in, 136-38; Warren court in relation to, 144-50
Model of restraint: doctrine of ripeness in, 128; limits placed on Court by acceptance of, 128-29; nature of decisions of justices adhering to, 127-31; range of judicial behaviors in, 136-38
Mosher, Edith K., 19, 20
Munger, Frank J., 15
Murphy, Jerome T., quoted (with Cohen), 311

National Association for the Ad-

vancement of Colored People (NAACP), 201, 211, 217
National Conference of Professors of Educational Administration (NCPEA), 12
National Defense Education Act (NDEA), 44, 111
National Education Association, 117
New Deal, cruciality of, in shaping modern federalism, 108-10
New federalism, Presidents Nixon and Ford in relation to, 112-18
New York City, Board of Education, guidelines of, quoted, 85
Nie, Norman H., 68
Nixon, Richard M., 112, 116, 303; leadership of, 111
Nunnery, Michael Y., 34, 53

O'Conner, Edwin, 66
Offensive evaluation, definition and illustration of, 301-3
Operational concepts of politics, central categories of, 23-27
Organizational change, focus of research on, 327-29

Parent-Teacher Association (PTA), 56, 74, 201, 211, 222, 281
Participation: forms of, 70-71; knowledge as prerequisite for, 75; voting as a form of, 71-72
Peterson, Paul, 321; quoted, 220
Piele, Philip K., 52, 72
Pitkin, Hannah F., 68, 79; quoted, 80
Policy information, studies of, 322
Policy impact, concerns of studies of, 324-26
Policy implementation, research on, 323-24
Policy making, concept of, associated with politics, 25-27. See also Decision making, Educational politics
Policy outputs, studies of, 322-23
Policy systems, basis of, 261-62
Political adjustment, political changes in education in relation to, 267-71
Political changes in education, discussion of, 267-71
Political culture, distinction between patterns of, 177-85
Political ideology, discussion of, 271-75
Political inquiry, policy studies in relation to, 321-26
Political learning, discussion of area of, 329-30
Political models: discussion of, 63-66; graphic summary of, 62
Political philosophy, dealing with big problems of, 333
Political processes and outcomes, linkages between, 320-21
Political-psychological models, use of, in study of educational politics, 60-61
Political science: emerging paradigm of, 288-90; ramifications of development of, for politics of education, 8-9; stages in the evolution of, 6-9
Politics: basic notion of, 22; early separation of education from, 4-5; evaluation in relation to, 287-318
Politics and education, issues neglected by, 330-31
Politics of education: expanded definition of, 294-99; research on, 326-33. See also Educational politics
Politics of evaluation, prognosis for, 314-18
Polsby, Nelson W., 54, 90
Polyarchal democracy, basic tenets of, 77
Popham, W. James, 308
Porter, David O., 121, 122
Porter, John, 311
Power: concept of, associated with politics, 24-25; exercise of, in education, 32-33
Power and politics in education, methods and models for the study of, 33-41; class power models, 43-46; comparative analysis, 40-41; comparative-descriptive models, 58-60; general systems models, 41-43; ideal typical models, 46-52; issue analysis, 35-38; political-psychological models, 60-61; public participation models, 52-58; reputational analysis, 34-35; socio-anthropological field analysis, 38-40; survey analysis, 33-34
Pressman, Jeffrey, 324
Price, David E., 322
Principals (school), evaluation of, opposed by principals, 304
Professionalism of education, chal-

lenge of teacher militancy, 11
Privatization in government, tendency toward, 271-72; definition of, 271
Provus, Malcolm, 292
Public participation models: discussion of, 52-59; use of, in study of educational politics, 52-58

Ramsey, Charles E., 25; quoted (with McCarty), 221
Ramsey, Margaret, 40
Rand Corporation, 317; analysis of federally supported program by, 91-92
Rawls, John, 125, 126
Record, Jane Cassels, 313
Redford, Emmette S., quoted, 78
Regions (American), school policy cultures of, 176-85
Representation: categories of, 79; definitions of, 68-69; kinds of, wanted by citizens, 81-82; research on, reported, 80-89
Representational style, three choices of, 80
Representatives: attitude of types of, toward constituencies and their demands, 84; practical and ethical dilemmas faced by, 80; roles of, 80-81; types of, 80-81
Reputational analysis, use of, in study of power structure, 34-35
Researchers, effect of, on schools, 60
Restraint and the minimization of costs, 137-40
Rice, Joseph M., 275
Right to Read, demands for program of, 197
Rivers, Wendell, 310
Rivlin, Alice M., 300
Rodriguez, Eric, 313
Rogers, David, 324
Roosevelt, Franklin D., innovative leadership of, 109
Rosenthal, Robert, 74
Rossi, Peter, 300, 313
Rossmiller, Richard A., 18

Salisbury, Robert H., 18, 188
Sanders, James R., 293; quoted (with Worthen), 291
Sarason, Seymour, 329
Savard, William G., quoted (with Carter), 52

Sayre, Wallace S., 15
Schattschneider, Elmer E., 25, 38, 93, 258, 259, 272, 279; quoted, 257, 260, 272-73, 273, 274
Scheiber, Harry N., 103
School administrator: dominant position of, in control, 85; service of, as political representative, 87
School board meetings (three districts): agenda dissimilarities (table), 234; correlation between statements and discussions of (table), 236; discussion initiated by actors in (table), 243; distribution of statements in (table), 234; intensity of discussion in (table), 237; intensity of participation in (table), 246; nature of communication in (table), 239; proposers of policy discussion in (table) 250; statements of, by source and topic (table), 248; summary of research on (table), 253; topics discussed in (table), 233; types of communication in (table) 238; voting behavior in (table), 231. See also School districts, School government
School boards: agenda of meetings of, 230-36; discussion and resolutions in meetings of, 31; participants in meetings of, 44-45; proposers of policy decisions of, 249-50; setting agenda for meetings of, 247-50. See also School board meetings, School governance
School centralization: scores of, by states (table), 173, (fig.), 174; scores of, on list of variables (table), 182-83; states with designated ranges of scores of (table), 173.
School centralization scores: distribution of, by political culture (table), 178; distribution of, by regions (table), 180
School districts (Grahamdale, Barwig Park, Leeville), 227-53; categorization of (table), 230; characteristics of (table), 228; discussion and resolutions in boards of education (table), 228. See also Boards of education, Board of education meetings

INDEX

School government: actors in operation of, 222; distribution of influence between board and superintendent in, 222-23; influence of community tensions on, 323. See also Board of education, Board of education meetings, Governance of education

School policy culture: patterns of, in American regions, 176-85; state decentralization in relation to, 164-87

School politics, models adhered to by Supreme Court in, 124-63

School revenues, decisions of the Burger Court in relation to, 153-54; tabular presentation of, by source, 116

Schools: direct democracy exemplified by, replaced by polyarchal democracy, 77; forces impinging on, 69-70; service of, to children in general, 331-32; social mobility in relation to, 86. See also Education

Scribner, Jay D., 17, 28, 42, 63

Scriven, Michael, 316; quoted, 291-92

Segregation, Warren Court in area of, 149-50

Seidman, Harold, 324

Self-government, participation, representation, and control in, 67-93

Servicemen's Readjustment Act of 1944, 110-11

Shields, Currin, 179

Simmons, J. L., 39

Simon, Herbert A., 26

Sjoberg, Gideon, 300

Smith-Hughes Act, 107

Smoley, Eugene R., 257

Social mobility, schools in relation to, 86

Social science discipline: politics of education becomes complement to, 12-13

Socio-anthropological field analysis, method of, in studies of politics and education, 38-40

Speizman, William L., 313

Sroufe, Gerald E., 18

Stake, Robert, 316

State and local education authority: data for analysis in study of, 171-72; paradigm for comparative research on, 167-70

State centralization, local consequences of, 185-87

State decentralization, school policy culture in relation to, 164-87. See also Centralization

State policy culture, a paradigm for (table), 168

State's role in education: background of, 165-69; paradigms for comparative research on, 167-69; research design for study of, 169-71

Strong, Josiah, quoted, 199

Stufflebeam, David L., 307, 310, 316; quoted, 291-92, 292, 293

Substantive representation, nature of, 79, 81

Suchman, Edward A., quoted, 306-7

Sundquist, James L., 322

Superintendent (school), dominating influence of, in educational decision making, 223

Supreme Court: decisions of, relating to schools, 154-55; inability of, to force compliance, 138; nature of decisions of, based on doctrine of restraint, 127-31; two important doctrines affecting decisions of, 124-63. See also Warren Court, Burger Court

Survey analysis methods, use of, in study of politics and education, 35-38

Sutthoff, John, 52

Symbolic representation, nature of, 79

Taft, Robert, advocacy of federal aid by, 110

Tax elections: reasons for failure of, 205-9; vote on, in Detroit (table), 206

Thomas, J. Alan, 17

Thompson, John Thomas, 26, 98

Tri-systems model, nature and use of, in study of politics and education, 42-43

Truman, David B., 25, 289

Trustee administrators, proportion of, in different types of communities, 88-89

Trustee position, low responsiveness of, to community preferences, 87

Tullock, Gordon, quoted, 288

Tyack, David B., quoted, 276

INDEX

Unitary community, doctrine of, 280-81
U.S. Department of Health, Education, and Welfare (HEW), 155
U.S. Office of Education, 19, 107, 114, 115, 263, 264
University Council for Educational Administration (UCEA), 12
Urban areas, issue of segregation and decentralization in, 209-13
Urban changes, political implications of, 199-217
Urban leadership, school boards in relation to, 202-4
Urban-rural biases model, 59-60

Values, kinds of, distributed by schools, 86
Verba, Sidney, 68-75
Vidich, Arthur J., 32
Voting: cumulative effect of, 24; limits on control by, 73-74; participation by means of, 71-72

Waldo, Dwight, 256; quoted, 257
Walker, David, quoted, 113
Walsh, John E., 30
Warner, W. Lloyd, 32, 42, 44, 45
Warren Court: activist doctrines of, in relation to education, 147; activist model exemplified by, 145; segregation dealt with by, 149-50; transmuting of Constitution by, 150; willingness of, to change role of Supreme Court, 146. *See also* Supreme Court, Burger Court
Wax, Rosalie, 39
Wayson, William, quoted, 120
Weber, Max, 23; models following lead of, 46
Wildavsky, Aaron B., 54, 324
Wilensky, Harold L., quoted, 317
Williams, Walter, quoted, 305, 313; evaluation of Head Start by, 305
Willower, Donald J., 258
Wilson, James O., 48, 49, 55
Wirt, Frederick M., 20, 21, 28, 42, 52, 84, 321; quoted (with Kirst), 262
Wirth, Louis, 55
Worthen, Blaine, 293; quoted (with Sanders), 291
Wright, Deil S., 97, 111

Yin, Robert K., 73

Zeigler, L. Harmon, 24, 47, 82, 83, 84, 88, 98, 222; quoted (with M. K. Jennings), 30, 55, 81, 83-84; 96-97, 98

CONSTITUTION AND BY-LAWS
OF
THE NATIONAL SOCIETY FOR THE STUDY OF EDUCATION

(As adopted May, 1944, and amended June, 1945, February, 1949, September, 1962, February, 1968 and September, 1973)

ARTICLE I

NAME

The name of this corporation shall be "The National Society for the Study of Education," an Illinois corporation not for profit.

ARTICLE II

PURPOSES

Its purposes are to carry on the investigation of educational problems, to publish the results of same, and to promote their discussion.

The corporation also has such powers as are now, or may hereafter be, granted by the General Not For Profit Corporation Act of the State of Illinois.

ARTICLE III

OFFICES

The corporation shall have and continuously maintain in this state a registered office and a registered agent whose office is identical with such registered office, and may have other offices within or without the State of Illinois as the Board of Directors may from time to time determine.

ARTICLE IV

MEMBERSHIP

Section 1. *Classes.* There shall be two classes of members—active and honorary. The qualifications and rights of the members of such classes shall be as follows:

(*a*) Any person who is desirous of promoting the purposes of this corporation is eligible to active membership and shall become such on payment of dues as prescribed.

(*b*) Active members shall be entitled to vote, to participate in discussion, and, subject to the conditions set forth in Article V, to hold office.

(*c*) Honorary members shall be entitled to all the privileges of active members, with the exception of voting and holding office, and shall be exempt from the payment of dues. A person may be elected to honorary membership by vote of the active members of the corporation on nomination by the Board of Directors.

(d) Any active member of the Society may, at any time after reaching the age of sixty, become a life member on payment of the aggregate amount of the regular annual dues for the period of life expectancy, as determined by standard actuarial tables, such membership to entitle the member to receive all yearbooks and to enjoy all other privileges of active membership in the Society for the lifetime of the member.

Section 2. *Termination of Membership.*

(a) The Board of Directors by affirmative vote of two-thirds of the members of the Board may suspend or expel a member for cause after appropriate hearing.

(b) Termination of membership for nonpayment of dues shall become effective as provided in Article XIV.

Section 3. *Reinstatement.* The Board of Directors may by the affirmation vote of two-thirds of the members of the Board reinstate a former member whose membership was previously terminated for cause other than nonpayment of dues.

Section 4. *Transfer of Membership.* Membership in this corporation is not transferable or assignable.

Article V

BOARD OF DIRECTORS

Section 1. *General Powers.* The business and affairs of the corporation shall be managed by its Board of Directors. It shall appoint the Chairman and Vice-Chairman of the Board of Directors, the Secretary-Treasurer, and Members of the Council. It may appoint a member to fill any vacancy on the Board until such vacancy shall have been filled by election as provided in Section 3 of this Article.

Section 2. *Number, Tenure, and Qualifications.* The board of Directors shall consist of seven members, namely, six to be elected by the members of the corporation, and the Secretary-Treasurer to be the seventh member. Only active members who have contributed to the yearbook shall be eligible for election to serve as directors. A member who has been elected for a full term of three years as director and has not attended at least two-thirds of the meetings duly called and held during that term shall not be eligible for election again before the fifth annual election after the expiration of the term for which he was first elected. No member who has been elected for two full terms as director in immediate succession shall be elected a director for a term next succeeding. This provision shall not apply to the Secretary-Treasurer who is appointed by the Board of Directors. Each director shall hold office for the term for which he is elected or appointed and until his successor shall have been selected and qualified. Directors need not be residents of Illinois.

Section 3. *Election.*

(*a*) The directors named in the Articles of Incorporation shall hold office until their successors shall have been duly selected and shall have qualified. Thereafter, two directors shall be elected annually to serve three years, beginning March first after their election. If, at the time of any annual election, a vacancy exists in the Board of Directors, a director shall be elected at such election to fill such vacancy.

(*b*) Elections of directors shall be held by ballots sent by United States mail as follows: A nominating ballot together with a list of members eligible to be directors shall be mailed by the Secretary-Treasurer to all active members of the corporation in October. From such list, the active members shall nominate on such ballot one eligible member for each of the two regular terms and for any vacancy to be filled and return such ballots to the office of the Secretary-Treasurer within twenty-one days after said date of mailing by the Secretary-Treasurer. The Secretary-Treasurer shall prepare an election ballot and place thereon in alphabetical order the names of persons equal to three times the number of offices to be filled, these persons to be those who received the highest number of votes on the nominating ballot, provided, however, that not more than one person connected with a given institution or agency shall be named on such final ballot, the person so named to be the one receiving the highest vote on the nominating ballot. Such election ballot shall be mailed by the Secretary-Treasurer to all active members in November next succeeding. The active members shall vote thereon for one member for each such office. Election ballots must be in the office of the Secretary-Treasurer within twenty-one days after the said date of mailing by the Secretary-Treasurer. The ballots shall be counted by the Secretary-Treasurer, or by an election committee, if any, appointed by the Board. The two members receiving the highest number of votes shall be declared elected for the regular term and the member or members receiving the next highest number of votes shall be declared elected for any vacancy or vacancies to be filled.

Section 4. *Regular Meetings.* A regular annual meeting of the Board of Directors shall be held, without other notice than this by-law, at the same place and as nearly as possible on the same date as the annual meeting of the corporation. The Board of Directors may provide the time and place, either within or without the State of Illinois, for the holding of additional regular meetings of the Board.

Section 5. *Special Meetings.* Special meetings of the Board of Directors may be called by or at the request of the Chairman or a majority of the directors. Such special meetings shall be held at the office of the corporation unless a majority of the directors agree upon a different place for such meetings.

Section 6. *Notice.* Notice of any special meeting of the Board of Directors shall be given at least fifteen days previously thereto by written notice delivered personally or mailed to each director at his business address, or by telegram. If mailed, such notice shall be deemed to be delivered when deposited in the United States mail in a sealed envelope so addressed, with postage thereon prepaid. If notice be given by telegram, such notice shall be deemed to be delivered when the telegram is delivered to the telegraph company. Any director may waive notice of any meeting. The attendance of a director at any meeting shall constitute a waiver of notice of such meeting, except where a director attends a meeting for the express purpose of objecting to the transaction of any business because the meeting is not lawfully called or convened. Neither the business to be transacted at, nor the purpose of, any regular or special meeting of the Board need be specified in the notice or waiver of notice of such meeting.

Section 7. *Quorum.* A majority of the Board of Directors shall constitute a quorum for the transaction of business at any meeting of the Board, provided, that if less than a majority of the directors are present at said meeting, a majority of the directors present may adjourn the meeting from time to time without further notice.

Section 8. *Manner of Acting.* The act of the majority of the directors present at a meeting at which a quorum is present shall be the act of the Board of Directors, except where otherwise provided by law or by these by-laws.

Article VI

THE COUNCIL

Section 1. *Appointment.* The Council shall consist of the Board of Directors, the Chairmen of the corporation's Yearbook and Research Committees, and such other active members of the corporation as the Board of Directors may appoint.

Section 2. *Duties.* The duties of the Council shall be to further the objects of the corporation by assisting the Board of Directors in planning and carrying forward the educational undertakings of the corporation.

Article VII

OFFICERS

Section 1. *Officers.* The officers of the corporation shall be a Chairman of the Board of Directors, a Vice-Chairman of the Board of Directors, and a Secretary-Treasurer. The Board of Directors, by resolution, may create additional offices. Any two or more offices may be held by the same person, except the offices of Chairman and Secretary-Treasurer.

Section 2. *Election and Term of Office.* The officers of the corporation shall be elected annually by the Board of Directors at the annual regular meeting of the Board of Directors, provided, however, that the Secretary-Treasurer may be elected for a term longer than one year. If the election of officers shall not be held at such meeting, such election shall be held as soon thereafter as conveniently may be. Vacancies may be filled or new offices created and filled at any meeting of the Board of Directors. Each officer shall hold office until his successor shall have been duly elected and shall have qualified or until his death or until he shall resign or shall have been removed in the manner hereinafter provided.

Section 3. *Removal.* Any officer or agent elected or appointed by the Board of Directors may be removed by the Board of Directors whenever in its judgment the best interests of the corporation would be served thereby, but such removal shall be without prejudice to the contract rights, if any, of the person so removed.

Section 4. *Chairman of the Board of Directors.* The Chairman of the Board of Directors shall be the principal officer of the corporation. He shall preside at all meetings of the members of the Board of Directors, shall perform all duties incident to the office of chairman of the Board of Directors and such other duties as may be prescribed by the Board of Directors from time to time.

Section 5. *Vice-Chairman of the Board of Directors.* In the absence of the Chairman of the Board of Directors or in the event of his inability or refusal to act, the Vice-Chairman of the Board of Directors shall perform the duties of the Chairman of the Board of Directors, and when so acting, shall have all the powers of and be subject to all the restrictions upon the Chairman of the Board of Directors. Any Vice-Chairman of the Board of Directors shall perform such other duties as from time to time may be assigned to him by the Board of Directors.

Section 6. *Secretary-Treasurer.* The Secretary-Treasurer shall be the managing executive officer of the corporation. He shall: (*a*) keep the minutes of the meetings of the members and of the Board of Directors in one or more books provided for that purpose; (*b*) see that all notices are duly given in accordance with the provisions of these by-laws or as required by law; (*c*) be custodian of the corporate records and of the seal of the corporation and see that the seal of the corporation is affixed to all documents, the execution of which on behalf of the corporation under its seal is duly authorized in accordance with the provisions of these by-laws; (*d*) keep a register of the postoffice address of each member as furnished to the Secretary-Treasurer by such member; (*e*) in general perform all duties incident to the office of secretary and such other duties as from time to time may be assigned to him by the Chairman of the Board of Directors or by the Board of Directors. He shall also: (1) have charge and custody of and be responsible for all funds and securities of the corporation; receive and give receipts for moneys due and payable to the corporation from any source whatsoever, and deposit all such moneys in the name of the corporation in such banks, trust companies or other depositories as shall be selected in accordance with the provisions of Article XI of these by-laws; (2) in general perform all the duties incident to the office of Treasurer and such other duties as from time to time may be assigned to him by the Chairman of the Board of Directors or by the Board of Directors. The Secretary-Treasurer shall give a bond for the faithful discharge of his duties in such sum and with such surety or sureties as the Board of Directors shall determine, said bond to be placed in the custody of the Chairman of the Board of Directors.

Article VIII

COMMITTEES

The Board of Directors, by appropriate resolution duly passed, may create and appoint such committees for such purposes and periods of time as it may deem advisable.

Article IX

PUBLICATIONS

Section 1. The corporation shall publish *The Yearbook of the National Society for the Study of Education*, such supplements thereto, and such other materials as the Board of Directors may provide for.

Section 2. *Names of Members.* The names of the active and honorary members shall be printed in the Yearbook in alternate years or, at the direction of the Board of Directors, may be published in a special list.

Article X

ANNUAL MEETINGS

The corporation shall hold its annual meetings at the time and place of the Annual Meeting of the American Association of School Administrators of the National Education Association. Other meetings may be held when authorized by the corporation or by the Board of Directors.

Article XI

CONTRACTS, CHECKS, DEPOSITS, AND GIFTS

Section 1. *Contracts.* The Board of Directors may authorize any officer or officers, agent or agents of the corporation, in addition to the officers so authorized by these by-laws to enter into any contract or execute and deliver any instrument in the name of and on behalf of the corporation and such authority may be general or confined to specific instances.

Section 2. *Checks, drafts, etc.* All checks, drafts, or other orders for the payment of money, notes, or other evidences of indebtedness issued in the name of the corporation, shall be signed by such officer or officers, agent or agents of the corporation and in such manner as shall from time to time be determined by resolution of the Board of Directors. In the absence of such determination of the Board of Directors, such instruments shall be signed by the Secretary-Treasurer.

Section 3. *Deposits.* All funds of the corporation shall be deposited from time to time to the credit of the corporation in such banks, trust companies, or other depositories as the Board of Directors may select.

Section 4. *Gifts.* The Board of Directors may accept on behalf of the corporation any contribution, gift, bequest, or device for the general purposes or for any special purpose of the corporation.

Section 5. *Dissolution.* In case of dissolution of the National Society for the Study of Education (incorporated under the GENERAL NOT FOR PROFIT CORPORATION ACT of the State of Illinois), the Board of Directors shall, after paying or making provision for the payment of all liabilities of the Corporation, dispose of all assets of the Corporation to such organization or organizations organized and operated exclusively for charitable, educational, or scientific purposes as shall at the time qualify as an exempt organization or organizations under Section 561(C)(3) of the Internal Revenue Code of 1954 (or the corresponding provision of any future United States Internal Revenue Law), as the Board of Directors shall determine.

Article XII

BOOKS AND RECORDS

The corporation shall keep correct and complete books and records of account and shall also keep minutes of the proceedings of its members, Board of Directors, and committees having any of the authority of the Board of Directors, and shall keep at the registered or principal office a record giving the names and addresses of the members entitled to vote. All books and records of the corporation may be inspected by any member or his agent or attorney for any proper purpose at any reasonable time.

Article XIII

FISCAL YEAR

The fiscal year of the corporation shall begin on the first day of July in each year and end on the last day of June of the following year.

Article XIV

DUES

Section 1. *Annual Dues.* The annual dues for active members of the Society shall be determined by vote of the Board of Directors at a regular meeting duly called and held.

Section 2. *Election Fee.* An election fee of $1.00 shall be paid in advance by each applicant for active membership.

Section 3. *Payment of Dues.* Dues for each calendar year shall be payable in advance on or before the first day of January of that year. Notice of dues for the ensuing year shall be mailed to members at the time set for mailing the primary ballots.

Section 4. *Default and Termination of Membership.* Annual membership shall terminate automatically for those members whose dues remain unpaid after the first day of January of each year. Members so in default will be reinstated on payment of the annual dues plus a reinstatement fee of fifty cents.

Article XV

SEAL

The Board of Directors shall provide a corporate seal which shall be in the form of a circle and shall have inscribed thereon the name of the corporation and the words "Corporate Seal, Illinois."

Article XVI

WAIVER OF NOTICE

Whenever any notice whatever is required to be given under the provision of the General Not For Profit Corporation Act of Illinois or under the provisions of the Articles of Incorporation or the by-laws of the corporation, a waiver thereof in writing signed by the person or persons entitled to such notice, whether before or after the time stated therein, shall be deemed equivalent to the giving of such notice.

Article XVII

AMENDMENTS

Section 1. *Amendments by Directors.* The constitution and by-laws may be altered or amended at any meeting of the Board of Directors duly called and held, provided that affirmative vote of at least five directors shall be required for such action.

Section 2. *Amendments by Members.* By petition of twenty-five or more active members duly filed with the Secretary-Treasurer, a proposal to amend the constitution and by-laws shall be submitted to all active members by United States mail together with ballots on which the members shall vote for or against the proposal. Such ballots shall be returned by United States mail to the office of the Secretary-Treasurer within twenty-one days after date of mailing of the proposal and ballots by the Secretary-Treasurer. The Secretary-Treasurer or a committee appointed by the Board of Directors for that purpose shall count the ballots and advise the members of the result. A vote in favor of such proposal by two-thirds of the members voting thereon shall be required for adoption of such amendment.

ANNUAL MEETINGS OF THE SOCIETY

During 1976 meetings of the Society were held in Atlantic City, Washington, D.C., Miami Beach, and San Francisco. At each of these meetings one part of the Seventy-fifth Yearbook was presented.

Part I

Part I (*The Psychology of Teaching Methods*) was presented on April 22 in San Francisco at a meeting cosponsored by the American Educational Research Association, with the following persons participating:

Presiding: N. L. Gage, Professor of Education and Psychology, Stanford University, Chairman of the Yearbook Committee, and member of the Board of Directors of the Society.

Presenting the Yearbook: David C. Berliner, Associate Laboratory Director for Research, Far West Laboratory for Educational Research and Development, and member of the Yearbook Committee.

Commenting on the Yearbook: Ernest R. Hilgard, Professor of Psychology, Stanford University; Frederick J. McDonald, Educational Testing Service; and Susan M. Markle, Office of Instructional Resources, University of Illinois, Chicago Circle.

Another presentation of this volume was made on September 15 in Washington, D.C. at a meeting of Division 15 (Educational Psychology) of the American Psychological Association, with the following persons participating:

Presiding: David C. Berliner.

Presenting the Yearbook: N. L. Gage.

Commenting on the Yearbook: Eva L. Baker, University of California (Los Angeles); Bruce J. Biddle, University of Missouri; and Lee S. Shulman, Michigan State University.

Part II

Part II (*Issues in Secondary Education*) was presented in Washington, D.C. on February 15 at a meeting cosponsored by the National Association of Secondary School Principals, with the following persons participating:

Presiding: J. Lloyd Trump, Associate Secretary Emeritus, National Association of Secondary School Principals, and member of the Yearbook Committee.

Presenting the Yearbook: William Van Til, Coffman Distinguished Professor of Education, Indiana State University, and chairman of the Yearbook Committee.

Commenting on the Yearbook: Robert D. Barr, Associate Professor of Education, Indiana University, and Vernon H. Smith, Professor of Education, Indiana University.

The volume was also presented on February 22 in Atlantic City at a meeting cosponsored by the American Association of School Administrators, with the following persons participating:

Presiding: Kenneth J. Rehage, Secretary-Treasurer of the Society.

Presenting the Yearbook: William Van Til.

Commenting on the Yearbook: Ronald T. Hyman, Professor of Education, Rutgers University, and George Young, Superintendent of Schools, St. Paul, Minnesota.

Another presentation of this volume was made on March 15 in Miami Beach at a meeting cosponsored by the Association for Supervision and Curriculum Development, with the following persons participating:

Presiding and presenting the Yearbook: William Van Til.

Commenting on the Yearbook: Arthur W. Combs, Professor of Education, University of Florida; Gordon F. Vars, Professor of Secondary Education, Kent State University, and member of the Yearbook Committee; and Harold G. Shane, University Professor of Education, Indiana University, and member of the Yearbook Committee.

SYNOPSIS OF THE PROCEEDINGS OF THE BOARD OF DIRECTORS OF THE SOCIETY FOR 1976

I. Meeting of April 18 and 19, 1976

The Board of Directors of the National Society for the Study of Education met at 7:30 P.M. Sunday, April 18, and again at 8 A.M. Monday, April 19 at the offices of the San Francisco Public School Commission in San Francisco with the following members present: Jeanne Chall, Luvern Cunningham (presiding), N. L. Gage, Harold G. Shane, Ralph W. Tyler, and Kenneth J. Rehage. A. Harry Passow and Jacob W. Getzels were unable to attend this meeting.

1. The Secretary presented a financial report for the first nine months of the current fiscal year together with projections of income and expenditures for the balance of the year. He reported that the following measures had been taken to reduce expenditures connected with the manufacture of yearbooks and the reprinting of earlier yearbooks: (a) fewer copies have been printed and bound on the initial run, (b) the practice of printing the names of members of the Society in one of the yearbook volumes has been discontinued and a separate publication of the list of members has been prepared for distribution to members upon request, (c) expenditures for reprinting have been sharply curtailed. Even with these economies it is expected that the cost of manufacturing and distributing the yearbooks will be greater in 1975-76 than in 1974-75, and further increases are anticipated in 1976-77. Similarly, the cost of the paperbacks distributed to those holding the Comprehensive Membership has risen and will be appreciably higher in 1976-77.

2. The Secretary reported on the volumes currently in preparation for the 1977 paperback series. The Board discussed the developments in this program since its inception in 1971, noting in particular the purposes that were envisaged for the program at that time. The Secretary was asked to undertake an inquiry, with the help of the Commission responsible for the program, on the impact of this activity to date.

3. The Secretary presented a report on membership in the Society as of April 1, noting that the number of paid memberships as of that date was approximately the same as the previous year. He also distributed a report of the returns from a questionnaire recently distributed to members. The report summarized the distribution of members by age, sex, professional position, and length of time as a member of the Society. It also included numerous suggestions from members for topics for future publications of the Society. The Board gave extensive consideration to the report on membership, emphasizing the need for the Society to continue its efforts to get new members. There was also

considerable discussion of the topics suggested for future publication efforts, both in the Yearbook series and in the paperback series.

4. The Board reviewed a proposal, prepared by the Secretary at its request, for a revision of the dues structure in the light of increasing costs. After a lengthy discussion the Board approved motions to (a) increase annual dues for the regular membership to $13, (b) increase annual dues for the comprehensive membership for 1977 to $27 (the $14 difference between regular and comprehensive memberships representing the actual cost to the Society for the three paperbacks to be distributed to those holding the comprehensive membership), (c) set the annual dues for members sixty-five years of age and older who have held continuous membership in the Society for not less than ten years at $10 (regular) and $20 (comprehensive), (d) set the annual dues for students at $10 (regular) and $20 (comprehensive) for the first year of membership.

5. The Board heard reports on the following yearbooks in process: *The Teaching of English* (1977), *The Politics of Education* (1977), *Education and the Brain* (1978), *The Law and Education* (1978), and *The Gifted and the Talented* (1979).

6. There was discussion of proposals for yearbooks on the following topics: the middle school, the governance of education, moral education, the economics of education, classroom management, and recurring problems in education. Action was deferred on these proposals.

7. Mr. Passow was named chairman of the Board for 1976-77.

8. The next meeting of the Board was set for September 10-11, 1976 in Chicago.

II. Meeting of September 10 and 11, 1976

The Board of Directors of the National Society for the Study of Education met at 7:30 P.M. Friday, September 10 and again at 8:30 A.M. on Saturday, September 11 at the O'Hare Hilton Hotel in Chicago with the following members present: Jeanne Chall, N. L. Gage, Jacob W. Getzels, A. Harry Passow (presiding), Harold G. Shane, Ralph W. Tyler, and Kenneth J. Rehage, Secretary-Treasurer.

1. The Secretary presented a report on the financial position of the Society at the close of the fiscal year 1975-76 and a membership report as of the close of the membership year (December 31, 1975) and as of August 31, 1976.

2. The Secretary presented a report on the Expanded Publication Program. During the discussion that followed it was pointed out that the program was initially conceived as a means of (a) providing an additional service to members of the Society and to the profession through the publication of a series of paperbacks on timely and often controversial subjects, (b) providing opportunities for more individuals

to write for the Society's publications, and (c) increasing the income of the Society. It was noted that there was as yet no clear evidence of the extent to which these purposes were being accomplished. There was discussion of whether the project should be continued beyond 1977, and if so in what form. The Board's view was that the initial purposes still had merit. Several suggestions were made for alternative ways of working toward those ends. It was agreed that further discussion of this matter should occur at the next meeting of the Board, at which time the Secretary is to make a detailed report on the program together with such recommendations as the Committee currently responsible for the program may wish to make.

3. The Secretary reported that the work on the manuscript for *The Teaching of English* (Part I of the Seventy-sixth Yearbook) was completed ahead of schedule and that the work on Part II (*The Politics of Education*) was behind schedule. Manuscripts for *The Law and Education* (Seventy-seventh Yearbook, Part I) have been promised for early January and manuscripts for Part II (*Education and the Brain*) are due on April 1. Work is proceeding satisfactorily on the volume on *The Gifted and the Talented* (Seventy-eighth Yearbook).

4. The Board authorized Messrs. Gage and Goodlad to proceed with plans for a volume on classroom management for publication in 1979. Mr. Passow was authorized to proceed with plans for a volume on the Middle School. The customary appropriation of $2,000 was made to meet expenses in connection with the preparation of each of these volumes.

5. The Board continued to express interest in a volume on educational governance, which had originally been proposed by Mr. Cunningham.

6. Mr. Shane was asked to explore possibilities for a volume on the philosophy of education and to report to the Board at its next meeting.

7. Mr. Gage was asked to communicate with Mr. Henry Levin regarding Mr. Levin's proposal for a volume on education and income.

8. Other topics for future yearbooks or paperbacks were considered but no action was taken pending receipt of formal proposals.

9. The next meeting of the Board was set for February 4-5 in Chicago.

REPORT OF THE TREASURER OF THE SOCIETY
1975-1976
Receipts and Disbursements

Receipts:

Membership dues and fees	$ 62,222.00
Sales, royalties, and permissions	57,788.56
Interest and dividends	7,208.86
Refund from McCutchan Publishing Corporation	880.00
Transfers	130.01
Miscellaneous	119.06
Transfer from savings	37,000.00
Total	$165,348.49

Disbursements:

Yearbooks:

Manufacturing	$ 53,804.94
Reprinting	873.51
Preparation	3,150.77
Mailing	3,919.08

Meetings of Board and Society	3,711.09

Secretary's Office:

Editorial, secretarial, clerical salaries	28,527.38
Supplies, equipment, telephone, promotion	6,478.18

New Publication Program

Cost of paperbacks	22,100.00
Preparation	801.21
Refunds/transfers	196.11
Bank charges	77.91
Miscellaneous	129.21
Transfer to savings	40,000.00
Total	$163,769.39
Excess of receipts over disbursements	$ 1,579.10
Cash on hand, June 30, 1975	$ 10,634.15
Cash on hand, June 30, 1976	$ 12,213.25

STATEMENT OF CASH AND SECURITIES
as of June 30, 1976

Cash:

    New University Bank, Chicago, Checking Account......$ 12,213.25

Savings Account:

    New University Bank, Chicago....................... 8,491.12

Savings and Loan Certificates:

    Chicago Federal Savings and Loan Association........... 10,000.00
    Home Federal Savings and Loan Association............ 10,000.00

Certificate of Deposit:

    New University Bank, Chicago 15,000.00

Bonds:

    American Telephone & Telegraph ($21,000, 1985)....... 14,679.42
    ML Corporate Income Fund (25 units)................. 25,925.25
    U.S. Government Bonds (H) due March, 1977.......... 15,000.00

Stock:

    First National Bank of Boston, 57 shares capital stock.... 1,300.00

    Total cash and securities on hand..................$112,609.04

Charges against Current Assets

Annual dues paid for 1977 & 1978.....................$ 232.00
Paid up Life Memberships 4,279.00
    Total ... .$ 4,511.00

Unencumbered assets $108,098.04

A Note to Members of the Society

The practice of including a list of members of the Society in one of the volumes of each yearbook has been discontinued. Instead, a booklet containing the names of members has been prepared. The booklet will be sent to any member upon written request to the Secretary-Treasurer.

KENNETH J. REHAGE
Secretary-Treasurer

INFORMATION CONCERNING
THE NATIONAL SOCIETY FOR THE STUDY OF EDUCATION

1. *Purpose.* The purpose of the National Society is to promote the investigation and discussion of educational questions. To this end it holds an annual meeting and publishes a series of yearbooks and a series of paperbacks on Contemporary Educational Issues.

2. *Membership.* Any person interested in the purpose of the Society and in receiving its publications may become a member by sending in name, title, address, and a check covering dues and the entrance fee (see items 4 and 5). Graduate students may become members, upon recommendation of a faculty member, at a reduced rate for the first year of membership. Dues for all subsequent years are the same as for other members.

Membership is not transferable. It is limited to individuals and may not be held by libraries, schools, or other institutions, either directly or indirectly.

3. *Period of Membership.* Membership is for the calendar year and terminates automatically on December 31, unless dues for the ensuing year are paid as indicated in item 6. Applicants for membership may not date their entrance back of the current calendar year.

4. *Categories of Membership.* The following categories of membership have been established:

> *Regular.* Annual dues are $13.00. The member receives a clothbound copy of each part of the current yearbook.
> *Comprehensive.* Annual dues are $27.00. The member receives a clothbound copy of the current yearbook *and* all volumes in the current year's paperback series on Contemporary Educational Issues.
> *Special Memberships for Retired Members and Graduate Students.*
> > *Retired members.* Persons who are retired or who are sixty-five years of age *and* who have been members of the Society continuously for at least ten years may retain their Regular Membership upon payment of annual dues of $10.00 or their Comprehensive Membership upon payment of annual dues of $20.00.
> > *Graduate Students.* Graduate students may pay annual dues of $10.00 for Regular Membership or $20.00 for Comprehensive Membership for their first year of membership, plus the $1.00 entrance fee in either case.
> *Life Memberships.* Persons sixty years of age or above may become life members on payment of a fee based on the average life expectancy of their age group. Regular life members may take out a Comprehensive Membership for any year upon payment of an additional fee of $10.00. For further information apply to the Secretary-Treasurer.

5. *Privileges of Membership.* Members receive the publications of the Society as described above. All members are entitled to vote, to participate in meetings of the Society, and (under certain conditions) to hold office.

6. *Entrance Fee.* New members are required to pay an entrance fee of one dollar, in addition to the dues, for the first year of membership.

7. *Payment of Dues.* Statements of dues are rendered in October for the following calendar year. Any member so notified whose dues remain unpaid on January 1 thereby loses membership and can be reinstated only by paying the dues plus a reinstatement fee of fifty cents ($.50).

School warrants and vouchers from institutions must be accompanied by definite information concerning the name and address of the person for whom the membership fee is being paid. Statements of dues are rendered on our own form only. The Secretary's office cannot undertake to fill out special invoice forms of any kind or to affix a notary's affidavit to statements or receipts.

Cancelled checks serve as receipts. Members desiring an additional receipt must enclose a stamped and addressed envelope therefor.

8. *Distribution of Yearbooks to Members.* The yearbooks, normally ready prior to the February meeting of the Society, will be mailed from the office of the distributor only to members whose dues for that year have been paid.

9. *Commercial Sales.* The distribution of all yearbooks prior to the current year, and also of those of the current year not regularly mailed to members in exchange for their dues, is in the hands of the distributor, not of the Secretary. Orders may be placed with the University of Chicago Press, Chicago, Illinois 60637, which distributes the yearbooks of the Society. Orders for paperbacks in the series on Contemporary Educational Issues should be placed with the designated publisher of that series. The list of the Society's publications is printed in each yearbook.

10. *Yearbooks.* The yearbooks are issued about one month before the February meeting. Published in two volumes, each of which contains 300 to 400 pages, the yearbooks are planned to be of immediate practical value as well as representative of sound scholarship and scientific investigation.

11. *Series on Contemporary Educational Issues.* This series, in paperback format, is designed to supplement the yearbooks by timely publications on topics of current interest. There will usually be three of these volumes each year.

12. *Meetings.* The annual meeting, at which the yearbooks are presented and critiqued, is held as a rule in February at the same time and place as the meeting of the American Association of School Administrators. Members will be notified of other meetings.

Applications for membership will be handled promptly at any time. New members will receive the yearbook scheduled for publication during the calendar year in which application for Regular Membership is made. New members who elect to take out the Comprehensive membership will receive both the yearbook and the paperbacks scheduled for publication during the year in which application is made.

KENNETH J. REHAGE, Secretary-Treasurer

5835 Kimbark Avenue
Chicago, Illinois 60637

PUBLICATIONS OF THE NATIONAL SOCIETY FOR THE STUDY OF EDUCATION

1. The Yearbooks

NOTICE: Many of the early yearbooks of this series are now out of print. In the following list, those titles to which an asterisk is prefixed are not available for purchase.

*First Yearbook, 1902, Part I—*Some Principles in the Teaching of History.* Lucy M. Salmon.
*First Yearbook, 1902, Part II—*The Progress of Geography in the Schools.* W. M. Davis and H. M. Wilson.
*Second Yearbook, 1903, Part I—*The Course of Study in History in the Common School.* Isabel Lawrence, C. A. McMurray, Frank McMurry, E. C. Page, and E. J. Rice.
*Second Yearbook, 1903, Part II—*The Relation of Theory to Pratice in Education.* M. J. Holmes, J. A. Keith, and Levi Seeley.
*Third Yearbook, 1904, Part I—*The Relation of Theory to Practice in the Education of Teachers.* John Dewey, Sarah C. Brooks, F. M. McMurry, *et al.*
*Third Yearbook, 1904, Part II—*Nature Study.* W. S. Jackman.
*Fourth Yearbook, 1905, Part I—*The Education and Training of Secondary Teachers.* E. C. Elliott, E. G. Dexter, M. J. Holmes, *et al.*
*Fourth Yearbook, 1905, Part II—*The Place of Vocational Subjects in the High-School Curriculum.* J. S. Brown, G. B. Morrison, and Ellen Richards.
*Fifth Yearbook, 1906, Part I—*On the Teaching of English in Elementary and High Schools.* G. P. Brown and Emerson Davis.
*Fifth Yearbook, 1906, Part II—*The Certification of Teachers.* E. P. Cubberley.
*Sixth Yearbook, 1907, Part I—*Vocational Studies for College Entrance.* C. A. Herrick, H. W. Holmes, T. deLaguna, V. Prettyman, and W. J. S. Bryan.
*Sixth Yearbook, 1907, Part II—*The Kindergarten and Its Relation to Elementary Education.* Ada Van Stone Harris, E. A. Kirkpatrick, Marie Kraus-Boelté, Patty S. Hill, Harriette M. Mills, and Nina Vandewalker.
*Seventh Yearbook, 1908, Part I—*The Relation of Superintendents and Principals to the Training and Professional Improvement of Their Teachers.* Charles D. Lowry.
*Seventh Yearbook, 1908, Part II—*The Co-ordination of the Kindergarten and the Elementary School.* B. J. Gregory, Jennie B. Merrill, Bertha Payne, and Margaret Giddings.
*Eighth Yearbook, 1909, Part I—*Education with Reference to Sex: Pathological, Economic, and Social Aspects.* C. R. Henderson.
*Eighth Yearbook, 1909, Part II—*Education with Reference to Sex: Agencies and Methods.* C. R. Henderson and Helen C. Putnam.
*Ninth Yearbook, 1910, Part I—*Health and Education.* T. D. Wood.
*Ninth Yearbook, 1910, Part II—*The Nurses in Education.* T. D. Wood, *et al.*
*Tenth Yearbook, 1911, Part I—*The City School as a Community Center.* H. C. Leipziger, Sarah E. Hyre, R. D. Warden, C. Ward Crampton, E. W. Stitt, E. J. Ward, Mrs. T. C. Grice, and C. A. Perry.
*Tenth Yearbook, 1911, Part II—*The Rural School as a Community Center.* B. H. Crocheron, Jessie Field, F. W. Howe, E. C. Bishop, A. B. Graham, O. J. Kern, M. T. Scudder, and B. M. Davis.
*Eleventh Yearbook, 1912, Part I—*Industrial Education: Typical Experiments Described and Interpreted.* J. F. Barker, M. Bloomfield, B. W. Johnson, P. Johnson, L. M. Leavitt, G. A. Mirick, M. W. Murray, C. F. Perry, A. L. Stafford, and H. B. Wilson.
*Eleventh Yearbook, 1912, Part II—*Agricultural Education in Secondary Schools.* A. C. Monahan, R. W. Stimson, D. J. Crosby, W. H. French, H. F. Button, F. R. Crane, W. R. Hart, and G. F. Warren.
*Twelfth Yearbook, 1913, Part I—*The Supervision of City Schools.* Franklin Bobbitt, J. W. Hall, and J. D. Wolcott.
*Twelfth Yearbook, 1913, Part II—*The Supervision of Rural Schools.* A. C. Monahan, L. J. Hanifan, J. E. Warren, Wallace Lund, U. J. Hoffman, A. S. Cook, E. M. Rapp, Jackson Davis, J. D. Wolcott.
*Thirteenth Yearbook, 1914, Part I—*Some Aspects of High-School Instruction and Administration.* H. C. Morrison, E. R. Breslich, W. A. Jessup, and L. D. Coffman.
*Thirteenth Yearbook, 1914, Part II—*Plans for Organizing School Surveys, with a Summary of Typical School Surveys.* Charles H. Judd and Henry L. Smith.
*Fourteenth Yearbook, 1915, Part I—*Minimum Essentials in Elementary School Subjects—Standards and Current Practices.* H. B. Wilson, H. W. Holmes, F. E. Thompson, R. G. Jones, S. A. Courtis, W. S. Gray, F. N. Freeman, H. C. Pryor, J. F. Hosic, W. A. Jessup, and W. C. Bagley.
*Fourteenth Yearbook, 1915, Part II—*Methods for Measuring Teachers' Efficiency.* Arthur C. Boyce.
*Fifteenth Yearbook, 1916, Part I—*Standards and Tests for the Measurement of the Efficiency of Schools and School Systems.* G. D. Strayer, Bird T. Baldwin, B. R. Buckingham, F. W. Ballou, D. C. Bliss, H. G. Childs, S. A. Courtis, E. P. Cubberley, C. H. Judd, George Melcher, E. E. Oberholtzer, J. B. Sears, Daniel Starch, M. R. Trabue, and G. M. Whipple.

*Fifteenth Yearbook, 1916, Part II—*The Relationship between Persistence in School and Home Conditions.* Charles E. Holley.
*Fifteenth Yearbook, 1916, Part III—*The Junior High School.* Aubrey A. Douglas.
*Sixteenth Yearbook, 1917, Part I—*Second Report of the Committee on Minimum Essentials in Elementary-School Subjects.* W. C. Bagley, W. W. Charters, F. N. Freeman, W. S. Gray, Ernest Horn, J. H. Hoskinson, W. S. Monroe, C. F. Munson, H. C. Pryor, L. W. Rapeer, G. M. Wilson, and H. B. Wilson.
*Sixteenth Yearbook, 1917, Part II—*The Efficiency of College Students as Conditioned by Age at Entrance and Size of High School.* B. F. Pittenger.
*Seventeenth Yearbook, 1918, Part I—*Third Report of the Committee on Economy of Time in Education.* W. C. Bagley, B. B. Bassett, M. E. Branom, Alice Camerer, J. E. Dealey, C. A. Ellwood, E. B. Greene, A. B. Hart, J. F. Hosic, E. T. Housh, W. H. Mace, L. R. Marston, H. C. McKown, H. E. Mitchell, W. V. Reavis, D. Snedden, and H. B. Wilson.
*Seventeenth Yearbook, 1918, Part II—*The Measurement of Educational Products.* E. J. Ashbaugh, W. A. Averill, L. P. Ayers, F. W. Ballou, Edna Bryner, B. R. Buckingham, S. A. Courtis, M. E. Haggerty, C. H. Judd, George Melcher, W. S. Monroe, E. A. Nifenecker, and E. L. Thorndike.
*Eighteenth Yearbook, 1919, Part I—*The Professional Preparation of High-School Teachers.* G. N. Cade, S. S. Colvin, Charles Fordyce, H. H. Foster, T. S. Gosling, W. S. Gray, L. V. Koos, A. R. Mead, H. L. Miller, F. C. Whitcomb, and Clifford Woody.
*Eighteenth Yearbook, 1919, Part II—*Fourth Report of Committee on Economy of Time in Education.* F. C. Ayer, F. N. Freeman, W. S. Gray, Ernest Horn, W. S. Monroe, and C. E. Seashore.
*Nineteenth Yearbook, 1920, Part I—*New Materials of Instruction.* Prepared by the Society's Committee on Materials of Instruction.
*Nineteenth Yearbook, 1920, Part II—*Classroom Problems in the Education of Gifted Children.* T. S. Henry.
*Twentieth Yearbook, 1921, Part I—*New Materials of Instruction.* Second Report by Society's Committee.
*Twentieth Yearbook, 1921, Part II—*Report of the Society's Committee on Silent Reading.* M. A. Burgess, S. A. Courtis, C. E. Germane, W. S. Gray, H. A. Greene, Regina R. Heller, J. H. Hoover, J. A. O'Brien, J. L. Packer, Daniel Starch, W. W. Theisen, G. A. Yoakam, and representatives of other school systems.
*Twenty-first Yearbook, 1922, Parts I and II—*Intelligence Tests and Their Use,* Part I—*The Nature, History, and General Principles of Intelligence Testing.* E. L. Thorndike, S. S. Colvin, Harold Rugg, G. M. Whipple, Part II—*The Administrative Use of Intelligence Tests.* H. W. Holmes, W. K. Layton, Helen Davis, Agnes L. Rogers, Rudolf Pintner, M. R. Trabue, W. S. Miller, Bessie L. Gambrill, and others. The two parts are bound together.
*Twenty-second Yearbook, 1923, Part I—*English Composition: Its Aims, Methods and Measurements.* Earl Hudelson.
*Twenty-second Yearbook, 1923, Part II—*The Social Studies in the Elementary and Secondary School.* A. S. Barr, J. J. Coss, Henry Harap, R. W. Hatch, H. C. Hill, Ernest Horn, C. H. Judd, L. C. Marshall, F. M. McMurry, Earle Rugg, H. O. Rugg, Emma Schweppe, Mabel Snedaker, and C. W. Washburne.
*Twenty-third Yearbook, 1924, Part I—*The Education of Gifted Children.* Report of the Society's Committee. Guy M. Whipple, Chairman.
*Twenty-third Yearbook, 1924, Part II—*Vocational Guidance and Vocational Education for Industries.* A. H. Edgerton and others.
*Twenty-fourth Yearbook, 1925, Part I—*Report of the National Committee on Reading.* W. S. Gray, Chairman, F. W. Ballou, Rose L. Hardy, Ernest Horn, Francis Jenkins, S. A. Leonard, Estaline Wilson, and Laura Zirbes.
*Twenty-fourth Yearbook, 1925, Part II—*Adapting the Schools to Individual Differences.* Report of the Society's Committee. Carleton W. Washburne, Chairman.
*Twenty-fifth Yearbook, 1926, Part I—*The Present Status of Safety Education.* Report of the Society's Committee. Guy M. Whipple, Chairman.
*Twenty-fifth Yearbook, 1926, Part II—*Extra-Curricular Activities.* Report of the Society's Committee. Leonard V. Koos, Chairman.
*Twenty-sixth Yearbook, 1927, Part I—*Curriculum-making: Past and Present.* Report of the Society's Committee. Harold O. Rugg, Chairman.
*Twenty-sixth Yearbook, 1927, Part II—*The Foundations of Curriculum-making.* Prepared by individual members of the Society's Committee. Harold O. Rugg, Chairman.
*Twenty-seventh Yearbook, 1928, Part I—*Nature and Nurture: Their Influence upon Intelligence.* Prepared by the Society's Committee. Lewis M. Terman, Chairman.
*Twenty-seventh Yearbook, 1928, Part II—*Nature and Nurture: Their Influence upon Achievement.* Prepared by the Society's Committee. Lewis M. Terman, Chairman.
Twenty-eighth Yearbook, 1929, Parts I and II—*Preschool and Parental Education,* Part I—*Organization and Development.* Part II—*Research and Method.* Prepared by the Society's Committee. Lois H. Meek, Chairman. Bound in one volume. Cloth.
*Twenty-ninth Yearbook, 1930, Parts I and II—*Report of the Society's Committee on Arithmetic.* Part I—*Some Aspects of Modern Thought on Arithmetic.* Part II—*Research in Arithmetic.* Prepared by the Society's Committee. F. B. Knight, Chairman. Bound in one volume.
*Thirtieth Yearbook, 1931, Part I—*The Status of Rural Education.* First Report of the Society's Committee on Rural Education. Orville G. Brim, Chairman.
Thirtieth Yearbook, 1931, Part II—*The Textbook in American Education.* Report of the Society's Committee on the Textbook, J. B. Edmonson, Chairman. Cloth, Paper.

PUBLICATIONS

*Thirty-first Yearbook, 1932, Part I—*A Program for Teaching Science*. Prepared by the Society's Committee on the Teaching of Science. S. Ralph Powers, Chairman.
*Thirty-first Yearbook, 1932, Part II—*Changes and Experiments in Liberal-Arts Education*. Prepared by Kathryn McHale, with numerous collaborators.
*Thirty-second Yearbook, 1933—*The Teaching of Geography*. Prepared by the Society's Committee on the Teaching of Geography. A. E. Parkins, Chairman.
*Thirty-third Yearbook, 1934, Part I—*The Planning and Construction of School Buildings*. Prepared by the Society's Committee on School Buildings. N. L. Engelhardt, Chairman.
*Thirty-third Yearbook, 1934, Part II—*The Activity Movement*. Prepared by the Society's Committee on the Activity Movement. Lois Coffey Mossman, Chairman.
Thirty-fourth Yearbook, 1935—*Educational Diagnosis*. Prepared by the Society's Committee on Educational Diagnosis. L. J. Brueckner, Chairman. Paper.
*Thirty-fifth Yearbook, 1936, Part I—*The Grouping of Pupils*. Prepared by the Society's Committee. W. W. Coxe, Chairman.
*Thirty-fifth Yearbook, 1936, Part II—*Music Education*. Prepared by the Society's Committee. W. L. Uhl, Chairman.
*Thirty-sixth Yearbook, 1937, Part I—*The Teaching of Reading*. Prepared by the Society's Committee. W. S. Gray, Chairman.
*Thirty-sixth Yearbook, 1937, Part II—*International Understanding through the Public-School Curriculum*. Prepared by the Society's Committee. I. L. Kandel, Chairman.
*Thirty-seventh Yearbook, 1938, Part I—*Guidance in Educational Institutions*. Prepared by the Society's Committee. G. N. Kefauver, Chairman.
*Thirty-seventh Yearbook, 1938, Part II—*The Scientific Movement in Education*. Prepared by the Society's Committee. F. N. Freeman, Chairman.
*Thirty-eighth Yearbook, 1939, Part I—*Child Development and the Curriculum*. Prepared by the Society's Committee. Carleton Washburne, Chairman.
*Thirty-eighth Yearbook, 1939, Part II—*General Education in the American College*. Prepared by the Society's Committee. Alvin Eurich, Chairman. Cloth.
*Thirty-ninth Yearbook, 1940, Part I—*Intelligence: Its Nature and Nurture. Comparative and Critical Exposition*. Prepared by the Society's Committee. G. D. Stoddard, Chairman.
*Thirty-ninth Yearbook, 1940, Part II—*Intelligence: Its Nature and Nurture. Original Studies and Experiments*. Prepared by the Society's Committee. G. D. Stoddard, Chairman.
*Fortieth Yearbook, 1941—*Art in American Life and Education*. Prepared by the Society's Committee. Thomas Munro, Chairman.
Forty-first Yearbook, 1942, Part I—*Philosophies of Education*. Prepared by the Society's Committee. John S. Brubacher, Chairman. Cloth, Paper.
Forty-first Yearbook, 1942, Part II—*The Psychology of Learning*. Prepared by the Society's Committee. T. R. McConnell, Chairman. Cloth.
*Forty-second Yearbook, 1943, Part I—*Vocational Education*. Prepared by the Society's Committee. F. J. Keller, Chairman.
*Forty-second Yearbook, 1943, Part II—*The Library in General Education*. Prepared by the Society's Committee. L. R. Wilson, Chairman.
Forty-third Yearbook, 1944, Part I—*Adolescence*. Prepared by the Society's Committee. Harold E. Jones, Chairman. Paper.
*Forty-third Yearbook, 1944, Part II—*Teaching Language in the Elementary School*. Prepared by the Society's Committee. M. R. Trabue, Chairman.
*Forty-fourth Yearbook, 1945, Part I—*American Education in the Postwar Period: Curriculum Reconstruction*. Prepared by the Society's Committee. Ralph W. Tyler, Chairman.
Forty-fourth Yearbook, 1945, Part II—*American Education in the Postwar Period: Structural Reorganization*. Prepared by the Society's Committee. Bess Goodykoontz, Chairman. Paper.
*Forty-fifth Yearbook, 1946, Part I—*The Measurement of Understanding*. Prepared by the Society's Committee. William A. Brownell, Chairman.
*Forty-fifth Yearbook, 1946, Part II—*Changing Conceptions in Educational Administration*. Prepared by the Society's Committee. Alonzo G. Grace, Chairman.
*Forty-sixth Yearbook, 1947, Part I—*Science Education in American Schools*. Prepared by the Society's Committee. Victor H. Noll, Chairman.
Forty-sixth Yearbook, 1947, Part II—*Early Childhood Education*. Prepared by the Society's Committee. N. Searle Light, Chairman. Paper.
Forty-seventh Yearbook, 1948, Part I—*Juvenile Delinquency and the Schools*. Prepared by the Society's Committee. Ruth Strang, Chairman. Cloth.
Forty-seventh Yearbook, 1948, Part II—*Reading in the High School and College*. Prepared by the Society's Committee. William S. Gray, Chairman. Cloth, Paper.
Forty-eighth Yearbook, 1949, Part I—*Audio-visual Materials of Instruction*. Prepared by the Society's Committee. Stephen M. Corey, Chairman. Cloth.
*Forty-eighth Yearbook, 1949, Part II—*Reading in the Elementary School*. Prepared by the Society's Committee. Arthur I. Gates, Chairman.
*Forty-ninth Yearbook, 1950, Part I—*Learning and Instruction*. Prepared by the Society's Committee. G. Lester Anderson, Chairman.
Forty-ninth Yearbook, 1950, Part II—*The Education of Exceptional Children*. Prepared by the Society's Committee. Samuel A. Kirk, Chairman. Paper.
Fiftieth Yearbook, 1951, Part I—*Graduate Study in Education*. Prepared by the Society's Board of Directors. Ralph W. Tyler, Chairman. Paper.
Fiftieth Yearbook, 1951, Part II—*The Teaching of Arithmetic*. Prepared by the Society's Committee. G. T. Buswell, Chairman. Cloth, Paper.

PUBLICATIONS

Fifty-first Yearbook, 1952, Part I—*General Education.* Prepared by the Society's Committee. T. R. McConnell, Chairman. Cloth, Paper.
Fifty-first Yearbook, 1952, Part II—*Education in Rural Communities.* Prepared by the Society's Committee. Ruth Strang, Chairman. Cloth, Paper.
*Fifty-second Yearbook, 1953, Part I—*Adapting the Secondary-School Program to the Needs of Youth.* Prepared by the Society's Committee: William G. Brink, Chairman.
Fifty-second Yearbook, 1953, Part II—*The Community School.* Prepared by the Society's Committee. Maurice F. Seay, Chairman. Cloth.
Fifty-third Yearbook, 1954, Part I—*Citizen Co-operation for Better Public Schools.* Prepared by the Society's Committee. Edgar L. Morphet, Chairman. Cloth, Paper.
Fifty-third Yearbook, 1954, Part II—*Mass Media and Education.* Prepared by the Society's Committee. Edgar Dale, Chairman. Paper.
*Fifty-fourth Yearbook, 1955, Part I—*Modern Philosophies and Education.* Prepared by the Society's Committee. John S. Brubacher, Chairman.
Fifty-fourth Yearbook, 1955, Part II—*Mental Health in Modern Education.* Prepared by the Society's Committee. Paul A. Witty, Chairman. Paper.
*Fifty-fifth Yearbook, 1956, Part I—*The Public Junior College.* Prepared by the Society's Committee. B. Lamar Johnson, Chairman.
Fifty-fifth Yearbook, 1956, Part II—*Adult Reading.* Prepared by the Society's Committee. David H. Clift, Chairman. Paper.
Fifty-sixth Yearbook, 1957, Part I—*In-service Education of Teachers, Supervisors, and Administrators.* Prepared by the Society's Committee. Stephen M. Corey, Chairman. Cloth, Paper.
Fifty-sixth Yearbook, 1957, Part II—*Social Studies in the Elementary School.* Prepared by the Society's Committee. Ralph C. Preston, Chairman. Cloth, Paper.
Fifty-seventh Yearbook, 1958, Part I—*Basic Concepts in Music Education.* Prepared by the Society's Committee. Thurber H. Madison, Chairman. Cloth.
Fifty-seventh Yearbook, 1958, Part II—*Education for the Gifted.* Prepared by the Society's Committee. Robert J. Havighurst, Chairman. Cloth, Paper.
Fifty-seventh Yearbook, 1958, Part III—*The Integration of Educational Experiences.* Prepared by the Society's Committee. Paul L. Dressel, Chairman. Cloth.
Fifty-eighth Yearbook, 1959, Part I—*Community Education: Principles and Practices from World-wide Experience.* Prepared by the Society's Committee. C. O. Arndt, Chairman. Cloth, Paper.
Fifty-eighth Yearbook, 1959, Part II—*Personnel Services in Education.* Prepared by the Society's Committee. Melvene D. Hardee, Chairman. Paper.
*Fifty-ninth Yearbook, 1960, Part I—*Rethinking Science Education.* Prepared by the Society's Committee. J. Darrell Barnard, Chairman.
Fifty-ninth Yearbook, 1960, Part II—*The Dynamics of Instructional Groups.* Prepared by the Society's Committee. Gale E. Jensen, Chairman. Cloth.
Sixtieth Yearbook, 1961, Part I—*Development in and through Reading.* Prepared by the Society's Committee. Paul A. Witty, Chairman. Cloth, Paper.
Sixtieth Yearbook, 1961, Part II—*Social Forces Influencing American Education.* Prepared by the Society's Committee. Ralph W. Tyler, Chairman. Cloth.
Sixty-first Yearbook, 1962, Part I—*Individualizing Instruction.* Prepared by the Society's Committee. Fred T. Tyler, Chairman. Cloth.
Sixty-first Yearbook, 1962, Part II—*Education for the Professions.* Prepared by the Society's Committee. G. Lester Anderson, Chairman. Cloth.
Sixty-second Yearbook, 1963, Part I—*Child Psychology.* Prepared by the Society's Committee. Harold W. Stevenson, Editor. Cloth.
Sixty-second Yearbook, 1963, Part II—*The Impact and Improvement of School Testing Programs.* Prepared by the Society's Committee. Warren G. Findley, Editor. Cloth.
Sixty-third Yearbook, 1964, Part I—*Theories of Learning and Instruction.* Prepared by the Society's Committee. Ernest R. Hilgard, Editor. Paper.
Sixty-third Yearbook, 1964, Part II—*Behavioral Science and Educational Administration.* Prepared by the Society' Committee. Daniel E. Griffiths, Editor. Paper.
Sixty-fourth Yearbook, 1965, Part I—*Vocational Education.* Prepared by the Society's Committee. Melvin L. Barlow, Editor. Cloth.
Sixty-fourth Yearbook, 1965, Part II—*Art Education.* Prepared by the Society's Committee. W. Reid Hastie, Editor. Cloth.
Sixty-fifth Yearbook, 1966, Part I—*Social Deviancy among Youth.* Prepared by the Society's Committee. William W. Wattenberg, Editor. Cloth.
Sixty-fifth Yearbook, 1966, Part II—*The Changing American School.* Prepared by the Society's Committee. John I. Goodlad, Editor. Cloth.
Sixty-sixth Yearbook, 1967, Part I—*The Educationally Retarded and Disadvantaged.* Prepared by the Society's Committee. Paul A. Witty, Editor. Cloth.
Sixty-sixth Yearbook, 1967, Part II—*Programed Instruction.* Prepared by the Society's Committee. Phil C. Lange, Editor. Cloth.
Sixty-seventh Yearbook, 1968, Part I—*Metropolitanism: Its Challenge to Education.* Prepared by the Society's Committee. Robert J. Havighurst, Editor. Cloth.
Sixty-seventh Yearbook, 1968, Part II—*Innovation and Change in Reading Instruction.* Prepared by the Society's Committee. Helen M. Robinson, Editor. Cloth.
Sixty-eighth Yearbook, 1969, Part I—*The United States and International Education.* Prepared by the Society's Committee. Harold G. Shane, Editor. Cloth.
Sixty-eighth Yearbook, 1969, Part II—*Educational Evaluation: New Roles, New Means.* Prepared by the Society's Committee. Ralph W. Tyler, Editor. Paper.
Sixty-ninth Yearbook, 1970, Part I—*Mathematics Education.* Prepared by the Society's Committee. Edward G. Begle, Editor. Cloth.
Sixty-ninth Yearbook, 1970, Part II—*Linguistics in School Programs.* Prepared by the Society's Committee. Albert H. Marckwardt, Editor. Cloth.

Seventieth Yearbook, 1971, Part I—*The Curriculum: Retrospect and Prospect*. Prepared by the Society's Committee. Robert M. McClure, Editor. Paper.
Seventieth Yearbook, 1971, Part II—*Leaders in American Education*. Prepared by the Society's Committee. Robert J. Havighurst, Editor. Cloth.
Seventy-first Yearbook, 1972, Part I—*Philosophical Redirection of Educational Research*. Prepared by the Society's Committee. Lawrence G. Thomas, Editor. Cloth.
Seventy-first Yearbook, 1972, Part II—*Early Childhood Education*. Prepared by the Society's Committee. Ira J. Gordon, Editor. Cloth, Paper.
Seventy-second Yearbook, 1973, Part I—*Behavior Modification in Education*. Prepared by the Society's Committee. Carl E. Thoresen, Editor. Cloth.
Seventy-second Yearbook, 1973, Part II—*The Elementary School in the United States*. Prepared by the Society's Committee. John I. Goodlad and Harold G. Shane, Editors. Cloth.
Seventy-third Yearbook, 1974, Part I—*Media and Symbols: The Forms of Expression, Communication, and Education*. Prepared by the Society's Committee. David R. Olson, Editor. Cloth.
Seventy-third Yearbook, 1974, Part II—*Uses of the Sociology of Education*. Prepared by the Society's Committee. C. Wayne Gordon, Editor. Cloth.
Seventy-fourth Yearbook, 1975, Part I—*Youth*. Prepared by the Society's Committee. Robert J. Havighurst and Philip H. Dreyer, Editors. Cloth.
Seventy-fourth Yearbook, 1975, Part II—*Teacher Education*. Prepared by the Society's Committee. Kevin Ryan, Editor. Cloth.
Seventy-fifth Yearbook, 1976, Part I—*Psychology of Teaching Methods*. Prepared by the Society's Committee. N. L. Gage, Editor. Cloth.
Seventy-fifth Yearbook, 1976, Part II—*Issues in Secondary Education*. Prepared by the Society's Committee. William Van Til, Editor. Cloth.
Seventy-sixth Yearbook, 1977, Part I—*The Teaching of English*. Prepared by the Society's Committee. James R. Squire, Editor. Cloth.
Seventy-sixth Yearbook, 1977, Part II—*The Politics of Education*. Prepared by the Society's Committee. Jay D. Scribner, Editor. Cloth.

Yearbooks of the National Society are distributed by

THE UNIVERSITY OF CHICAGO PRESS, CHICAGO, ILLINOIS 60637

Please direct inquiries regarding prices of volumes still available to the University of Chicago Press. Orders for these volumes should be sent to the University of Chicago Press, not to the offices of the National Society.

2. The Series on Contemporary Educational Issues

In addition to its Yearbooks the Society now publishes volumes in a series on Contemporary Educational Issues. These volumes are prepared under the supervision of the Society's Commission on an Expanded Publication Program.

The 1977 Titles

Early Childhood Education: Perspectives and Issues (Bernard Spodek and Herbert J. Walberg, eds.)

The Future of Big City Schools: Desegregation Policies and Magnet Alternatives (Daniel U. Levine and Robert J. Havighurst, eds.)

Educational Administration: The Developing Decades (Luvern L. Cunningham, Walter G. Hack, and Raphael O. Nystrand, eds.)

The 1976 Titles

Prospects for Research and Development in Education (Ralph W. Tyler, ed.)

Public Testimony on Public Schools (Commission on Educational Governance)

Counseling Children and Adolescents (William M. Walsh, ed.)

The 1975 Titles

Schooling and the Rights of Children (Vernon Haubrich and Michael Apple, eds.)

Systems of Individualized Education (Harriet Talmage, ed.)

Educational Policy and International Assessment: Implications of the IEA Assessment of Achievement (Alan Purves and Daniel U. Levine, eds.)

The 1974 Titles

Crucial Issues in Testing (Ralph W. Tyler and Richard M. Wolf, eds.)

Conflicting Conceptions of Curriculum (Elliott Eisner and Elizabeth Vallance, eds.)

Cultural Pluralism (Edgar G. Epps, ed.)

Rethinking Educational Equality (Andrew T. Kopan and Herbert J. Walberg, eds.)

All of the above volumes may be ordered from

McCutchan Publishing Corporation
2526 Grove Street
Berkeley, California 94704

The 1972 Titles

Black Students in White Schools (Edgar G. Epps, ed.)

Flexibility in School Programs (W. J. Congreve and G. L. Rinehart, eds.)

Performance Contracting—1969–1971 (J. A. Mecklenburger)

The Potential of Educational Futures (Michael Marien and W. L. Ziegler, eds.)

Sex Differences and Discrimination in Education (Scarvia Anderson, ed.)

The 1971 Titles
- *Accountability in Education* (Leon M. Lessinger and Ralph W. Tyler, eds.)
- *Farewell to Schools???* (D. U. Levine and R. J. Havighurst, eds.)
- *Models for Integrated Education* (D. U. Levine, ed.)
- PYGMALION *Reconsidered* (J. D. Elashoff and R. E. Snow)
- *Reactions to Silberman's* CRISIS IN THE CLASSROOM (A. Harry Passow, ed.)

Titles in the 1971 and 1972 series may be ordered from
Charles A. Jones Publishing Company
Worthington, Ohio 43085